CRITIQUE AND POSTCRITIQUE

CRITIQUE
AND
POSTCRITIQUE

ELIZABETH S. ANKER & RITA FELSKI, EDITORS

DUKE UNIVERSITY PRESS *Durham and London* 2017

Typeset in Minion Pro by Westchester Publishing Services

Library of Congress Cataloging-in-Publication Data
Names: Anker, Elizabeth S. (Elizabeth Susan), [date]—editor. |
Felski, Rita, [date]—editor.
Title: Critique and postcritique / Elizabeth S. Anker and Rita
Felski, editors.
Description: Durham : Duke University Press, 2017. | Includes
bibliographical references and index.
Identifiers: LCCN 2016042487 (print)
LCCN 2016043715 (ebook)
ISBN 9780822363613 (hardcover : alk. paper)
ISBN 9780822363767 (pbk. : alk. paper)
ISBN 9780822373049 (e-book)
Subjects: LCSH: Criticism. | Criticism—Methodology. |
Hermeneutics.
Classification: LCC PN81 .C853 2017 (print) | LCC PN81 (ebook) |
DDC 801/.95—dc23
LC record available at https://lccn.loc.gov/2016042487

Cover art: Alma Thomas, *Hydrangeas Spring Song*, 1976.
Acrylic on canvas. 198.1×121.9 cm. Courtesy of Charles
Thomas Lewis and the Philadelphia Museum of Art,
Object Number 2002201. 125th Anniversary Acquisi-
tion. Purchased with funds contributed by Mr. and
Mrs. Julius Rosenwald II in honor of René and Sarah
Carr d'Harnoncourt, The Judith Rothschild Foundation,
and with other funds being raised in honor of the 125th
Anniversary of the museum and in celebration of African
American art, 2002.

CONTENTS

INTRODUCTION

Elizabeth S. Anker and Rita Felski

It would have been hard to imagine, only a few years ago, that the idea of *postcritique* would be gaining significant traction in literary and cultural studies. We are currently in the midst of a recalibration of thought and practice whose consequences are difficult to predict. There is little doubt that debates about the merits of critique are very much in the air and that the intellectual or political payoff of interrogating, demystifying, and defamiliarizing is no longer quite so self-evident. Even those who insist on the continuing salience and timeliness of critique are now often expected to defend and justify what was previously taken for granted. Meanwhile, we are seeing the flourishing of alternatives to a suspicious hermeneutics. In this respect, the "post-" of postcritique denotes a complex temporality: an attempt to explore fresh ways of interpreting literary and cultural texts that acknowledges, nonetheless, its inevitable dependency on the very practices it is questioning.

This volume, then, offers perspectives by well-known scholars on the past, present, and future of critique in literary studies and beyond. Located in American studies, queer theory, postcolonial studies, feminist criticism, and related fields, our contributors draw on these intellectual and political commitments, while sharing an interest in rethinking established methods. One aim of the volume is descriptive: What does critique look like as a style of academic argument? What kind of rhetorical moves and philosophical assumptions does the activity of critique deploy? Does critique entail a distinctive disposition, tone, attitude, or sensibility? And, if so, does postcritique require a different ethos or affect? In literary and cultural studies, critique is widely invoked but less frequently examined as a specific set of interpretive conventions, expectations, and orientations; by looking closely at critique and recasting it, our authors shed fresh light on what have become ubiquitous ways of reading. While some contributions to this volume focus on critique as a contemporary genre and mood, other essays take a more historical approach, tracing the eighteenth-century origins of critique or explaining its recent evolution in terms of the lingering influence and mentality of the Cold War. And finally, our authors all reckon with both the benefits and the shortcomings of critique as a mode of reading and analysis. What has critique made possible, and what are its most salient achievements? Where are its oversights or liabilities located, and what are their consequences for literary studies and for the humanities more generally?

These questions in turn inspire a number of the volume's contributors to reimagine the aims and practices of literary and cultural studies. Some of the different topics addressed in the following pages include: the promise of ordinary language philosophy; Bloch's notion of utopian thought; the significance of tragedy and translation; the force of cliché; and the need to endorse, rather than just to complicate or dismiss, notions of objectivity. While all the essays raise questions about critique, most of them are less concerned with hammering home a "critique of critique" than with testing out new possibilities and intellectual alternatives. In this sense, the collection as a whole captures a rethinking of literary studies that is currently taking place: one that involves new conceptions of literary value, of the critic's interpretive labor, and of the public role of the humanities. While individual essays take varying perspectives on the continued merits of critique, they all agree on the need to reassess styles and approaches to reading that have become routine over the past few decades, along with the histories and justifications devised to support them.

This volume therefore carries out a threefold project: it offers an assessment of the legacy and status of critique; it explores a range of alternative methods and orientations; and it presents multiple perspectives on the value of a postcritical turn. Our hope is that the collection will serve as a valuable resource and reference point for readers interested in the "method wars" in which many areas of literary and cultural studies are currently embroiled. A tendency has arisen in some quarters to portray—or rather to caricature—any ambivalence about critique as inherently conservative or anti-intellectual. The following essays offer a different picture of the political and institutional bearings of postcritique, conceiving it as linked to, rather than at odds with, progressive commitments. In the rest of the introduction, we set forth a framework designed to help readers make sense of current debates about critique. We begin by cataloging the recurring qualities of critique as a distinct academic genre in order to then examine three alternate, if intersecting, angles from which critique is now being questioned: affect, politics, and method. These insights will enable a reflection on the larger intellectual and historical contexts that have motivated a rethinking of the aims of literary and cultural studies. Finally, we conclude by sketching out some future directions and agendas for scholarship today.

Critique as Genre

It is important to note that the meanings and uses of critique vary dramatically across intellectual fields, disciplines, and schools of thought. These permutations render a comprehensive account of critique an impossible task, even if we limit ourselves to key debates in the humanities over recent decades. Within literary studies, for example, some scholars see critique as synonymous with literary and cultural theory, due to a shared emphasis on the values of destabilization and estrangement. Thus Jonathan Culler, in his widely read primer, defines the main practical effect of theory as a disputing of "common sense," such that the reader is schooled to become suspicious of whatever is identified as natural and taken for granted.[1] Other scholars, however, are more inclined to underscore critique's debts to specific philosophical genealogies. Paul Ricoeur offered what is perhaps the most widely cited account of critique's historical origins when he identified Marx, Nietzsche, and Freud as its primary architects, whose imprint on contemporary scholarship remains indelible. Nonetheless, virtually every field in literary and cultural studies—from American studies to animal studies, from feminist theory to New Historicism—has developed local inflections of, and variations on, critique, whether in relation to its central terms of reference, in-house debates, or styles of argument.

So if critique is, for some scholars, shorthand for theory itself, what exactly are its critics objecting to? And if critique is too multiform to be grasped via a single definition or a unified account, how are we to gain an understanding of its modes of operation? We have adopted two strategies to delineate some of its especially salient features. In a later section of this introduction we catalogue some influential objections to critique, offering a point of entry into its various functions and meanings. That these objections come from diverse angles testifies to the many-sidedness of how scholars have understood critique as both an intellectual project and a style of interpretation.

We want to start, however, with a consideration of critique as genre, in order to register some of its most distinctive aesthetic, affective, and analytical components. Critique is, among other things, a form of rhetoric that is codified via style, tone, figure, vocabulary, and voice and that attends to certain tropes, motifs, and structures of texts at the expense of others. Genre theory, meanwhile, has developed sophisticated ways of conceptualizing similarities and differences across large groups of examples. Rather than signaling a set of core criteria to which all models must conform, genre is now widely understood via the Wittgensteinian idea of family resemblances: individual instances of a genre may be related in disparate ways, but without necessarily possessing any single set of features that are common to all.[2] A genre, in other words, is not an exclusive or internally homogeneous class, but a fluid constellation of discontinuous as well as overlapping modes. In highlighting some characteristic modalities of critique, then, we are not implying that they are present in every case. Nonetheless, attending to the diagnostic, allegorical, and self-reflexive facets of critique will allow us to better understand why it has proven such an enduring as well as gratifying approach.

The *diagnostic* quality of critique is often unmistakable. Diagnosis, of course, has its origins in the practice of medicine, even as the term is frequently applied to other domains (the mechanic examining a defective car, the pundit weighing in on the state of the economy). In a clinical context, diagnosis refers to the act of identifying an illness by investigating and interpreting symptoms. Three aspects of diagnosis seem especially pertinent: the presence of an *expert* (doctor, scientist, technician) who is engaged in the *scrutiny* of an object in order to decode certain *defects* or flaws that are not readily or automatically apparent to a nonspecialist perspective. A diagnosis is both a speech act and a stance or orientation: one that is predicated on the revelatory force of an examining gaze. To diagnose is to look closely and intently, in the belief that such scrutiny will bring problems to light that can be deciphered by an authoritative interpreter. The stance is one of judicious and knowledgeable detachment.

Psychoanalysis, above all, played the role of mediator between a clinical context and a literary one. From the 1970s onward, critics trained themselves to read as Freudian analysts, even when their own commitments were political rather than purely psychoanalytical. Treating the text as a patient, the critic sought to identify buried symptoms that would undercut explicit meaning and conscious intent. For the Freudian reader, what defines the symptom is its unintended or involuntary status: the text unwittingly reveals an often shameful or scandalous truth that it would prefer to deny. In classic Freudian interpretation, repression is the mechanism by which such truths are hidden from view, creating a contrast between manifest meaning and what lurks beneath. This schismatic model has frequently been combined with more political, and often allegorical, analysis: a text's "symptoms"—such as puzzling plot elements, stylistic incongruities, startling motifs, or other oddities—are traced back to social inequities or ideological struggles that cannot be openly acknowledged.

A subsequent generation of Lacanian critics challenged this spatial topology of the self, with its dichotomy of surface and depth, deceptive façade and hidden truth. Yet they retained key elements of the diagnostic model, underscoring a text's unawareness of its own contradictions, slippages, and elisions. It is a fundamental premise of this line of thinking that a patient cannot adequately diagnose herself; the third-person perspective of the critic/analyst will always trump the self-understanding of the text/patient. For Lacanian theorists, another key property of the symptom is its resistance to remedy or cure: hence Slavoj Žižek famously enjoined his readers to "Enjoy your symptom!" in the title of his 1992 study of Hollywood cinema. This fundamental incurability of the symptom also renders the labor of critical interpretation an infinite task; the result can be what Tim Dean describes as a universalization of the symptom, which subsumes anything of interest into its explanatory grid.[3]

The broad impact of Foucault on literary and cultural studies, especially via New Historicism, had the effect of both questioning and reinforcing such a diagnostic impulse. Foucault's work inspired an acute awareness of the entanglement of knowledge with power, showing how the human as well as medical sciences have normalized behaviors and legitimized truths via regimes of classification and categorization. After Foucault, it was no longer possible to overlook the role of the "clinical gaze" as a modern technology of perception that shapes the very objects it claims to interrogate or discover. At the same time, however, Foucauldian scholars internalized and reproduced the characteristic qualities of this same gaze in their own methods of analysis, tracing out hidden capillaries of power in the dispassionate manner of clinicians diagnosing the pathologies of the social body. For the Foucauldian critic, like the scientific expert, critical insight relies on a stance of equanimity and judicious neutrality.

That Marxist criticism in the United States became so closely associated with the diagnostic gaze of symptomatic reading speaks to the exceptional influence of Fredric Jameson: other key figures in Marxist aesthetic theory—Georg Lukács, Walter Benjamin, Raymond Williams—rely, after all, on quite different orientations and methods. In a vast body of commentary on literature, film, visual art, and popular culture, Jameson reads texts as fragments of social totalities that crystallize, often involuntarily, the defining elements of such totalities. In *The Political Unconscious*, Jameson describes his own approach as the "diagnostic revelation of terms or nodal points implicit in the ideo-logical system which have, however, remained unrealized in the surface of the texts, which has failed to become manifest in the logic of the narrative, and which we can therefore read as what the text represses."[4] Meanwhile, yet another reason that Jameson's work has often served as a lightning rod for recent debates lies in his unapologetic embrace of allegorical and homological modes of reading.

Diagnosis defines a relationship between text and critic; *allegory*, however, speaks to the links between text and world. In allegory, the specific gestures or alludes to the general; characters, narratives, or poetic figures are freighted with, and held to stand for, broader philosophical meanings or social struc-tures. Here, allegory overlaps with metaphor. However, while metaphor sees, allegory thinks, having much closer ties to conceptual or abstract thought. In this respect, allegory also claims kinship with homological readings that explain literary forms as echoing the structures of larger sociopolitical realities. Such modes of analysis often contend that literature helps to naturalize or lend ideological support to real-world institutions and practices due to shared ge-nealogies and underlying conceptual structures.

One major contribution of ideology critique was to uncover and demon-strate how allegory can operate in literature as a manifestation of larger social hierarchies and inequalities. Subjecting the literary canon to scrutiny, femi-nist and minority critics maintained that members of certain groups were far less likely to be depicted in terms of their complex particularities, serving instead as abstract ciphers and bearers of negative symbolic meaning (the de-monic, the primitive, the nonrational). We might think here, for example, of Abdul JanMohamed's critique of Manichean allegories in colonialist fiction or Judith Fetterley's evisceration of representations of women in the mainstream U.S. literary tradition.[5] Racial and sexual differences, these critics argued, com-monly translate into moral and metaphysical inferiority via a continuum of pejorative associations.

Critique, however, not only discovers previously unnoticed and politi-cally pernicious allegories in literary works; it also brings allegorical modes of analysis to bear on texts so as to unearth what Jameson refers to as their "repressed" meanings. As Angus Fletcher points out, allegory is intrinsically double-sided: while it can be created by the author, it also requires an act of interpretation by the critic. Yet in their desire to establish parallels between individual works and social structures, critics can risk imputing layers of gen-erality even in the absence of clear textual warrants. In its less happy forms, allegorical interpretation can thus devolve into an all-too-predictable style of reading, where characters in novels or films are reduced to the indexical function of signaling some larger social injustice (sexism, imperialism, heteronormativity). In this context, Jameson's claim that all Third World literatures function as national allegories triggered considerable resistance by postcolonial theorists who complained that Jameson oversimplified the social meanings and thereby discounted the formal complexities of non-Western art.[6] Likewise, Žižek's tendency to explain everything from caffeine-free Diet Coke to characters from popular films in allegorical terms inspired objections to the reductive nature of such analysis.[7]

The dissemination of deconstructive ideas in the 1970s and 1980s led to an intensifying skepticism about such modes of political interpretation, which were condemned for presuming, in naive fashion, a clear parallel between a signifier inside and a signified outside the text. Allegory became a cause for suspicion, accused of imposing false unities and hierarchical structures onto literature: the allegorically minded critic, it was argued, did not know how to read. Gordon Teskey, for example, hailed allegory as "the logocentric genre par excellence": one that strives to subdue the ambiguities and incoherencies of literature by yoking it to a transcendental structure of meaning.[8] Yet allegory did not disappear in deconstructive readings; rather, it shifted from the realm of identity politics to that of language and rhetoric. What defines literature, in this line of thought, is its capacity to engage in self-conscious commentary on the indeterminacies and aporias of language, thereby eluding the overconfident reader. By staging refusals of closure, resolution, or truth, literary works serve, in Paul de Man's words, as "allegories of the impossibility of reading."[9]

Meanwhile, allegory also persisted in literary studies at another level: in prevailing accounts of the role of the critic. In the mid-1980s, Evan Watkins described a recurring ethical allegory in which the critic's role is one of "heroic resistance to all the social pressures toward conformity, mass culture homogeneity, utilitarian demands and the bureaucratization of knowledge within the university."[10] In recent decades, such allegories of the defiant critic have become increasingly influential, especially in highly politicized fields such as American studies, queer theory, and postcolonial studies, where the hermeneutic project is often conceived in terms of an ethical disclosure of structures of Otherness or oppression. The novel ideas, insights, and perspectives emerging from these fields were accordingly tied to a trust in the transgressive or oppositional impact of critique. Indeed, Fletcher's observation that allegory relies on narratives of progress as well as the schismatic, adversarial logic of battle is often confirmed in the tenor of such criticism. Meanwhile, the current questioning of critique, as we will see, extends from growing doubts both about such claims of political efficacy and about the romantic image of the critic as heroic dissident.

Finally, the influence of poststructuralist ideas helps explain a third generic feature of critique: its strong investment in modes of *self-reflexivity*, in terms of both methodology and the critic's preferred objects of analysis. While the association of critique with self-questioning extends back to Kant, it is heightened and intensified in the "dramas of exposure" that characterize contemporary forms of interpretation.[11] Whatever is natural, taken for granted, essentialized, or transparent become the critic's target: such qualities are seen as not only theoretically inadequate (in failing to acknowledge the linguistic and cultural construction of reality), but also politically troubling (in "naturalizing" social phenomena and thereby rendering them immune to criticism and change). As a result, critique has encouraged a recurring preoccupation with second-order or meta-analysis and a seemingly inexhaustible relay of skepticism and disclosure: hermeneutic insight emerges only to become the object of further suspicion, lest it fall prey to the stable, authentic, or authoritative knowledge that critique seeks to challenge. Demanding a hypervigilance on the part of the critic, critique thus requires stringent self-critique and continued attempts to second-guess or "problematize" one's own assumptions.

This self-reflexive dimension is evident in the proliferation of suspicious readings of suspicious readings; poststructuralism, especially, has helped transform critique into a condition of metacritique. Whereas Freudian, Marxist, and feminist thought were once the preferred mechanisms of hermeneutic unmasking, they were unmasked in turn, disparaged for being insufficiently attuned to the complexity or otherness of their objects and themselves invested in metanarratives, logocentrism, or a will to power. In *Gender Trouble*, for example, Judith Butler reproaches feminism for failing "to understand how the category of 'woman,' the subject of feminism, is produced and restrained by the very structures of power through which emancipation is sought."[12] This tendency toward metacritique manifests itself in a favored vocabulary: a rhetoric of defamiliarization that underscores its distrust of anything that does not persistently call its own assumptions into question. As a result, analysis often proceeds through a "hide the ball" structure; rather than espouse stable terms or conclusions, the critic undermines his or her own claims at the very moment when they might appear to reach a stopping point. In its resistance to normative assertions, critique thus unfolds through a spiraling loop of self-complicating questions and reservations. The use of scare quotes, italicization, and qualifiers like *so-called* or *self-styled* can thus highlight the critic's awareness of the constructed and artificial nature of representation.[13]

This tendency for critique to transmute into self-critique has often lead to a penchant for the "new," as theory has revised and reinvented itself through a series of frequently exuberant movements and "turns." Homi Bhabha, for instance, begins *The Location of Culture* by reclaiming the "beyond" of the "post" as an invitation to dwell in the borderlines of a present that marks a revisionary time of invention and intervention.[14] For Bhabha, the "post-" of postmodernism, postcolonialism, and posthistory signals not belatedness or impossibility but the opportunity for creative openings and interstitial discoveries. Yet the modernist impetus toward the new underlying this self-reflexivity has also imbued much critique with an overwhelming mood of self-doubt, contributing to a posture of vigilant self-scrutiny, as the critic scours her own thought processes to expose their lurking ideological biases and limitations. Gayatri Spivak thus prefaces *A Critique of Postcolonial Reason* with multiple reminders of the need to productively acknowledge one's own complicity: we need, she writes, to "look around the corner, to see ourselves as others would see us."[15] Self-critique is one necessary response to the constant risk of co-optation, such that even fields like postcolonial studies can become an alibi for political inaction unless subjected to a "persistent dredging operation" that, for Spivak, derives its methodology from deconstruction.[16]

Critique's propensity for self-reflexivity has also influenced its choice of texts in arguably restrictive ways, as a number of critics have noted. Especially in the fields of contemporary literature and culture, critics are often drawn to texts that exhibit levels of self-consciousness mirroring their own. Within postcolonial studies, for example, critics were often enthralled with texts that "wrote back" to empire, foregrounding their own compromised position within literary history while subverting the ideological biases of their literary forebears.[17] More generally, the self-reflexive mode has led to an entrancement with works of metafiction; highly self-referential texts and allusions probe the nature of the author's and critic's labor, exposing the various pretensions and fantasies (of mastery and redemption) informing those endeavors. Needless to say, this preference for the self-reflexive and metafictional has often gone along with a cult of formal as well as philosophical difficulty.

Mood, Tone, Affect

Given this inherently self-critical dimension of critique, what exactly is new or distinctive about its current reappraisal? How do recent debates differ from a long-standing tradition of self-scrutiny in theoretical inquiry? One difference, we would suggest, is a striking shift in the sensibility, as well as the scope, of current reassessments of critique. It is no longer just a matter of engaging in critiques of critique—thereby prolonging the very style of thinking that is at issue. Rather, influential arguments over the last two decades suggest that the language game of critique may have played itself out: that there is a need not just for different kinds of thinking but for an alternative ethos, mood, or disposition. In what follows, we offer a tentative taxonomy of these various objections to critique. Rather than homogenizing what is increasingly referred to as postcritical thought, we seek to emphasize the diverse range of arguments, attitudes, and reservations that are in play.

Some reassessments of critique have been informed by the recent "turn to affect" that has influenced not only literary and cultural studies but also such disciplines as anthropology, history, sociology, geography, and political theory. Accounts of feelings and emotion, of course, have a long history, whether in the eighteenth-century philosophy of Hume or Smith, the writings of nineteenth-century sentimentalists, Freudian and Darwinian accounts of the emotions, or a substantial body of twentieth-century philosophy from Nietzsche to Jean-Paul Sartre to Martha Nussbaum. However, recent theories of affect, while drawing on these precursors, have typically been skeptical about traditional notions of empathy, sympathy, and shared or universal emotions. In addition, the new affect studies often include attempts to push beyond the psychoanalytic framework that, for a number of decades, was the dominant approach to theorizing drives, desires, and emotional or visceral registers of experience. Psychoanalysis, its critics argue, is limited by its reliance on a logic of depth and repression, its emphasis on etiology and the psychic dramas of early childhood, and its insufficient attention to the phenomenological texture and complexity of feelings.

Eve Sedgwick's 1995 essay "Shame in the Cybernetic Fold: Reading Silvan Tomkins," coauthored with Adam Frank, represents an early and influential example of a turn to affect grounded in pointed objections to critique—objections that continue to inform much affect studies scholarship.[18] The essay begins by rehearsing the antiessentialisms, antibiologisms, and antinaturalisms that define much theory after poststructuralism, with its emphasis on the social construction of subjectivity. For Sedgwick and Frank, constructivism remains caught up in the very dualisms that it strives to oppose. They therefore draw out the less salutary aspects of the linguistic turn, with its absolutizing of a semiotic model of analysis, its dismissal of biology and physiology, and its flattening out of the thickness, complexity, and unpredictability of affective life. In the work of psychologist Silvan Tomkins, by contrast, the authors find a model of exemplary and patient attention to the distinctiveness of, and qualitative differences between, specific affects—shame, interest, surprise, joy, anger, fear, distress, disgust, and contempt—as well as to the "combinatorial complexity" of their interactions.

Sedgwick and Frank's essay voiced reservations that have been echoed by other affect theorists who challenge the rationalism of critique and its frequent neglect of emotion, mood, and disposition. Such scholars have looked to—and in some cases looked back to—a range of intellectual traditions. Phenomenology—frequently dismissed as a naive or outdated form of philosophical thinking—has experienced a dramatic renaissance, as we see, for example, in the work of intellectual historians such as Michael Gubser and Knox Peden. Within film studies, the work of Vivian Sobchack and her followers has been highly influential, triggering a range of inquiries into the experiential and embodied dimensions of the viewing experience. Meanwhile, literary studies are seeing a growth of interest in Maurice Merleau-Ponty, Henri Bergson, and other phenomenological thinkers. Here, of course, we should acknowledge that feminist thinkers continued to highlight the importance of feeling and embodiment even when such approaches fell out of favor; key examples would include Iris Young's work in political theory and the phenomenology of the body; Donna Haraway's work on the intertwining of love and knowledge; Jane Tompkins's emphasis on the affective dimensions of reading; and bell hooks's focus on the raced as well as gendered aspects of emotional life. Such approaches have recently been revitalized by critics like Sara Ahmed, who appropriates and extends phenomenology as a valuable resource for elaborating the affective textures of personal and transpersonal experience, or what Ahmed calls "economies of touch" that unfold *"the social experience of dwelling with other bodies."*[19]

Recent work on affect often defines itself against what it describes as the pervasive pessimism of academic thought. The chronic negativity of critique has been widely noted, whether in Jacques Rancière's argument that critique is predicated on shame in critics about their own culpability and denials or in Eve Sedgwick's influential discussion of paranoid reading.[20] In response to this perceived cynicism or fatalism, some scholars have sought to reclaim negative emotions, drawing out their creative or generative force. This, for instance, is the thrust of Ann Cvetkovich's study of depression, which seeks to "move past the work of critique or the exposure of social constructions" by depathologizing negative feelings and demonstrating their productive role in engendering political action and agency.[21] Other affect theorists are more invested in stressing the reparative or productive value of positive emotions such as hope, joy, or happiness. Jonathan Lear, for example, argues in his analysis of the collapse of the Crow civilization that "radical hope" is the only appropriate stance in the face of cultural devastation.[22] Another influential example of this embrace of the affirmative is the late Jose Muñoz's galvanizing *Cruising Utopia: The Then and There of Queer Futurity*; for Muñoz, idealism, utopia, and "the anticipatory illumination of art" serve as much-needed antidotes to the tone of fatalism and disappointment that is often endemic to critique.[23]

To be sure, not all affect theorists see themselves as working outside or against the tradition of critique. In *Cruel Optimism*, for example, Lauren Berlant explores how affective attachments structure common fantasies of upward mobility, job security, political equality, and durable intimacy. Linking her study of present-day affects to a tradition of Marxist theory, for Berlant an emphasis on the notion of crisis offsets the overly buoyant or celebratory tenor of many recent appeals to affect, maintaining what she describes as a necessary realism about the more problematic costs of attachment. Likewise, Ahmed's phenomenology of affective states remains firmly tied to a critical analysis of the social dimensions of emotion, even while she defends the political importance of embodied experience. And in her influential analysis of "ugly feelings" as well as more recent work on the zany, cute, and interesting, Sianne Ngai situates changing affective states in relation to larger social forces such as those of late capitalism.[24] There is thus a noteworthy divergence between those thinkers who hail the turn to affect as a means of breaking with critical or skeptical modes of analysis and others who insist on the inescapable entanglement of power with affective life and a resulting need for ongoing critique.

Critique and Politics

What, then, are the *political* stakes of the current reassessment of critique? What are its relations to capitalism, democracy, radicalism, revolution, or social change? If critique is political, what are its politics? And is it possible to question the legitimacy of critical analysis without forsaking a concern with the social dimensions of art, theory, and interpretation? Critique is, of course, deeply intertwined with political and philosophical thought, being closely linked to the diverse traditions of Kantianism, Marxist thought, the Frankfurt School, and post-'68 French theory. Long before its importation into literary and cultural studies, critique encompassed a lengthy history of debate about governance, freedom, conflict, and the relations between the individual and the state, even as it has taken on fresh meanings with reference to an array of new social movements. The twentieth century, moreover, witnessed an intensifying affinity between critique and the ethos of the avant-garde: that is to say, an ever greater emphasis on critique's oppositional, marginal, and embattled status and a concomitant distrust of any form of institutionalization as a sign of co-optation.

This history is reanimated in one recent objection to critique: the claim that critique has been normalized, domesticated, or defanged through its own popularity. The sheer success of critique in disseminating and reproducing itself, in this line of thought, is a sign of its ultimate failure: no longer marginal, it is now part of the mainstream, at least within academia. Safely housed in the Routledge anthology and the freshman composition class, critique has become just another familiar pedagogical tool and research method in the neoliberal university. For Michael Hardt, critique has become "the primary mode of practicing theory"; yet this very dominance has deprived theory of both its militancy and its urgency.[25] Likewise, for Robyn Wiegman, American studies confronts a conundrum—namely, that it continues to look to critique for social and political transformation despite the wholesale institutionalization of critique as a methodology.[26] Such objections, while forceful and impassioned, also reveal a continuing commitment to the ethos of critique: contemporary forms of reading and reasoning are called to account for being insufficiently radical or oppositional. The ideals of critique are thus invoked in order to accuse critique of licensing or being oblivious to its own compromised and co-opted status.

Another complaint is that critique's methodologies and commitments betray a Eurocentric bias. The rationalism of critique, it is argued, reveals its roots in a particular tradition of Enlightenment thought,[27] often causing critique to reproduce the logic that has historically supported Northern hegemony, albeit in subtle ways. For Talal Asad, critique is thus tied to the logic of modernity, with its goal of the progressive expansion of human freedom; such an equation, meanwhile, reinforces the status of non-Western populations as deficient in the qualities needed for moral and political autonomy. While critique purports to be secular and value-neutral, Asad argues, it produces specific

(Judeo-Christian) versions of truth while destroying competing conceptions of meaning.[28] In this context, one important standpoint for challenging the Eurocentrism of critique has been work on the postsecular. Saba Mahmood, for example, argues that the "semiotic ideology" informing critique has produced an "impoverished understanding of images, icons, and signs": one that denies or underestimates the crucial role of affective and embodied practices in creating spiritual meaning.[29] As Mahmood further suggests, echoing the concerns of Frank and Sedgwick, critique's indebtedness to linguistic models ties it to a particular epistemology: one that privileges analytical modes of interpretation while paying scant attention to vectors of experience that resist or exceed such an explanatory frame. This rationalist orientation means that critique is poorly equipped to engage seriously with spiritual beliefs, sacramental practices, and attachments to the sacred that remain central to the lives of countless individuals, especially in the global South.[30]

In a related vein, there is dissatisfaction with critique's frequent rendering of the thoughts and actions of ordinary social actors as insufficiently self-aware or critical. This concern helped inspire the emergence of British cultural studies, which took issue with the mass culture theory associated with the Frankfurt School and its assumption that ordinary readers or viewers are dupes or dopes, prisoners of their own naïveté, gullibility, and false consciousness. A related line of inquiry has recently been reanimated in the work of the French pragmatist sociologists Luc Boltanski and Laurent Thévenot, who claim critical thinking as part of the everyday experience of individuals forced to negotiate between conflicting spheres of value in complex societies.[31] Such arguments call into question the mistrust of ordinary language and thought endemic to critique, as well as the frequent assumption that public speech is invariably reactionary, opportunistic, or commodified. As these debates suggest, suspicion of the commonplace and everyday risks entrenching the notion that critical thinking is the unique provenance of intellectuals—enclosing it within the rarefied space of the academy.

The perception that critique is automatically aligned with the Left—a sine qua non of progressive thought—has also been shaken up in recent decades. One early argument along these lines was made by Peter Sloterdijk in the 1980s in *Critique of Cynical Reason*, where Sloterdijk attributed the dissolution of the 1960s student movements to the "metamorphosis of hope into realism, of revolt into a clever melancholy."[32] For Sloterdijk, a pervasive mood of irony and world-weariness has impeded rather than furthered radical social change; cynicism has become a form of "enlightened false-consciousness" in its endless tactics of problematizing and self-questioning. Modes of unmasking are widely practiced, Sloterdijk notes, but they seem to make little or no political difference. To similar ends, in his much-cited essay in *Critical Inquiry*, Bruno Latour contends that a hermeneutics of suspicion has become the preferred weapon of conservative thinkers and conspiracy theorists alike. Tactics forged by the Left—skepticism about the status of facts, exposure of the problematic motives of scientists—now drive the arguments of the Right, evident in positions such as climate change denial. It is time, Latour declares, to adopt new tools; to move from a spirit of debunking to one of assembling, or from critique to composition.[33] Meanwhile, Stefano Harney and Fred Moten's complaint about the reactionary nature of critique, or its tendency to "endanger the sociality it is supposed to defend," responds to similar fears that an overreliance on critique can become self-sabotaging. In its place, Harney and Moten underscore the urgent need to safeguard what they term the "sociopoetic force" of the undercommons.[34]

It is no longer feasible, in short, to assume that critique is synonymous with leftist resistance or that rethinking critique implies a retreat to aestheticism, quietism, belle-lettrism, or other much maligned "-isms" of literary studies. Indeed, the shift away from suspicion may conceivably inspire a more nuanced vision of how political change comes about. As a form of "strong" social theory (Sedgwick), critique can encourage a paranoid vision that translates every possible phenomenon into yet another sign of the ubiquity of ideology or disciplinary power. It leaves little room, in short, for attention to contradictions or qualitative differences in social or political conditions. Impatient with incremental or piecemeal political change, critique insists that real-world, pragmatic progress is nothing but a strategy for disguising the persistence of structural inequality, rendering any form of optimism at best overly credulous or misplaced and at worst a craven capitulation. At the same time, critique's commitment to exposure can exaggerate its own power to transform the social world, a tendency that is especially evident among many literary and cultural critics.

The Method Wars

Recent efforts to rethink critique have often emphasized method: the ways in which established practices of reading limit the inquiries, experiences, and insights available to the critic. Critique, it is argued, implies a methodological orientation that encourages certain kinds of interpretation while leaving little room for others. In particular, a persistent concern with drawing out shadowy, concealed, or counterintuitive meanings can lead to a neglect of the formal qualities of art and the sensual dimensions of aesthetic experience. In what might appear to be a reprise of Susan Sontag's well-known argument in "Against Interpretation"—a stirring manifesto for an erotics rather than a hermeneutics of art—critics have questioned the value of reducing art to its political utility or philosophical premises, while offering alternative models for engaging with literary and cultural texts.

For example, Stephen Best and Sharon Marcus argue that symptomatic reading, as one of the most influential forms of critique, relies on questionable metaphors of depth, concealment, and hiddenness. Against this assumption that the essential meaning of a text resides in a repressed or unconscious content that requires excavation by the critic, they urge greater attention to what lies on the surface—the open to view, the transparent, and the literal. Along related lines, Heather Love contends that the very idea of interpretation, whether in critical or affirmative mode, relies on misguided assumptions about concealed truths that the critic is expected to retrieve. By contrast, Love calls for a model of what she calls "thin description" and for renewed attention to empiricism "after the decline of the linguistic turn."[35]

Other critics emphasize the need to adopt a more generous posture toward the text. Eve Sedgwick's account of paranoid reading, for example, culminates with an acknowledgment of the value of a reparative impulse that is "additive and accretive," aiming "to assemble and confer plenitude."[36] In a similar vein, Sharon Marcus's *Between Women* questions how a suspicious hermeneutics has been enlisted to expose a hidden reality of repressed lesbian sexuality in Victorian England. Instead, Marcus develops a model of "just reading" that attends carefully to what is given by a text, "without construing presence as absence or affirmation as negation," as it seeks to discover a vibrant and complex history of female affective and sexual bonds.[37] Meanwhile, Ann Laura Stoler argues that historians have tended to treat archives as inherently skewed and biased sources. By contrast, Stoler asserts the need "to explore the grain with care and read along it first," being attuned to what she terms its "watermarks" and productions of common sense.[38] In spite of their differences, these critics are all committed to treating texts with respect, care, and attention, emphasizing the visible rather than the concealed in a spirit of dialogue and constructiveness rather than dissection and diagnosis.

Jacques Rancière's thought is also salient in this regard. Like the foregoing critics, Rancière insists on art's resistance to established modes of political analysis. For Rancière, aesthetics is a capacious category that extends beyond literary or artistic texts to involve broader reconfigurations of seeing, doing, and sensing. At the same time, the differentiation of art as a distinct regime of meaning cannot be undone; art and politics, he insists, embody two different "distributions of the sensible" that are related yet far from identical. Works of art thus allow for specific configurations of perception and experience that resist translation into the norms or calculus of political strategy, even as art has its own unique metapolitics. There is, Rancière argues, "no criterion for establishing a correspondence between aesthetic virtue and political virtue."[39] While Rancière rejects any idea of emancipation based on the intellectual's unmasking of ideology, for instance via endless demonstrations of the secret machinery of capital, he shows how instances of aesthetic dissensus can reshape established capacities for political expression—enabling disagreement and disruption that may emerge in the most unexpected places.[40]

Another common feature of the methodology of critique involves a tendency to read individual texts as reflections, indices, or symptoms of larger cultural or social wholes. The appeal of such a style of interpretation is evident: it allows literary critics to reconcile the spheres of literature and politics, enlisting their expertise and training in close reading in the service of combatting social injustice. Yet it is not at all obvious that literary analysis offers a direct conduit to a sharper understanding of the social, or that individual texts can be seen as microcosms of broader ideological structures or cultural forces. Objections to this approach have been voiced by critics such as Lawrence Grossberg, who has long lamented the literary-critical practice of "reading the world in a grain of sand," as he calls it. By contrast, the cultural studies notion of "articulation" provides for Grossberg an alternative way of grasping the social lives of texts: one that emphasizes the radically contingent and changing relations between texts and social constituencies and contexts, as well as the need for empirical analysis, multiple forms of evidence, and the willingness of the critic to be surprised.[41] A similar line of argument has been raised by scholars affiliated with actor-network theory, who replace the notion of "society" with an emphasis on networks of associations, conceiving of the artwork as embedded within multiple chains of mediation rather than serving as a microcosm of a social totality. Close reading, in this line of thought, will reveal very little about the social life of works of art. The politics of a text are not dictated by its form, structure, or internal dynamics; rather, they are forged in the history of its various and diverse entanglements.[42]

Contextualizing Postcritique

To be sure, this emphasis on the contingencies of how texts circulate in the world does not sit well with some scholars' insistence on the big picture: namely, the increasingly pervasive influence of neoliberalism and economic rationality in recent decades, both within and outside the academy. Current debates about method and interpretation, they insist, must be situated and understood within this larger historical framework. We are witnessing, after all, an extended assault on the autonomy of universities: a growing emphasis on profit and utility at the expense of humanistic inquiry, declining state support for the liberal arts, the adjunctification of the professoriate, and the quantification of scholarly thought and research. Within such a context, the "postcritical turn" is read by some as an ominous sign of defeatism, exemplifying a failure of nerve on the part of intellectuals who are no longer prepared to embrace the role of gadflies and oppositional figures. Offering a stirring defense of universities as centers of critique, Terry Eagleton declares: "There is no university without humane inquiry, which means that universities and advanced capitalism are fundamentally incompatible."[43] In this line of thought, there would seem to be only two options: a stance of opposition, negation, and critique, or else the consent to, and co-option by, a larger system.

Hal Foster, for example, has recently expressed his alarm at the postcritical turn within art history. He concedes that there is a growing sense of fatigue with critique, admitting that "its moral righteousness can be oppressive, and its iconoclastic negativity destructive."[44] Ultimately, however, the turn away from critique is explained by Foster not in terms of its own internal problems or intellectual limits, but as a direct and unmediated reflection of larger political trends. He traces the growing interest in affirmation back to the politics of the Bush administration and its suppression of oppositional thought: "Bullied by conservative commentators, most academics no longer stress the importance of critical thinking for an engaged citizenry."[45] Appraising the influence of Rancière, Foster condemns him for encouraging passivity and wishful thinking ("the new opiate of the art world"); meanwhile, Latour is taken to task for a fetishism that treats objects as quasi-subjects and emphasizes the agency of nonhumans. Insisting on the increased necessity of critique in bleak times, Foster concludes that the contemporary moment is a very inopportune time to go postcritical.

There are, however, other ways of framing the historical meanings of the current reassessment of critique: viewing it not as an unwitting symptom of current exigencies but as an active and purposeful response to them. At a time when higher education is under siege, it seems urgent to articulate more compelling accounts of why the humanities matter and to clarify to larger audiences why anyone should care about literature, art, or philosophy. Accustomed to a rhetoric of dismantling and demystification, critique lacks a vocabulary and set of established rationales for mounting such defenses. Meanwhile, it has often encouraged an antagonistic and combative attitude toward the public world; in the wake of poststructuralism, especially, critique has often been synonymous with a pronounced aversion toward norms and an automatic distrust of instrumentality and institutions. One result of this spirit of marginality is to keep serious thought sequestered in the ivory tower, thereby working to ensure its lack of impact or influence on the public sphere.

Rethinking critique can thus forge stronger links between intellectual life and the nonacademic world. Such links are not simply a matter of capitulation or collusion, but can offer a vital means of influencing larger conversations and intervening in institutional policies and structures. In this respect, much recent talk of a "public humanities" differs in tone and tenor from the more familiar model of the radical public intellectual, whose public stance entailed a uncompromising indictment of a "neo-liberal culture of idiocy and illiteracy."[46] That the political ambitions of critique have not led to a more prominent public voice for literary critics is surely not unrelated to such rhetoric: a presumption—undergirded by prevailing theories of ideology or language—that the attitudes of the majority require diagnosis or denunciation rather than thoughtful engagement. As long as critique gains its intellectual leverage from an adversarial stance, it will continue to presume a populace deluded by forces that only the critic can bring to light. Such a mind-set, however, is hardly likely to influence or persuade that same populace.[47]

In this context, we are seeing a greater willingness to work within, while striving to modify, institutional structures both inside and outside the university; a recognition that scholars have much to learn from engagement with nonacademics, even those who do not share their convictions; and a more variegated sense of the current intellectual-political landscape. Some critics have also called for a language that better communicates the specific contributions of the arts and the power of imaginative innovation to the public.

"Art's work in the world," writes Doris Sommer, "is not yet a core concern for an academic field that remains skeptical and pessimistic."[48] Social change, she suggests, is unlikely to be brought about by political sermonizing or the jaundiced rhetoric of high theory. Rather, a more productive path lies in yoking political involvement to the forms of value, play, and pleasure cultivated by an aesthetic education.

Where, then, do these arguments leave us? And what do they suggest for the future of criticism? A recurring theme in discussions of postcritique is the urgency of crafting new rationales—and updating our old ones—for the value of the arts and humanities. We can no longer assume that a stance of negativity and opposition is sufficient to justify the aesthetic or social importance of literature or our practice as critics. Rather, we are in urgent need of more powerful and persuasive justifications for our commitments and endeavors. The current moment in literary and cultural studies, as this volume shows, thus involves a broad interest in exploring new models and practices of reading that are less beholden to suspicion and skepticism, more willing to avow the creative, innovative, world-making aspects of literature and criticism. What gets built and shaped when a critic reads? What affordances and opportunities does literary form and experience open up?

Meanwhile, our authors share a continuing concern with the social and political work of both literature and criticism, challenging the frequent assumption that any defense of literary value must be a sign of belle-lettrism or an apolitical formalism. These and other attempts to craft new accounts of the value of art and literature often insist on the role of affect in criticism: that interpretation and argument are a matter not just of better or worse insights, but also of ethos or disposition. The concern is that a pervasive mood of suspicion, ennui, or irony, in this regard, can easily become debilitating, both intellectually and politically. In response, some recent scholarship not only discusses affect as a theme but itself models and explores differing affective styles and tonal registers of writing—as we see, for example, in the work of both Latour and Sommer.

It seems undeniable that the ethos of critique is losing its allure for a significant number of younger scholars as well as many established critics. On the one hand, this disillusionment is unfolding hand in hand with a larger sense of crisis in the humanities and of institutional retrenchment. On the other hand, the current moment in literary and cultural studies is also one of significant energy, excitement, and revitalization, as scholars confront and reimagine the reigning paradigms of the field. This volume, we hope, will help harness and direct this energy, as both an introduction to and a sustained exploration of the merits of critique and postcritique.

The collection opens with a set of essays that explore various counterhistories and "countertraditions of critique" that have been neglected in the mainstream of literary and cultural studies. Contemporary critique, Moi observes, often implies a specific vision of language and reading: namely, the assumption that texts have hidden meanings to be uncovered by the critic. Drawing on Wittgenstein and Cavell's thought, Moi challenges such a view. Just as there is no "approach" to language, there is no method in literary criticism. Whereas the suspicious critic is convinced that texts lead us astray, for Wittgenstein the fault lies in our own propensity to get lost in our unacknowledged assumptions. Moreover, because Wittgensteinian thought treats a text as an utterance—an action rather than an object—its meanings cannot be understood via metaphors of surface or depth. Instead, the key question for criticism now becomes "Why this?" We are thus inspired by our puzzlement to look more closely at how and why words are being used. Turning to two exemplars of suspicious readers—the detective and the psychoanalyst—Moi argues that the surface/depth distinction tells us nothing about how Sherlock and Freud actually engage in interpretation. Meanwhile, Kierkegaard offers an example of strenuous thinking that takes place outside the hidden/shown parameters of the hermeneutics of suspicion. The "Why this?" question, Moi concludes, opens up a much wider range of affective as well as interpretative possibilities, allowing for forms of admiration as well as critique.

In another reassessment of the history of critique, Heather Love's "The Temptations: Donna Haraway, Feminist Objectivity, and the Problem of Critique" begins by reflecting on the polarized responses triggered by Latour's widely cited "Has Critique Run Out of Steam? From Matters of Fact to Matters of Concern." While evincing conflicting visions of the politics of critique, these responses index larger fractures within academia, including disciplinary prejudices about the relative merits of humanistic versus scientific scholarship. A return to the work of Donna Haraway allows Love to negotiate those tensions, given Haraway's interest in mixing methodologies from different disciplines as well as her simultaneous commitment to both critique and care. Haraway's embrace of a robust and self-reflexive notion of objectivity, especially, has often been overlooked by feminist critics. As Love argues, Haraway's writing offers an exceptionally rich resource for bridging current methodological divides, in particular the frequent stand-offs between proponents of critique and defenders of empiricism. As Love asserts: "Critique need not be only corrosive, but it can also represent a commitment to tracing social arrangements in-the-making; and the careful examination of the world as it appears does not imply a capitulation to *the way things are*."

Looking back to the eighteenth century, Simon During offers a revisionist account of the origins of critique. During first explains Nietzsche's *The Birth of Tragedy* as exhibiting a number of the features associated with critique: its reliance on standards or criteria, its scale, and its style or affect. Within Nietzsche's writing, moreover, the tone of critique is one of combined skepticism, denunciation, and prophecy, while Nietzsche also enlists satire. Nietzsche's thought thereby suggests an alternate genealogy of critique that challenges its typical alignment with the enlightenment project of reason and progress. During subsequently turns to an analysis of Reinhart Koselleck's narrative of the historical fortunes of critique as a gradual degradation—a vision often echoed in critiques of critique today. Finally, the concluding section of During's essay examines two specific episodes in eighteenth-century British letters that further illustrate the many parallels between contemporary critique and Nietzsche's thought. He focuses, first, on a pamphlet war between Richard Steele and Jonathan Swift in 1713–14 and, second, on parson John Brown's 1757 book criticizing social conditions. For During, these varied texts draw attention to underrecognized aspects of critique that characterized its eighteenth-century presence: namely, its grounding in polemic, irony, insult, and even laughter

The next section of this volume turns to questions of interpretation and to different "styles of reading" associated with both critique and postcritique. In "Romancing the Real: Bruno Latour, Ian McEwan, and Postcritical Monism," Jennifer L. Fleissner stages a dialogue between Bruno Latour's thought and Ian McEwan's 1997 novel *Enduring Love*. McEwan's novel, she proposes, offers an allegory of competing styles of reading, pitting suspicious or symptomatic interpretation versus surface and fact-based reading. In particular, one of McEwan's characters favors literal readings and justifies his preference through appeals to chemistry and biology. For Fleissner, this link raises questions about whether the backlash against critique should also be explained as a turn to science and realism—in other words, as deeply antiromantic. Like Love, Fleissner attributes this shift to science in part to the increasing influence of Latour. While Latour seeks to collapse what is often termed the "two cultures" divide, he also complains that humanists have enforced this split and failed to recognize what the humanities can gain from the sciences. An analogous conflict plays out in *Enduring Love*, which demonstrates the need for the continuing coexistence—and also the difference—of the sciences and the humanities. Here, Fleissner affirms her sympathy with certain veins of Eve Sedgwick's thought, namely her attention to the productive limits of both critical-pessimistic and reparative or reformist projects.

While a postcritical turn might seem to signal the waning of symptomatic reading, Ellen Rooney robustly defends such an interpretive approach as involving far more than a hermeneutics of suspicion. Rather, styles of symptomatic reading ultimately require a particular kind of engagement with form, a term that for Rooney extends beyond the literary. She notes that Althusser credited Marx with devising a new mode of reading that views all interpretations as bringing their own problematics to bear on a text, in ways that both render them guilty and invariably focus attention on other possible readings or counterreadings. Moreover, for Althusser the "reading effect" of form confounds both interpretation and writing to entail a play on words: a style that Althusser enacts through his own writing with its frequent use of puns, paradox, doubling, and irony. These various tactics add up, for Rooney, to an account of symptomatic reading that is predicated on its receptiveness to surprise, with consequences for both subjectivity and history.

For C. Namwali Serpell, cliché provides a helpful category for thinking about the styles of both critique and postcritique. Typically, cliché denotes instances of repetition, predictability, and unoriginality: the familiar targets and adversaries of critical thinking and reading. But cliché is also an indispensable component of both literature and criticism that cannot be wholly eschewed. Serpell thus canvasses cliché's origins, history, and forms in order to grasp its centrality. Rather than either defending or deriding cliché, Serpell's essay stages an appeal to phenomenologically informed habits of reading as an approach best geared to engaging with it. In this respect, cliché involves a materialist, manifest *experience* of language, which she theorizes by drawing on both Barthes's *A Lover's Discourse* and reader-response theory. The essay then moves to a reading of Jim Thompson's 1952 noir thriller *The Killer inside Me*, which Serpell analyzes both to demonstrate the limits of existing critical insights into cliché and to model an alternative style of engagement with the material and affective affordances of the text.

For Elizabeth S. Anker, J. M. Coetzee's oeuvre—particularly his 2013 novel, *The Childhood of Jesus*—serves to illustrate key features of critique, as a style not only of interpretation but also of fiction writing. As a novelist, Coetzee frequently engages in self-conscious dialogue with theoretically minded readers and critics, and Anker asks whether his fiction itself aspires to the status of theory. This blurring of the boundaries between literature and theory is reflective of a growing body of contemporary writers who have absorbed and creatively responded to the lessons of critique. In particular, Anker explains *The Childhood of Jesus* as an "allegory of reading" that both problematizes certain conventions of interpretation and illustrates why critique can devolve into a kind of hermeneutic game. One favored approach to Coetzee's fiction has been via deconstructive ethics, leading Anker to challenge many of the assumptions underlying ethics-based approaches to literary analysis. Although a deconstructive ethics might appear distinct from critique, Anker shows how an ethics-based framework can nevertheless be understood as an unexpected style and modality of critique.

The final section addresses affects, politics, and institutions. In the first essay, Christopher Castiglia focuses on the disposition of critique: a distinctive and widespread attitude of mistrust, indignation, and complacency that he dubs "critiquiness." The effect of critiquiness, Castiglia argues, is to promote an automatic skepticism about ethical ideals and utopian imaginings, a disposition he traces back to the era of Cold War politics and the state's explicit cultivation of vigilance, suspicion, and distrust. A revitalized critique, he insists, must be willing to embrace hopefulness, idealism, and imagination. And here literature can be a valuable ally, as a training ground in the unreal that expands our vision of what is possible. Invoking the thought of Deleuze as well as Rancière to support this notion of critical hopefulness, Castiglia also turns to the past for examples of its actualization: nineteenth-century spiritualism and stories of divine visitation, in which the otherworldly serves to validate existing possibilities. Literary studies, in short, needs new dispositions that can take us not beyond "critique," but beyond critiquiness.

In his essay, Russ Castronovo examines the relations between academic critique and a broader sphere of politics. Juxtaposing the works of Edward Said and Matthew Arnold, he shows that they share, despite obvious differences, a commitment to criticism and a common vision of the intertwining of politics and culture. And yet critique as an intellectual practice, ironically, is often attacked on two opposed fronts: it is simultaneously accused of being too political (with scholars reproached for overstepping their areas of scholarly expertise) and of not being political enough (in relation to more urgent and immediate real-world struggles). This fraught position, Castronovo suggests, may actually be the point: the status of critique is inherently contradictory, its effects uncertain. What he describes as the weak messianic power of critique thus resists a narrative of progress or a clear-cut telos. It is only by miscalculating, mistaking, or missing out on the political, Castronovo concludes, that critique retains its political promise.

John Michael's "Tragedy and Translation: A Future for Critique in a Secular Age" offers an account of the politics of critique in a context where secularism and rational thought are increasingly under siege. On the one hand, he argues, modern narratives of social transformation and emancipation have lost much of their power; on the other hand, there is a sharpened sense of the inescapability of belief and the limits of disenchantment. Meanwhile, art plays an increasingly marginal role in either reproducing or subverting the social order, such that the usual political justifications for critique seem increasingly tenuous. In the work of Whitman, Michael finds inspiration for an alternative vision of criticism-as-translation: a practice of reconstituting and redescribing meanings and experiences by moving them from one context to another. Attending to questions of aesthetic pleasure as well as social use, this practice of translation also possesses a tragic aspect in its recognition of the inevitable limits of criticism.

Eric Hayot's chapter, "Then and Now," concludes the volume by meditating on the past, present, and future of critique, especially in terms of its institutionalization. The essay first maps the diverse intellectual currents and political ambitions that came together to inaugurate the theory era in the academy. Hayot thus aims to capture the excitement and bold promise of theory in its heyday. However, these reflections are a prelude to the essay's attempts to reckon with the profound disappointment that has come to characterize the current intellectual climate. Hayot zeroes in on the historical arguments commonly invoked to explain what he identifies as a crisis in criticism, which he contrasts with other temporal arcs and patterns: those of the lives both of institutions and of human biology. These competing time frames operate according to different scales, rhythms, and logics of succession, Hayot argues, and call for new and more complex modes of historicizing. The essay accordingly advocates a "beyond" to critique, although one predicated on both greater attunement to the contemporary and an abandonment of the logic of crisis and temporal succession that has, for too long, underpinned practices of criticism.

Notes

1 Jonathan Culler, *Literary Theory: A Very Short Introduction* (Oxford: Oxford University Press, 2011), 4.

2 Alastair Fowler, *Kinds of Literature: An Introduction to the Theory of Genres and Modes* (Cambridge, MA: Harvard University Press, 1985), 41.

3 Tim Dean, "Art as Symptom: Žižek and the Ethics of Psychoanalytic Criticism," *diacritics* 32, no. 2 (2002): 22.

4 Fredric Jameson, *The Political Unconscious: Narrative as a Socially Symbolic Act* (Ithaca, NY: Cornell University Press, 1982), 48.

5 Abdul R. JanMohamed, "The Economy of Manichean Allegory: The Function of Racial Difference in Colonialist Literature," *Critical Inquiry* 12, no. 1 (1985): 59–87; Judith Fetterley, *The Resisting Reader: A Feminist Approach to American Fiction* (Bloomington: Indiana University Press, 1981).

6 Fredric Jameson, "Third-World Literature in the Age of Multinational Capitalism," *Social Text* 15 (1986): 65–88; Aijaz Ahmad, "Jameson's Rhetoric of Otherness and the 'National Allegory,'" *Social Text* 17 (autumn 1987): 3–25.

7 See, e.g., Slavoj Žižek, *The Fragile Absolute* (New York: Verso, 2000).

8 Gordon Teskey, *Allegory and Violence* (Ithaca, NY: Cornell University Press, 1996), 3, 23.

9 Paul de Man, *Allegories of Reading: Figural Language in Rousseau, Nietzsche, Rilke, and Proust* (New Haven, CT: Yale University Press, 1982), 205.

10 Evan Watkins, "The Self-Evaluations of Critical Theory," *boundary* 2, nos. 12/13 (1984): 366.

11 The phrase comes from Eve Kosofsky Sedgwick, "Paranoid Reading and Reparative Reading, or, You're So Paranoid, You Probably Think This Essay Is about You," in *Touching Feeling: Affect, Pedagogy, Performativity* (Durham, NC: Duke University Press, 2003), 7.

12 Judith Butler, *Gender Trouble: Feminism and the Subversion of Identity*, 10th anniv. ed. (New York: Routledge, 1999), 5.

13 See, for instance, Judith Butler, "Subjects of Sex/Gender/Desire," in *Gender Trouble*; Dipesh Chakrabarty, introduction to *Provincializing Europe: Postcolonial Thought and Historical Difference* (Princeton, NJ: Princeton University Press, 2000); Gayatri Chakravorty Spivak, *A Critique of Postcolonial Reason* (Cambridge, MA: Harvard University Press, 1999), 112–13; Homi Bhabha, *The Location of Culture* (New York: Routledge, 1994).

14 Bhahba, *Location of Culture*, 1, 7.

15 See *A Critique of Postcolonial Reason*, xii–xiii. Indeed, it is this tendency toward shame that, for Jacques Rancière, has divested critique of "any hope" of real-world payoff. *The Emancipated Spectator* (London: Verso, 2009), 40.

16 Rancière, *The Emancipated Spectator*, 1.

17 For a helpful discussion of the postcolonial canon, see Neil Lazarus, "The Politics of Postcolonial Modernism," in *Postcolonial Studies and Beyond*, ed. Ania

Loomba, Suvir Kaul, Matti Bunzl, Antoinette Burton, and Jed Esty (Durham, NC: Duke University Press, 2005), 423–38.

18 Adam Frank and Eve Kosofsky Sedgwick, "Shame in the Cybernetic Fold: Reading Silvan Tomkins," *Critical Inquiry* 21, no. 2 (winter 1995): 496–522.

19 Sara Ahmed, *Strange Encounters: Embodied Others in Post-Coloniality* (New York: Routledge, 2000), 47–49; and see also her *Queer Phenomenology: Orientations, Objects, Others* (Durham, NC: Duke University Press, 2006).

20 Jacques Rancière, "The Misadventures of Critical Thought," in *The Emancipated Spectator* (New York: Verso, 2009); Sedgwick, "Paranoid Reading and Reparative Reading."

21 Ann Cvetkovich, *Depression: A Public Feeling* (Durham, NC: Duke University Press, 2012), Kindle location 69, 219.

22 Jonathan Lear, *Radical Hope: Ethics in the Face of Cultural Devastation* (Cambridge, MA: Harvard University Press, 2008).

23 Jose Estaban Muñoz, *Cruising Utopia: The Then and There of Queer Futurity* (New York: New York University Press, 2009), 292. See also Michael D. Snediker, *Queer Optimism: Lyric Personhood and Other Felicitous Persuasions* (Minneapolis: University of Minnesota Press, 2008).

24 Lauren Berlant, *Cruel Optimism* (Durham, NC: Duke University Press, 2011); Ahmed, *Cultural Politics of Emotion*; Sianne Ngai, *Ugly Feelings* (Cambridge, MA: Harvard University Press, 2007).

25 Michael Hardt, "The Militancy of Theory," *South Atlantic Quarterly* 110, no. 1 (winter 2011): 19.

26 Robyn Wiegman, "The Ends of New Americanism," *New Literary History* 42, no. 3 (2011): 385–407.

27 See Achille Mbembe, *On the Postcolony* (Berkeley: University of California Press, 2001), 4–5.

28 Talal Asad, "Free Speech, Blasphemy, and Secular Criticism," in *Is Critique Secular?*, Kindle location 989, 623.

29 Asad, "Free Speech," 841–42.

30 See also Charles Hirschkind, *The Ethical Soundscape: Cassette Sermons and Islamic Counterpublics* (New York: Columbia University Press, 2006).

31 Luc Boltanski and Laurent Thevenot, *On Justification: Economies of Worth*, trans. Catherine Porter (Princeton, NJ: Princeton University Press, 2006).

32 Peter Sloterdijk, *Critique of Cynical Reason*, trans. Andreas Huyssen (Minneapolis: University of Minnesota Press, 1988), 89.

33 Bruno Latour, "Why Has Critique Run Out of Steam? From Matters of Fact to Matters of Concern," *Critical Inquiry* 30, no. 2 (2004): 225–48, and "The Compositionist Manifesto," *New Literary History* 41, no. 3 (2010): 471–90.

34 Stefano Harney and Fred Moten, *The Undercommons: Fugitive Planning and Black Study* (New York: Autonomedia, 2013), 19.

35 Best and Marcus, "Surface Reading," 1–21; Heather Love, "Close Reading and Thin Description," *Public Culture* 25, no. 3 (2013): 404.

36 Sedgwick, *Touching Feeling*, 149.

37 Sharon Marcus, *Between Women: Friendship, Desire, and Marriage in Victorian England* (Princeton, NJ: Princeton University Press, 2007), 75.

38 Ann Laura Stoler, *Along the Archival Grain: Epistemic Anxieties and Colonial Common Sense* (Princeton, NJ: Princeton University Press, 2010), 50. For another version of the "with the grain" motif, see Timothy Bewes, "Reading with the Grain: A New World in Literary Criticism," *differences* 21, no. 3 (2010): 1–33.

39 Jacques Rancière, *The Politics of Aesthetics*, trans. Gabriel Rockhill (London: Bloomsbury, 2013), 62.

40 Jacques Rancière, *Dissensus: On Politics and Aesthetics*, trans. Steven Corcoran (New York: Continuum, 2010).

41 See Lawrence Grossberg, *Bringing It All Back Home: Essays in Cultural Studies* (Durham, NC: Duke University Press, 1997), 107; see also Rita Felski, "Modernist Studies and Cultural Studies: Reflections on Method," *Modernism/Modernity* 10, no. 3 (2003): 501–18.

42 See, e.g., Antoine Hennion, "Pragmatics of Taste," in *The Blackwell Companion to the Sociology of Culture*, ed. Mark D. Jacobs and Nancy Weiss Hanrahan (Oxford: Blackwell, 2005).

43 Terry Eagleton, "The Death of Universities," *The Guardian*, December 17, 2010.

44 Hal Foster, "Post-Critical," *October*, no. 139 (2012): 6.

45 Foster, "Post-Critical," 3.

46 Henri Giroux, *Neoliberalism's War on Higher Education* (Chicago: Haymarket, 2014), 8.

47 Jeffrey Wallen, *Closed Encounters: Literary Politics and Public Cultures* (Minneapolis: University of Minnesota Press, 1998).

48 Doris Sommer, *The Work of Art in the World: Civic Agency and Public Humanities* (Durham, NC: Duke University Press, 2014), 6.

PART I. COUNTERTRADITIONS OF CRITIQUE

"Nothing Is Hidden"

From Confusion to Clarity; or, Wittgenstein on Critique

TORIL MOI

Critique, Method, Reading

It used to go without saying that the purpose of literary studies was to produce critique, and that to do so, one had to practice some form of the "hermeneutics of suspicion."[1] These assumptions long ruled unchallenged. Already in the late 1990s, Eve Sedgwick observed that the hermeneutics of suspicion had become "nearly synonymous with criticism itself."[2] Recently, Rita Felski has shown how the mind-set—the mood or attitude—characteristic of the hermeneutics of suspicion came to dominate literary studies. Whether they are deconstructionists, Marxists, feminists, Foucauldian historicists, or something else, Felski writes, most literary critics share the same suspicious—"knowing, self-conscious, hardheaded, tirelessly vigilant"—attitude.[3] To suspicious critics, then, the text is never what it seems, or never *only* what it seems.

The reasoning behind this belief seems impeccable. To engage in critique is to expose ideology and the workings of power, encourage resistance, and generally contribute to social and political change. Practitioners of critique must therefore be fundamentally suspicious of anything that appears to be ordinary and commonsensical, and anything that presents itself as an "established fact," including the so-called facts of the text. The conclusion imposes itself: radical, committed, political, left-wing critics must read "against the grain."

By now, critique has begun to lose its status as the self-evident goal and method of literary studies. We no longer believe that power always seeks to cover its tracks. Well before terrorists began to release videos of their atrocities— well before they began to commit their atrocities in order to release their videos—Eve Sedgwick asked: "What does a hermeneutics of suspicion and exposure have to say to social formations in which visibility itself constitutes much of the violence?"[4] Moreover, she argued, the hermeneutics of suspicion's obsession with the opposition between *the hidden* and *the shown* encourages paranoid readings.[5] Bruno Latour notes that the techniques of critique are no longer the exclusive province of radicals. In particular, its trademark skepticism about "established facts" has long since been hijacked by everyone from defenders of the Iraq War to climate change deniers.[6] For him, critique removes us from the things we actually care about: instead of writing about the things we cherish, we focus on their conditions of possibility. When we have exposed them as socially constructed, and thus as contingent, we feel that our work is done. But, Latour asks, what good does it do to know that something we love is contingent, or socially constructed? Is that really all we can say about the objects of our affection and admiration?

Despite their misgivings, neither Sedgwick nor Latour is against critique. Sedgwick wants there to be room for "reparative" readings alongside the usual paranoid readings.[7] Latour wants us to get closer to the facts, to "cultivate a stubbornly realist attitude" by turning to the "matters of concern we cherish."[8] For critique to renew itself, they both imply, we must learn to recognize situations in which suspicion is *not* called for, situations requiring us to speak up for the things we care about. Sometimes skepticism and suspicion will simply be less politically useful than admiration, care, love. Even Stephen Best and Sharon Marcus, who in their 2009 essay "Surface Reading" controversially argued that critique—"political activism by another name"—can't conceivably be the only purpose of literary studies, consider that "surface reading broadens the scope of critique."[9]

As a feminist, I too am convinced that we still need to produce compelling critiques of injustice and oppression. But let's remember that it is perfectly possible to produce critical readings without invoking terms like *the hermeneutics of suspicion*, or *symptomatic reading*. Before intellectuals began to speak of the hermeneutics of suspicion, Simone de Beauvoir took apart the sexism in the writing of Henry de Montherlant, Paul Claudel, D. H. Lawrence, and André Breton, and Kate Millett's blistering political critique of writers from Lawrence to Henry Miller and Norman Mailer proceeded quite without reference to hidden depths.[10] Such examples remind us of the obvious: critical readings existed well before professional literary critics began to believe that critique requires a particular vision of language, meaning, and texts, or a particular method of reading.

In "Surface Reading," Best and Marcus don't use the term *hermeneutics of suspicion*. They prefer "symptomatic reading," a term first elaborated by Marxist thinkers, notably Louis Althusser and Fredric Jameson. In Jameson's words, symptomatic readings set out to "seek a latent meaning behind a manifest one [and] rewrite the surface categories of a text in the stronger language of a more fundamental interpretive code."[11] Over time, Best and Marcus note, the term has come to name any reading that "[takes] meaning to be hidden, repressed, deep, and in need of detection and disclosure by an interpreter."[12] In their view, we should oppose the idea that the task of literary criticism is to disclose the hidden and the deep. We should reject symptomatic reading, or "depth" reading, and embrace "surface reading" instead.

The essay provoked innumerable, more or less irate responses. In a particularly well-argued essay, the Marxist critic Carolyn Lesjak accuses Best and Marcus of positing a "benign" and "culturally conservative" reader who is "neutral, objective, self-effacing, humbled before the text."[13] The surface reader, Lesjak argues, "accommodates herself to the given, to common sense, against the now discredited excesses of the theory years."[14] Lesjak, who is certainly not alone, is convinced that critique or symptomatic reading requires critics to probe beneath the surface of the text. In this way, a specific picture of texts (as things with surfaces and depths) gets entangled in a political project: to undo an oppressive status quo, to raise our political consciousness. This logic leads to the idea that critics who refuse to accept this specific picture of texts and reading must be conservative or reactionary, whatever their actual political views may be.

But if we look more closely at the disagreement between Best and Marcus and Lesjak, it's easy to see that they share the same picture of the text, namely as a thing or object with surface and depths. While Lesjak prefers depths, and Best and Marcus surfaces, all agree that there are two different methods of reading, namely one that delves beneath the surface, and one that more or less contentedly accepts the same surface.

In this chapter I challenge these views. To get beyond the by now exhausted terms of the debate about surface reading and critique, we need to learn how to think differently about texts, reading, and language. This is where Wittgenstein comes in. This may sound surprising, for Wittgenstein doesn't write about reading, or literary criticism. His philosophy has yet to be widely disseminated among literary scholars. It is also true that it can be fiendishly difficult to grasp what his concerns are, and even harder to figure out the implications of his philosophy for literary studies. But Wittgenstein repays the effort. His philosophy enables us to look at old questions in fresh ways, to raise new questions and escape from the pictures that have held us captive for so long.

I shall show that there is no need to think of texts and language as hiding something. This goes against the grain of the post-Saussurean assumption that language itself, just by being language, is always hiding something; that words, sentences, utterances themselves always wear masks; that there is always something else beneath or behind our words, a shadow of meanings covered up by the words themselves. This picture of language and meaning, which is far from compulsory, helps to shore up the idea that texts have surfaces and depths, and thus that it makes sense to oppose surface reading to depth reading.

I shall also show that critics who think they are uncovering hidden truths don't read any differently from critics who don't share this picture of reading. In fact, even the most suspicious critics, the very poster-figures for the hermeneutics of suspicion—Sherlock Holmes and Sigmund Freud—don't do anything special. They simply look and think. There simply is no special "suspicious" as opposed to a "gullible" method of reading. Readers—and readings—may of course be more or less subtle and sophisticated, more or less knowing or naive, but that has nothing to do with "method." Finally, I want to oppose the idea that only "suspicious" or "symptomatic" readings are capable of acknowledging and exploring difficulty and obscurity. I do this by turning to Søren Kierkegaard's practice of reading in *Fear and Trembling*.

In my view, literary criticism—by which I mean what we now call "reading"—doesn't have anything we can plausibly call competing methods, at least not in the sense widely used in the sciences and social sciences: a set of explicit strategies for how to generate new knowledge. This is why literary critics often have trouble explaining their "method" to colleagues in other disciplines. Insofar as grant application forms take the procedures of the natural sciences as their norm, they force literary critics to discuss their "method" whether or not they really have anything to say about it. ("Reading" alone somehow never seems sufficiently "scientific" in such contexts.)

When Rita Felski discusses critique, she rightly refrains from calling it a method, and rather defines it by using terms such as mood and mind-set, and by focusing on characteristic rhetorical patterns. Critics clearly have specific thematic interests and political investments. But whether I do a postcolonial or a feminist or a psychoanalytic reading, methodologically I do the same sort of thing: I look and think in response to particular questions. In literary studies (as opposed to criticism) the methodological alternatives to reading are things like conducting interviews, setting up focus groups, chemical analysis of paper quality and watermarks, or computer crunching of big data.[15]

Most handbooks and courses in "method" either provide useful instructions in how to do research (how to use archives and bibliographies, how to read seventeenth-century handwriting), or turn out to be overviews of various kinds of theory. But a theory is not a method. If we think of "deconstruction" or "feminist theory" as methods, we simply encourage students to take a given theory and apply it to a text. As I have argued elsewhere, this is truly the last thing we should teach our students to do.[16]

The way we (literary critics) talk about what we do (often under headings such as "method" or "approach" and the like) is at odds with what we actually do. We mistake political and existential investments for methods, specific practices of reading. Whether they speak of depths or surfaces, readers do pretty much the same sort of thing regardless of their understanding of what they are doing. What we—literary critics—call different "methods of reading" are really different thematic and political interests, and different views of what is important in literature (and in life).

The implications are radical: the fetishization of the hidden and the deep does *no work* for literary critics. This is why Best and Marcus are right to challenge the ubiquitous invocations of depth and hiddenness. But it is also why Best and Marcus are wrong to believe that a call for "surface reading" will liberate us from the metaphor of depth. After all, the two are inextricably linked: any talk of surfaces calls forth thoughts of depths. In my view, claims about hiddenness and depth in literary criticism are empty. They don't underpin anything, not even critique.

This is a liberating insight, for it follows that radical critics no longer have to feel bound to the hermeneutics of suspicion. We can reject its characteristic oppositions—latent/manifest, hidden/shown, depth/surface—without losing anything at all. By "reject," I don't mean "exclude from our vocabulary." There can be no point in forbidding literary critics from using the word *deep*, for example (in this chapter, I use precisely that word about Kierkegaard's reading of the sacrifice of Abraham). I mean rejecting the belief that these oppositions tell us something interesting about how to read or not to read a literary text. Abandoning this view leaves the field of reading wide open. In the encounter with the literary text, the only "method" that imposes itself is the willingness to look and see, to pay maximal attention to the words on the page. What we do next, what we choose to focus on, is up to us. We are responsible for our own reading. This is liberating, but it is daunting too.

"Nothing Is Hidden," or, From Confusion to Clarity

The suspicious reader assumes that language itself hides its meanings from us. This belief is rooted in the post-Saussurean idea that the sign is split into a purely formal or material part (the signifier, the visible surface), and a buried or hidden part (the signified, the meaning). On the theory of the "split sign," any attempt to establish meaning will per definition become a hunt for the hidden—the sign here, the meaning there. Or, as Wittgenstein dismissively puts it: "Here the word, there the meaning. The money, and the cow one can buy with it."[17] Critics who accept the idea of the split sign build the idea of the hidden into their very idea of language. And once they do that, they will find it impossible to break with the hermeneutics of suspicion.

Wittgenstein flatly denies that language hides anything: "How does a sentence manage to represent? . . . How does a sentence do it?—Don't you know? After all, nothing is hidden" (§435). The main reason he insists that sentences don't hide anything is that for him, the meaning of a word isn't divorced from its use. In this essay, I can't go into what he means by "use."[18] Let me just say that when Wittgenstein insists that nothing is hidden, he does not mean that everything is self-evident. He means that we shouldn't go around thinking that language itself—our sentences, our utterances—hides something just because it *is* language. Sometimes we lie, deceive, cheat; sometimes we are honest and truthful. This isn't something "language" does. It is something *we* do. We, as speakers, are responsible for our words. Language itself can't be blamed for our prevarications.

Wittgenstein thinks of utterances as actions, as something we *do*. If we think of a poem, a play, a novel as a particularly complex action, or intervention, we immediately escape the hold of some of the hermeneutics of suspicion's most entrenched beliefs. Actions aren't objects, and they don't have surfaces or depths. To understand an action isn't the same thing as to open the lid of a box. The "death of the author" doesn't apply to actions, for actions aren't divorced from their doers in the same way as objects from their makers. Think of the simplest of actions, such as reaching for a pen, or jumping over a puddle in the road. To understand the action *is* to understand why I or you do this particular thing in this particular situation, and to grasp the implications of doing it.

On this view, to understand an utterance requires us to ask about the speaker's motivations, reasons, and intentions; to ask about the repercussions, ramifications, consequences, and effects of the utterance; and to consider issues of responsibility, ethics, and politics arising in and through the action. From now on I'll refer to the whole range of such questions and investigations as the "Why this?" question.

Stanley Cavell, whose pioneering understanding of Wittgenstein has profoundly shaped my own, notes that "a certain sense of the question 'Why this?' is essential to criticism."[19] We can't ask it unless we have noticed something, seen something that surprises or strikes us. In this way, a specific word, a way of applying paint strokes, a surprising camera angle can become the starting point for an investigation. "Why this?" is unrelated to the metaphysics of the hidden: it neither presupposes anything in particular about surfaces and depths nor prescribes any particular critical mood or attitude. We can ask "Why this?" in a spirit of confusion, or a spirit of really wanting to know. But we can also ask it in a spirit of suspicion. (To ban suspicion is no better than to generalize it.) The point is to be able to show why suspicion is called for in a particular case.

The suspicious reader is convinced that the text leads us astray. Wittgenstein thinks that we get lost in our own words, in our own unacknowledged or imperfectly understood assumptions. In *Philosophical Investigations*, Wittgenstein shows that philosophical problems arise when we let our words drift away from their ordinary use, yet still trade on that use. The result is not meaning, but the illusion of meaning. If I tell you, "I hid the car keys," you will usually understand. But what if you replied: "And I hid the meaning of my words"? It would take me aback, puzzle me, make me wonder what you mean. There simply is something odd about your use of this verb *here*, in this particular sentence, in these particular circumstances. In philosophy, Wittgenstein writes, we easily end up doing something similar, namely using ordinary words (*see*, for example), while twisting their usual meanings. Problems arise when we don't discover the problem: "A *picture* held us captive. And we couldn't get outside it, for it lay in our language, and language seemed only to repeat it to us inexorably" (§115). Then we are lost in the fog of our own language.

For Wittgenstein, philosophy begins in the acknowledgment of this lostness: "A philosophical problem has the form, 'I don't know my way about'" (§123). Note the difference between assuming that a text is hiding something from us, and assuming that the problem is *in me, in us*. If Wittgensteinian philosophy is a kind of therapy, it is a therapy not of others but of ourselves.[20] If we assume that the work of reading is akin to the work of philosophy, then reading isn't an excavation but a self-examination. The work of philosophy is to dispel the fog and get to a clear view of the particular problem that troubled us. In literary criticism, we can begin by asking, "Why this?" We begin, then, not with a method, but with our own sense of confusion. If the critic doesn't have a problem, if nothing really puzzles her about the text, she really has no reason to investigate it. A reading is an attempt to get clear on something.

To give an example: I began writing a paper on *Hedda Gabler* because I was struck by three different moments when Hedda remains puzzlingly or shockingly silent.[21] The paper is an attempt to answer the question: "Why these silences?" The answer wasn't obvious, at least not to me. Nor was it self-evident where or how the reading would end. To bring out the meaning—value, mode—of Hedda's silences, I chose to contrast Ibsen's modern and Kierkegaard's romantic notion of despair. I can certainly imagine moving in some other direction. I can also imagine asking different questions. Why does Hedda say such awful things about Aunt Julie's hat? What does this tell us about her relationship to language? Different questions lead to different kinds of investigations. I don't think there is any way of deciding in advance of the reading what the *best* option would be, as if the path was already there, waiting for us. We just have to risk it. There are no guarantees.

A Clear View, or Description According to Wittgenstein

"Why this?" questions arise every time we are confused by a word, a sentence, an utterance. To find the answer, we try to get clear on how the word or sentence is used in this particular case. This can be so hard that we begin to feel we are banging our head against a brick wall. We may get stuck, feel we go around in circles. Then we get bumps on our understanding, as Wittgenstein puts it.[22] When we reach this point, a "grammatical investigation" is called for. The aim of the investigation is to reach a clear overview—a "surveyable representation" (*übersichtliche Darstellung*; §122)—of the way we use our words. Wittgenstein often refers to such an overview as a *description*. Think of something like an engineer's drawings of a machine, which lays out the different parts and their connections as clearly as possible. But note also that such drawings won't do anything for us unless they are offered in response to a confusion.

Here surface/depth metaphors no longer work. Of course, we can say that the drawings reveal how the machine is put together. Maybe you want to say that it unveils the inner workings of the machine (although that would be a bit odd). Yet it makes no sense to think of the machine itself as somehow hiding its own construction or structure. The drawings simply remind us of what was already there. We began by being confused, by failing to realize why the engine stopped working, but now we see what went wrong. The clear view allows us to relax, to stop worrying about this particular problem. It "gives philosophy peace," Wittgenstein writes (§133). At least for a while, until we begin to feel confused about something else.

In Wittgenstein's understanding of philosophy, then, a description is the therapy we need to see clearly. To describe, for him, is to point out connections, do comparisons, pay attention to distinctions, and so on. In literary studies, however, description has long been a contentious term. Proponents of "description" have been accused of being empiricists, of taking language to be "transparent," or of believing that texts have only one "literal" meaning. In *The Political Unconscious*, Jameson imagines an "ordinary reader" who "when confronted with elaborate and ingenious interpretations [objects] that the text means just what it says."[23] According to Jameson such a reader can only be a mystified victim of ideology.[24] When Best and Marcus bravely declared that "surface reading . . . strives to describe texts accurately," they knew that they were asking for trouble.[25]

In "Live Free or Describe," her wittily entitled response to Best and Marcus, Ellen Rooney goes for the jugular: "Description . . . celebrates obviousness, that which (allegedly) lies in plain view; it consequently embraces (the form of) paraphrase. Paraphrase is precisely a reading practice that disavows reading's own formal activities, which are thus rendered transparent in the sense of 'neutral' . . . , allowing a paradoxical mediation without (the complicating factor of) mediators."[26] According to Rooney, description simply reiterates the obvious, that which is in plain view; it is no more than paraphrase. Paraphrase, in its turn, is a reading practice that wrongly takes itself to be neutral, even objective, as if it weren't an interested, ideologically suspect exercise in its own right. Whether we talk about "description" or about "what the text says," we are, according to Jameson and Rooney, dealing with quintessential cases of the kind of self-understanding, and the kind of language, that truly cries out for critique, unveiling, demystification.

Such critiques have no purchase on Wittgenstein's notion of description as *übersichtliche Darstellung*, simply because a Wittgensteinian description is a response to a confusion, not an unmotivated call for an empirical survey. Wittgenstein, moreover, doesn't believe that human beings can ever escape their own embodied point of view. To him, we always speak as fallible creatures. All utterances are situated: to understand an utterance is to understand how it is used in a specific situation, for a particular purpose. Yet it doesn't follow that all utterances are equally biased or equally unreliable. We can still get some things right, still get clear on a specific problem. Moreover, some utterances *are* more neutral, or more objective than others. Even enthusiastic proponents of critique will denounce their opponents for providing "flagrantly biased" accounts. But in so doing, they implicitly invoke the idea of a better—more accurate, more objective, more illuminating—account. Or at least I hope they do, for otherwise critique would be pointless.

Nevertheless, in literary studies "description" still invites misunderstandings. My use of the term may be easier to follow if I stress that until relatively recently the English-language editions of *Philosophical Investigations* translated *übersichtliche Darstellung* as a "clear view." The description *is* the clear view. This is why I also use expressions such as "provide a clear view," "get clear" on something, or simply talk about reaching some kind of clarity.

When Wittgenstein declares that nothing is hidden, or that everything is in plain view, he doesn't mean that everything is obvious, in the sense of easily grasped, self-evident, or banal. If something really is obvious to us, we will not feel confused. Then we don't have a philosophical problem. Maybe we *should* have a philosophical problem. For what we take to be obvious may be precisely the picture that holds us captive. But as long as we haven't discovered that we are held captive, we are not in a position to realize that. So we still don't have a philosophical problem. To do philosophy—to engage in critical thinking—we must begin with our own personal experience of intellectual trouble. Unless *something* grates, gives us a headache, wakes us up from the conviction that our current view works just fine, we'll never realize that we *are* confused.

Adherents of the hermeneutics of suspicion try to avoid the inevitable appeal to the critic's own experience of the text, the critic's own act of reading, by recommending constant suspicion. The result is a radical narrowing of the literary critic's register of attitudes, and, in the worst cases, a permanent pose of knowing cynicism. And it won't help. For even the most suspicious critic will never be able to see her own blind spots. Wittgenstein helps us to understand that this is an inevitable part of the very process of thinking. For him, philosophy isn't a steady state of eternal vigilance, but rather a series of new forays, new efforts to clear up new confusions.

When the fog in our head lifts, we often feel that we should have seen what the problem was all along. For then the solution often seems excruciatingly obvious. How *could* we have missed it? It was never hidden. We just failed to see it. This is like Edgar Allan Poe's purloined letter: what we seek is hiding in plain view. But to see it is nevertheless not that easy. It requires self-therapy, a change in outlook, an escape from the picture that held us captive. This has nothing to do with empiricism.

Wittgenstein's notion of description—a clear view—thus stands in no specific relationship to paraphrase. Yet paraphrase has been unjustly maligned. There is no point in being either for or against paraphrase as such. A paraphrase can be an indispensable aid to understanding. As Cavell has shown, metaphors *demand* paraphrase, while other kinds of poetic language absolutely resist it.[27] Like all the other tools in the critic's toolbox, paraphrase can be illuminating when it is offered as a response to a genuine problem. The question, as always, turns on use. Nobody is in favor of bad uses of paraphrase. The challenge is to distinguish good uses from bad ones.

Looking and Thinking: Sherlock and Freud

I now want to show that reading practices that are routinely described as quintessential cases of the hermeneutics of suspicion don't in fact require us to think in terms of the traditional oppositions. The implications are revolutionary, for it follows that metaphors of depth and surfaces, hidden and shown, don't actually describe what readers are doing, or how reading works. Whether a critic takes herself to be digging beneath the surface or not makes no difference to her actual reading practice.

To clarify what I mean, I'll give two examples. The first concerns a detective, one of the favorite figures of the hermeneutics of suspicion. My example comes from the TV series *Sherlock*. How does it represent Sherlock's detection process? In the first episode, Sherlock examines the body of a woman dressed in a pink suit, sprawled on the floor of an empty warehouse.[28] He notices that there is humidity on the inside of her collar. He looks at her umbrella, which is dry. He examines her jewelry, takes off her wedding ring and looks carefully at the inside. He notices small splatterings of mud on her calves.

During this process, Sherlock doesn't say anything. He is just looking, touching, smelling, and thinking. To convey a sense of action—his hectic process of thinking—words in Courier font, styled to look like rough data output, flash across the screen. "Umbrella: dry," for example. At the end of the scene, Sherlock declares that the woman has just arrived from Cardiff, where it rained that morning; she is a serial adulterer; there has to be a missing pink suitcase; and so on.

Is Sherlock uncovering the hidden? Well, if you like you can say so, but then it becomes your responsibility to explain why you think that metaphor captures what Sherlock is doing better than the alternatives. I prefer to say that Sherlock is *looking and thinking* in response to a specific question: Why this? What brought this woman to her death in this dismal place? What Sherlock notices is already there, in plain view. The other characters—the police detective, Watson—simply fail to take an interest in the features that grab Sherlock's attention. It's not that the others look at the surface, whereas Sherlock looks beneath it. It is that he *pays attention* to details they didn't think to look at. Wittgenstein's "Nothing is hidden" explains Sherlock's activities better than metaphors of hiding/showing. Sherlock is a master in his field because he pays meticulous attention to what is there. Master readers do the same thing.

My second example comes from one of the founding fathers of the hermeneutics of suspicion, namely Freud. Freud regularly used metaphors of the hidden and the buried to describe the unconscious, and drew on the language of archaeology and detection to explain his method of interpretation. In the famous "Dora" case, Freud writes that his strategy was to "follow the example" of great archeologists who "bring to the light of day after their long burial the priceless though mutilated relics of antiquity." Like such archeologists, he too has "restored what is missing."[29]

Freud's metaphors stress the hidden/shown opposition. But his account of what he actually does is at odds with the imagery of burial and excavation. He has set himself the "task of bringing to light what human beings keep hidden within them . . . by observing what they say and what they show."[30] It turns out to be easier to discover human secrets than one thinks: "He that has eyes to see and ears to hear may convince himself that no mortal can keep a secret. If his lips are silent, he chatters with his finger tips; betrayal oozes out of him at every pore."[31] Our secrets are all too evident: all it takes to reveal them are "eyes to see and ears to hear." The psychoanalyst observes and listens. Freud isn't digging under the surface. He looks at and listens to his analysand's expressions, and thinks.

Wittgenstein thought that human beings are, as Cavell puts it, "condemned to expression, to meaning."[32] The famous aphorism "The human body is the best picture of the human soul" is an attempt to make us stop thinking of the body as something that *hides* the soul, to make us realize that the body is *expressive* of soul, which means that it is expressive also of our attempts to hide, disguise, or mask our feelings and reactions.[33] For Wittgenstein, gestures and activities inflect our words: language cannot be isolated from our tone, our facial expressions, or from what we do with our bodies as we speak or remain silent. Silence can be as easy—or as hard—to read as words.

In Freud's celebrated model analysis of one of his own dreams, the so-called Dream of Irma's injection, he shares his method of interpretation with his readers. He begins by writing down the dream as soon as he wakes up. This writing is the "dream-text," the text to be analyzed. The "specimen dream" concerns a patient Freud calls "Irma," a woman who despite Freud's psychoanalytic therapy still complained of pains. To analyze the dream, Freud breaks the dream-text up in small fragments. Some of the fragments are full sentences, others are single words, or, in one case, a chemical formula. Then he produces, as fully as he can, his thoughts and associations to each fragment. The aim of the process is to figure out what the dream means. The effort is crowned with success. Freud concludes that the dream shows that "I was not responsible for the persistence of Irma's pains, but [my colleague] Otto was."[34] The famous conclusion follows: a "dream is the fulfillment of a wish."[35]

This strategy can easily be redescribed as a version of the "Why this?" question. Here, as in his other interpretations of dreams, or jokes, or literary texts, Freud is looking for motivations and intentions, showing *why* the individual elements of the dreams are as they are, why each word, each sentence appears where it does, what work it does, and so on. Sherlock does the same thing: he explains *why* the umbrella is dry, while the inside of the coat collar is humid, and so on.

How do the surface/depth metaphors fit Freud's method? What is hidden here? The dream-text is not hidden. On the contrary, it is the text to be interpreted. The new associations and thoughts produced by Freud are not hidden either. He has to prod himself to produce them, but once they appear, they are neither "deeper" nor more "superficial" than the dream-text itself. What *is* hidden, according to Freud, is the meaning of it all—let's call it his *conclusion*—namely that the dream expresses his wish to blame Otto for Irma's pain. He himself was not aware of this wish. What is hidden, then, is the unconscious. But this is a claim about the human mind, not about language, texts, or interpretation.

The Italian historian Carlo Ginzburg would say that Sherlock and Freud behave like master hunters who know how to piece together a detailed picture of the animal from its traces. The master hunter does not move from surface to depth, but rather from details, scattered traces and clues, to an idea of the whole. When Freud discovers the meaning of his dream, when Sherlock uncovers the murderer, they are like the brothers in the oriental fable who "demonstrate[d] in a flash how, by means of myriad small clues, they could reconstruct the appearance of an animal on which they have never laid eyes."[36]

For Ginzburg, both Sherlock and Freud practice *conjectural knowledge*. They are among the early practitioners of a new "evidential paradigm" which began to enter European intellectual life in the 1870s and 1880s. Rooted in medicine, jurisprudence, historiography, and philology, the conjectural paradigm soon became the very foundation of the emerging human sciences. Any "highly qualitative" discipline, any form of knowledge concerned with "individual cases, situations and documents," Ginzburg writes, will build its cases in this conjectural way.[37] Where Ginzburg writes "conjecture," others might want to say "interpretation." But whatever we call it, Ginzburg shows that it is possible to write about interpretation without thinking in terms of metaphors of surface and depth.

The Difficult, the Dark, and the Deep: Kierkegaard

We have seen that partisans of critique believe that the only alternative to "deep" reading is banal paraphrase, simplistic and superficial descriptions. I have already shown that Wittgenstein's search for clarity doesn't entail a rejection of difficulty. Now I want to show that the language of the hidden and the shown, of mystery and revelation, isn't the private property of the hermeneutics of suspicion, but can be used in other, different ways. To show what I mean, I'll turn to Søren Kierkegaard, a magnificent reader of difficult texts, but in no way a hermeneuticist of suspicion.

I choose Kierkegaard as my example because he is almost obsessed with revelation and recognition. And, as he himself stresses: "Whenever and wherever it is possible to speak of recognition, there is *eo ipso* a prior hiddenness."[38] In *Fear and Trembling*, he reminds us that ancient Greek drama is constructed on the model of the hidden and the shown. In Aristotle's *Poetics*, recognition (*anagnorisis*) is an unveiling, a discovery, a disclosure, as when Oedipus suddenly realizes that *he* is the one who brought the plague to Thebes. For Aristotle, anagnorisis is something a tragic hero experiences when he realizes who he is, what he has done. In the moment of recognition, the hero moves from ignorance to knowledge. This can also be experienced as a conversion: "I was blind, but now I see." Wittgenstein's search for the path from confusion to clarity is not alien in this company.

For Kierkegaard, the hiddenness of the Greek drama connects to the Greeks' sense of the "dark, mysterious source" of dramatic action.[39] But it lingers on in modern drama, which depends on recognition and hiddenness for its very existence. (He is thinking of nineteenth-century melodramas, in which the plot almost always turns on sudden revelations of identity: "Ah, so *you* are my long-lost son!") We note that neither the Greek recognitions nor the modern revelations are hidden from the audience; on the contrary, they take the form of explicit dramatic action, there for all to see.

The Bible's story of Abraham's willingness to sacrifice Isaac is remarkably simple. God tells the old Abraham to sacrifice his only son. Abraham takes his son, a knife, and some firewood to Mount Moriah, and begins to prepare the sacrifice. At the last minute, an angel stays Abraham's hand. Abraham suddenly notices a ram caught in a nearby bush, and sacrifices the ram instead. In this story, nothing is hidden and nothing is revealed. God's intervention isn't the revelation of a secret, it's just what God does. Yet this simple story disturbs Kierkegaard's sense of reason. He simply can't understand how Abraham can *do* such a thing.

Kierkegaard's method for getting clear on what this story means is fascinating. He begins *Fear and Trembling* by rewriting it four times. In each retelling he makes an enormous effort to imagine what the situation must have felt like to the different protagonists, how they might have experienced it, what it might have been like. To him, such a literary rewriting—a retelling or recounting— of the story is an act of intense interpretation. (Why don't we ask our students to do this sort of thing more frequently?) By supplying new contexts, adding details about the characters' feeling and experiences, he tries to get closer to understanding Abraham's action. Then, in the rest of the book, which is much longer, he meditates on the philosophical—religious, ethical, existential— confusion this story throws him into.

Kierkegaard's various retellings are attempts to understand a text that challenges him totally, as a thinker and as a human being. As he struggles to get clear on Abraham's relationship to God, he keeps returning to the idea that faith is "distress, anxiety and paradox."[40] At the end of the book, the story of Abraham still defeats him, not because it is obscurely written, or particularly puzzling in style or form, but because it presents us with a fundamentally incomprehensible act, one that will only ever make sense to a great religious soul, a "knight of faith." The effort to bring Abraham's act back to human (social, ethical) categories of understanding will always fail.

Few texts come close to equaling *Fear and Trembling* in its strenuous, iconoclastic, imaginative, deeply philosophical effort to read a difficult text as thoughtfully and intensely as possible. *Fear and Trembling* exemplifies a form of reading that fully acknowledges difficulty, obscurity, and mystery without falling under the categories of the hermeneutics of suspicion.

I find that I want to say that Kierkegaard's reading of the story of Abraham is deep. What does the word mean here? In his reading of *Walden*, Cavell writes: "A deep reading is not one in which you sink away from the surface of the words. Words already engulf us. It is one in which you depart from a given word as from a point of origin; you go deep as into the woods."[41] Kierkegaard's reading sends us deeper into the woods, to a place we have never been before. In such a place new discoveries can be made, at least by those who know how to read the signs. We are back to Ginzburg's hunter, back to what he calls "the oldest act in the intellectual history of the human race: the hunter squatting on the ground, studying the tracks of his quarry."[42]

"Why This?": Critique, Admiration, Responsibility

As we have seen, Cavell notes that "a certain sense of the question 'Why this?' is essential to criticism."[43] But to ask "Why this?" in relevant and interesting ways is difficult. It takes extensive training and experience to become a good critic. If you know nothing about metaphors in romantic poetry, you will fail to notice anything puzzling or unusual about a specific metaphor in a particular poem. And if you notice nothing special, you won't be in a position to begin an investigation: "The best critic will know the best points," Cavell writes. "Because if you do not see *something*, without explanation, then there is nothing further to discuss."[44] A good critic stakes herself—her experience, her judgment—in her observations. That's why the very work of criticism can conjure up anxiety, fear of exposure, dread of being misunderstood.

We can ask "Why this?" about anything. This doesn't mean that the words of the text can be made to *mean* just anything. It just means that we can do more than one thing with texts. A Marxist may be interested in the class struggle, or in modes of production or ideology; a feminist in women, their social status, their relationships, their actions and expressions; and so on. Different interests will inspire different questions. As Cavell notes: "What you need to learn will depend on what specifically it is you want to know; and how you can find out will depend specifically on what you already command."[45] If we want to know whether the Marxist or the feminist reading is better, the answer will depend on the particular case. They are not necessarily mutually exclusive. In any case, we shouldn't lay down requirements about what thematic interests, what worldview, what politics the critic should deploy in advance of the reading. The reading—the critic's expression of her reading—either justifies itself or it doesn't. The best critic will not just know the best points, and ask the best questions; she will also choose to work on the best texts, by which I mean the texts that best responds to her own interests and purposes, the texts to which she herself responds most fully.

Wittgenstein, J. L. Austin, and Cavell can be formidable allies for anyone interested in unmasking pretense, deceit, and illusions.[46] But *we* are the ones who decide to unmask or not to unmask. Whether we write literary criticism to critique or to admire, to investigate or to explore, is up to us. The politics of literary criticism does not lie in the method, or in the way we picture texts. It lies in the critic. *We* are responsible for our words, for our own practice. Our readers will always be justified in asking, as Sartre did: "What aspect of the world do you want to disclose? What change do you want to bring into the world by this disclosure?"[47] They will also always be justified in asking how far our reading genuinely illuminates the text, how far it helps us to understand something we didn't understand before. In literary criticism, both politics and aesthetics are matters of response, judgment, and responsibility.

The *doxa* of critique makes us fear that if we were to write in admiration, were to reveal what we cherish, we may come across as blindly submissive and unthinkingly accepting, as if picking fault with a text was always more difficult, more challenging, more serious than giving an account of why it deserves our full attention. This is to confuse critique with critical thinking. Once we learn to read beyond the traditional parameters of critique and suspicion, we will find it easier to show why literature matters, why people should care about it, and why it is important to create a society that takes it for granted that such things are to be cherished and preserved.

Notes

An early version of this chapter was presented at the MLA Convention, Vancouver, Canada, January 8, 2015. Chaired by Rita Felski, the panel was called "Rethinking Critique." The other panelists were Ellen Rooney and Ankhi Mukherjee. I am grateful to Elizabeth Anker, Rita Felski, Niklas Forsberg, and Hugo Strandberg for useful feedback on earlier versions of this chapter.

1   Paul Ricoeur was the first to call Marx, Nietzsche, and Freud "masters of suspicion," in *Freud and Philosophy*, trans. Denis Savage (New Haven, CT: Yale University Press, 1970), 33.

2   Eve Kosofsky Sedgwick, "Paranoid Reading and Reparative Reading, or, You're So Paranoid, You Probably Think This Essay Is about You," in *Touching Feeling: Affect, Pedagogy, Performativity* (Durham, NC: Duke University Press, 2003), 124. A version of this text originally appeared as the introduction to Sedgwick, *Novel Gazing: Queer Readings in Fiction* (Durham, NC: Duke University Press, 1997).

3   Rita Felski, *The Limits of Critique* (Chicago: University of Chicago Press, 2016), 6.

4   Sedgwick, "Paranoid Reading and Reparative Reading," 140.

5   See Sedgwick, "Paranoid Reading and Reparative Reading," 125.

6   See Bruno Latour, "Why Has Critique Run Out of Steam? From Matters of Fact to Matters of Concern," *Critical Inquiry* 30, no. 2 (winter 2004): 225–48, esp. 228–32.

7   See Sedgwick, "Paranoid Reading and Reparative Reading," 126.

8   Latour, "Why Has Critique," 231, 248.

9   Stephen Best and Sharon Marcus, "Surface Reading: An Introduction," *Representations*, no. 108 (2009): 1–21, 2, 1.

10   See Simone de Beauvoir, *The Second Sex*, trans. Constance Borde and Sheila Malovany-Chevallier (New York: Knopf, 2010), and Kate Millett, *Sexual Politics* (Garden City, NY: Doubleday, 1970).

11   Fredric Jameson, *The Political Unconscious: Narrative as a Socially Symbolic Act* (Ithaca, NY: Cornell University Press, 1981), 60.

12   Best and Marcus, "Surface Reading," 1.

13   Carolyn Lesjak, "Reading Dialectically," *Criticism* 55, no. 2 (2013): 248.

14   Lesjak, "Reading Dialectically," 241. I discuss common sense and critique at length in chapter 7 of my forthcoming book, *Revolution of the Ordinary: Literary Studies after Wittgenstein, Austin, and Cavell*.

15   In *The Limits of Critique*, Felski considers Latour's actor-network theory to be a new method for literary criticism. Given my definition of "method," I would call it a method if the theory provides ways for the critic to do something else or something more than reading, thinking, judging.

16   Toril Moi, "The Adventure of Reading: Literature and Philosophy, Cavell and Beauvoir," *Literature and Theology* 25, no. 2 (June 2011): 125–40, esp. 125–27.

17   Ludwig Wittgenstein, *Philosophical Investigations: The German Text, with an English Translation*, translated by G. E. M. Anscombe, P. M. S. Hacker, and Joachim Schulte, rev. 4th ed. (Malden, MA: Wiley-Blackwell, 2009; first published 1953), §120. Further quotations are cited parenthetically in the text, marked with §.

18   The best account of Wittgenstein's vision of language is Stanley Cavell's "Excursus on Wittgenstein's Vision of Language," in *The Claim of Reason: Wittgenstein, Skepticism, Morality, and Tragedy* (New York: Oxford University Press, 1999), 168–90. But see also chapters 1 and 2 in my forthcoming book, *Revolution of the Ordinary: Literary Studies after Wittgenstein, Austin, and Cavell*.

19   Stanley Cavell, "A Matter of Meaning It," in *Must We Mean What We Say?* (Cambridge: Cambridge University Press, 2002), 227.

20   "There is not a single philosophical method, though there are indeed methods, different therapies, as it were" (§133, box).

21   See Toril Moi, "Hedda's Silences: Beauty and Despair in Hedda Gabler," *Modern Drama* 56, no. 4 (2013): 434–56.

22   "The results of philosophy are the discovery of some piece of plain nonsense and the bumps that the understanding has got by running up against the limits of language. They—these bumps—make us see the value of that discovery" (§119).

23 Jameson, *The Political Unconscious*, 60.

24 See Jameson, *The Political Unconscious*, 61.

25 Best and Marcus, "Surface Reading," 16.

26 Ellen Rooney, "Live Free or Describe: The Reading Effect and the Persistence of Form," *differences* 21, no. 3 (2010): 116.

27 See Stanley Cavell, "Aesthetic Problems of Modern Philosophy," in *Must We Mean What We Say?*, esp. 78–79.

28 Sherlock (BBC-TV series), "A Study in Pink" (season 1, episode 1, first broadcast July 25, 2010, 88 min.), dir. Paul McGuigan, written by Steven Moffat, with Benedict Cumberbatch and Martin Freeman.

29 Sigmund Freud, "Fragment of an Analysis of a Case of Hysteria ["Dora"]" (1905), in *The Standard Edition of the Complete Psychological Works*, ed. and trans. James Strachey, 24 vols. (London: Hogarth, 1953–74), 7:12.

30 Freud, "Fragment of an Analysis of a Case of Hysteria," *Standard Edition* 7:77.

31 Freud, "Fragment of an Analysis of a Case of Hysteria," *Standard Edition* 7:77–78.

32 Stanley Cavell, *The Claim of Reason: Wittgenstein, Skepticism, Morality, and Tragedy* (New York: Oxford University Press, 1999; first published 1979), 357.

33 Wittgenstein, "Philosophy of Psychology—A Fragment" (formerly called "Part II" of Philosophical Investigations), §25.

34 Sigmund Freud, "The Method of Interpreting Dreams: An Analysis of a Specimen Dream," in *The Interpretation of Dreams* (1900), *Standard Edition* 4:118.

35 Freud, "The Method of Interpreting Dreams," *Standard Edition* 4:121.

36 Carlo Ginzburg, "Clues: Roots of an Evidential Paradigm," trans. Anne C. Tedeschi and John Tedeschi, in *Clues, Myths, and the Historical Method* (Baltimore: Johns Hopkins University Press, 1992), 102.

37 Ginzburg, "Clues," 106.

38 Søren Kierkegaard, *Fear and Trembling. Repetition*, ed. and trans. Howard V. Hong and Edna H. Hong (Princeton, NJ: Princeton University Press, 1983), 83.

39 Kierkegaard, *Fear and Trembling*, 84.

40 Kierkegaard, *Fear and Trembling*, 63, 65.

41 Stanley Cavell, *The Senses of Walden* (Chicago: University of Chicago Press, 1981).

42 Ginzburg, "Clues," 105.

43 Cavell, "A Matter of Meaning It," 227.

44 Cavell, "Aesthetic Problems of Modern Philosophy," 93.

45 Stanley Cavell, "Must We Mean What We Say?," in *Must We Mean What We Say?*, 20.

46 For a discussion of Austin as an unmasker, see Stanley Cavell, "Austin at Criticism," in *Must We Mean What We Say?*, 113.

47 Jean-Paul Sartre, "What Is Literature?," in *What Is Literature? and Other Essays*, ed. Steven Ungar (Cambridge, MA: Harvard University Press, 1988), 37.

2

The Temptations

Donna Haraway, Feminist Objectivity,

and the Problem of Critique

HEATHER LOVE

Wars. So many wars. Wars outside and wars inside. Cultural wars, science wars, and wars against terrorism. Wars against poverty and wars against the poor. Wars against ignorance and wars out of ignorance. My question is simple: Should we be at war, too, we, the scholars, the intellectuals? Is it really our duty to add fresh ruins to fields of ruins? Is it really our task to add deconstruction to destruction? More iconoclasm to iconoclasm? What has become of the critical spirit? Has it run out of steam?

—BRUNO LATOUR, "Why Has Critique Run Out of Steam? From Matters of Fact to Matters of Concern"

Bruno Latour's 2004 article "Why Has Critique Run Out of Steam? From Matters of Fact to Matters of Concern" opens with a reflection on the militarization of theory.[1] Addressing the culture of skepticism in the contemporary humanities and social sciences, the essay protests against rote forms of critical thought and calls for a renewed empiricism. Arguing that the dominance of large-scale structural explanations and slash-and-burn ideology critique makes it difficult for scholars to account for their objects, Latour suggests that such approaches are not only ineffective but also dangerous. A comment on the state of contemporary thought by a veteran of the science wars, "Why Has Critique Run Out of Steam?" is also retrospective on the history and reception of science studies. Latour's efforts, since *Laboratory Life: The Construction of Scientific Facts* (coauthored with Steve Woolgar [1979]), to redefine research practices have been interpreted as attempts to discredit scientific knowledge.[2] Latour attributes this misunderstanding partly to his failure to emphasize the constructive (rather than deconstructive) aspects of his method. "The mistake we made, the mistake I made, was to believe that there was no efficient way to criticize matters of fact except by moving *away* from them and directing one's attention *toward* the conditions that made them possible."[3] As a countermeasure, Latour asks scholars to take a break from critique and to collectively cultivate a "*stubbornly realist attitude.*"[4]

A historical irony has emerged in the decade since the publication of "Why Has Critique Run Out of Steam?": Latour's cease-fire has led to a spectacular academic flame war. The essay has inspired a number of scholars to experiment with a range of postcritical and posthermeneutic forms of analysis, but it has also raised critical hackles in equal measure.[5] Many have seen Latour's polemic against polemic as an act of aggression, a violent refusal of the resources of poststructuralism, Marxism, and cultural studies. For such critics, Latour's new empiricism sounds a lot like the old empiricism: "neutral" (i.e., apolitical), positivist, and willfully naive regarding questions of language, subjectivity, representation, and power.[6] Eve Kosofsky Sedgwick articulated an earlier argument against critique in her 1996 article "Paranoid Reading and Reparative Reading," using the work of Melanie Klein to argue for a more generous orientation toward scholarly objects of knowledge. Although the response to Sedgwick's essay has been less ambivalent, the fact that essays lamenting the violence of criticism have led to an arms race around critique and postcritique might be a sign that aggression is an ineradicable attribute—if not of *Homo sapiens*, then at least of *Homo academicus.*[7] To outsiders, the polemical energies generated by the debate over critique must seem somewhat surprising, given that they often turn on fine methodological points. Still, for combatants in the field, the stakes could hardly be higher.

Latour has continually upped the ante in his writing on critique, tying the failures of critical thought to pressing contemporary issues including climate change, violence, and the future of democracy. In *An Inquiry into the Modes of Existence* (2013), he champions postcritical methods by arguing that they are necessary to "ward off the worst," by which he means the mutual destruction of species and planet ("If there is only one Earth, and it is against us, what are we going to do? No polemology prepares us for conflicts so asymmetrical that we are helpless in the face of Gaia, which is helpless before us").[8] Latour's claims have not impressed his critics, who tend to ignore or discount the explicit focus on politics in recent works such as *Reassembling the Social, The Politics of Nature,* and *An Inquiry into the Modes of Existence*; for scholars of political economy, Latour's focus on objects and networks skirts crucial questions of power, inequality, and social structure.

Proponents of critique do not see this approach as exhausted or ineffective; instead, in their view, critique is the only viable means of resistance in a world ruled by market forces and given over to enlightened cynicism. If Latour focuses on the destruction of planet Earth, critical academics counter with the immiseration of the world's population, casting postcritical scholarship as the indulgence of a narrowly professional, disengaged professoriate. In a 2012 article responding to Stephen Best and Sharon Marcus's essay on "surface reading" (another influential and controversial indictment of critical hermeneutics), early modernist scholar Crystal Bartolovich argues that their focus on what a text says is inadequate because it does not "move beyond the level of individual—and social—limitations so that we might approach truth."[9] Bartolovich sets a high bar for literary critics, suggesting that readings fail if they do not aspire "to assemble the scattered body of truth," to ask questions "whose pursuit will result in contention that can be resolved only by structural change beyond the literary institution," and to "reassert the value of the humanities" in order to address "how we might at last create a sustainable world in which the 'free development of each is the condition for the free development of all.'"[10] For Bartolovich, scholarship without revolution as its ultimate horizon betrays the legitimate aims of the humanities.

It is possible that the fate of the earth and its peoples depends on the resolution of these questions of method. However, it often seems that the most salient context for these debates is not global survival but rather the university, with its long-standing fractures along disciplinary lines.[11] The critique debates repeatedly invoke the divergent epistemologies, methodologies, and values in the humanities, the sciences, and the social sciences. Key terms in these debates—objectivity, truth, reality, description, interpretation, relativism, representation, and skepticism—recall a long history of such tensions; the real stakes seem to be less about geopolitics than about local struggles over the future of close reading, the rise of cognitive science, the closing of national language programs, funding for digital humanities projects, and the uses of big data. Scholars invoke canonical methodological and epistemological debates, but also draw on familiar characterizations of humanists and scientists, trading blows about positivism and aestheticism, naive empiricism and blasé knowingness.[12] Attending carefully to the rhetoric of these debates may teach us more about the state of the contemporary university than they do about Gaia or Google Earth.

In this essay, I return to the early work of the feminist science studies scholar Donna Haraway to adjudicate the question of critique. As is so often the case, there is a feminist predecessor whose contributions to this question have gone mostly unremarked. Writing in the 1980s, Haraway addressed both the uses and limits of critique a decade before the beginning of the current debates (which we might date to Sedgwick's essay on paranoid and reparative reading). Furthermore, Haraway pursued an account of critique as a problem of the disciplines, one inseparable from persistent conflicts between the humanities, the sciences, and the social sciences. In developing a robust interdisciplinary methodology for feminist science studies, Haraway situated her research in the context of a contradictory field of knowledge production, riven by tensions between representation and reality, interpretation and description, values and facts. Haraway's commitment throughout her work to epistemological disruption and social transformation aligns her with the protocols of literary and cultural studies, and has made her a hero to critical humanities scholars. Yet she is deeply engaged with the epistemology and methods of scientific inquiry; while critical of positivism, she remained committed to alternative and feminist versions of objectivity. Haraway's investments in scientific methods and epistemologies have been largely forgotten by scholars in feminist and cultural studies, who read her work as a critique of scientific objectivity and as a wellspring of alternative epistemologies and ontologies.

This essay reads Haraway's early work on scientific epistemology and her magisterial 1989 volume *Primate Visions* to emphasize her dual investment in the anchoring and the destabilization of reality. I argue that her attention to the "temptations" of positivism and skepticism, as well as her strong commitment to both scientific practice and to social transformation, make her an early and indispensable arbiter of the problem of critique. The complex and ambivalent position that Haraway staked out in this work has been simplified in her identification with feminist critique. Haraway's defining role in feminist science studies depends on her use of mixed methods and, in particular, her dream of cultivating a feminist version of objectivity. Through this work, Haraway suggests that critique and care are not mutually exclusive and that descriptions of the world as it is should not be confused with an endorsement of the status quo.

Gender-in-the-Making

The fact that Latour's lament about the militarization of theory and criticism has resulted in escalating conflicts about critique and postcritique would hardly surprise Haraway. In her essay "Modest_Witness@Second_Millennium" (1997), she discusses the martial rhetoric of "mainstream science studies," noting that its accounts of the production and dissemination of scientific facts tends to focus disproportionately on tactics, strategic allies, and takeovers.[13] Latour in particular is cited as an example of the militarization of method; Haraway contends that his tracings of the construction of scientific knowledge tend to emphasize feats of epistemological strength and to overinvest in the fates of winners and losers. But the fact that mainstream science studies is linked to a masculinist and martial rhetoric does not lead her to reject its methodology. Instead, in a move that is characteristic of her feminist engagement with the resources of both science and science studies, Haraway adopts the methodology of tracing science "in-the-making" order to pursue different ends. In "Modest_Witness," Haraway suggests that a thoroughgoing attention to the techniques of knowledge production would yield a fuller account not only of the construction of scientific facts but also of social categories.

"Modest_Witness" opens with a discussion of Steven Shapin and Simon Schaffer's 1985 book *Leviathan and the Air Pump*, in which they trace the significance of the values of invisibility and modesty to the construction of scientific objectivity in modernity. Freeing himself not only of bias, but also of all traces of subjecthood, the "modest witness" or scientific observer must embody the foundational virtue of "transparency" (26) in order to underwrite the reign of the fact or the modern "'culture of no culture'" (23).[14] Haraway explains, "This is the culture within which contingent facts—the real case about the world—can be established with all the authority, but none of the considerable problems, of transcendental truth" (23). Within technoscientific modernity, adopting the stance of modesty reaps substantial (and immodest) rewards: "epistemological and social power" (23–24). But these rewards are not distributed evenly, since cultivating transparency is contingent on belonging to the "'unmarked category'" (23). As Haraway argues, "Colored, sexed, and laboring persons still have to do a lot of work to become similarly transparent to count as objective, modest witnesses to the world rather than to their 'bias' or 'special interest'" (32). Furthermore, the "world of scientific gentlemen" (28) not only determined who could participate in these new practices of knowledge making, it also forged gendered (and sexed and raced and classed) norms about what would count as knowledge. Modern forms of scientific objectivity were in Haraway's view a technology of gender, which helped to establish "what counted as objective and subjective, political and technical, abstract and concrete, credible and ridiculous" (29) and which was "instrumental in both sustaining old and in crafting new 'gendered' ways of life" (28).

One of the key products of the "experimental way of life" was a new form of masculinity defined not by heroic or violent action but rather by "measure, moderation, solicitude, studied equilibrium, and reticence in command" (231). With reference to the work of David Noble, Elizabeth Potter, and Bonnie Wheeler, Haraway considers the rise of the figure of the *vir modestus*, how practices of "disciplined ethical restraint" (31) and "gendered self-renunciation" (31) prevented scholarly, retiring men from being labeled soft or feminine. Haraway draws a connection between the early modern period and the present day, arguing that mainstream science studies reinvests in the myth of the modest witness even as it challenges the ideology of scientific objectivity and philosophical realism. However, in an analysis of what she calls a "relentless, recursive mimesis" (34), or a mirroring between method and object of study, she notes that work in the field represents a throwback to older forms of masculine prowess. In a reading of Latour's *Science in Action* (1988), Haraway argues that his methodology in the book "intensifies the structure of heroic action . . .—both in the narrative of science and in the discourse of the science studies scholar," which casts technoscience as warfare (234). Haraway continues, "The action in science-in-the-making is all trials and feats of strength, amassing of allies, forging of worlds in the strength and numbers of forced allies. All action is agonistic; the creative abstraction is both breathtaking and numbingly conventional. Trials of strength decide whether a representation holds or not. Period" (34). Haraway's point in "Modest_Witness" is not simply to call out the masculinist or violent rhetoric of particular critics. Rather, she looks beyond the apparent differences between Shapin and Latour to offer a more sweeping account of the formation of modern gender. She argues that the constitution of new objects of scientific knowledge is inseparable from the creation of modern forms of gender and gendered inequality.

Shapin and Schaffer's account of the origins of scientific objectivity is crucial to Haraway's argument about the gendered politics of knowledge; she draws on their concept of science-in-the-making to offer an account of "gender-in-the-making" (28). However, she parts ways with mainstream science studies because of its failure to extend this account of the constitution of categories to gender and other categories of social identity. Haraway argues, "Science studies scholars . . . have mistaken other narratives of action about scientific knowledge production as functionalist accounts appealing in the tired old way to preformed categories of the social, such as gender, race, and class" (35). Haraway detects an irony in the fact that these scholars—committed as they are to demonstrating the construction of all categories in material and social processes—take categories of social difference and hierarchy as givens. "This is a strange analytical aberration, to say the least," she observes wryly, "in a community of scholars who play games of epistemological chicken trying to beat each other in the game of showing how all the entities in technoscience are constituted *in* the action of knowledge production, not before the action starts" (29). Haraway puzzles over this failure to extend the interrogative methods of science studies to social categories; she concludes, "Either critical scholars in antiracist, feminist cultural studies of science and technology have not been clear enough about racial formation, gender-in-the-making, the forging of class, and the discursive production of sexuality through the constitutive practices of technoscience themselves, or the science studies scholars are not reading or listening—or both" (235).

Haraway's quarrel with mainstream social science clarifies an important aspect of the critique debates, which often turn on the question of social determination. In "Why Has Critique Run Out of Steam?," Latour objects to explanations that treat "society, discourse, knowledge-slash-power, fields of forces, empires, capitalism" as secret operators, "powerful agents hidden in the dark."[15] Latour's travesty echoes many accounts of critique as a paranoid, reductive mode of interpretation that reifies both objects of analysis and the formidable—but static and one-dimensional—social forces that determine them. But as Haraway's discussion in "Modest_Witness" would suggest, Latour is not interested in restoring complexity and dynamism to these social forces. Instead, he protests the reification of these forces by refusing to engage them at all. Latour assents to the reductive account of social forces which, in his view, proponents of critique have offered, and then drops those categories from his analysis altogether. Through his method of actor-network theory, Latour sidesteps questions of large-scale social determination, choosing instead to focus on concrete objects in situations of complex, contingent interdependency. Latour frames his refusal of social explanations as a matter of ethics, casting critique as a betrayal. He argues that scholars might cultivate more intimate, respectful, and productive relations with their objects of study by installing "matters of concern" at the heart of their inquiry rather than "matters of fact."

Citing Haraway, Latour asks, "Can we devise another powerful descriptive tool that deals this time with matters of concern and whose import then will no longer be to debunk but to protect and to care, as Donna Haraway would put it? Is it really possible to transform the critical urge in the ethos of someone who adds reality to matters of fact and not subtract reality?"[16] In the turn from critique to care, Latour hopes to light up his objects, making their complexity, richness, and in-the-making qualities visible. Haraway also embraces this central science studies methodology, yet she draws the line between object and context differently. While Latour seeks to suspend determination in order to give it full attention, Haraway imagines extending attention from the object to its contexts, seeing how *all* of the entities in technoscience—including gender, and other forms of social determination—are "constituted *in* the action of knowledge production, not before the action starts." Haraway treats gender as a matter of concern, not a static background against which matters of concern can be defined. In this context, explanation via social "context" is not necessarily reductive; rather, explanations along these lines can be caring engagements both with our objects and with their determinants in the social world.

If Latour scants attention to the in-the-making quality of social categories, the same cannot be said of critics in cultural studies, who have fully absorbed an understanding of gender as, in Haraway's term, a "relationship" (228). Accounts of the role of gendered inequality in shaping modern knowledge (as well as the definition of public and private spheres, the senses, the meaning of labor and the body, etc.) have demonstrated the expansiveness and dynamism of gender as a category. But outside the context of feminist science studies, many accounts of the in-the-making quality of gender fail to reckon with its imbrication with a complex and uneven field of technoscience. Instead, Western scientific modernity is treated as a monolith, an unvarying story of masculinist domination rather than an entity in-the-making. By reifying modernity, critics fail to acknowledge the variety and contingency of scientific practices of objectification, experiment, and verification. Tracking the history of objectivity reveals a diverse field of practices, conceptual frameworks, ideologies, and ethical commitments.[17] Recent debates about method and critique have repeatedly turned on the question of the novelty of the new empiricism: is this just positivism by another name? Meanwhile, the divergent trajectories of the *old* empiricism have been left to one side.

In "Modest_Witness," Haraway writes, "I am at least as invested in the continuing need for stabilizing contingent matters of fact to ground serious claims on each other as any child of the Scientific Revolution could be" (33). Haraway's critique of the flattening of categories of gender, race, class, and sexuality in both technoscience and mainstream science studies constitutes her central contribution to feminist cultural studies. But she also insisted on the importance of reckoning with technoscience both as a major force in modernity and as a resource. Over the past several decades, mainstream science studies scholars have failed to acknowledge the complexity of accounts of gender, race, class, and sexuality by feminist science studies scholars (as well as other critical humanists). During the same time, the feminist reception of Haraway has failed to account for her commitment to the rhetoric, methods, and culture of the sciences. In "Modest_Witness," Haraway suggests how the resources of the critical humanities can be combined with those of science and science studies. This engagement with the resources (or what, in *Primate Visions*, she calls the temptations) of these disparate disciplines constitutes Haraway's contribution to the critique debates. That contribution is visible only from a robust interdisciplinary perspective; attempting to frame Haraway either within feminist cultural studies or in science studies renders her tense, dynamic engagement of the problem of critique invisible.

Concrete Objectivity

In her essay "Situated Knowledges: The Science Question in Feminism and the Privilege of Partial Perspective" (1988), Haraway narrates her intellectual trajectory, describing the psychic and epistemological costs of a commitment to a strong form of social constructionism. Reflecting on the rise of feminist science studies, she writes,

> I, and others, started out wanting a strong tool for deconstructing the truth claims of hostile science by showing the radical historical specificity, and so contestability, of every layer of the onion of scientific and technological constructions, and we end up with a kind of epistemological electroshock therapy, which far from ushering us into the high stakes table of the game of contesting public truths, lays us out on the table with self-induced multiple personality disorder. We wanted a way to go beyond showing bias in science (that proved too easy anyhow) and beyond separating the good scientific sheep from the bad goats of use and misuse. It seemed promising to do this by the strongest possible constructionist argument that left no cracks for reducing the issues to bias versus objectivity, use versus misuse,

science versus pseudoscience. We unmasked the doctrines of objectivity because they threatened our budding sense of collective historical subjectivity and agency and our "embodied" sense of the truth, and we ended up with one more excuse for not learning any post-Newtonian physics and with one more reason to drop the old feminist self-help practices of repairing our own cars. They're just texts anyway, so let the boys have them back.[18]

Years before Latour articulated his concern about the elision of social construction with deconstruction, Haraway voices deep reservations about a critical viewpoint that, in aiming for historical specificity, contestability, and the cultivation of new forms of agency, ends up as "epistemological electroshock therapy." In language that recalls Clifford Geertz's oft-cited assertion that it is "turtles all the way down," Haraway recalls the effort to unpeel every layer of the onion of technoscientific epistemology and practice, and its unintended consequences.[19] Haraway questions what will be left once all these layers have been removed. The danger of such an approach is that it will limit the participation of feminist scholars in public forums where urgent matters of technoscience are decided, and that it will end by dismissing important forms of practice, from physics to car repair.[20]

Haraway identifies this endless questioning of reality as one of "two poles of a tempting dichotomy on the question of objectivity" that has "trapped" feminists (576). She associates this seduction with the work of social constructionists in science studies, who focus on the material processes and rhetoric of science in order to challenge the "ideological doctrines of disembodied scientific objectivity" (576). They argue that no practicing scientists ever embraced that line anyway, which is just a distraction from "the real game in town" (577), the work of persuasion. Haraway writes, "The strong program in the sociology of knowledge joins with the lovely and nasty tools of semiology and deconstruction to insist on the rhetorical nature of truth, including scientific truth" (577). Making all truth into a matter of rhetoric calls up a powerful resistance in Haraway, who suggests the importance of being able to "talk about reality":

So much for those of us who would still like to talk about reality with more confidence than we allow the Christian Right when they discuss the Second Coming and their being raptured out of the final destruction of the world. We would like to think our appeals to real worlds are more than a desperate lurch away from cynicism and an act of faith like any other cult's, no matter how much space we generously give to all the rich and always historically specific mediations through which we and everybody else must know the world. But the further I get in describing the radical social constructionist program and a particular version of postmodernism, the more nervous I get. The imagery of force fields, of moves in a fully textualized and coded world, which is the working metaphor in many arguments about socially negotiated reality for the postmodern subject, is, just for starters, an image of high-tech military fields, of automated academic battlefields, where blips of light called players disintegrate (what a metaphor!) each other to stay in the knowledge and power game. Technoscience and science fiction collapse in the sum of their radiant (ir)reality—war. (577)

The strong program in the sociology of knowledge threatens to replace reality with an image of a "fully textualized and coded world." As in "Modest_ Witness," Haraway worries about the fact that such accounts cast the entire social world as a battlefield. In this instance, however, Haraway blames not just the martial metaphors that subtend science-in-action, but also the powerful concoction of postmodernism and "the acid tools of critical discourse" (577). In language that emphasizes her ambivalence regarding this temptation, Haraway allies critique with skepticism, suggesting that such "lovely and nasty tools" have made it impossible to have important conversations about reality.

In owning her desire to continue to talk about real worlds, Haraway characterizes herself as one of those who have "tried to stay sane in these disassembled and disassembling times by holding out for a feminist version of objectivity" (578). Rather than seeing this desire simply as a corrective to postmodernism gone wild, however, Haraway discusses it as the "other seductive end of the objectivity problem" (578), a temptation that must be balanced along with a keen awareness of mediation. Alongside a critical understanding of historical contingency, radical difference, and semiotic play, feminists need a "no-nonsense commitment to faithful accounts of a 'real' world" (579). Identifying a strand of "feminist empiricism" (579) that she credits to Evelyn Fox Keller and to Sandra Harding's concept of a "successor science," Haraway suggests the importance of "enforceable, reliable accounts of things" (580).[21] "Situated Knowledges" considers how such accounts, or the desire for them, can be brought into conversation with critique. In formulating her concept of feminist objectivity, Haraway must distinguish a "no-nonsense commitment to faithful accounts of a 'real' world" (579) from the kinds of limited and limiting ideologies of objectivity that she critiques in "Modest_Witness," which she refers to here as the "god trick of seeing everything from nowhere" (581). As Haraway argues, "Feminist objectivity means quite simply situated knowledges" (581); it means admitting bias as inevitable, acknowledging the limits of reason, and cultivating an "embodied, therefore accountable, objectivity" (588).

In "Situated Knowledges," Haraway argues that a robust and self-reflexive concept of objectivity would allow feminists to intervene more effectively in both the semiotic and material practices of science. In her historical and sociological research, she turns up a diversity of practices in both the past and the present. That diversity is crucial to Haraway's history of twentieth-century primatology, *Primate Visions: Gender, Race, and Nature in the World of Modern Science* (1989).[22] In her introduction to the book, which overlaps with "Situated Knowledges," Haraway multiplies the two poles of the objectivity problem to four. She describes her aim in the book to "enter current debates about the social construction of knowledge without succumbing completely to any of *four* very tempting positions" (6, my emphasis). These positions include: the rejection of epistemological realism (which she associates with Latour and his version of science studies); the analysis of power through Marxist, feminist, and anticolonial frameworks; the perspective of the scientists themselves, who suggest that their extended observations of primates in the field is "getting at" the reality of that world; and what she calls the "master temptation," "the temptation to look always through the lenses ground on the stones of the complex histories of gender and race in the constructions of modern science around the globe" (8). Haraway acknowledges that these temptations are "also major resources for the approaches for this book" (6), the very perspectives out of which she builds her argument. Her treatment of the four temptations is not simply a matter of balance or integration; rather she plays these polarities off against each other, mining the tensions between them as well as their moments of intersection or complementarity.

The dynamism and ambivalence of Haraway's method has been lost in her reception, which has been selective in its account of her methodology. Haraway's uptake within postmodern feminism has succumbed to the temptation to identify her wholly with the positions she characterizes as the first, but especially the second and fourth temptations; but in this context there has been scant attention to her investment in the third temptation—which includes not only respect but also love for the practices and epistemological orientation of working primatologists. In feminist and cultural studies, *Primate Visions* is remembered mostly for its widely cited chapter, "Teddy

Bear Patriarchy," a masterpiece of ideology critique that traces the story of the founding of the American Museum of Natural History. Haraway considers the reign of "'naked eye' science" during the early twentieth century, focusing on the creation of the museum's anthropological and ethological displays: "perfectly suited to the camera," and aimed toward the "possession, production, preservation, consumption, surveillance, appreciation, and control of nature" (45). Such limited forms of objectivity, in which ideological neutrality conceals projects of resource extraction and domination, are the primary target of *Primate Visions*.

This ideological version of objectivity does not exhaust the possible meanings of the term for Haraway. Objectivity also refers to the "concrete objectivity" (13) that insists on the "interests and stakes" that go into making scientific observations. Objectivity is also the "twin" or dialectical partner of empathy; they are in "constant productive tension" in the "western scientific tool kit" (293). Objectivity can also refer to the "art of observation" undertaken in the field, which (according to Haraway) Jane Goodall described as requiring "years of patience and yielding quiet triumphs" (136). Practices of observation in the field are an object of particular interest to Haraway. She describes the naturalistic field as "primate science's privileged semiotic center" (368), considering the "kinds of objects of knowledge which historically can exist and are made to exist by the mundane practice of science in the world really structured by war, capitalist economic organization, and male-dominant social life" (110–11). The field is also the site for extended practices of attention, for experiments in producing new objects of knowledge, and for experiments in cohabitation and care. No one can escape the histories that condition scientific practice, or start fresh, constituting "meanings by wishing them into existence," since "discourse is a material practice" (111). Every practice of knowledge production is both a compromise with multiple histories and an insecure venture in an unjust world: Haraway insists this is equally true of field primatology and postmodern feminism.

Haraway's most extended discussion of her own relation to practices of scientific objectivity is in the context of the third temptation. She writes,

> The third temptation comes from the siren call of the scientists themselves; they keep pointing out that they are, among other things, watching monkeys and apes. In some sense, more or less nuanced, they insist that scientific practice "gets at" the world. They claim that scientific knowledge is not simply about power and control. They claim that their knowledge some-

how translates the active voice of their subjects, the objects of knowledge. Without necessarily being compelled by their aesthetic of realism or their theories of representation, I believe them in the strong sense that my imaginative and intellectual life and my professional and political commitments in the world respond to these scientific accounts. Scientists are adept at providing good grounds for their belief in their accounts and for action on their basis. Just how science "gets at" the world remains far from resolved. What does seem resolved, however, is that science grows from and enables concrete ways of life, including particular constructions of love, knowledge, and power. That is the core of its instrumentalism and the limit to its universalism. (8)

In this remarkable passage, Haraway performs her ambivalent attachment to scientific practice and epistemology. Rehearsing the defense of scientific objectivity as told by the scientists themselves, who believe they are "getting at" reality though their sustained observations, she questions what such access might mean. But she also avows the strength of her imaginative, intellectual, professional, and political investment in these practices. Haraway admires the persuasiveness of scientific accounts: scientists are good at demonstrating the grounds for their beliefs, and effective in acting on them; they thus provide a model for feminists and demonstrate another important aspect of objectivity. But even more, she recognizes science as growing from and enabling "concrete forms of life." Haraway describes science not as an ideology of objectivity but as a way of life, an extensive, prolific praxis. If we are to understand science and to critique it responsibly, we have to see it as a dynamic field, bound up with love, knowledge, *and* power, and not reducible to any one of these dimensions.

For Haraway, scholarship means yielding to and resisting temptations. As a feminist science studies scholar, Haraway brings to the table the deconstructive resources of postmodern feminism and the attention to practice and knowledge-in-the-making of science studies. As a trained scientist, she also brings a commitment to observational and experimental methods, to the practices of objectification, description, and testing that attempt to make contact with the real world. She suggests that *all* the "lovely and nasty tools" at our disposal—social construction, semiology, objectification, feminism, empirical observation, anticolonial thought, verification, and storytelling—need to be taken up and held at bay. Like Latour, Haraway tracks the tension between productive and critical or disruptive modes of knowledge, but she identifies this tension as ineradicable: "It is specifically the permanent tension between construction and deconstruction, identification moves and destabilization moves, that I see, not as uniquely feminist, but as inherent to feminism—and to science. Both feminist and scientific discourses are critical projects built in order to destabilize and reimagine their methods and objects of knowledge in complex power fields" (324).

Writing in 1989, Haraway insisted that the tension between construction and deconstruction is a permanent and vital aspect of both scientific and feminist practice. Haraway offers a crucial perspective in the context of the contemporary debates about critique, where practices of stabilization are routinely equated with an attachment to the status quo, and where practices of destabilization are dismissed either as relativist or, more recently, as corrosive and irresponsible. Haraway suggests that there is no stable connection between forms of knowledge production and particular ethical attitudes or political commitments; there are different kinds of critique, just as there are different kinds of objectivity, and one cannot judge in advance whether empirical research or Derridean deconstruction will do justice to its objects, or will make an opening for social transformation. Instead, for Haraway, any form of research is an ongoing process of semiosis—or "politics by other means" (111)—in a dense historical and material field. Haraway helps us to see both critique and anticritique as the tempting poles of the objectivity debate, attempts to stake out fixed positions rather than engaging in the risky business of destabilizing and restabilizing knowledge in a field permanently in flux.

The Way Things Are

In her work on objectivity, critique, and method, Haraway avoids totalizing positions by adopting a dynamic approach that sets classic oppositions in the humanities and sciences in productive tension with one another. Haraway's approach avoids many of the faults that have been associated with postcritical and posthermeneutic modes of reading, which are often identified as flattening and static. Carolyn Lesjak's 2013 essay "Reading Dialectically" critically examines a range of postcritical reading methods, including new formalism, "narratological, cognitive, and other data-based versions of literary criticism," Elaine Scarry's humanist empiricism, David Bordwell's "middle-level research," Best and Marcus's "surface reading," and my own elaboration of a "close but not deep" reading practice.[23] In these practices, Lesjak sees a common acceptance of the reduced conditions of the humanities in the neoliberal university, legible in the diminished ambition of these practices as well as their tendency to take at face value. Drawing on Latour's concept of matters of concern, Lesjak turns to the work of Fredric Jameson and Eve Kosofsky Sedgwick to develop a spatial, sensory mode of reading that avoids the pitfalls of both ideology critique and surface reading.

Nathan K. Hensley has also critiqued the flattening effect of recent post-critical modes of reading. In his essay "Curatorial Reading and Endless War," he points to the material conditions of humanities research in the present what he sees as the instrumentalist and scientistic nature of some recent new methods. Hensley is particularly concerned with the "so-called new materialism," which he sees as both insufficiently materialist and positivist, betraying an ideological "faith in appearances."[24] Hensley focuses on object-centered approaches in the humanities, which he suggests are linked to critical passivity, appeals to common sense, and the "evacuation of the category of the . . . political."[25] Hensley argues that "in scholarship and teaching both, deferring uncritically to objects also ensures a reiterative, even positivistic relationship to the items under observation, since any merely descriptive method must perforce narrate in other terms what already is, however rich or variegated that extant reality might be."[26] This descriptive account of what already exists is, in Hensley's view, not only tautological but also politically bankrupt, a capitulation to the given rather than a way of reaching toward new possibilities not yet materialized in the social world. In a footnote, Hensley assesses Latour's call for a new empiricism, for "another powerful descriptive tool" which would allow us "no longer to debunk but to protect and care."[27] In Hensley's view, Latour's "stubbornly realist attitude" is a form of tourism, an analytic mode that sees things as "inert objects to be observed like scenery."[28]

After critiquing the reduction of critical agency in new modes of reading, Hensley proposes an alternative, which he calls "curatorial reading," which he frames as a "rapprochement" between Latourian methods and Marxist critique. Drawing a distinction between intrinsic forms of engagement (with one's objects of study) and extrinsic forms of engagement (with real-world politics), Hensley argues that a curatorial mode of reading might stay close to its objects while still maintaining a vigilant critical attitude toward injustice and violence in the social world. He writes, "My effort is to remain 'paranoid' (to adapt Eve Sedgwick's term) or critical about extrinsic matters of historical violence (politics) while adopting a 'reparative' or positive dispensation toward the individual objects of its intrinsic acts of reading."[29] Hensley takes Sedgwick as a model because even in her uptake of a postcritical or reparative reading practice, her work remained explicitly engaged; one might also point to the fact that, because her concept of paranoid and reparative reading was indebted to Melanie Klein's account of the depressive position, she did not see either paranoid or reparative reading as programmatic; rather, she regarded both as temporary positions to be taken up and discarded depending on circumstances.[30] Although it is not clear whether Latour-inspired critics adopt an apolitical position across the board, Hensley's suggestion that Latour's attention to objects might be compatible with structural forms of critique is salutary.

Sedgwick's work is Hensley's key example of curatorial reading, but we might look to Haraway for a model of scholarship that combines concern and critique. In *Primate Visions*, Haraway outlines an approach that combines a meticulous, faithful attention to her objects of study with powerful indictments of colonial, racial, sexual, gender, and capitalist oppression. In her dual commitment to the anchoring and destabilization of reality, Haraway exemplifies the value of attentive, close, careful attention to objects, the form of attention that adds reality rather than taking it away, and she resists what Hensley calls "the positivist's bias" toward "the way things are."[31] In its critique of positivism and belief in the transformative power of critique, Haraway's work is consonant with Hensley's. However, she differs from him in defining both empiricism and objectivity more capaciously: while these approaches may coincide with positivist approaches, Haraway's interest extends to a range of practices of observation that are empiricist without being positivist. She situates the practices of field primatologists in the context of long histories of colonial domination, semiotic codes of nature and women, and the elision of whiteness with universal humanity. Yet Haraway nonetheless extols the patience, fidelity, reflexivity, and care that characterize their acts of observation, recording, and description. She opens a gap between science and scientism, suggesting that description is not always "mere description," that there are forms of looking in field sciences that dynamize the landscape rather than turning it into a cabinet of curiosities or a picture postcard. For this reason, Haraway argues that feminists should not give up the claim to truth. In going without a frame, we might be able to see *what else is out there*; such experiments in ways of looking are in the spirit of the critique of objectivity.

In *An Inquiry into the Modes of Existence*, Latour opens a similar gap between empiricism and positivism, gesturing toward the liberation of science from Science. He writes, "Wouldn't sciences delivered from Science, finally capable of deploying their chains of reference without insults on their lips, be lovelier—I mean more objective, more respectable?"[32] Feminists and others may object to Latour's embrace of the values of a peculiarly feminized beauty and respectability. In addition, his consistently scathing comments about critique will alienate many of his readers. Latour's insistence that it is impossible to integrate large-scale structural critique with careful attention to one's objects is dogmatic, as much an instance of Haraway's temptations as the conflation of science and scientism. However, the fact that Latour is dogmatic in his stance against critique does not suggest that his work is positivist. To the contrary, Latour is one of the strongest allies humanists have against positivism; he has done as much as anyone to question the reign of the fact (and has been attacked for it by scientists). If Latour's claim that pluralized antipositivist "sciences" would be more objective rather than less so unsettles those who see objectivity and positivism as identical, it is important to remember that his call for a renewed objectivity echoes several decades of feminist science studies. To the extent that such a renewed objectivity can help to disrupt things as they are, it is in part because of the science studies methodology that Latour helped to develop—what Haraway glosses as the "game of showing how all the entities in technoscience are constituted *in* the action of knowledge production, not before the action starts." For Haraway, this method is sound; she only faults the masculinism of mainstream science studies scholars for failing to pursue the full consequences of this approach, and as a consequence failing to recognize the processual and unfinished quality of all social categories. In his recent work, Latour has emphasized the productive and positive rather than critical aspects of this program, but his turn from (positivist) "matters of fact" to (empiricist) "matters of concern" is a continuation of his earlier work on science-in-the-making, a shift of emphasis rather than a break.

It is striking that across all of these methods and approaches, care remains a consistent goal and an unquestioned value. From Haraway's extension of a feminist ethics of care into contexts of field biology, ecology, and interspecies intimacies; to Sedgwick's account of reparative reading (drawn from a psychoanalytic theory assessing the possibilities for care in wartime); to Hensley's focus on care in the arts of curation; to Latour's attempt to accord respect to his objects by treating them as matters of concern—all of these approaches, whether critical or postcritical, treat care as a desideratum of scholarship, what in the words of poststructuralist, Marxist, anticolonial, feminist critic Gayatri

Spivak's words we "cannot not want."[33] Spivak uses this phrase in the context of an interview in which she addresses the utility of deconstruction; she presents deconstruction not as corrosive or destructive, but rather as a sustained interrogation of values:

> Deconstruction does not say there is no subject, there is no truth, there is no history. It simply questions the privileging of identity so that someone is believed to have the truth. It is not the exposure of error. It is constantly and persistently looking into how truths are produced. That's why deconstruction doesn't say logocentrism is a pathology, or metaphysical enclosures are something you can escape. Deconstruction, if one wants a formula, is, among other things, a persistent critique of what one cannot not want.[34]

Deconstruction, according to Spivak, does not attempt to destroy or undermine values but rather provides critical tools to interrogate the values that scholars continue to invest in—the subject, truth, history. Her method for investigating them echoes the key method of science studies, the "constant and persistent" investigation into how knowledge is made. Reading Spivak alongside Haraway's investigation into situated knowledges and Latour's recent turn toward "new empiricism" suggests that the affective and political valences of "persistent critique" cannot be determined in advance: they too are established in-the-making.

While we may find common ground in this account of critique as productive rather than destructive, it is nonetheless the case that the gulf between empirical practices of observation and description and textual practices of interpretation and evaluation remains deep. Since this tension is constitutive of the disciplinary divisions of the modern university, there is no reason to expect that it will be resolved anytime soon. As I have suggested in my account of Haraway's method, making those differences explicit and placing them at the center of our research is ultimately more useful than either ignoring them or papering them over through weak claims to interdisciplinary cooperation; such sidelining of disciplinary conflict results in displaced flame wars about critique and other matters. I have suggested that apocalyptic rhetoric about the destruction of planet Earth fails to grapple with more local conflicts and dangers; however, it is true that scholars across disciplines are concerned with the question of care—how to care for our objects of knowledge, and for the world beyond.

Such conversations would be well served by attention to care-in-the-making, that is to say, by a genealogy of this term's emergence as an unquestioned scholarly value (despite persistent critiques of the empathy and care in the humanities and social sciences). This essay is not the place to unfold this history. Instead, my aim is to question some persistent assumptions in the humanities about the epistemology, ethics, and politics of research in the sciences and social sciences, and to suggest that while the tools of empiricism can be used in the service of social control, the stabilization of meaning, and assent to the status quo, their applications vary. Work on the subject, truth, and history is compatible with care both for our objects of knowledge and for the social and natural world; critique need not be only corrosive, but it can also represent a commitment to tracing social arrangements in-the-making; and the careful examination of the world as it appears does not imply a capitulation to *the way things are.*

Notes

1   Bruno Latour, "Why Has Critique Run Out of Steam? From Matters of Fact to Matters of Concern," *Critical Inquiry* 30, no. 2 (winter 2004): 225–48.

2   Bruno Latour and Steve Woolgar, *Laboratory Life: The Construction of Scientific Facts* (Princeton, NJ: Princeton University Press, 1986 [1979]).

3   Latour, "Why Has Critique," 231; italics in original.

4   Latour, "Why Has Critique," 231; italics in original.

5   The bibliography on critique and postcritique is now extensive. Latour has had a significant influence in literary studies, although Eve Kosofsky Sedgwick's concept of "reparative reading," first articulated in 1997, has had the greatest impact in the field. Sedgwick's essay "Paranoid Reading and Reparative Reading; or, You're So Paranoid, You Probably Think This Introduction Is about You," inspired the articulation of a host of new reading methods across the discipline. Some influential examples include Sharon Marcus's just reading, Stephen Best and Sharon Marcus's surface reading, Cannon Schmitt's literal reading, and Timothy Bewes's reading with the grain. Rita Felski's book *The Limits of Critique* offers both a retrospective on this theoretical moment and a powerful argument on behalf of postcritical modes of thought. There have also been a number of defenses of critique in the wake of these writings, a few of which I discuss in this essay. Eve Kosofsky Sedgwick, "Paranoid Reading and Reparative Reading; or, You're So Paranoid, You Probably Think This Introduction Is about You," in *Novel Gazing: Queer Readings in Fiction,* ed. Sedgwick (Durham, NC: Duke University Press, 1997): 1–37; Sharon Marcus, *Between Women: Friendship, Desire, and Marriage in Victorian England* (Princeton, NJ: Princeton University Press, 2007); Stephen Best and Sharon Marcus, "Surface Reading: An Introduction," *Representations* 108, no. 1 (2009): 1–21; Cannon Schmitt, "Tidal Conrad (Literally)," *Victorian Studies* 55, no. 1 (2012): 7–29; Timothy Bewes, "Reading with the Grain: A New

World in Literary Criticism," *differences* 21, no. 3 (2010): 1–33; and Rita Felski, *The Limits of Critique* (Chicago: University of Chicago Press, 2015).

6   The distinction between positivism (aimed toward the discovery of truth) and empiricism (an additive practice aimed toward a better view of the object) is important in this essay.

7   A recent cluster of essays on affect, psychoanalysis, and interpretation in *Feminist Theory* explore the persistence of interpretation and aggression in postcritical and reparative modes of reading. The central essay by Robyn Wiegman ("The Times We're In: Queer Feminist Criticism and the Reparative 'Turn'") takes up questions of temporality and affect in recent criticism in order to consider the persistence of the interpretive drive within forms of reparative reading. Two responses to Wiegman's essay put pressure on the equation of reparation with love: considering the defunding of the university, Clare Hemmings suggests that we might see reparative reading as a "spectacular avoidance tactic" (29), an attempt to focus on the privilege of academics rather than their marginalization; Jackie Stacey argues both that reparative reading collapses affect and method and that, by attempting to ground critical practice in love and care, it fails to account for the ambivalence that Melanie Klein (among others) sees as fundamental to reparation. Robyn Wiegman, "The Times We're In: Queer Feminist Criticism and the Reparative 'Turn,'" *Feminist Theory* 15, no. 1 (2014): 4–25; Clare Hemmings, "The Materials of Reparation," *Feminist Theory* 15, no. 1 (2014): 27–30; Jackie Stacey, "Wishing Away Ambivalence," *Feminist Theory* 15, no. 1 (2014): 39–49; see also Love, "Truth and Consequences: On Paranoid Reading and Reparative Reading," *Criticism* 52, no. 2 (spring 2010): 235–41.

8   Bruno Latour, *An Inquiry into the Modes of Existence: An Anthropology of the Moderns*, trans. Catherine Porter (Cambridge, MA: Harvard University Press, 2013), 485–86.

9   Crystal Bartolovich, "Humanities of Scale: Marxism, Surface Reading—and Milton," *PMLA* 127, no. 1 (2012): 115–21, 119, 120.

10 Bartolovich, "Humanities of Scale," 120.

11 To articulate such skepticism is not to step outside the battle lines that have been drawn in the debates over critique, postcritique, and new reading methods. The localization of debates to institutional contexts has been seen as reflective of a narrow professionalism produced by the downsizing of intellectual life in the era of neoliberalism. Bartolovich makes a related argument about the work of Stanley Fish and its focus on the institutional conditions of knowledge production.

12 These tensions are perhaps most evident in the way that commenters on both sides characterize (or caricature) each other. In *An Inquiry into Modes of Existence*, Latour associates Derridean deconstruction with the "temptations of the critical spirit" (156), and, in a discussion of the Magritte painting *This Is Not a Pipe*, he describes the standard response toward its ironic motto as "the knowing blasé chuckle of the critical connoisseur" (147). It is not merely the epistemology of critical humanism that is being travestied here, but also its ethos and

style—a languid hauteur more at home in the café than in the laboratory. Critics in the humanities give back as good as they get, identifying Latour's empirical method as narrow and positivist. In the recent special issue of *Victorian Studies* that they edited, "The Ends of History," Lauren M. E. Goodlad and Andrew Sartori assess Latour's influence, arguing that his method is a poor fit with both the methodological and political commitments of a properly historicist literary criticism. Latour's sociology, they argue, "seeks to resolutely exclude abstractions from the domain of knowledge. . . . We do not doubt that Latour is providing a useful method, perhaps a bracing tonic for some sclerotic critical habits. His focus on the tangible and local—on providing a detailed snapshot of a set of objects in a given place—offers great clarity. But that clarity comes courtesy of the narrowing space and, more strikingly yet, the freezing of time." In contrast to the figure of the worldly café habitué conjured by Latour, here the science studies scholar appears not as an anti-dualist philosophe but as a tinkerer, hobbyist, or even a quack doctor. Long-standing resentments between humanists and scientists underwrite these exaggerated portraits. Lauren M. E. Goodlad and Andrew Sartori, "The Ends of History: Introduction," special issue, *Victorian Studies* 55, no. 4 (summer 2013): 591–614, 604.

13 Donna Haraway, "Modest_Witness@Second_Millenium," *Modest_Witness@ Second_Millennium: FemaleMan©_Meets_OncoMouse™* (New York: Routledge, 1997): 23–39, 34. Further quotations from this work are cited parenthetically in the text.

14 Haraway borrows the term from the work of Sharon Traweek.

15 Latour, "Why Has Critique," 229.

16 Latour, "Why Has Critique," 232.

17 The key history emphasizes the significance (and diversity) of practices of objectivity. See Lorraine Daston and Peter Galison, *Objectivity* (New York: Zone Books, 2010).

18 Donna Haraway, "Situated Knowledges: The Science Question in Feminism and the Privilege of Partial Perspective," *Feminist Studies* 14, no. 3 (fall 1988): 575–99, 578. Further quotations from "Situated Knowledges" will be cited parenthetically in the text.

19 Clifford Geertz, "Thick Description: Toward an Interpretive Theory of Culture," in *The Interpretation of Cultures* (New York: Perseus, 1973), 3–30, 29. See my essay "Close Reading and Thin Description," where I offer a reading of Geertz's essay that resonates with this essay's reading of Haraway. Geertz has been taken up in literary and cultural studies as offering a justification of research practices that do not assume a solid reality that anchors representation; scholars in these fields have ignored his defense (in this same essay) of empirical field research. Geertz warns against "aestheticism" as a form of scholarship that would lose itself in a world of textuality, thus risking loss of contact with the "hard surfaces of life" (30). See Heather Love, "Close Reading and Thin Description," *Public Culture* 25, no. 3 (2013): 401–34, esp. 409–12.

20 Haraway's reference to car repair recalls Latour's frequent turns to the quotidian practices that connect scientific positivism to more diffuse and less dogmatic forms of realism; in "Why Has Critique Run Out of Steam?" he mentions "painting, bird-watching, Shakespeare, baboons, proteins, and so on" (241). Haraway's mention of post-Newtonian physics and car repair in the same breath anticipates this strategy, suggesting the varied uses of sturdy forms of realism. However, while Latour often alludes to such attachments in the context of personal hobbies, Haraway invokes them in the context of collective social transformation, arguing for the importance for women of access to technoscientific epistemology and practice.

21 In the wake of Haraway's article, Harding articulated the concept of "strong objectivity"—a form of objectivity that is made stronger by being "socially situated." Sandra Harding, "Rethinking Standpoint Epistemology: What Is 'Strong Objectivity?,'" in *Feminist Epistemologies*, ed. Linda Alcoff and Elizabeth Potter (New Brunswick, NJ: Rutgers University Press, 1993), 49–82, 50.

22 Donna Haraway, *Primate Visions: Gender, Race, and Nature in the World of Modern Science* (New York: Routledge, 1989). Further quotations from this work are cited parenthetically in the text.

23 Carolyn Lesjak, "Reading Dialectically," *Criticism* 55, no. 2 (spring 2013): 232–77, 266n16.

24 Nathan K. Hensley, "Curatorial Reading and Endless War," *Victorian Studies* 56, no. 1 (autumn 2013): 59–83, 62.

25 Hensley, "Curatorial Reading and Endless War," 63.

26 Hensley, "Curatorial Reading and Endless War," 63.

27 Cited in Hensley, "Curatorial Reading and Endless War," 79n8.

28 Hensley, "Curatorial Reading and Endless War," 79n8.

29 Hensley, "Curatorial Reading and Endless War," 64.

30 Stacey develops this account in "Wishing Away Ambivalence."

31 Hensley, "Curatorial Reading and Endless War," 64.

32 Latour, "An Inquiry into the Modes of Existence," 125.

33 Gayatri Spivak, "Bonding in Difference: Interview with Alfred Arteaga," in *The Spivak Reader*, ed. Donna Landry and Gerald MacLean (New York: Routledge, 1996), 28.

34 Spivak, "Bonding in Difference," 27–28.

3

The Eighteenth-Century Origins of Critique

SIMON DURING

When his *The Birth of Tragedy* was republished in 1886, over a decade after its first appearance, Friedrich Nietzsche added an introduction he called "Versuch einer Selbstkritik" ("An Attempt at Self-critique").[1] It is a remarkable document in which Nietzsche gradually loses control of his critical impulse, although in such a way as to expose the conditions that make his critique possible to start with. Nietzsche wants to make it clear that he no longer agrees with the book— his own book—that readers have in front of them. That is because, under Arthur Schopenhauer's sway, he there critiqued the concept of *Wissenschaft* (science/knowledge) from the perspective of art. What he should have done, he now realizes, was to examine Wissenschaft from the perspective of life. And, in a move which depends on a kind of philology, Nietzsche tells us that book's falsity is expressed in its style, which was also, it seems, adopted by a particular, now rejected, critical persona.[2]

The Birth of Tragedy was, he says, written in "a strange voice" by the disciple of an as-yet "unknown god" who "concealed himself beneath the cowl of a scholar . . . a spirit with strange needs, nameless as yet, a memory brimming over with questions, experiences, hidden things."[3] Such a persona—who seems to draw as much on memories of monks and prophets as of philosophers and critics—cannot fully understand the Greeks, however. To do that one needs to understand the Greek capacity not just to affirm "all that is fearsome, wicked, mysterious, annihilating, and fateful at the very foundations of existence" but to recognize that tragedy and fearsomeness and death are healthy. At the same time, one needs to grasp the converse of this: that the modern requirement— Nietzsche thinks of it as romanticism's requirement—to console oneself imaginatively by avoiding the actual conditions of life, and, most of all, the modern requirement to be democratic, reasonable, emancipatory, utilitarian, optimistic—to be "moral"—are signs of exhaustion. Once inspected from the perspective of "life," modern morality, with its will to critical judgment, becomes "a secret instinct for annihilation . . . the beginning of the end" (9).

Having reached this point, Nietzsche flips again. Without warning, he turns against the argument and persona that he has adopted so far, whom he brusquely addresses thus: "But, Sir, if *your book* is not Romanticism, what on earth is?" (11). Isn't its ruthless criticism of the present itself in the end just a form of critique as consolation? Doesn't it itself harbor a certain unearned optimism? Isn't the only form of critique that escapes the false elevation and comfort of the critical position itself simply *laughter*? To put this in terms that depart only slightly from Nietzsche's own: pessimism, which is the affect that best bears critique once progressivism is revealed as an expression of exhaustion and weakness, can itself be best expressed as something that at least on the surface looks like critique's opposite—laughter. And, importantly, in this turn, critique separates itself from rhetoric. It gives up (ostensibly, at least) on its effort to *persuade*.

Several features of this remarkable performance seem especially relevant in considering critique as a historical formation. First, Nietzsche recognizes that critique requires division. The critic and her object are divided from one another on terms that require the critic to align with certain values or allegiances or purposes, if sometimes unknowingly. This is also to say that criticism is criterion-based. A critic is required to choose or, at least, to assume, standards by which to assess a particular object or field. In *The Birth of Tragedy*, aesthetic criteria examine and test the kind of knowledge that is based on (putatively) Greek reason. But Nietzsche also implicitly recognizes that any set of criteria can be used to test any object whatsoever, and that the strongest criteria are those which extend furthest. Hence, perhaps, his mature preference for life rather than art as a criterion to test knowledge—or, rather, for life *as* art. Life, after all, covers much.

It is apparent, too, that critique involves further issues of scale: in this case Nietzsche's object—the first edition of *Birth of Tragedy*—quickly becomes an example of something much larger: a cultural or social state. And it is apparent, I think, that Nietzsche's particular critical style, his persona, is chosen partly in order to make this scalar leap persuasive. There might be different styles and modes for a critique whose object was just a particular and discrete thing—a specific text, for instance, as against a critique of a large structure, a mode of production, say. Looking back, we can also see that modern critique, like Nietzsche's here, most often deploys a particular scalar structure:

a discrete and small thing (a text, an image, an event) is examined as an example of or portal into a larger structure (an ideological formation, a mode of production).

At any rate, Nietzsche recognizes that critique is issued by *critics* who may be swept away by, or adopt, various moods, disguises, styles, voices, and vehicles, but whose habitual pose is an elevated one in which, as we might put it, skepticism, denunciation, and prophecy encounter one another. Although he does not point it out here, his argument implies that the figure of the critic thought like this has a long genealogy, one that includes, for instance, the Old Testament Prophets and, perhaps more pertinently still, the Greek Cynics, who in their practice of philosophical living set themselves against established conventions (the *Nomos*) and recommended denunciation as a public practice.[4] In this lineage, crucially, critique can take place as laughter or performance or insult or satire. It certainly isn't, and can't be, a matter just of sober and careful philosophical analysis, or at least not unless its play is to be confined to the protocols of reason or Wissenschaft itself, and, for Nietzsche of course, like many before and after him, those protocols themselves demand critique.

Nietzsche recognizes, last, that both because there is no limit to critique and because it is always perspectival and divisive, it can turn against itself too. No critique would seem to be secure from its own undoing, not even one like his self-criticism here which attempts to immunize itself by embracing joyful affirmation.

It is perhaps unsurprising that the accounts of critique that have had most purchase in the modern academy have taken a more restricted view of the topic than did Nietzsche.

On the one side that is because, after Michel Foucault (and 1968), they often think of critique as much in relation to the critic herself as in relation to its object. On this account, critique aims for "the desubjectification of the subject" and does so by focusing on the "government of individualization" through which the modern subject is (supposedly) formed precisely as a bounded individual.[5] Here critique is deemed more an ethical than a social force, tied to a politics searching for new subjectivities. As such, fairly obviously, it has little purchase, for instance, on the practical problems of life under contemporary capitalism. In effect (to use terms that will become clearer below), this is a new form of coterie critique, or, if you'd prefer, a recent symptom of critique's internal limits.

But most work on critique remains under the spell of a more established model that connects critique to the enlightenment project. From this point of view, criticism and reason may be considered as intertwined, even as versions of one another. Under this view, critique appears to be, as Raymond Geuss put it, "a reflective theory which gives agents a kind of knowledge productive of enlightenment and emancipation."[6] From this perspective, it is also considered to be an agent of progressive, historical development—like rationality. In addition, it is routinely considered to be a form of discourse that requires—and justifies—liberal rights to "free speech." Critique becomes a significant social agent on the side of improvement and liberty. Under this account, however, the full range of critical personas, styles, values, and intentions fall from view, especially angry or cynical or exalted or burlesque ones. At the same time, the history in which modern critique emerged as much *against* liberal enlightenment as on its behalf falls from view.

To avoid lapsing back into a history of emancipatory reason, careful histories of critique (of which there exist remarkably few) have characteristically come at their topic askew, whether or not they endorse the enlightenment project itself. Perhaps most usefully, the history of critique has been treated via historical sociology, that is by describing twists and turns in critique's social and political conditions of possibility. (That is partly because, as Harmut Rosa has argued, sociology itself "springs from a critical impulse.")[7] Historical sociology was the method used by what has been arguably the most influential history of critique so far, Reinhart Koselleck's perceptive *Kritik und Krise: Eine Studie zur Pathogene der bürgerlichen Welt* (1959), a book which I think has come to ground an orthodoxy on the topic. It (among other works) stands behind Jürgen Habermas's critical theory of the bourgeois public sphere, for instance, although Koselleck's politics and conceptual presuppositions and intent, which are broadly Schmittean, differ from those of others, like Habermas, who affirm critique as a component of enlightened reason.[8]

Because it comes to critique via history; because it has become, more or less, orthodoxy; and also just because it is so far removed from Nietzsche's more searching if vaguer view, Koselleck's thesis is worth describing at a little length.

Koselleck begins by arguing that the early modern absolutist state—which he thinks was enlightened critique's most important early target—also forms critique's condition of possibility. That is because the absolutist state divided the subject or citizen from the bourgeois person. The first is merely obedient and has no power; the second is an owner of private property, who in his or her private social relations is required to act and talk reflectively and morally. In a word, absolutism sets into place the key division which supports modern critique historically: that between the public and the private, where it organizes, and is organized by, a further division—that between the state and civil society. This structure is a nursery of enlightenment just because the state, as the guardian of social stability, operates by virtue of sheer force at least in its relation to other states, whereas private citizens are required, as I say, to be moral. (Koselleck's argument here has been countered by more recent scholarship that focuses on how neostoicism and natural law theory, especially as articulated in Hugo Grotius's *De jure belli ac pacis* [1625], provided grounds for principles that were universal across states and periods.)[9] That civil societies were nurseries of ethical deportment was the starting point of the period's various "moral reformation" movements, which were put into place across all confessions, and whose success can be measured by our tendency to corral critique inside ethos and "civility."

Under absolutism, then, politics—or rather governmentality—is disjunct from morality, just as it is in Thomas Hobbes's *Leviathan* (1651), absolutism's most important theoretical justification. But then history stirs: the civil realm, thought of as an association of private persons, gradually begins to test and censure the state. For Koselleck, it does so first in England, where a "mixed" constitution, in which formal sovereignty was shared by Parliament, was put into place after 1688. This constitution encouraged citizens not just to act morally and civilly but to set up institutions of sociability and communication (which Habermas was to call the "public sphere") where judgments of government flourished in ways that had been impossible under absolutism. In the process, citizens also formed loose "factions" or "parties" in which those holding different visions of government and, at least sometimes, different religio-moral allegiances, organized attempts to gain power. (Koselleck, however, plays down the actual limits to tolerance in Britain at the period: on this, more below.) For Koselleck the enlightenment forms when conjunct private judgments in a politically divided society begin to claim for themselves a certain universality and neutrality which is then deemed an instrument of reason itself. It is in this way that, as he puts it, "civic morality becomes a public power."[10]

This fusion of reason, civil society, and private judgment, which begins in England circa 1688, spreads across Europe through the next century. For Koselleck, it is enabled by interstate relations, in the first instance because civil society gains legitimacy as the ultimate provider and owner of the public debt required by states to maintain their military forces. Civil society comes ideologically and rhetorically, if not formally, to control the state via the finance capital that it generates and which states required to secure their position against other states. As we have begun to see, at the same time, reason, private judgment, and civil society also join together because civil judgment is "innocent" in comparison to the Hobbesian relations between states.

But, importantly, these larger sociopolitical structures assign authority and power to forms of judgment and knowledge—to critique—that were developed elsewhere: in relation to Christianity and then in relation to (what we would call) culture.

Especially in its early days, criticism was bound to ecclesiastical philology. In particular, Roman Catholicism began to develop new means of ascertaining textual authenticity and accuracy through techniques of what the Oratorian priest, Richard Simon, was already calling "critique" in the 1670s. It did so originally (although Koselleck passes over this) in order to clear itself of "superstitious" accretions in hagiography (scholars like the paleographer and diplomatist Jean Mabillon, connected to the Benedictine monastery in Saint-Germain-des-Prés, were particularly important here), and then, more influentially, following Simon's own pioneering work, to test the authority of the Bible so as to curtail the vernacular scriptures' status as revelation (that status being a prop of Protestantism, of course).[11] By the early eighteenth century, a critical and pyrrhonian philology had become autonomous from both theology and philosophy, as becomes dramatically clear in the Jesuit priest and scholar, Jean Hardouin's radical claim that most classical and patristic texts had been forged by thirteenth-century monks, this claim being made on nuministic evidence alone. As early as in Spinoza's *Theological-Political Treatise* (1669–70) critique in this mode was thought to require no "other light than natural reason," and indeed, for Spinoza, without natural reason and its tool, logic, the meaning of the sacred texts could not be sufficiently secured as to safeguard "salvation and happiness."[12] Here what is in question is less the critical assessments of private persons than a disciplined form of critical knowledge that was first designed to strengthen Christianity (or a particular confession within it) but then turns against revealed religion and its documentation as such.

Koselleck himself places more emphasis on the European republic of letters than religion as the site in which private judgment and opinion were transformed into rationality. For him, the key text here is Pierre Bayle's *Dictionaire historique et critique* (1697), in which the limited practices of early modern humanists and philologists were extended across "all areas of human knowledge and history" in what Koselleck calls "an infinite process of relativization," so that, indeed, one constitutive division of modern criticism—that between reason and religion—is first articulated.[13] In Bayle too, older forms of denunciation and mockery—satire, prophecy, burlesque, and so on—become barred to criticism, which is limited to what is reasonable, serious, sincere. Nonetheless, Bayle does not turn the apparatus of critique, already a combination of philology and logic, against the state. That jump is made by Voltaire, who can perform it, surprisingly, because of the authority granted to him by his skill in "literary, aesthetic and historical criticism" (113). In effect here (although Koselleck does not put it like this) the political authority of the critic is founded on criticism's development not just in the republic of letters but in the everyday and usually local exercise of judgment and censure directed toward plays, concerts, artworks, and books, in urban and commercial centers—in this case, Paris.

Critique becomes organized against established authority—whether political, rational, philosophical, or aesthetico-cultural—only in mid-eighteenth-century France, where the absolutist state was both weak and repressive. In this culmination of Enlightenment critique, the Encyclopedists—particularly Denis Diderot—bring the operations of critique to bear on a historical and political situation they named one of "crisis." The division between critique and its objects is now energized by a perception of a divisive instability at the level of the state itself. Koselleck passes over Rousseau's crucial role in this history, even though it is Rousseau more than anyone who brings critique into connection with emancipation on the grounds that any society that is not just (i.e., governed by the general will) is not legitimate. This means that universal justice becomes critique's principal criterion, and also that critique is bound to a social crisis which may lead to revolution in the modern sense.[14]

At any rate, once the crisis of absolutism is resolved, which is to say, once the absolutist state falls, critique begins its slow decline. In telling his story, Koselleck therefore also underplays the importance of the politics of emancipation that came to a head in 1848 and which had been prepared for intellectually not just in Rousseau but in the work of young left-Hegelians such as Bruno Bauer, Moses Hess, and Karl Marx in their postrevolutionary attempts to define relationships between political and human emancipation.[15] For Koselleck, it was Kant who was the first "to bring the Enlightenment process to an end" (109), presumably because his new concept of critique—as an examination of the foundations of knowledge itself—did not just suck practical force from critique, but, paradoxically, announced critique's separation from reason, in making it clear that all critique that was not "transcendental" and true a priori, was arbitrary. Kant's metaphysicalization of critique opens up the path that will lead to Nietzsche, or—to give another resonant example—to Theodor

Adorno's valiant attempt to imagine and exercise an "immanent critique," that is, a multiscalar critique without criteria or presuppositions or, indeed, practical purpose.

Koselleck offers a history of critique that tells of its topic's historical degradation. It is, finally, a posthumous history, and as such is a precursor to the more recent "critique is dead" literature.[16] That is the ultimate force of an analysis which insists that critique, as a practice of rationality, drove an emancipation project that was primarily aimed at the authoritarian state and whose basic conditions have been met in the democratic era, at which point the critical persona becomes all but otiose. To sense difficulties in this thesis, all we have to do is to remind ourselves of how Nietzsche went about his lively self-criticism in regard to *The Birth of Tragedy*.

Indeed, a different line of entry into critique's history can also take us beyond orthodoxy because the conditions under which modern critique emerges are not adequately presented by Koselleck—or by Habermas, for that matter. If, as Koselleck suggests, absolutism provides critique's enabling social structures (i.e., the separation of civil society from the state), critique as a practice appeared in absolutism's wake. It did so, as he suggests, in late seventeenth-century- and early eighteenth-century England but in forms that undercut what will come to be critique's own understanding of itself as a use of plain reason in the service of freedom and justice. In support of this line of thought, I will now offer a brief but general account of the English public sphere in the period, focusing on two authors—Jonathan Swift and John Brown—and two texts—Swift's *A Tale of a Tub* and Brown's *An Estimate of the Manners and Principles of the Times*. This will enable us to recognize that critique was plural, self-conscious, and hedged from its beginning. Why Swift and Brown? Swift is useful here because he helped articulate that complex and productive threshold at which (party) polemic, irony, and insult abutted modern critique in its emergent form. Brown is useful because *An Estimate* (1757) was one of the first general philosophico-sociological critiques of actual society, but it too is already haunted by a sense of critique's limits. And both show how critique was, from its modern origins, as much conservative as progressive.

So to the English emergence of modern critique. The 1660 restoration of a Stuart king after Cromwell's protectorate established a monarchy committed to tolerating Christian confessional differences.[17] While Anglicanism was mandated as the official religion, citizens could adhere to other Protestant

Confessions or even to Roman Catholicism, at the cost, admittedly, of attracting civil penalties as mandated by the so-called Test Acts. This tolerant state did not, however, elicit wholehearted consent so that its governmental structures were under constant contestation. Two issues dominated these contestations, both concerning Anglicanism's constitutional status. The first concerned the state's relation to nonepiscopal Protestant denominations. For over a century politics were dominated by efforts to weaken or overturn the Test Acts. The second concerned the Anglican Church's response to the Stuart family's personal Catholicism, which became especially intense when, after his accession to the throne in 1685, James II attempted to place Catholics in positions of authority. That led to the 1688 revolution, in which sovereignty was transferred to Parliament. But it was only after the failure of the 1745 Jacobite rebellion, which aimed to return a Stuart to the throne, that efforts to restore the Stuarts, and scale back the "tolerant" Protestant state were put to rest.

These tensions led to the establishment of the world's first political parties—the Whigs and the Tories. On the one side, the Whigs were anti-Stuart and, in an emergency, willing to resist sovereign authority. On the other side, the Tories preached the Lutheran principles of "passive obedience" and "nonresistance," in practical terms, adhesion to Stuart sovereignty even by Protestants. As Koselleck acknowledges, this factionalism provides one condition for critique's emergence since it not only encouraged but *required* debate, denunciation, dismantling of the other party's policies and principles.

Nonetheless—and this cannot be overemphasized—this factionalism had no sanction. Factionalism was conceived of not as a basis of a political structure but as an urgent social problem—a party system was only fully accepted in the last decades of the eighteenth century, when, under Edmund Burke's intellectual leadership, the so-called Rockingham Whigs made that case. The parties' uncertain status was not helped by the fact that the distinction between Whig and Tory was itself unstable. After about 1700 most political players were Whigs in the original denotation of the term, since the 1688 settlement, if not all its concrete terms, met with widespread agreement. Jacobites were few and concealed. At this point Tories then came to oppose Whigs on other grounds. Even this is a little simple, however, because "Whig" and "Tory" were identities and groupings that, however powerful, sheltered other interests: the country interest, the church interest, the city interest, and alike, which often actually motivated political allegiance but still did not quite determine which party one would adhere to at any moment. There was, for instance, a Tory "country interest" *and* a Whig one.

Organization of a rudimentary kind happened at a quite other level, that of the coterie. Thus, until the end of his career Swift, for instance, might call himself either a Whig or a Tory depending on his mood and context even though between 1709 and 1714 he was a Tory propagandist attached to Robert Harley and Henry St. John's administration. His more concrete and vital connections were with groups of friends and patrons, wits, politicians, churchmen, of which the most famous was the "Scriblerus Club," which included the poets Alexander Pope and John Gay as well as Harley and St. John and whose written publications specialized in mocking the broad sweep of contemporary culture. Coteries were important just because it was not yet accepted that individuals might make judgments against society and culture *purely as individuals*. Because individual critical elevation lacked legitimacy, critique often addressed the public as if it had been formulated less by a private person than among a group of friends, that is, among a coterie.

If critique emerges under the messy conditions of political toleration that led to political divisions formed mainly in struggles over how to join—or disjoin—church and state, two other conditions, neither independent of this larger structure, also underpinned its early development.

First, after 1660 book-trade production and distribution expanded quite rapidly. They did so under commercial market conditions that were themselves triggered and shaped by institutional support for printed propaganda and sermonizing, whether in narrow confessional or political interests or in the service of the broader moral reformation movement. This provided critique's infrastructure. As Mark Knights has recently argued in his illuminating *Representation and Misrepresentation in Later Stuart Britain: Partisanship and Political Culture*, this mass of printed discourse changed the language itself. It caused both an "anxiety about words" along with a widespread discursive ambiguation, just because factional identities were bound to the language in which values and ideals were expressed (i.e., the language of unity, liberty . . .), but that language was, in most cases, shared between factions who could not (to make things more complicated) confess themselves as factions.[18]

Second, after 1690 an opposition between the ancient and the modern entered public discourse, when, on the back of a Parisian pamphlet war, the Whig statesman Sir William Temple published his *Essay upon Ancient and Modern Learning*. Temple himself took the side of the ancients in order to critique the ethos of the new protoprofessional (post-Baconian and post-Cartesian) science as well as the new critical philology. As recent scholarship has made clear, this opposition did not, however, correspond to the current sense of what is and is not modern, and today intellectual historians often dismiss it as fundamentally trivial.[19] But especially after William Wotton responded to Temple in his book-length *Reflections upon Ancient and Modern Learning* (1694) by arguing unambiguously for intellectual and social progress, the ancient/modern debate brought history's weight to bear on contemporary thought and erudition.[20] In this historical conjuncture, intellectual positions—including the positions from which critique could be enunciated—could be assessed as being either on the side of progress or not. That, of course, markedly increased critique's gravity and functionality.

This new positive function of critique was articulated most clearly at the cutting edge of "modern" thought, by the English Deists, who drew, in particular, on Bayle and John Locke. Locke is relevant here more as a theorist of government than as an epistemologist. Indeed the post-1688 British state formation was given theoretical grounding not so much by Hobbes, whom Koselleck (following Carl Schmitt and Leo Strauss) regards as the key theorist of modern "liberal" state in which critique becomes possible, but by Locke. In their philosophical legitimations of the modern state, both Hobbes and Locke appeal to a conjectural history in which individuals living in a state of nature create what Locke called a "civil society."[21] But Hobbes cited a need for security as the motive for this move, while Locke cited a need for justice. At the same time, Hobbes thought of the state of nature primarily in Calvinist terms of struggle and harshness between vulnerable individuals, while Locke (in the Anglican-scholastic lineage) thinks of it as ordered by God's law, which created individuals as free and equal, as well in terms of those capabilities and appetites, which (supposedly) make the species property owners by nature.

Locke's theory matters to us because his insistence on a natural law that mandates equality and autonomy provides a basis for a new understanding of truth and critique. This new understanding appears after 1694, when John Toland, drawing on Locke (to the latter's discomfort), publishes *Christianity Not Mysterious*, the first English Deist tract. There Toland contended, radically, that Christian revelation can only be true insofar as it is available to rational inspection. This argument is more fully joined to Lockean natural law in Anthony Collins's *Discourse on Freethinking* (1713), which makes the (Habermasian) argument that truth can only be uncovered in public debate and critique. It is to be understood as the outcome of a transparent and free process. In other words, for Collins epistemology is civil and procedural rather than theological or philosophical. He makes the social and political conditions in which critique is protected and encouraged and truth appears necessary to human progress. With that, we are the beginning of an "enlightened" era in which it will be possible to believe that critique is essential to human flourishing.

Swift

Although for most of his career Swift was a parson in the Irish Church, he wrote at the center of the political and intellectual order that I have been sketching. His first well-known book, *A Tale of a Tub* (1704), written while he was employed as Temple's secretary, was a contribution to the ancient and modern debate on the side of the ancients. But Swift polemicized very widely. When *A Tale of a Tub* appeared he was already active as a political pamphleteer, first as a Whig, and, after 1709, when the Whigs made it clear that they wished to weaken the Test Acts in Ireland, as a Tory. Indeed, as a journalist for St. John's journal *The Examiner,* and as the author of *The Conduct of the Allies* (1711), he became the most important Tory propagandist of the moment, urging an end to the War of Spanish Succession, which secured the Treaty of Utrecht. It was to make this case that, for instance, he articulated the relationship between military enterprise and finance capital that established the terms on which Whig governments would long be denounced as creating an oligarchic order known as "Old Corruption." At the same time, he wrote against irreligion: in 1713 he published an ironical critique of Collins's *A Discourse of Free-thinking* itself. And he extended this conventional attack on "atheism" to the "new philosophy" that had been introduced by Bacon, Descartes, Hobbes, and others. He also denounced the commercial spirit that encouraged entrepreneurial "project" after "project." Like the famous third Earl of Shaftesbury, he upheld the canons of "polite" manners and forms, in particular against discursive confusion and vulgarization. In his first contribution to *The Examiner,* for instance, he insisted that political division was distorting language itself, which, as he put it, now sheltered those "perpetual Misrepresentations" through which friends cannot be distinguished from enemies and "truth" is buried.[22] Not least, he wrote critically of criticism: his "Digression concerning Critics" in *A Tale of a Tub* presents criticism as a form of modern pride and overweeningness, as does his allegory of "Criticism" in *The Battel of the Books,* where it forms a team with Ignorance, Opinion, Noise, Impudence, Vanity, and Pedantry.[23]

In 1724 he published his summa, *Gulliver's Travels,* which by its adroit manipulation of physical scale allowed him to combine and extend his various critical targets. In its last book, of course, Gulliver travels to the land of rational horses and, when he returns to England, tries to imitate them, condemning himself to a kind of insanity that allows Swift movingly to bewilder his readers by demonstrating the limits of rationality itself.

So Swift is instructive for a history of critique just because, in writing from the center of social and discursive order in which critique becomes prolific, he bitterly condemns what he regards as the dominant tendencies of his own times, including—crucially—those that enable and enact enlightened critique itself. One way of stating this is that he is a critic who does not believe in the kind of reason that sanctioned critique of the kind that Locke and Collins developed, namely, rationality capable of winnowing truth and improving the world. What does Swift believe, then? What supports his anticritique critique? Appeals to ordinariness. To common sense. To letting things stay as they are. And, most of all, to Anglicanism's authority. But, of course, these could not easily withstand the evidence-based and rational critical examination promulgated by the new philosophy, particularly by the English Deists. This means that Swift's critique, unable to rely on his enemies' tools of reason, logic, and evidence, takes rhetorical flight into satire, abuse, mockery, irony. As a result, we might say, critique becomes *literature*.

Swift first made his mark in 1704 when he published a short book that included *A Tale of a Tub* along with another contribution to the ancient/modern debate (against William Wotton), "A Full and True Account of the Battel fought last Friday between the Ancient and Modern Books in Sir James's Library," as well as a burlesque of materialism, "A Discourse Concerning the Mechanical Operation of the Spirit. A Fragment." Like almost everything that Swift wrote, the book was published anonymously, not (this time) so much to protect him from the libel laws as to escape the impropriety of publishing a provocation of this kind as a named individual and churchman. He did not—could not—present himself openly in a critical persona, so he made his mark obliquely through those coteries that were aware that he was indeed *A Tale of a Tub*'s author. And *A Tale of a Tub* had such an impact not just because of its rhetorical and imaginative force but because of its breadth. Here the modern order as such becomes a grotesque totality: vicious, proud, mad.

In *A Tale of a Tub* form *is* critique. Indeed, that had to be the case, because by Swift's own program and values, the persona of the critic was barred to him. So *A Tale of a Tub* passes itself off as a mimesis of the debased books that the trade was publishing. It presents itself as an imaginary and disorganized manuscript by a nameless hack author that has accidently been delivered to its bookseller, who has organized its publication. A welter of preliminary matter to this manuscript further disorganizes the book: it begins with a letter (apparently in praise) to the Whig statesman Lord Somers, which is followed by a preface from the bookseller, a dedicatory epistle, a preface, and, last, an introduction. In its later editions, Swift writing as the actual author (if still anonymously) began the book with a formal "Apology," which defends the book against complaints that it was irreligious and which roundly declares that "it celebrates the Church of England as the most perfect of all others in Discipline and Doctrine."[24] In these later editions, A Tale of a Tub also includes explanatory footnotes (Swift thought of footnotes and indexes as vices of contemporary bookmaking) stolen, to heighten the irony, from one of the first edition's critics, none other than William Wotton. A Tale of a Tub is, then, an imitation of the book trade's most cynically produced commodities. And it might seem to be a protective and immunizing mimesis against modernity's contagions as they shape book production were it not for the way in which its exorbitant exaggerations undo that which it mimes.

Even its title contains a crude pun. "Tub" refers to the barrels that whalers threw overboard to distract aggressive whales, in this case (tellingly) Hobbes's Leviathan. But it turns out that the title also refers to the tubs which street orators mounted to address their audience, and by extension any "machine" used by those who want to get up and address their fellows "without interruption."[25] The conjunction of these two meanings is unsettling. This is a book itself written from a tub—it claims the right to address the public from a position of elevation—but that tub, a decoy, is just an illusion. It is as if it is designed to lure readers away from more serious matters, from the Hobbesian/Lockean model of sovereignty in particular, but at the cost of presenting itself as a nothing, a mere lure, written by somebody with no sanction to address us.

At its heart lies an esoteric narrative allegory that, symptomatically, nothing in the preliminary matter has prepared us for. It tells a story about a man who bequeaths a coat to each of his three sons—Peter, Martin, and Jack—in a will promising that, if the coats are well cared for and not altered, they will last forever. The allegory of the Reformation is obvious: Peter stands for the Roman Catholic Church; Martin, the Lutherans (and thus the Anglicans as Swift sees it); and Jack, Calvinism. Much of the rest of the story tells how the sons (particularly Peter and Jack) ignore their father's will in ways that can be mapped onto Latin Christianity's post-Reformation history. Jack becomes possessed by "Enthusiasm"—that is, the belief that he as an individual can have direct inspired access to God and his truths—while Peter falls into a rigid formalism. The story is told, then, in Martin's interest. But its main point is one that will become central to later conservatisms: that the Reformation is the primal scene of the West's fall into divisive factionalism, error, and politics.

This story, however, important as it is, is not enough to fill the book out. So the hack author interrupts it with a series of eccentric digressions—each on a particular topic, usually concerning the book trade. Only one—"A Digression concerning the Original, the Use, and Improvement of Madness in a Commonwealth"—is connected to the tale of a tub allegory, and critics have, rightly, paid special attention to it. Here, once more, the author's wrongheadedness is simultaneously ironized and endorsed. The section is structured like this: the digression is inserted at the point in the allegory of Latin Christianity's history when Jack (the Calvinist) has reduced his coat to "a Meddley of *Rags*, and *Lace*, and *Rents*, and *Fringes*."[26] Why? Because, in the grip of enthusiasm, he has lost his wits. And in the digression the author draws a moral from this. Many great actions in the world have been caused by "revolutions" in individual minds. In particular: "*The Establishment of New Empires by Conquest: the Advance and Progress of New Schemes in Philosophy; and the contriving, as well as propagating of New Religions.*"[27] The hack author reveals his intellectual incompetence by explaining this in the terms of a muddled Cartesianism: "Semen, raised and inflamed, became adust, converted to Choler, turned head upon the spinal Duct, and ascended to the Brain."[28] But a basic point stands: imperialism, the various reductive metaphysical and esoteric systems, and Protestant evangelicalism are all of a piece—they are all cases of "enthusiasm," as is the new philology as practiced by Bentley and Wotton.

The hack author more than accepts all this; he bravely affirms it. For him, the moderns may be mad, but madness is a form of happiness because it allows the imagination and illusion to triumph. Reason itself, "a very light rider," becomes *their* instrument. It is at this point that he writes what will become one of the most famous sentences in the English language: "Last week I saw a Woman *flay'd*, and you will hardly believe, how much it altered her Person for the worse"—a sentence that joins the author's closeness to the reader's here and now ("last week") to his affirmation of illusion, madness, and the modern.[29] The point is that happiness is the "perpetual possession of being well deceived," and whatever, like the lash, penetrates the surface (which modern knowledge based on the senses does not) disrupts happiness. In the modern world, surfaces trump depths; deception trumps truth; happiness trumps salvation. The digression on madness ends with the author putting on his projector's hat to recommend that a government commission find out who is crazy and promote them to those offices where their brilliance and imagination might be most useful for the commonwealth, declaring himself to be someone whose reason too is subsumed by imagination and illusion.

We might call this too a summa of Swift's critique of the modern even if it comes near the beginning of his career. At any rate, by its end, *A Tale of a Tub* has achieved its implicit claim to contain *in petto* the corruptions of its time—Calvinism, natural philosophy after Descartes and Hobbes, the commercialized book trade, the new philology, governmental structures, and so on. All these elements cohere to a single regime in which reason, imagination, and a will to critically intervene are joined in dangerous, potentially disastrous ways. Correcting this totality requires not more reason and more imagination but less, just because reason has become the instrument of destructive wills and purposes. It follows that the hack author's thin allegory is expressive of modern culture's hollowness and craziness, but in its extraordinary imaginative and linguistic energy, its liberation from classical rhetorics and contemporary politeness, its embrace of insult, allegory, puns, and irony, so too is Swift's book.

Brown

John Brown was a parson loosely attached to a coterie of Anglican divines whom David Hume called the "Warburtonian school" because they were under the patronage of the prominent scholar and polemicist William Warburton, bishop of Gloucester.[30] At the risk of exaggerating their unity and purposefulness, we can say that their project was to use their church offices, their support from the Whig establishment, and their capacity to address themselves to the Anglican faithful to take up positions of cultural and social critique on the back of, and in revision of, Scriblerian/Popean practices of denunciation. When his *Estimate* became one of the century's smash hits (eleven editions in two years, and remembered for another generation at least), Brown himself was just a country parson, best known for a book-length critique of Shaftesbury's *Characteristics*.[31] He had recently received a living in Essex at the favor of the Court Whig magnate, Lord Hardwicke, from whom patronage had been solicited for him by Warburton.[32] Brown himself had originally come to Warburton's attention through his poem *An Essay on Satire: Occasioned by the Death of Mr Pope* (1745), a panegyric addressed to both Pope and Warburton. It argued that satire was useful to correct what Brown called "perverted Shame," that is, to check contagions of debased, irreligious values that ran through those committed to mere worldly pride and vanity, whose sense of shame had thus become perverted. But, according to Brown, satire's corrective force was limited. It could not do what Shaftesbury thought it could in the theory of ridicule that he had famously spelled out in the first volume of *Characteristics*. It could not work as reason's good-humored practical instrument in the public sphere.[33] Brown sets Shaftesbury's promotion of irony, burlesque, and wit against Warburton (and George Berkeley's) commitment to truth. (A critique of Swift is also implied, I suspect.) Satire works best, Brown contends, when it makes a historical turn, that is, when it compares the past to the debased present.[34] Otherwise it is potentially dangerous, since it can so easily evade order and fairness and become prey to mere enthusiasms.

Brown's attack on satire was taken further in his book-length critique of Shaftesbury published in 1751. There he argued more philosophically for the move that, according to Koselleck, is one of modern critique's necessary conditions: its displacement from humor. He also there contests Shaftesbury's attempt to critique religious enthusiasm in favor of a secular enthusiasm proper to poets and artists and alike. Brown's *Essays on "Characteristics"* can be understood as a contribution to a more general project under way among the circle around Warburton at the time, that is, to reconfigure the terms on which Anglican learning divided itself off from the society around it, by reconciling elements of post-Cartesian/Lockean thought to Christian revelation and Anglican hegemony. For this project, friendships or factions based on wit and worldly politeness were dangerous, as were all cultural forms limited to the mundane and the secular. As I say, Warburtonian critique reached out to the Anglican national public, not to a coterie or party.

Thus, just to give one instance, throughout the 1750s, those in Warburton's orbit were among those who formed a new cultural-intellectual formation that would later be called "romanticism."[35] This involved a demotion of rhetoric and classic *imitatio* (the key text here is by the prominent Warburtonian Richard Hurd—the introduction to his 1751 edition of Horace); the promotion of the gothic (as in Hurd's famous 1762 essay on the topic); the recovery of "primitive" poetry (most influentially in Thomas Percy's *Reliques of English Poetry* [1765]); and a series of attacks (by Brown) on Shaftesbury's theory that an innate moral sense, bound to sociability, tied communities more solidly and naturally than those institutions, in particular the church, which emphasized rootedness and creaturely fallibility.

To cite two further examples of Brown's particular involvement in this larger project: in the early 1750s he wrote one of the first appreciations of what he called the Lake District's "beautiful and romantic scenes," which unified "Beauty," "Horror," and "Immensity."[36] And in his conjectural history *A Dissertation on Poetry and Music* (1763), he turned to the lifeways of the Huron and Iroquois to make the case that poetry and music were the expressive basis of what gradually became religion and manners, a case which is to be understood as a riposte to the Scottish Enlightenment's faith not just in sociability but in commerce's civilizing capacity.[37]

Brown's critique of satire has only a loose connection to his preromanticism. But in 1757, he published a sophisticated philosophical critical examination of current society that reveals the larger parameters of his thought. Like Swift's Tory journalism, it was a response to war. England and France went to war in 1756 over France, Austria, and Russia's designs on Protestant Prussia but also because they were competitors for global trade, and particularly for control of the North American river systems, as John Pocock has argued.[38] In its first three years, the war went badly for England, which was gripped by invasion panics. This looming defeat was the occasion for Brown to write a bleak but innovative account of English society.

An Estimate was neither satirical nor (as Brown had earlier recommended) historical. It was not multiscalar either: it was directed straight at "manners and principles" (i.e., at society). Which is to say that it is written from a more elevated position than Swift's, one for whom a critical distance was more secure, by a persona who, in removing himself from satire, abuse, and corporeality, is nonetheless as much a gentlemanly parson as a philosophical social analyst. His church office now enabled his critical elevation.

An Estimate synthesizes various intellectual genealogies. As Pocock has also pointed out, it belongs to the civic republican tradition: its preference for the early Roman Republics against the Roman Empire, its identification of asceticism with virtue, and its (sexist) description of England's weakness as "effeminacy" all flow from there.[39] At the same time, it has a clear (if disjunct) relation to the sermonizing that emerged from the moral reformation movement, which pictured society as dominated by vice, luxury, and irreligion and which itself fed on earlier forms like the premodern "morality play," with its comic allegories of Luxury and Avarice. It takes on a prophetic mode, too, in terms enabled by Warburton's and Hurd's work on esotericism.[40] In his *Sermons on Prophecy* (1771), for instance, Hurd, following the method established in Warburton's *Divine Legation of Moses* (1737), was to argue that the strange allegories deployed by the Old Testament prophets could be decoded precisely as critiques of contemporary conditions. To cite his own words:

these prophecies were "profitable" "for reproof, for correction, for instruction," just as Spenser's and Virgil's epics were.[41] This was to understand large
swathes of the inherited canon as primarily critical in intent in terms that
legitimated Brown's binding the critic to the priest. Last, Brown had taken on
the "sociological" understanding most influentially set out in Montesquieu's
De l'esprit des lois (1748) but also in Voltaire's widely read histories published
in the 1750s, as well as David Hume's *Political Discourses* (1752), in which (to
use modern terms) the economy's shaping power over society is laid out.

By bringing these genealogies together, Brown could articulate a surprisingly sophisticated, if admittedly rather thin, model of society. What is the
model? Like Montesquieu, Brown recognizes that the state and civil society
are mutually constitutive: the organization of the one reciprocally determines
the organization of the other. He further supposes that different kinds of state/
civil society have different affective hegemonies. A society that is basically
commercial (like Holland) will be dominated by "Avarice." A society that is
"mixed" between commerce and agrarian production will be dominated by
effeminacy, by which Brown means a lack of commitment to honor and virtue.
"Effeminacy" (a term which, sexist though it is, is not here applied to women)
causes a breakdown in the authority of inherited institutions such as the universities and the Anglican Church. This is to say that avarice and effeminacy,
as determined by social structures, have become not just vices but agents of
social transformation.

For Brown, societies are also constituted by different and often oppositional ranks and interests. England in particular is divided in three: between
the commercial interest, the landed interest, and the people, who alone have
avoided effeminacy, so that Brown's critique is also a celebration of plebeian
resilience and virtue. The reason for the people's residual virtue is that the expansion of commerce and finance is producing something like Marx's "surplus
value," although Brown, of course, does not have to hand the Marxian concept
of exploitation. The people are exempt from avarice and luxury because they
have no share of surplus value. Among the polite only, then, commerce, via its
dangerous surpluses, is undoing religion, where Brown, like other Warburto-
nians, thinks of religion not as a suite of private beliefs, not as enthusiasm, but
as institution ultimately based in more or less esoteric revelation supporting
national unity and order. So it is not so much that irreligion of the kind propagated in Hume's *History of England* is increasing in contemporary society; it
is that, among the upper classes, "religion" is now a "ghost" of its former self.[42]
Its life has been sucked out of it by the affective regime set in place by the

political economy, and in ways in which, especially during the present military crisis, endanger the nation.

The sociological force of Brown's critique leads to an impasse. He understands that expanding trade is necessary to secure not just the modern nation's prosperity but its security. But he also views commerce as undoing those subjectivities and institutions that maintain the social order and virtue and that make security and prosperity valuable to start with. (This is a version of the "cultural contradictions of capitalism" argument that Daniel Bell developed after the Vietnam War defeat in 1970s America.) What to do about this? How can the process be "countered by opposite Manners or Principles" (200)? Only, it seems, by state "coercion" (219). A stronger central authority, more "Police," would appear to be necessary. That might require Britain to become more like absolutist France, where the state, at least for the moment, prevents the upper classes from taking full advantage of commercial profits (204–6). But in the end these are idle hopes. Finally, in a move that ties Brown himself to irreligion, all the critic can in fact do is deliver himself up to sheer "Necessity"—not Providence (220). In the end, criticism is otiose: its denunciations will be absorbed into a futurity on which it makes little or no impact and which may—or may not—deliver us from society's self-cancellation; no one can tell.

Parsing Brown in this way makes it all the easier to return to this essay's beginning, that is, to Nietzsche and Koselleck's critiques of critique. In Brown, critique, after having sloughed off satire and abuse; after having reconstituted an elevated, polite, prophetic, critical persona; and after having established new protocols of philosophico-social analysis finds itself appealing passively, hopelessly even, to contingency, to history's unpredictable passages. Brown's critique comes up with, well, almost nothing. In that way, he, who stands near modern critique's beginning, points the way to Koselleck's death-sentencing of critique. To notice this is also to see why the Nietzschean and Swiftian options—critique as laughter, critique as mask, critique as abuse, critique across scales, styles, and voices—is so difficult to move beyond. Rhetorics and personas like Nietzsche's survive critique's self-cancellations. They even survive the latest such—Luc Boltanski and Eve Chiapello's functionalist argument that capitalism endlessly encourages critique because it is so useful to its own survival.[43] Perhaps, then, one lesson of this examination of critique's eighteenth-century origins is that critique's most persistent (and perhaps most valuable) modes are those in which it is not very nice, not very acceptable, not very progressive. As I say, more like Swift and Nietzsche than Brown and Habermas, in fact. More conservative and literary than rational or ethical.

Notes

1   The German word *Kritik* is used variously and loosely to denote "critic," "criticism," and (in our current sense) "critique." In English, *critique* was borrowed from the French in the seventeenth century, where, however, it too meant, among other things, both "critic" and "criticism." So the English word *critique* has no exact equivalent in either French or German.

2   I am using the term *persona* more lightly and loosely than it is now sometimes used by intellectual historians, by Ian Hunter and others, for instance, in the collection *The Philosopher in Early Modern Europe: The Nature of a Contested Identity*, ed. Conal Condren, Stephen Gaukroger, and Ian Hunter (Cambridge: Cambridge University Press, 2006). I mean it simply to indicate the characterless and ethically insubstantial person implied by a textual voice.

3   Friedrich Nietzsche, *The Birth of Tragedy and Other Writings*, trans. Ronald Speirs (Cambridge: Cambridge University Press, 1999), 6. Further quotations from this work are cited parenthetically in the text.

4   For the relationship between denunciation and critique, see Peter Sloterdjik, *Rage and Time: A Psychopolitical Investigation*, trans. Mario Wenning (New York: Columbia University Press, 2010). For the Cynics (who were likely the Greek philosophical school that had most impact on the historical Jesus Christ as social critic), see Michel Foucault, *The Courage of Truth*, trans. Graham Burchell (London: Palgrave, 2011), 166–74, and Donald R. Dudley, *A History of Cynicism from Diogenes to the 6th Century A.D.* (Cambridge: Cambridge University Press, 1937).

5   I have taken this summary of Foucault's account of critique from Thomas Lemke's "The Risks of Security: Liberalism, Biopolitics and Fear," in *The Government of Life: Foucault, Biopolitics, and Neoliberalism*, ed. Vanessa Lemm and Miguel Vatter (New York: Fordham University Press, 2014), 72.

6   Raymond Geuss, *The Idea of a Critical Theory: Habermas and the Frankfurt School* (Cambridge: Cambridge University Press, 1981), 2.

7   Harmut Rosa, "Kritik der Zeitverhältnisse: Beschleunigung und Entfremdung als Schlüsselbegriffe einer erneurten Sozialkritik," in *Was ist Kritik?*, ed. Rahel Jaeggi and Tilo Wesche (Frankfurt am Main: Suhrkamp, 2009), 24, my translation.

8   For a perspective contextualization of Koselleck's work see Niklas Olsen, *History in the Plural: An Introduction to the Work of Reinhart Koselleck* (New York: Berghahn, 2011). Habermas also owes much to Alexandre Beljame's *Le public et les hommes de lettres en Angleterre au XVIII siècle* (1881), as did Q. D. Leavis's *Fiction and the Reading Public* (1932), which Habermas may also have known.

9   For neostoicism and internationalism see Jonathan Scott, *Algernon Sidney and the English Republic, 1623–1677* (Cambridge: Cambridge University Press, 1988), 18–20.

10 Reinhard Koselleck, *Critique and Crisis: Enlightenment and the Pathogenesis of Modern Society* (Cambridge, MA: MIT Press, 1988), 59.

11 For the history of ecclesiastical philological critique in this period, see Jonathan Sheehan, *The Enlightenment Bible: Translation, Scholarship and Culture* (Princeton, NJ: Princeton University Press, 2005), 93–118, and James Turner, *Philology: The Forgotten Origins of the Modern Humanities* (Princeton, NJ: Princeton University Press, 2014), 91–123.

12 Benedict Spinoza, *Theological-Political Treatise*, ed. Jonathan Israel (Cambridge: Cambridge University Press, 2007), 111.

13 Koselleck, *Critique and Crisis*, 108–9. Further quotations from this work are cited parenthetically in the text.

14 For this understanding of Rousseau, see also Bernard Yack, *The Longing for Total Revolution: Philosophical Sources of Social Discontent from Rousseau to Marx and Hegel* (Berkeley: University of California Press, 1992).

15 For emancipation and critique in this juncture, see Gopal Balakrishnan, "The Abolitionist—1," *New Left Review* 90 (November–December 2014): 101–38.

16 This literature is large and nuanced. For one influential example see Bruno Latour, "Why Has Critique Run Out of Steam? From Matters of Fact to Matters of Concern," *Critical Inquiry* 30, no. 2 (winter 2004): 225–48.

17 This state formation was to be given theoretical grounding not so much by Hobbes, whom Koselleck (following Schmidt and Strauss) regards as the key theorist of modern "liberal" state in which critique is possible, but by Locke. The key difference between the two philosophers in this context being that while, in their efforts to legitimate the modern state, both appeal to a conjectural history in which individuals living in a state of nature create what Locke calls a "civil society," Hobbes contends that the motive for this move was a need for security, Locke a need for justice. At the same time Hobbes thinks of the state of nature just in terms of struggle and harshness between vulnerable individuals, Locke in terms of the natural law in which God created individuals as free and equal.

18 Mark Knights, *Representation and Misrepresentation in Later Stuart Britain: Partisanship and Political Culture* (Oxford: Oxford University Press, 2005), 29, 49.

19 For the sui generis nature of the debate see Joseph Levine, *The Battle of the Books: History and Literature in the Augustan Age* (Ithaca, NY: Cornell University Press, 1991). For dismissal of its cogency see Dimitri Levitin, *Ancient Wisdom in the Age of the New Science: Histories of Philosophy in England, c. 1640–1700* (Cambridge: Cambridge University Press, 2015), 225.

20 For a revisionary account of Wotton's contribution, see David Wootton, *The Invention of Science: A New History of the Scientific Revolution* (New York: HarperCollins, 2015), 454–58.

21 John Locke, *Two Treatises of Government*, ed. Peter Laslett (Cambridge: Cambridge University Press, 1988), 100.

22 Jonathan Swift, *The Prose Works of Jonathan Swift*, vol. 3, ed. Herbert Davis (Oxford: Basil Blackwell, 1940), 12.

23 Jonathan Swift, *A Tale of a Tub and other Works*, ed. Marcus Walsh (Cambridge: Cambridge University Press, 2010), 154.

24 Swift, *A Tale of a Tub*, 7.

25 Swift, *A Tale of a Tub*, 26.

26 Swift, *A Tale of a Tub*, 93.

27 Swift, *A Tale of a Tub*, 105.

28 Swift, *A Tale of a Tub*, 106.

29 Swift, *A Tale of a Tub*, 112.

30 David Hume, "My Own Life," in *Essays: Moral, Political and Literary*, ed. Eugene F. Miller (Indianapolis: LibertyClassics, 1987), xxxvii.

31 An Estimate was published as "by the Author of Essays on the Characteristics" in its early editions.

32 The most thorough account of Brown is to be found in William Roberts, *A Dawn of Imaginative Feeling: The Contribution of John Brown (1715–66) to Eighteenth Century Thought and Literature* (Carlisle, PA: Northern Academic Press, 1996), 3–83.

33 John Brown, *An Essay on Satire: Occasion'd by the Death of Mr. Pope* (London: R. Dodsley, 1745), 6.

34 Brown, *An Essay on Satire*, 7.

35 I am here accepting the (contested) category of "preromanticism" as first spelled out in Marshall Brown's *Preromanticism* (Stanford, CA: Stanford University Press, 1993).

36 See Malcolm Andrews, *The Search for the Picturesque: Landscape Aesthetics and Tourism in Britain, 1760–1800* (Stanford, CA: Stanford University Press, 1989), 177–79.

37 John Brown, *A Dissertation on the Rise, Union, and Power, the Progressions, Separations, and Corruptions of Poetry and Music* (London: L. Davis and C. Reymers, 1763), 28. For the Scottish Enlightenment see Warburton's letter to Richard Hurd asking him to reply to Hume's infidel History of England. William Warburton, *Letters from a Late Eminent Prelate to One of His Friends*, ed. Richard Hurd (London: T. Cadell and W. Davies, 1809), 207.

38 J. G. A. Pocock, *Barbarism and Religion*, vol. 1: *The Enlightenments of Edmund Gibbon, 1737–1764* (Cambridge: Cambridge University Press, 1999), 113. See also Carol Watts, *The Cultural Work of Empire: The Seven Years' War and the Imagining of the Shandean State* (Edinburgh: Edinburgh University Press, 2007), 12, for insightful comments on the war's cultural fallout.

39 J. G. A. Pocock, *The Machiavellian Moment, Florentine Political Thought and the Atlantic Republican Tradition* (Princeton, NJ: Princeton University Press, 1975), 484–85.

40 See Arthur M. Melzer's *Philosophy between the Lines: The Lost History of Esoteric Writing* (Chicago: University of Chicago Press, 2014), 429–33, for a good account of Warburton's contribution to discussions about esotericism.

41 Richard Hurd, *An Introduction to the Study of the Prophecies in Twelve Sermons* (London: T. Cadell, 1772), 435.

42 [John Brown], *An Estimate of the Manners and Principles of the Times by the Author of Essays on Characteristics, &c* (London: L. Davis and C. Reymer, 1757), 176. Further quotations from this work are cited parenthetically in the text.

43 See Luc Boltanski and Eve Chiapello, *The New Spirit of Capitalism*, trans. Gregory Elliott (London: Verso, 2007), for capitalism's endless capacity to turn critique to its own advantage.

PART II. STYLES OF READING

4

Romancing the Real

Bruno Latour, Ian McEwan, and Postcritical Monism

JENNIFER L. FLEISSNER

There is a desire for the literal. Dare one say, for the real? We are losing, it appears, the ability to see what is right in front of us: the purloined text, as it were.[1] So eager to see *through* it, to what lies behind, we refuse its apparent solidity—that quality so evident that we are certain it must be a ruse, a way to distract us from what's really going on. *Ceci n'est pas une pipe*: the motto of the humanities in the waning years of the twentieth century.

With the dawning of the twenty-first, the object has returned, announcing, scandalously enough, that it may in fact be *what it seems*. Along with the object, the body; along with the body, the text. The literal text, the text as construed by historians of the book, its front and back matter as much a part of its meaningful existence as that part where we had thought the answers lay. We are enjoined to look—not behind, not through, not around, but to take the thing for what it is. Like Edgar Allan Poe's policemen, we are told, we will find that the truth for which we so assiduously dug was waiting patiently to be noticed, given its due, the whole time.

While one cannot simply conflate them, a striking range of recent polemics on the subject of interpretation—by Bruno Latour, Heather Love, Sharon Marcus and Stephen Best, Talal Asad, Anne-Lise François, and others—encourage us, along these lines, to mend our ways.[2] In one way or another, all ask a version of the question Latour poses: "Why has critique run out of steam?" Literary and cultural studies have proceeded for too long, they assert, as a curious concatenation of Freudian, Marxian, and biblical hermeneutics, for which what you saw before you was always but a sign, if not an actual mask, for something else: hidden, even nefarious motives; a larger historical narrative; or disavowed depths. The new work thus proclaims a sea change: a new attention to surfaces, to "the given," to the task—a far harder one than we had imagined—of simply describing.

Perhaps, however, critique, in the particular form to which Latour and others drew attention, had begun to huff and puff a bit for some time. Despite his claims for a radical shift, Latour's article in many ways restated points he had been making at least as long ago as *Pandora's Hope* (1999)[3]—and even *We Have Never Been Modern* (1991), which includes a brief section on "The Crisis of the Critical Stance."[4] In the former text, he can already be heard specifically making the case for "presence, deployment, affirmation, and construction" against what he terms the "postmodern" insistence on "absence," "debunking," "negation," and "deconstruction."[5] And as we will see in a moment, the context in which these arguments initially arose forms my particular interest here.

Alongside Latour, it turns out, the standoff between suspicion and its alternatives was allegorized in remarkably similar form in a novel published around the same time as *Pandora's Hope*, Ian McEwan's 1997 *Enduring Love*. Repeatedly, in that book, we find identical events explained by one member of a couple, Joe, in "flat," literal terms, while the other, Clarissa, insists on ferreting out occluded meanings everywhere. It would appear, moreover, that she does so for the same reasons we did for so long: she is a literary critic, who when not discerning Freudian undercurrents in her lover's every gesture can be found poring over the language of Romantic poetry.

The lover himself, meanwhile, the surface reader, is by training a scientist. Hence, his anti-Freudian accounts of human behaviors, including his own, are often biological ones, aiming at precise descriptions of *what* is happening, chemically, when a creak in an empty house makes him jump, not *why* he may be particularly jumpy.[6] He shares this descriptive habit, notably, with the neurosurgeon hero of McEwan's later and more celebrated *Saturday* (2006). Indeed, if both novels can seem like fictional mirrors of the debates spurred by Latour, Best and Marcus, Love, and so on, there may well be good reason: both *Enduring Love* and *Saturday* have been said to mark a contemporaneous "turn" in novel writing, one that can itself be mapped onto a longer-brewing turn in the field of human psychology, and that in each case tracks quite well with the turn against symptomatic reading. As Love writes, that turn eschews a "depth" approach to human "consciousness" and "motivation," instead offering "descriptions of surfaces, operations, and interactions."[7] Similarly, both in what Marco Roth has dubbed the new "neuro-novel"[8] as well as in psychology departments today, Freudian views of self and symptom as shaped by buried traumas and disowned desires have given way to a focus on brain chemistry: a focus, again, in both etiology and treatment, on the *what*, perhaps the *how*, but not the why.[9] The result (notably stranger in the case of the novel) is a psychology with far greater ties to the hard sciences than to the humanistic fields that once took Freud as a source of hermeneutic inspiration. (Indeed, *Enduring Love* provided McEwan with the opportunity for a kind of Sokal hoax in reverse: the novel concludes with an appendix posing as an article from the *British Journal of Psychiatry*—which, when McEwan submitted it to a similar journal in real life, received a positive response.)[10] This leads, then, to a question: Should we give some thought to the fact that the turn against critique can appear, not infrequently, as a turn toward science?

This characterization will no doubt surprise many advocates of the postcritical turn. Isn't the rejection of suspicion frequently linked to a reaffirmation of the specifically literary or aesthetic, to our pleasurable engagement with artistic works for their own sake, or for the sake of the feelings they genuinely evoke? Certainly, this seems to be the case (though one might note that a number of these very arguments, in their contemporary form, themselves rely on the findings of neurology and so forth).[11] More broadly, however, what seems most to call out for further explanation is the fascinating way in which postcritique can appear as *both* a humanist retrenchment, in the form of a return to aesthetic experience as such, *and* a new scientism, a move toward finally closing what C. P. Snow famously dubbed the "two cultures" divide, at one and the same time. While these projects can of course remain strongly at odds—from either side—my interest in this essay lies more in the ways in which they have become newly able to appear as a shared project. Consider, after all, critique's insistence that nothing was ever what it appeared to be. What looked like truth was really ideology. What looked like nature was really culture. What looked like art was really "art," a historically and socially produced category, a form of power. What, in all these instances, was being disavowed? Both, we could say, the idea of something ineffable (what might have appeared to be such could always be brought back down to earth via the exposure of its sordid or merely mundane underpinnings) *and* the idea of something concrete, something that is simply what it appears to be. In these two opposed senses, then, to move beyond critique means no more or less than confronting the thing in itself.

The Kantian resonances here are quite intentional. If, as Stanley Cavell has argued, we may identify the rise of Romanticism (as well as, importantly, skepticism) with the "Kantian settlement" that bracketed the "thing in itself" off into an unreachable noumenal realm, the turn against critique, this essay argues, can thereby be understood as a fundamentally anti-Romantic turn.[12] (This aspect is perhaps already evident in the refusal of depth, which would necessarily entail a lack of interest in allegory and symbolization.) This is one way, and perhaps the most important, of understanding a certain self-identification with "realism" on the part of some of its most notable practitioners. This realism, I will suggest, needs to be thought of in relation to the significant role played by science in the postcritical turn. Both "science" and "realism" take distinct and complex forms here, however, which is what we now need to try to understand.

I

Ironically, perhaps, some of the most straightforward insistences that the road forward from critique will be paved by the epistemological protocols of the sciences have come from within literary studies. As stated, some of the most unapologetic new formalisms have justified their turn toward beauty and other long-maligned universals by reference to what neurology can tell us about the habits of the reading brain. More broadly, Marcus and Best express their hope that the methods of what they call surface reading might stand a better chance of "attain[ing] what has almost become taboo in literary studies: objectivity, validity, truth."[13] Similarly, Love depicts her own project of meticulous flat description as a complement to the "distant reading" techniques of Franco Moretti, which also "experimen[t] with scientific and social-scientific methods," from data mining to cognitive science, as a means of reaping the gains of "scientific authority, generality, knowledge, legitimacy."[14] As Marcus and Best explain, whereas the heyday of critique grew up in tandem with the insistence on criticism as a forthrightly political act, data mining and other digital humanities techniques work from the opposite perspective; they aim to "correct for [the critic's] subjectivity, by using machines to bypass it, in the hopes that doing so might produce more accurate knowledge about texts."[15]

Several assumptions thus come into play here that do differ starkly from those animating literary studies over the past few decades: (1) There is a set of objective facts out there to be discerned; (2) Our task as critics is to get at them as "accurately" as possible; (3) Our own "subjectivity," our interestedness, can only be a liability in doing so. Thus broadly stated, these are "realist" positions in the sense used by philosophers, particularly philosophers of science; they can be opposed to the kinds of perspectives one might usually associate with literary studies, such as the belief that no "truths" can be accessed that are not mediated by human conceptual schemas such as language and culture. Perhaps unsurprisingly, then, one can find arguments against critique and in favor of what is termed a new "realism" being made within Continental philosophy circles as well.[16]

Aside from these self-proclaimed new philosophical "realists," the figure who has perhaps done most to argue for the postcritical turn as a turn toward realism—indeed, in his words, a "more 'realistic realism'"—is Bruno Latour.[17] Latour's centrality within the postcritical turn possesses particular importance for my argument here, since he, of course, works neither in literary studies nor in philosophy, but in science studies, a field that by definition can be said to make science its raison dêtre yet to place scientific claims under scrutiny at the same time. Latour thus frequently describes his own project as entailing a refusal of the split between the two cultures, a reaction against the attempt by scientists and humanists alike to "purif[y]" or "purg[e]" their fields of the claims made on the other side of the campus (18). As a result, he has written strongly, including in the "Critique" essay, against precisely the sorts of neurological and evolutionary reductionisms that can at times characterize recent humanist borrowings from the scientific realm, casting the belief in bare facts as a kind of mirror image of critique's insistence that no facts exist at all.

Yet despite this laudable balancing act—and even ironically, given that science studies has most often appeared to its critics to be overly critical of science—Latour finally devotes more of his rambunctious energy, as he himself will readily acknowledge, to combating the claims of humanists. This imbalance begins to explain why the *Critical Inquiry* piece makes critique, not the invocation of fact, its core target. As I mentioned, after all, Latour had been arguing against humanists' allegiance to critique for over a decade. Thus, already in the 1990s, he will admit that "we [in science studies] can rightly be accused" of spending "*much more*" time "fight[ing] the humanists" than the scientists, for the simple reason that while the latter "spend only a fraction of their time purifying the sciences" (18–19), humanists *define what they do* as a project of saving "human" values from a "world of science" bent on reducing "a rich lived world of intentional stances" to a "cold," "inhuman" (9) realm of dispassionate objectification, "reification" (19), and rational calculation.[18]

We have seen the perspective here attributed to the humanities before in Latour's work. In *We Have Never Been Modern* (1991), it is that of the "antimodern," who strives mightily to save "souls, minds, interpersonal relations, the symbolic dimension, human warmth, local specificities, hermeneutics," and so forth from "the cold breath of the sciences," the "soulless" techno-world.[19] (And, once again, as with the humanists, Latour is finally much more critical of these "antimoderns" than of the scientists he posits as modernity's champions.)[20] Latour's characterization thus has the valuable feature of helping us see the extent to which "critique" as we are understanding it here might in fact be understood as having its roots in the critique of *modernity* (a term Latour himself refuses), and, specifically, that understanding of modernity for which the calculating propensity that Max Weber once called "rationalization" plays a crucial role. (Latour in fact quite often uses Weber's terminology, as well as that of his student Georg Lukács, to characterize the kinds of arguments he targets.)[21] By rationalization, Weber intended to evoke the transformation of all manner of things into what we would today call "data," to be managed via mathematics and other forms of systematization, as the core tendency of modern capitalism, on the one hand, and modern science in its applied mode as technology, on the other. And Weber indeed worried that a world dominated by such values would be an "iron cage" filled with "specialists without spirit, sensualists without heart."[22]

Why, however, associate such a point of view with the humanities? Would any humanist recognize her- or himself in Latour's portrayal? (Weber, after all, was a social scientist.) Here the relation Latour underscores between this perspective and the larger historical development of *critique* can be of help. On the one hand, Weber's stance harks back to that of the Marx, who characterized capitalist modernity as "the icy water of egotistical calculation," in which "the most heavenly ecstasies of religious fervor, of chivalrous enthusiasm" and "sentimen[t]" were "drowned."[23] At the same time, the work of Weber's student Lukács on capitalist "reification" would form an important touchstone for the later generation of what came to be known as "critical theory" in the work of the Frankfurt School. Finally, during the same era as Weber, others such as Friedrich Nietzsche and Sigmund Freud and, slightly later, the phenomenologists Edmund Husserl and Martin Heidegger were voicing their own doubts about what they saw as the self-congratulatory stance of modern rationalism. We have here, in other words, all the members of the "school of suspicion" as it was first identified by Paul Ricoeur—as well as, of course, many figures crucial to the critical projects of literary studies during the latter decades of the twentieth century.

And yet Latour's way of invoking, and dismissing, this line of thought uniquely depends, I would argue, on an understanding of all of it as fundamentally Romantic in its assumptions.[24] Specifically, it is described as Romantic in the same sense we saw earlier in Cavell: it is said to conceive a tragic divide between a lost or occluded truth of things, what really matters, and the world we see before us, which we are condemned to inhabit instead—with the hope, of course, that one utopian day, the two will reunite into a whole.[25] Indeed, Latour's characterization of the humanities thus strongly resembles that of C. P. Snow in his original "Two Cultures" lecture; Snow, too, portrayed "literary intellectuals" as "natural Luddites," who from the 1800s forward had been able to respond to the advent of industrial modernity only with "screams of horror."[26]

On the one hand, then, Latour often simply replaces these apocalyptic scenarios with images that are realist in an aesthetic sense as well, in at least two respects. First, morally speaking, they aim to replace hypostatized villains such as Science or Capitalism with "some poor scientist tinkering in his lab," "some small-business owner hesitatingly going after a few market-shares," and so on.[27] Modernity: it is the world not of George Orwell, it turns out, but of William Dean Howells. Second, rather than look forward to an infinitely deferred moment of redemption, or backward to an idealized lost past, they emphasize that such yearnings can make it very hard to see what simply lies before us *now*, in our own present: realism's time. "Is it asking too little," Latour asks, "to ratify in public what is already happening?"[28]

Yet finally, I would argue, Latour seems best understood not as arguing for realism *rather* than romance, any more than he wishes to be construed as arguing for the sciences over the humanities. For him, the problem, as he again and again presents it, lies *in the split itself.* Hence, it seems more accurate to see Latour as, in both cases, denying the divide entirely. For Latour, that is, one needn't turn to the aesthetic, the mystical, or any sort of projected future in order to find what Romanticism was looking for, because it's already present, *in "the real" before us.*[29] "Transcendences abound," as Latour puts it.[30] And, as has not been sufficiently recognized, Latour and others have taken the inspiration for this position from an alternate strain of thinking within the same late nineteenth-, early twentieth-century period that would so inspire the discarded project of critique. They draw, that is, on the writings of figures like William James, Gabriel Tarde, and Alfred North Whitehead, all of whom are experiencing something of a recuperation in the postcritical moment, precisely for their (at least at times) much more affirming take on the era's fascination with rendering the sciences and other forms of thought part of a single whole.[31]

In this sense, it is quite correct to identify postcritique, as Stephen Best has, as *monist,* in the sense that it has no use for the notion of two incommensurate poles of inquiry.[32] And yet as we saw above, however, Latour's mode of refuting the two-cultures split nonetheless has the effect of producing a new sort of sciences/humanities divide, in which the humanists now become the ones who believe such a split exists, indeed *whose work is (said to be) predicated* on the assertion of its existence, whereas the scientists have, in effect, moved on, for what Latour describes as a couple of reasons. First, they are too busy doing their actual work, and second, that work increasingly appears in new "hybrid" zones that no longer aim to cordon a purified science off from "politics," "markets," "ethics," and so on: "neuropsychology, sociobiology, primatology, computer sciences, marketing, cryptology, soil science, genome mapping," among other nascent fields.[33]

What seems needed, then, is a perspective that can both affirm the scholarship already taking place among literary "new materialists" that does overlap with these burgeoning fields, while nonetheless preserving a space that can enable a critical perspective on "what is already happening"—one that need not, indeed, take the form Latour and others rightly question. Such a perspective, which this essay aims to frame, also has important roots in the same turn-of-the-century epoch so crucial to the modes of critique Latour dismisses, in the writings of others within it, from Weber to W. E. B. Du Bois to Henry Adams and Henry James. Figures like these can begin to show how it might be possible to take Romantic questions seriously from a vantage point that can acknowledge their pitfalls as well. This stance, I argue, can then be taken as an alternate model for humanistic scholarship in the present, one that requires the sciences to think more with the humanities as much as the other way around.[34]

With the other James brother, Henry, for example, the question of these realist and romantic modes as they help to constitute the *novel* comes back in as an issue—as does the question of the relation of these debates about the status of science to literary production in the present moment, the moment of postcritique. When I suggested at the outset that Latour had in fact been thinking through these questions since at least the late 1990s, I also stated that some novelists had been as well: perhaps preeminently among them, Ian McEwan. McEwan's *Enduring Love* offers an ideal terrain for thinking through the various arguments this essay aims to make: first, that Latour's critique of humanists' allegiance to the two-cultures split needs to be taken seriously; second, that this critique is more important than we have recognized to the ideas animating a wide range of postcritical interventions; third, that, to the extent those interventions work against this split, they might be said to work against a certain understanding of Romanticism, often on behalf of a certain realism;

and, finally, that reframing Latour's divide in these more literary terms might also allow us to move toward a different, indeed more genuinely dialectical alternative to our present monism as well.

II

In *Enduring Love,* we will see, reading symptomatically isn't just a bad idea. To the extent it involves dismissing what lies right before you, it turns out it could endanger your life.

For most readers, however, McEwan's 1997 novel endures most for a single, powerfully visualized set piece: its riveting opening chapter, in which the narrator, Joe Rose, witnesses a man fall to his death while trying to ground a wild hot-air balloon with a terrified child inside. The odd thing about the book, however, is how little relation that scene can seem to bear to the storyline that succeeds it, save as a means for Joe and his romantic partner, Clarissa, to first encounter Jed Parry, the man who will become his nemesis. Instead, the bulk of the novel recounts Joe's stalking by the religious fanatic Parry, as he struggles to convince Joe to admit his supposedly suppressed love both for Parry and for God.

Enduring Love's classification as a "neuro-novel" stems largely from the diagnosis of Parry (both by Joe and by the faux-scientific documents that appear as appendices to his story) as suffering from a specific condition called de Clerambault's syndrome. As, no doubt, did McEwan himself, Joe diligently researches actual clinical accounts of this state in order to arrive at the scientifically backed conclusion that it can explain the odd behavior of Parry, who, like other "de Clerambaults," harbors the deluded, obsessive conviction of having become the object of a stranger (Joe)'s passion. With this reassuring sense of a concrete diagnosis, however, comes a fresh concern for Joe: "Well over half of male de Clerambaults in one survey had attempted violence on the subjects of their obsessions" (152). And as the novel progresses, Joe tries with increasing desperation to convince those around him of the threat the besotted Jed does turn out to pose: in one scene, he hires a gunman to shoot Joe (unsuccessfully) in a restaurant, and the nightmare finally invades the most everyday reality when Joe returns home one day to find Parry holding Clarissa at knifepoint on their couch.

The suspense and dread *Enduring Love* generates thus derives directly from the fact that nobody besides Joe will take Parry seriously as a danger—least of all, Clarissa herself. Where Joe attempts to direct her to the statistics he's unearthed, she persists to the end (even *after* the knife episode!) in viewing the entire situation as primarily an outgrowth of Joe's inner conflicts—thus, seeing the story's real obsessive as Joe himself. As she puts it to Joe at one point, "[Parry]'s not the cause of your agitation, he's a symptom" (90). Indeed, as I suggested earlier, the rift over how to interpret the Parry problem turns out to emblematize a broader divide between the two lovers that maps directly onto that which we now adduce between surface and symptomatic or suspicious modes of reading. Thus, for example, Clarissa will stand before Joe, reading his expression accusingly as a mask over deep, dark "calculations that I'll never know about," when in fact he is merely thinking for the umpteenth time, "How *did* such an oversized, average-looking lump as myself land this pale beauty?" (111).

More commonly, however, given Joe's training as a physicist and Clarissa's as a literary critic, readers have tended to understand the standoff between the two lovers as representing that between Snow's two cultures. Clarissa, in particular, often frames their disagreements in just these terms. So what did this mean, at least initially, when literary critics chose to interpret McEwan's novel as a whole? Wait for it: yes, they were quite sure the literary critic had to be right. The striking result is that these essays can at times read as if Clarissa had written them. Joe's attachment to rationality should be understood as an "attempt to stave off his insecurities" about masculinity, one writer states; for another, Joe demonstrates Foucault's point that reason produces madness, both Jed Parry's and Joe's own.[35] A third critic begins his essay telling us that, in his personal view, Darwinism has become our culture's "new fundamentalism," yet by the end it's made clear that he has in fact taken this characterization word for word from Clarissa herself, in an argument with her husband over what she considers the baleful cultural influence of the sociobiologist E. O. Wilson (74).[36]

Most amusingly, perhaps, McEwan himself confronted an instance of such readings when his own son was assigned *Enduring Love* by his English teacher. When McEwan Jr. failed to identify Clarissa as the "moral center of the book," he was given a D. "The teacher didn't care what I thought," McEwan complained to an interviewer. "Well. I mean, I only wrote the damn thing." What *he* thought, he explained, was that "Clarissa's got everything wrong." This assertion, it should be noted, appeared as part of a 2009 profile, written in the wake of *Saturday*, that portrays McEwan as having moved increasingly in the direction of the sciences over the course of his career—in tandem with a generic shift from a more gothic mode (which had earned him the sobriquet "Ian Macabre") to a Jamesian realism. "At first, he studied perversity;

now he studies normality," the interviewer summarizes. "His first god was Freud. Now it is Darwin."[37] Indeed, by 2005, McEwan was participating directly in the shift toward postcritique by contributing an essay to *The Literary Animal,* a volume of Darwinist literary criticism, and a few years later could be heard nominating as a "book that [has] helped shape my novels" Edward Slingerland's *What Science Offers the Humanities,* praising it as "an assault on the various assumptions and presumptions of postmodernism—and its constructivist notions of the mind."[38] Already in 1998, however, he was ready to proclaim Clarissa's bugbear Wilson his "intellectual hero," and the writings of Wilson, Steven Pinker, and other popular science writers dominate the acknowledgments page of *Enduring Love.*[39] Like C. P. Snow, McEwan has stated that intellectuals generally tend to rank the arts above the sciences—that what is missing is sufficient attention to the latter, not the former, in our view of what matters. Joe, his hero in *Enduring Love,* then makes these arguments in nearly identical terms (46, 81).

When literary critics persisted in positioning Clarissa as the "moral center" of McEwan's novel, then, did we merely attest to our own self-centeredness? A somewhat kinder reading might entail, rather, seeing such accounts as proof of Latour's point: like Clarissa herself, humanists have a tendency to hew to the two-cultures split—one often conceived, indeed, as a moral battleground. This tendency, however, may have significantly prevented us from considering the alternate possibility: that *Enduring Love* represents *not* a brief for the sciences *over* the humanities, but, rather, a critique, like Latour's, of the split itself. Put otherwise, the point of McEwan's decision to embody the two cultures in the form of a sparring couple who break up and must find out how to get back together by the book's end is to make an argument very much akin to that of both Snow and Latour: that is, less to plump for the arts' viewpoint *or* that of the sciences, and more to insist that the *real* danger lies in a perspective that sees the two as inhabiting separate worlds.

What can make this hard to recognize is that, again like Latour, *Enduring Love* associates the allegiance to this split *with* the humanities. Thus, it falls to those on what looks like the "science" side to represent the more inclusive view. Joe is a science *writer,* after all, and McEwan himself has in fact been invoked as a literary representative of what has been called the "third culture."[40] What interests him, clearly—as evidenced in his essay in *The Literary Animal*—is the possibility for the sciences and humanities to join forces in a new endeavor of exploring our "common nature" (and in this, he is clearly influenced by Wilson's notion of "consilience" or a "jumping together" of disparate fields).[41] In McEwan's case, however, we can also begin to see how this newly conceived joint project can dovetail with the traditionally conceived mission of the realist novelist. Within *Enduring Love*, for example, it is key that Joe, not Clarissa, has the capacity to take the omniscient perspective and narrate an entire chapter sympathetically from Clarissa's point of view (ironically providing fodder for the critics who see the entire book from that perspective).[42] And the flipside of this, then, is that when Clarissa fears the new popular science McEwan and Joe laud as a "new fundamentalism," Joe decides "she had spent too much time lately in the company of John Keats," with his famous fear that Newton's science threatened to take all the beautiful "mysteries" out of the rainbow (75).

This is an important moment, because it suggests that in making Clarissa a Keats scholar, McEwan, too, may be said to recast the two-cultures split as a divide between realism and Romanticism. Clarissa is smitten by the hope of recovering an unposted letter from the gravely ill Keats to his beloved Fanny Brawne, described as "a cry of undying love not touched by despair" (238). One of the central lessons of McEwan's novel is that in real life, however, stress does not bring us together but more often undoes us, as their conflict over Joe's stalker does Joe and Clarissa; this is the kind of stark truth recognized alike by realist novels and scientists repeatedly zapping lab rats with electronic prods. (When the pair reunite at book's end, the Darwinist implication is that their shared desire for children may have played the largest role.) By contrast, rather brutally, *Enduring Love* assigns the flame of "undying love not touched by despair" to Joe's insane stalker, Jed Parry, whose rapturous professions of undiminished devotion from within his new asylum home provide the book's final lines.

By aligning Clarissa with the clearly deranged Parry, indeed, McEwan makes plainest what he thinks of those who imagine a fallen world awaiting reenchantment. Parry, too, is certain that Joe's scientific work amounts to but a cover for his unworked-through emotions, seeing his writings as "add[ing] up to a long cry of loneliness" (146), a plea to be "set free" from what Parry, unexpectedly channeling Max Weber, terms Joe's "little cage of reason" (144). "Describing how the soup is made isn't the same as knowing why it's made, or who the chef is," Parry writes to Joe. "One day you'll be glad to say, 'Deliver me from meaninglessness'" (146). Clarissa, too, fears "some larger meaning [being] lost" in E. O. Wilson's evolutionary account of love; in the case of her own lover, Joe, the rationalist perspective on distressing events similarly appears as a narrowing, a means of avoiding one's buried emotions (74–75, 89).

For both of them, then, the antidote to the scientist's stripping away of meaning is to find it everywhere—to read symptomatically, which, as Marcus and Best remind us, is a practice with its roots in biblical hermeneutics. Hence, for Parry, the accident, in bringing him together with Joe, unquestionably bespeaks a higher, indeed divine purpose: his mission "to return [Joe's] love and to 'bring him to God'" (253). Like the woman described by de Clerambault himself who "believed King George V was in love with her," Parry is more broadly committed to reading secret meanings in everything Joe does, from the way he draws his curtains to the very "indifference" with which he responds to Parry's attentions (250–51). And as the book proceeds, we see Clarissa do this more and more as well—treating a drawer left open in their apartment as "a statement, a message . . . a signal" to be interpreted: a Freudian slip, in effect (141).[43]

Hence, what Clarissa wants to do, in the face of all the couple's conflicts, is take the Freudian approach, and talk things through. (Joe, naturally, describes himself as more of a behaviorist: having "lost faith in the talking cure," he tells us, he prefers in times of turmoil "to drive my car" [107].) For Clarissa, indeed, even the Parry problem could have been resolved through dialogue; had Joe just taken her advice and invited his stalker over for tea, she insists, the violent mania might well have subsided into mutual understanding (235). Again like Parry himself, then, Clarissa believes that all Joe's stress would end should he just reveal what lies inside—in her words, lay bare his true "heart" (111). And this shows another way in which McEwan reconceives the two cultures here not simply as the rift between "surface" readers and "symptomatic" ones, but as that dividing realists from romantics. For McEwan as an heir to George Eliot and Henry James, this doesn't mean simply sticking as a writer to the world we know ("It's enough to try and make some plausible version of what we've got, rather than have characters sprout wings and fly out the window," he has stated in an interview);[44] it entails, further, a dismissal of others who perceive literary representation in more personal terms as what McEwan calls "expression of the self," of "me."[45] The point here, which is developed more fully through the linkage of Clarissa and Parry, is twofold: the insistence on inner feelings can amount to an excuse for self-aggrandizement, and, further, it also can license a refusal of the hard task of confronting what's really there.

And yet what, in the case of *Enduring Love*, *is* really there? Here we can return, finally, to that indelible opening scene of the balloon accident. There, too, we see Clarissa struggling afterward to insist that such an event "must mean something," that their task as witnesses lies in trying to "make sense" of it all. To Joe, in contrast, this approach denies that such deaths appall us precisely for being so utterly "pointless" (for, indeed, once his doomed savior has fallen, the child manages to land the balloon safely in a field twelve miles away) (36). Its "meaning," scientifically considered, lies only in its revelation of a larger meaninglessness. "No special dispensation for flesh, or bravery, or kindness," as the man drops, Joe thinks. "Only ruthless gravity" (17). Crows squawk by "indifferent"; a nearby sheep "barely looked up from its chewing" (21). Joe, along with Parry, confronts this gap in its most direct form: he walks over to where the man has fallen, and is forced to realize: "*There was no one there. The quietness was that of the inanimate, and I understood again, because I had seen dead bodies before, why a prescientific age would have needed to invent the soul. The closing down of countless interrelated neural and biochemical exchanges combined to suggest to a naked eye the illusion of the extinguished spark*" (25, emphasis mine). Ever broad-minded, Joe sympathizes with such an illusion, but, "postscientific" himself, he cannot participate in it. He, like McEwan, is always the realist—or is he?

In fact, McEwan gives two versions of this moment. In the second, Joe describes himself as attempting to use the thoughts just quoted as a form of "protec[tion]" as he edges toward viewing the corpse from the front: "What I saw I only glimpsed. Though the skin was intact, it was hardly a face at all, for the bone structure had shattered, and I had the impression, before I looked away, of a radical, Picassoesque violation of perspective. Perhaps I only imagined the vertical arrangement of the eyes. I turned away and saw Parry coming toward me" (26). The scene concludes, then, with Joe's first direct encounter with the deranged man who will later try to take Joe's own life.

This second glimpse of death, paired with the encroaching threat of an insidious madness, reveals that McEwan has not simply left "Ian Macabre" behind. To be sure, he does begin moving away, around this period, from writing entire novels along the lines of *The Cement Garden*, in which four siblings come perversely of age in a house otherwise inhabited only by their mother's interred corpse. Even the more fully realist *Saturday*, however, displays the relish he still consistently displays in upending a complacent bourgeois everydayness with all the chaos it must bracket in order to persist.

At this moment in *Enduring Love*, then, this appears as a kind of eruption of modernism—the Picasso-like face—into the realist space, where it appears, as indeed it would, as a source of horror. And yet it is a horror we see both Joe and McEwan, as writer, drawn toward and yet repulsed by—"I glimpsed . . . I looked away . . . I turned away"—at the same time. So the question becomes why, if McEwan's allegiances so resemble Latour's, if he is equally concerned to reframe the two-cultures split, he never does quite embrace the sorts of plots championed by realists like Howells, the antimelodramatic story of "some poor scientist tinkering in his lab"—nor even, despite Joe's Latour-like insistence that science can bring "wonder" to things rather than stripping it away, the enchanted-realist alternative in which "transcendences abound." McEwan, rather, keeps being drawn to the gothic—at times, it seems, against his own realist impulses.

To think through this dimension further, I would argue, can not only suggest ways in which Latour, and postcritique, might possess such an aspect as well. Moreover, to acknowledge this can finally enable us to consider the possibility of an alternative "dualism," one that is no more committed to transcendence than to its contrary, and for which the novel as a form may play a particularly significant role.

III

Confronting the opening scene of *Enduring Love*, it is hard not to wonder whether McEwan might have had in the back of his mind perhaps the most canonical discussion of realism versus romance in the history of the novel: Henry James's 1907 preface to *The American* (1877). There the famed realist James, too, acknowledges that this early work's flaws could be seen to stem from its unabashedly romantic mode. And in explaining why romance is so hard to pull off successfully, James draws on an image remarkably pertinent to McEwan's novel: that of a hot-air balloon, in its unsteady relation to the ground.[46]

The romancer, James explains, must "cut the cable" that ties us down to earthly matters, and send us soaring into a realm unbeholden to their laws—and yet he must do so craftily, "without our detecting him," else the thing be a failure.[47] James's critique of his own youthful production is less that it *is* romantic, then, than that it too readily reveals itself to be. And yet this seems at once an inherent danger, given that romance itself, as James defines it, depends on a certain overdramatization of life's events. For James, importantly, this heightening is less about the presence of "pistols and knives" and "ghosts" and so on, than about the moral economy that lies behind such imaginings: the notion of the "'power' of bad people that good get into," or, in other words, the victimization of virtue, the idea of imperiled innocence.[48] This latter idea, James explains, is what led him to ramp up overmuch the opposition his hero faced in *The American*, and thereby too showily to cut his balloon's cord.

What would it mean to bring *this* conception of romance versus realism to bear on *Enduring Love*, and thereby on the larger issue of readerly stance, itself mapped onto the two-cultures split, that I've been arguing the novel embodies? At one point in the novel, Joe states in frustration of Clarissa, "*What was stopping her from being on my side?*" (114). This is a crucial question—yet one only answerable if we pose it, as Joe of course cannot, to the novel itself. For what is stopping her is really less Clarissa's "Romantic" way of seeing things than the "romance" aspects, in James's specific sense, of *Enduring Love* as a whole. McEwan's novel, that is, *does* set up rationality, in the form of Joe, as a kind of "innocence" (as Clarissa at one point suggests)—but precisely in the romantic sense of being in the position of lone, virtuous truth-teller battling the forces of unreason. Hence, no less than James does with his protagonist in *The American*, McEwan *has* to stack the deck against anyone being on Joe's side: the police have no record the ballooning accident ever happened, Parry tends handily to vanish from view the moment Clarissa appears.[49]

The broader irony, then, is that McEwan's very sense of a virtuous reason under threat is what gives *Enduring Love* its "romance" structure as James defines it: its tendency to heighten, to the point of implausibility, the forces conspiring against his beleaguered hero. Yet as its own version of the hot-air balloon dilemma reveals, what results is a kind of opposite of the scenario James himself envisions, where the would-be romancer faces the difficulty of cutting the cord of the "balloon of experience" without the reader noticing him doing so. On the windy hills of *Enduring Love*, after all, what turns out to be hardest of all is not releasing the balloon, but, rather, securing it to the ground. Might we not read this as a reversal of James's concern: that is, as a vision of the plight of the would-be realist? If so, then the urgent quest to secure the balloon—a quest that both McEwan's recent writing, and the realist turn of which it forms a part, could be said to represent—appears to risk the very opposite, as we watch it drift away into the clouds.

Within the Joe/Clarissa/Parry plot of the rest of the book, then, we can see a version of this same paradox at work in exactly the tendencies that the Freudian Clarissa notes in Joe as the narrative unfolds. For Joe, unquestionably, *does* grow increasingly manic and obsessive in tandem with his stalker—not to mention enamored of the paranoid vision of himself as a "wronged" innocent (156). Clarissa's error, then, lies in deciding that this affective cast to Joe's quest for truth merely negates it, removing any need to engage it further. This same error is then extended by most of the book's critics, for whom the revelation of obsessional tendencies on the part of reason itself—a familiar enough Romantic trope, it might be noted, from *Frankenstein* forward—is enough simply to discredit Joe's entire worldview. Whereas, if we are to take the book's brief for rationality seriously, as McEwan seems to want us to do, what we may really need to consider is that the scientist here may be obsessive, deaf to interpersonal nuances, *and* mostly right about things *at the same time*.

If we remain unable to see this, we ourselves fall prey to exactly the stance that produces Joe's own obsessiveness: the belief that the quest for truth must be innocent in order to be valid. Indeed, a brief reference to Lewis Carroll and "the darling objects of his own obsessions" near the very end of the novel suggests that one of our most enduring obsessions may be with innocence itself (a further truth that the author of *The Turn of the Screw* surely knew). In the end, the potential to lapse into a sense of "wounded" "self-righteous[ness]," to use Joe's words for Clarissa, may in fact be what ties the book's lovers together. It is, I would claim, a liability equally able to strike both the "surface" and the "symptomatic" reader as well.

To suggest that this can happen in symptomatic reading or critique, of course, merely echoes the point already made by a number of its critics, from Marcus and Best forward, who note the way critique's portrayal of its own stance as one of detached truth-telling may in fact harbor a desire for heroism— or perhaps simply for a belief in one's own goodness.[50] James's discussion can help us see how this revelation amounts to an account of critique's essentially Romantic moral universe. The danger, however, of *simply* making this point in this manner is that such readings thus continue to read symptomatic reading itself symptomatically. Again, then, this risks rendering their own intellectual space as that of a kind of idealized innocence, untainted by any such covert motivations. Indeed, it is hard not to feel, in the presence of some "postcritical" writings, that the critic is striving even *more* mightily to occupy such a space of purity: a childlike or indeed *pre*critical, prelinguistic wonder in the face of aesthetic or affective experience;[51] an unfiltered openness to all experience; a freedom simply to enjoy, to be, to be present. Critical mindfulness, in effect.

The old sort of symptomatic reading, when it simply dominated all other possibilities, *did* make such encounters more difficult. And so it is a good thing to make space for them. The postcritical mode, however, risks being a bit disingenuous in its fervent ingenuousness. Latour offers an ideal example in this regard. Again, from *We Have Never* to the more recent essay on critique, his proposed positive engagement always depends on a great deal of the debunking he supposedly wants to eschew; it's just that what is getting debunked are, again, supposedly those other kinds of critics who want to debunk. There is something, dare one say, *affectively* curious about the result of this: the relentlessly chipper tone combined with the breezy razing of entire fields of intellectual pursuit, as if this were not really what was taking place. And yet I would actually venture to say that, jarring though this may be to the sense of Latour's work as purely *constructive*, it in fact possesses no small role in producing that work's energy and enjoyability for the reader. It's just not clear that Latour, for all his certainty that his approach can blanket and account for everything, has fully mastered this dimension of his own criticism.[52]

What we need to be able to do is to talk about this dimension without it simply being disqualifying. Just as for *Enduring Love*, the recognition of a certain ineluctable excess to the pursuit of the real needs to be able to coexist with the genuine attempt at getting it right, at a "more realistic realism." One critic who, like Latour, saw critique's limitations early on and did a particularly good job of this was Eve Sedgwick. With Sedgwick, indeed, we move toward a different perspective, one in keeping with James's (and, finally, McEwan's) sense of the novel itself as a space making possible the uneasy coexistence of realism and romance.

We should take more time, at the present juncture, to consider the still very distinctive way Sedgwick wrote about critique and its alternatives. In her parlance, suspicious reading was "paranoid," but its opposite number, "reparative" reading, focused on healing versus on threat, was "depressive." Have we insufficiently considered the importance of this gesture, with its offhanded characterization of *all* critical engagement via a language usually reserved for pathology, for a radically incomplete self-knowledge?

In fact, I would argue, this aspect was crucial to Sedgwick's overall aim, which lay less in replacing one critical mode (suspicion) with the other (description), and more in showing how each one had its place. This assertion's seeming modesty, however, belies how difficult a lesson it has been to retain. Instead, in the years since Sedgwick's essay, the reparative mode has become much more associated with the very opposite of the "depressive": with, rather, the same apparently untroubled, self-avowedly depthless cheeriness we see in Latour.[53] From one perspective, this is quite understandable. After decades of the stern protocols of critique, scholars seem to have been galvanized by Sedgwick's invocations of "hope," aesthetic "pleasure," and the "additive and accretive"—a tendency very akin to Latour's—to put forward readings suffused by sheer positivity and happy proliferation.[54] Yet while such a mode typically presents itself as a model of pure, unfiltered openness, Sedgwick's own more nuanced analysis helps us see how, no less than did critique, it depends for its very force as much on what it brackets as what it includes.

What may make this especially hard to see, in the case of postcritique, is that what is bracketed is the very notion of limitation: specifically, that of limitation as productive. We notice, to begin with, that what has been lost from Sedgwick's own construal of the reparative is its link to the "merely reformist" (to the extent, indeed, that she inquires whether there might be goods worth salvaging in liberalism after all).[55] To acknowledge this dimension would require recognizing the extent to which the reparative in Sedgwick constitutes a "realist" position, in the particular sense in which James uses the term in his *American* preface: that is, the sense one gets from a realist novel. (And this may well be no accident, given how astute a reader Sedgwick was of James.) James defines the real as "the things we cannot possibly *not* know, sooner or later, in one way or another," and later, in contrast to the romantic, as experience "attach[ed]" to existing conditions.[56] Realism, that is to say, is the experience of a limit. Importantly, in this sense, it represents a response to *the same reality* that generates its opposite number: paranoia or critique, in Sedgwick; in James, romance. That reality, as Sedgwick describes it, must be acknowledged as, among other things, "a world full of loss, pain, and oppression."[57] So, she explains, the point is not that paranoia is "pessimistic" where the reparative is "optimistic"; the difference, rather, lies in the fact that the former mode can imagine solace only in an absolute transformation of the given, whereas the latter tries to make do, meaningfully—and even beyond that, to find real satisfactions—in what is there.[58]

Again, however, the key difference between Sedgwick's take on this distinction and the way it often appears elsewhere in postcritique rests in her acknowledgment of the value of *both* of these responses—a position that, crucially, requires *maintaining the difference between them*. This is to say, however, that we find ourselves back in the realm of the "Kantian [or 'modernist'] settlement" Latour decries. Consider the epistemological way James demarcates the real as what we have no choice but to know, in contrast to which romance becomes the name for what "we never *can* directly know; the things that can reach us only through the beautiful circuit and subterfuge of our thought and our desire."[59] To write as Sedgwick and James do, of romance and realism as two reactions to the same reality—one that refuses the limits it imposes, that is sure there must be more, and another that, facing the same limit, makes its peace with what it finds[60]—becomes no longer an option if one has decided, as Latour does, merely to collapse these sides, to insist on the real itself as a space of infinite possibility.

In understanding the two sides' inability to make a whole, it becomes useful to consider the other version of their collapse proffered by the speculative realists, who insist on the real, rather, as a space of radical opacity. (They thus deny the Kantian split from the opposite direction, giving everything a fathomless depth.) Less the "real," then, than what Lacanians term the "Real": the void, the gap, the space of an absolute, shattering contingency. McEwan, in his "Ian Macabre" mode, is clearly drawn again and again in this direction; we can see it at work in the opening scene of *Enduring Love*. We might, indeed, say that his novel unfolds according to a properly Lacanian framework, in which the symptoms we can now adduce in Joe, Clarissa, and Jed Parry alike have their root in the brief glimpse of a Real that cannot be lived, finally, except through one's symptomatic response. Yet this also enables a riposte to the view of symptomatic reading that sees it as always about uncovering some deeper truth that is hidden by the symptom—and that, further, necessarily entails separating the diagnosable (generally, in ideology critique, "anxious") from the reasonable and sane. In Lacan, to the extent that symptoms form our only means of access to an unlivable Real, they are both generalizable across the human population and, hence, not going anywhere anytime soon.[61] James, it appears, may be thinking something not so dissimilar, for what is this "circuit and subterfuge" of "thought" and "desire" through which we experience what we never can "know" otherwise, if not the channels of displacement that constitute the symptom?

McEwan thus reveals, finally, his difference from the Latourians and the speculative realists alike: he will acknowledge both the horror and the attraction of an abyssal Beyond that may also be a deeper Real, while nonetheless recognizing the need to patch together a life that holds it at bay. As his work shows, in more ways than one, there seem to be mirrored dangers in acceding too wholly to either of these. James, too, suggests as much, finally honoring most those writers in whom, he states, the complete "deflexion toward either quarter"—that is, toward the realist or the romantic—"has never taken place."[62] He mentions a few candidates in this regard: Walter Scott, Honoré de Balzac, and Émile Zola. Sedgwick seems equally appreciative of a similar facility not only in James himself, but also in his contemporary Proust.

Here, finally, seems to be a different way to consider humanists' relation to the two-cultures split. The novel, these writers suggest, can offer a space in which what James terms the different systems of "value" of realism and romance are both given their due, even as we recognize their ineradicable differences.[63] One hears here a surprising echo of James's contemporary, Weber, who deserves better than to be remembered as the somber voice of modern "disenchantment." As I suggested at the outset, the late nineteenth and early twentieth centuries have most commonly been remembered as the high-water mark of modernity critique; the recent work of Latour and others thus deserves real credit for recalling us to a counterstrain within the same era, in the writings of William James, Tarde, Whitehead, and others, whose monist project resembles their own. Neither of these perspectives, however—neither the strong, arguably Romantic critique of modernity (and modern science in particular) nor the cheerier explorations of the pragmatists and their kin—can account for those during this era who, like Weber, like Henry James, and like a number of others (again, Adams and Du Bois come to mind) framed the same situation as one of a confrontation between irreconcilable worldviews, or "value spheres," that were both taken seriously.[64]

In Weber, we see this perspective expressed most strongly in his 1918 talk "Science as a Vocation," which at one level clearly dedicates itself to countering the Romantically inclined youth of the day, who feel science amounts to factory-like procedures of calculation devoid of "'heart and soul,'" and yearn for a "prophet" in the classroom to enflame their deadened minds.[65] Against such claims, Weber first insists on the role played by "inspiration" and "intuition" in scientific discovery no less than in its purported opposites, faith and art (136). He goes on, however, to note that the Romantic youth are not merely mistaken in their concerns, for science does have its decisive differences from its others: faith, art, and indeed philosophy as well. Unlike art, it is of necessity "chained to the course of progress," planned to be obsolescent, as it were (137). And, as Tolstoy lamented, it cannot address the questions of the larger *point* of what we do, the questions "'What shall we do and how shall we live?'" (143). The "objectivity" for which Weber finally argues, then, looks closer to that embodied at present by the humanities than by the sciences, for it is the perspective, akin to that of the novel as theorized by James, that can produce a space in which these differing value systems might be able to come forward— in which, indeed, their "irreconcilable conflict with each other" can make evident to the student the need to *choose* that they necessarily entail (147).[66]

Fascinatingly enough, then, Latour himself, in his most recent writings, which focus on religion, ends up arriving at a place not so different from Weber's here. Attempting to make room for religious utterance, while honoring the work of the sciences, he ends up describing the two as distinct "universals," both of which demand our respect, but which, precisely for this reason, "we have to maintain as incommensurable."[67] Indeed, for Latour no less than for Weber, the real danger lies in mistaking the one for the other: demanding that faith produce evidence, or that science cover over its own workings and present its findings in the guise of unmediated illumination. Thus is a split reintroduced into our present monism, and with it, another reason to affirm a model of the university that will necessarily involve contention as much as the laudable goal of finding common ground.

Notes

1   See Sharon Marcus and Stephen Best, "Surface Reading: An Introduction," *Representations* 108 (fall 2009): 1–21, 18.

2   Bruno Latour, "Why Has Critique Run Out of Steam? From Matters of Fact to Matters of Concern," *Critical Inquiry* 30, no. 2 (winter 2004): 225–48; Heather Love, "Close but Not Deep: Literary Ethics and the Descriptive Turn," *New Literary History* 41, no. 2 (spring 2010): 371–91; Talal Asad, Wendy Brown, Judith Butler, and Saba Mahmood, *Is Critique Secular? Blasphemy, Injury, and Free Speech* (New York: Oxford University Press, 2013); Anne-Lise François, *Open Secrets: The Literature of Uncounted Experience* (Stanford, CA: Stanford University Press, 2007).

3   Bruno Latour, *Pandora's Hope: Essays on the Reality of Science Studies* (Cambridge, MA: Harvard University Press, 1999).

4   Bruno Latour, *We Have Never Been Modern*, trans. Catherine Porter (Cambridge, MA: Harvard University Press, 1993), 5. Subsequent references will appear parenthetically in the body of the text.

5   Latour, *Pandora's Hope*, 21. Further quotations from this work are cited parenthetically in the text.

6   Ian McEwan, *Enduring Love* (New York: Anchor, 1998), 140. See also, e.g., 93, 109, 4, 54. Further quotations from this work are cited parenthetically in the text.

7   Love, "Close but Not Deep," 6.

8   Marco Roth, "The Rise of the Neuro-Novel," *n+1* (fall 2009). Roth also mentions novels by Richard Powers, Mark Haddon, and Jonathan Lethem, among others, including McEwan's *Saturday* as well as *Enduring Love*.

9   For example, a book on obsessive-compulsive disorder from a neurological perspective dismisses entirely the Freudian notion that such manifestations "conceal important parts of yourself," describing them instead in strongly antihermeneutic terms as "random thoughts without special meaning": Ian Osborn, *Tormenting Thoughts and Secret Rituals: The Hidden Epidemic of Obsessive-Compulsive Disorder* (New York: Pantheon, 1998), 220. On the broader shift to biomedical forms of explanation within the field of psychiatry, see T. M. Luhrmann, *Of Two Minds* (New York: Vintage, 2004).

10 Laura Miller, "Ian McEwan Fools British Shrinks," *Salon*, September 21, 1999. http://www.salon.com/1999/09/21/mcewan_2/.

11 Hence, we see many invocations of cognitive science, neurology, and evolutionary psychology which seek to base the appeal of art in shared biological structures. See G. Gabrielle Starr, *Feeling Beauty: The Neuroscience of Aesthetic Experience* (Cambridge, MA: MIT Press, 2013); Paul B. Armstrong, *How Literature Plays with the Brain: The Neuroscience of Reading and Art* (Baltimore: Johns Hopkins University Press, 2013); Suzanne Keen, *Empathy and the Novel* (New York: Oxford University Press, 2010); Lisa Zunshine, *Why We Read Fiction* (Columbus: Ohio State University Press, 2006). Similarly, the turn to affect has been described as accompanied by a new attention to biology, physics, cognitive science, and neuropsychology. See Constantia Papoulias and Felicity Callard, "Biology's Gift: Interrogating the Turn to Affect," *Body and Society* 16, no. 1 (March 2010): 29–56, 330.

12 Stanley Cavell, *In Quest of the Ordinary: Lines of Skepticism and Romanticism* (Chicago: University of Chicago Press, 1994).

13 Marcus and Best, "Surface Reading," 17.

14 Love, "Close but Not Deep," 374.

15 Marcus and Best, "Surface Reading," 17.

16 Indeed, one finds statements remarkably similar to Marcus and Best's here in a contemporaneous anthology heralding the turn toward "materialism and realism" in Continental philosophy. As its back cover states, all the authors featured eschew "an obsession with the critique of written texts," preferring to put forward a "positive ontology." Or, as the editors more dramatically assert in their introduction, "By contrast with the repetitive continental focus on texts, discourse, social practices, and human finitude, the new breed of thinker is turning once more toward reality itself." Once more, this new "realism" depends crucially on a rapprochement with STEM fields, whether in the form of neuroscience or, as the editors suggest is the case for Alain Badiou, "taking mathematics to be the discourse of being," as a means of "resuscitat[ing] the question of truth, which was formerly a term of derision in much continental philosophy." Levi Bryant, Nick Srnicek, and Graham Harman, eds., *The Speculative Turn: Continental Materialism and Realism* (Melbourne: re:Press, 2011), back cover, 3 (emphasis mine), 5.

17 Latour, *Pandora's Hope*, 35. Subsequent references will appear parenthetically in the text.

18 This characterization is not very different from that invoked by Love, or, in more positive terms, by the humanist Jane Thrailkill in *Affecting Fictions: Mind, Body, and Emotion in American Literary Realism* (Cambridge, MA: Harvard University Press, 2007), 54–55.

19 Latour, *We Have Never*, 123, 115.

20 See, e.g., Latour, *We Have Never*, 134.

21 See, for example, Latour, *We Have Never*, 120, and the entire section (beginning on 114) titled "Small Mistakes Concerning the Disenchantment of the World."

22 Max Weber, *The Protestant Ethic and the Spirit of Capitalism*, trans. Talcott Parsons (London: Routledge, 1992; first published 1904–5), 181–82.

23 Karl Marx and Friedrich Engels, "The Communist Manifesto," in *The Portable Karl Marx*, ed. Eugene Kamenka (New York: Penguin, 1983), 206.

24 See, e.g., Latour, *We Have Never*, 124. After all, it is with Romanticism that complaints first emerge that "the general propositions of the sciences . . . never caught the actual living, palpitating reality of life": Isaiah Berlin, *The Roots of Romanticism* (Princeton, NJ: Princeton University Press, 2001; first published 1965), 41. For Berlin, this view reverberates, in the twentieth century, in the "division" obtaining between two realms of knowledge: one, the sciences, "where objective truth obtains," and another, "in ethics, aesthetics, and the rest," where "objective truth has been compromised" (138–40). For an argument on Marxism's Romantic aspects, see Frederick Löwy and Robert Sayre, *Romanticism against the Tide of Modernity*, trans. Catherine Porter (Durham, NC: Duke University Press, 2001). See also Robert Pippin's discussion, in *Modernism as a Philosophical Problem*, of what he terms the "Romanticism-to-modernism cycle" running from Kant through Nietzsche and Heidegger (London: Blackwell, 1989), 3.

25 Indeed, while Latour prefers the term modernist settlement to Cavell's Kantian settlement (see *Pandora's Hope*, 14, 96, 134, 193, 214, 294, 298, 310), Kant is as crucial for his account as he is for Cavell, providing what Latour calls the most "canonical" case of the splitting of object from subject, nature from society, and—crucially for the new turn to "surface reading"—of outside from depth (*We Have Never*, 56).

26 C. P. Snow, *The Two Cultures* (Cambridge: Cambridge University Press, 1998; first published 1959), 25.

27 Latour, *We Have Never*, 125–26.

28 Latour, *We Have Never*, 144.

29 Latour expresses this view directly in *Reassembling the Social's* idea of "practical metaphysics": e.g., 48. *Reassembling the Social: An Introduction to Actor-Network Theory* (Oxford: Oxford University Press, 2007).

30 Latour, *We Have Never*, 133. This perspective denies the split, but, as Latour himself suggests, it nonetheless does so, as I've suggested, from a position that importantly understands itself as "realist." The compass of the real is simply broadened (along the lines of Latour's "more realistic realism"). This is how such writings might be distinguished from, for example, those of object-oriented ontology (ooo), which similarly conflate the two sides of the divide into a "monist" whole, but could be said to do so from the "Romantic" perspective. We could put this in Kantian terms: while for Latour, there is no "Thing-in-itself" because "things" are quite enough, for ooo, in perhaps a more modernist vein, every single thing is a Thing-in-itself. Objects, that is, gain intellectual heft by being essentially granted the qualities Romanticism once reserved for subjects, and phenomenology, for what Heidegger called things. Graham Harman's work is a good example.

31 See, e.g., on Tarde, Bruno Latour and Vincent Antonin Lepinay, *The Science of Passionate Interests: An Introduction to Gabriel Tarde's Economic Anthropology*

(Chicago: Prickly Paradigm, 2010); Matei Candea, ed., *The Social after Gabriel Tarde: Debates and Assessments* (New York: Routledge, 2012); on Whitehead and William James, see Latour's contribution to Nicholas Gaskill and A. J. Nocek, *The Lure of Whitehead* (Minneapolis: University of Minnesota Press, 2014); as well as Isabelle Stengers, with a foreword by Latour, *Thinking with Whitehead: A Free and Wild Creation of Concepts* (Cambridge, MA: Harvard University Press, 2014).

32 Stephen Best, "Well, That Was Obvious," response to the *Representations* special issue "Technically, Denotatively, Literally," no. 125 (winter 2014), http://www.representations.org/responses/. William James, of course, is more famously known for his invocations of pluralism, but it is his later work—essays like "Does Consciousness Exist?," in which the contents of mind and world alike are subsumed under the general category of "experience"—to which I here allude as evidence for his relation to monism.

33 Latour, *Pandora's Hope*, 19. The invocation of these new areas of inquiry can begin to demonstrate the reach of Latour's work, which in the two decades since *Pandora's Hope* has led more and more scholars even in the purportedly blinkered humanities to link their scholarship to these very kinds of interdisciplinary innovations. Indeed, much of the groundbreaking work presently transpiring under the rubric of "new materialisms," including writings in animal studies, ecocriticism, and other "posthumanist" fields, may be said to draw energy very much from these sorts of new intellectual formations, as championed not only by Latour but by others he considers to be fellow travelers, such as Donna Haraway.

34 The absence of positivism from Latour's references to the interventions of phenomenology is typical of a broader tendency to dismiss any possible sense of the encroachments of scientific onto humanistic territory with a wave of a hand, as in *Pandora's* brief reference to "the averaged-out orthodoxies of a few neurophilosophers."

35 Rhiannon Davies, "Enduring McEwan," and Sean Matthews, "Seven Types of Unreliability," both in Ian McEwan's *Enduring Love*, ed. Peter Childs (London: Routledge, 2007), 69, 106.

36 James M. Mellard, "'No Ideas but in Things': Fiction, Criticism, and the New Darwinism," *Style* 41, no. 1 (spring 2007): 8, 22.

37 Daniel Zalewski, "The Background Hum," *New Yorker*, February 23, 2009. As sources close to McEwan describe, the novelist's split with his first wife (teacher of a class called "Mediation, Healing, Astrology, and Creativity"), right before writing *Enduring Love*, then combined with his later shock at 9/11 to produce a hardcore rationalist who began to outdo his friends Richard Dawkins and Christopher Hitchens in his contempt for religion and his fascination with the new neuroscience and evolutionary theory. Notably, over this same period his take on Clarissa in *Enduring Love* shifts dramatically: contrast a 1998 *Salon* interview with Dwight Garner where he states, "There is something about Clarissa's take on the world that Joe badly needs," to the *New Yorker* piece a decade later.

38   "Books That Have Helped Shape His Novels," http://fivebooks.com/interview/ian
     -mcewan-on-books-that-have-helped-shape-his-novels/?utm_expid=301755490
     .sAau5xAZR_uQq_U9zw1Xgw.0&utm_referrer=http%3A%2F%2Ffivebooks
     .com%2F%3Fs%3DMcEwan%26post_type%3Dinterview, accessed August 8, 2016.

39   Mellard, " 'No Ideas but in Things,' " 1.

40   In a more recent essay, Curtis D. Carbonell makes a version of this argument: "A
     Consilient Science and Humanities in Ian McEwan's *Enduring Love*," CLCWEB:
     Comparative Literature and Culture 12, no. 3 (2010).

41   Ian McEwan, "Literature, Science, and Human Nature," in *The Literary Animal:
     Evolution and the Nature of Narrative*, ed. Jonathan Gottschall and David Sloan
     Wilson (Evanston, IL: Northwestern University Press, 2005).

42   This is apparently, however, an unexpected enough stance that it remains hard to
     see. In a scathing essay on the even more neurologically inflected *Saturday*, for
     example, Elaine Hadley thus indicts that book for the well-worn crime—at least
     among contemporary English professors—of believing that the universal truths
     of literature can save us from our differences ("On a Darkling Plain: Victorian
     Liberalism and the Fantasy of Agency," *Victorian Studies* 48, no. 1 [autumn 2005]:
     92–102). Yet while Matthew Arnold's "Dover Beach" does have a heroic role to
     play in that novel, Hadley's account seems curiously indifferent to the fact that,
     in the book as a whole, the real exemplar of Arnoldian "disinterestedness" and
     "capaciousness of vision" turns out to be not the youthful poet who recites "Dover
     Beach" but her father, the neurosurgeon, whose Joe Rose–like musings on the
     commonalities shared by our human brains shape the novel's vision, and who
     is shown putting aside his personal feelings to operate on the thug who threat-
     ened his family. This latter conception, indeed, seems to embody the one toward
     which McEwan can be seen already moving in *Enduring Love*.

43   The most damning case of the wrongheadedness of this approach comes, how-
     ever, in the form of Jean Logan, the aggrieved widow who mistakenly believes
     her entirely noble husband to have been at the park because he was having an
     affair.

44   Zalewski, "Background Hum."

45   Laura Miller, "The Salon Interview: Ian McEwan," *Salon*, April 9, 2005, http://
     www.salon.com/2005/04/09/mcewan_5/.

46   Henry James, "The American," in William Veeder and Susan M. Griffin, eds.,
     The Art of Criticism: Henry James on the Theory and Practice of Fiction (Chicago:
     University of Chicago Press, 1986), 281.

47   James, "The American," 281.

48   James, "The American," 279, 283.

49   The larger cultural stakes behind these plot decisions only appear fully in a scene
     that might otherwise seem like a throwaway, when Joe visits an old friend living
     on the margins of society in order to acquire a gun for self-protection. The friend
     leads him to three hapless drug dealers, who turn out to represent all that McEwan
     finds intellectually impoverished in contemporary culture: when Joe feigns an al-

lergy to mask his nervous laughter, the lowlives, each in turn, somberly chalk up his symptoms to "frustrated needs in early childhood," astrology, and the baleful effects of the Industrial Revolution. The utter implausibility of this moment should be a sign of its overdetermination by considerations being imported from without into the story being told. For Joe is confronted here by, in effect, three paradigmatic forms of symptomatic reading: Freudianism, mysticism, and historicism of the antimodernity variety—precisely the tendencies that, in both his interviews and his contribution to the volume of Darwinist criticism, McEwan positions (along with social constructionism) against the new truths of neuroscience and evolutionary theory.

50 See also Asad et al., *Is Critique Secular?*

51 See Papoulias and Callard's discussion of this aspect in "Biology's Gift."

52 As in his characterization of humanists as Luddites, Latour no less than McEwan can seem to be channeling C. P. Snow when he briefly sets up the fight against critique as one of good against evil: see Latour, *We Have Never*, 125–26, Snow, *The Two Cultures*, 7–8.

53 In *The Affect Theory Reader*, editor Melissa Gregg briefly admits to having been forced by a reencounter with Sedgwick to realize that affect is not always either positive or utopian. Melissa Gregg and Gregory J. Seigworth, eds., *The Affect Theory Reader* (Durham, NC: Duke University Press, 2010), 23.

54 On Latour's self-confessedly "obsessive" list-making tendencies, and the difficulties they run into when one wants to address what works against connectivity, see Sianne Ngai, "Network Aesthetics," in *American Literature's Aesthetic Dimensions*, ed. Cindy Weinstein and Christopher Looby (New York: Columbia University Press, 2012), 367–92.

55 Eve Sedgwick, "Paranoid Reading and Reparative Reading, or, You're So Paranoid, You Probably Think This Essay Is about You," in *Touching Feeling: Affect, Pedagogy, Performativity* (Durham, NC: Duke University Press, 2003), 144, 141.

56 James, "The American," 279–80.

57 Sedgwick, "Paranoid Reading and Reparative Reading," 138.

58 Sedgwick, "Paranoid Reading and Reparative Reading," 138.

59 James, *The American*, 279.

60 For a particularly eloquent defense of the reparative position as Sedgwick presents it here, see François, *Open Secrets*.

61 On this alternative construal of the symptom, see, e.g., Colette Soler, "The Paradoxes of the Symptom in Psychoanalysis," in *The Cambridge Companion to Lacan*, ed. Jean-Michel Rabaté (Cambridge: Cambridge University Press, 2005). As Soler explains, Lacan's "second return to Freud," in which he realizes that "the symptom is [also] a mode of satisfaction," entails what we might see as a collapse between Freud's initial distinction between the symptom, "which implies repression," and sublimation, where some other thing is said to be "produced, invented" in the face of the impossibility of desire (87, 91).

62 James, *The American*, 279.

63 Lukács, describing Scott's invention of the novel as an alternative mode of history, called this capacity the novel's form of "objectivity": both its recognition of the irreducible reality of our present situation and, as a consequence, its tribute paid to the genuine losses that situation's achievement entailed: the presence of what is absent, as it were. Such losses can then, in the context of what has become reality, begin to take the form of myth; as Lukács puts it, in what might otherwise appear a paradoxical formulation, this "objectivity . . . only enhances the true poetry of the past." Georg Lukács, *The Historical Novel*, trans. Hannah Mitchell and Stanley Mitchell (Boston: Beacon, 1963), 55.

64 See Adams, *The Education of Henry Adams* (New York: Library of America, 2009), and Du Bois, "Sociology Hesitant," *boundary 2* 27, no. 3 (2000): 37–44.

65 Max Weber, "Science as a Vocation," in *From Max Weber: Essays in Sociology*, ed. and trans. H. H. Gerth and C. Wright Mills (New York: Oxford University Press), 135, 153. Further quotations from this work are cited parenthetically in the text.

66 For this reason, Weber's greatest critique of the romantic youth turns out to result not from their embrace of irrationality but from their distinctly modern mysticism, which imagines a kind of happy marriage of the rational and irrational at one and the same time. (One imagines he might well have had similarly little patience with the American variant of this mode, New Thought, which William James had embraced.)

67 Bruno Latour, *Rejoicing: or, The Torments of Religious Speech*, trans. Julie Rose (Cambridge: Polity, 2013), 51.

5

Symptomatic Reading Is a Problem of Form

ELLEN ROONEY

... no denunciation without its proper instrument of close analysis ...
—ROLAND BARTHES, *Mythologies*

What Now?

The advent of a postcritical turn in contemporary discourse is generally
imagined as the displacement if not the disavowal of symptomatic reading.
On this account, attentiveness and receptivity, description, and reenchantment
represent an escape from the theory-laden gestures of suspicion, mastery, and
contempt aligned with the posture of critique. In contrast, I will argue that
symptomatic reading invites us to read to the letter, intimately and yet aloud,
in the contentious, invigorating, and unpredictable company of other readings. Symptomatic reading cannot be reduced to either philosophical critique
or a hermeneutics of suspicion, not least because of its irreducible engagement
with form, its dependence on the text from which it nonetheless ineluctably
distinguishes itself. Symptomatic reading embraces an oxymoronic intention to be surprised that inscribes the reader in an encounter that cannot be
known in advance. Provisional, guilty, and lacking guarantees, it embodies a
reading effect that will in its turn emerge as symptom, a reading effect that, as
Barthes might say, "is scarcely concerned to last."[1]

The "critique of critique" and the contemporary crisis of the humanities are
coeval and inexorably connected. The nature of the crisis of the humanities is
not so much in dispute as profoundly over-determined, uneven, and deeply
mystified, and I will not attempt to summarize the wide-ranging discussion
that accompanies it.[2] But perhaps the many parties to the debate can at least
be said to agree that the humanities are (once again) on the defensive, los-

ing enrollments (though even this observation is challenged by those who have looked most searchingly at the data) and facing the summary closings of departments and dissolution of majors. Humanities scholars have literally been called out by the president of the United States, as devoted to less-than-ideal objects of study (an apology to the field of art history was dutifully issued; POTUS majored in political science) and are fading in the competition with STEM fields for research support, if not yet (in absolute numbers) for students. They have responded to the "crisis" with STEAM, celebrations of liberal learning from university presidents and television pundits,[3] and various, less explicitly crisis-driven, proposals and polemics concerning the future directions of humanistic scholarship, the essential character of the humanities, and what the practice of the humanities can do in the world we inhabit and the world to come.

Such is the institutional terrain on which the discourse of the postcritical emerges. Every quarrel about the future is always also a quarrel about the past. What our past efforts have accomplished, where they have led or failed to lead, how our habitual practices and familiar theories have brought us to our present conjuncture: these questions structure inquiry into what is to be done now, on the threshold of the era "after critique."[4] Lloyd Pratt has recently argued that "when you're a critic, one of your main tasks is to get the timing right."[5] "Antiquation" is his term for the rhetorical and political gesture that surveys the present conjuncture and pronounces certain projects over, on the grounds that they are out of date. Offering terse, elegant analyses of Matthew Arnold, Walter Benjamin, and Barbara Christian, each of whom he shows to have been acutely aware of the "necessary timeliness of an effective criticism," Pratt observes that "one of the main reasons it is so important to get the timing right is that the critic's statement of what ails the present determines what comes to be understood as the character of that present."[6] A certain amount of scholarly attention is regularly given to this question, but crisis intensifies efforts to think the problem of timing and the relation of present practice to future prospects. Pratt proposes that we attend to how the gesture of antiquation is undertaken, not least because any diagnosis of the present may be mistaken, and, as a result, what he designates as our "unfinished business" may be thrown out with the bathwater:

> Revisiting terms that once received a great deal of notice but that have more recently faded from view, while also paying attention both to how the fortunes of those terms have been made to wax and wane and to why,

avoids the naturalizing of such waxings and wanings, which are often represented as simply one feature of the normal course of intellectual life. The critical lexicons that we construct, endorse, and then routinely subject to antiquation constitute the main site of memory for the critical-intellectual fields we inhabit. The revisions we make to them determine how we end up deciding what should be the function of criticism at the present time: the choice of lexicon determines what can be said and seen about the present time.[7]

The antiquation of particular lexicons and practices often accompanies the proclamation of the new—the new Americanists, the new eighteenth century, the new materialism, even the New Historicism—as both long overdue and redemptive, and antiquation is very much at work in debates concerning critique. Overlapping and contending assertions concerning "the way we read now," our uncertain passage into an era "after critique," whether critique has "run out of steam," or if, perhaps counter-intuitively, "*now* is *then*," are subtended by interpretations (and critiques) of the present state of the humanities and the university, as well as of their disciplinary presuppositions, histories, and powers, and of the impact (or lack thereof) of critique on a wider, explicitly political world.[8] Together, these forces condition the very existence of the postulate that we have passed—or ought now to hurry—into a postcritical age.

Not Your Doktor Vater's Critique

I begin with the proposition that the possibility of rethinking critique entangles us with the question of reading. And once we turn to the question of reading, we confront the question of form. The problem of form as an effect of reading is thus integral to my understanding of what it might mean to rethink critique. Indeed, *reading* is for my purposes a more inclusive term than *critique* and the more suggestive and powerful theoretical object. In what follows, I argue that "symptomatic" reading remains the most supple problematic for rereading critique, taking as my proof text Louis Althusser's account of "guilty" reading and his own (guilty) attention to form, especially to the figure he calls "the play on words itself."[9] Symptomatic reading proceeds for Althusser in the most intimate way; in his practice, reading and writing are confounded in the work of form. This is the reading effect.

The view that reading is a more inclusive term than critique and the more suggestive and powerful theoretical object is far from universally embraced.

Rethinking critique is a cross-disciplinary challenge, but disciplines have distinctive preconceptions about the nature of critique and divergent experiences of its power. Insofar as the argument about how we read—about what reading can do—involves a judgment on the efficacy of critique beyond any disciplinary boundary, these distinctions will come under scrutiny. Disciplinary traditions are, as we know, the opposite of airtight, wholly autonomous realms; they do not differ absolutely. Indeed, I claimed above that the question of reading is always already a problem of form—not *literary* form, but form in a more general and capacious sense, a sense that many critics believe has purchase beyond literary studies.[10] At the same time, many literary scholars—I am one—have taken powerful lessons from philosophy, anthropology, science studies, and so forth. Some of these same scholars figure critique in ways that do not foreground its critical articulation with reading and form, where reading cannot be taken merely as a synonym for critique. In such cases, where we find a forgetting of the ways in which reading is distinguishable from critique, what often follows is a forgetting of form.[11]

Symptomatic reading imbricates critique with reading and thus with form and demonstrates the non-identity of these terms. As the problem of critique "as such" has become a more urgent and generally debated topic, the forgetting of reading as a matter of form has led literary studies into contortions that might be less knotted if we were to recall the ways in which the intimate relation of reading to form complicates our disciplinary borrowings, specifically in relation to critique.[12] Disciplines committed to notions of communication or reason that are ill-equipped to address the potentially unruly effects of form are consequently unable to register either the unpredictable capacity of form both to determine and to be determined or the impossibility of registering that capacity save through contingent reading practices that are irreducible to critique. Symptomatic reading, I argue, combines critique with an attention to the work of form that displaces the apparently purely propositional or conceptual movement of critique as such: symptomatic reading breaks with the givenness of the text yet remains profoundly attached to positing its forms.[13]

Reading Althusser as a theorist of forms obviously betrays my disciplinary formation. He stresses disciplinary heterogeneity when he distinguishes the philosopher's reading of *Capital* from those performed by "economists," "historians," "logicians," or "philologists." The philosophers, he argues, "posed the question of [*Capital's*] *relation to its object,* hence both the question of the specificity of its object and the question of the specificity of its relation to that object, i.e., the question of the nature of the type of discourse set to work to handle this object."[14] From the perspective of literary studies, the question of the object is both conceptual and formal, theory and figure entwined; so, too, in the mode of reading Althusser advances. Whether grappling with the categories of ideology and the subject, theorizing the "existence of the structure in its effects" (188), or questioning the "seductive" (26) metaphor of terrain, Althusser discloses the problem of reading as a problem of form, of the "nature of the type of discourse set to work" (14). Form may appear a detour from Althusser's central arguments, but it is a fundamental figure in his work, one that gives symptomatic reading its distinctive relation to critique.[15]

Althusser enables us to think symptomatic reading in excess of philosophical critique by means of his claim that reading is productive. This productivity defines the specificity of reading and entails its acceptance of what Althusser calls its "guilt," including its relation to other readings and to form. In this account, no reading is innocent, emphatically including his own. He pronounces his reading of *Capital* "the opposite of an innocent reading. It is a guilty reading, but not one that absolves its crime on confessing it. . . . It is therefore a special reading which exculpates itself as a reading by posing every reading the very question that unmasks its innocence, the mere question of its innocence: *what is it to read?*" (15).[16]

Reading that embraces its guilt never addresses only "the text itself" but always also the other reading or what Althusser calls the problematic. This relation to another reading constitutes critical history, the trace of many readers and of their irresolvable disputes, as much as their consensus.[17] The other reading is a counter-reading and thus a kind of "making difficult," a contestation, though reading against the other reader is always also reading with the other reader, as reading against the text is always also reading with the text. The model here is play, as Althusser acknowledges when he insists: "I am interested in the *play on words* itself" (40). Playing against is playing with. As we shall see, the other reading makes it impossible for me to forget that I am also a symptom. At the same time, insofar as this play with the other reading itself brings form into being, rather than simply discovering it, it cannot pose as purely empirical or merely descriptive. Called upon to explain its break with what Althusser calls "obviousness," the apparent givenness of the text, reading falls into theoretical explicitness. "The *play on words* itself" announces a reading that is also a moment of unabashed theorization. Innocence proves untenable once reading contests the other reading by means of its own artifice, its production of form.

Reading in the sense that I have been sketching here encompasses the problematic of critique but is not limited to it. It enacts critique through its attention to form, in the way that it takes form as a mode of address to the other reading (reader). The result is a formal productivity or "reading effect" that surprises. The most powerful way surprise makes itself felt in reading is through the apprehension of form; yet, as we shall see, this apprehension unsettles any notion of the knowing subject as the ground of reading.

What Is It to Read?

This is Althusser's question. He proposes to answer by reading *Capital* "to the letter. To read the text itself, complete, all four volumes, line by line, to return ten times to the first chapters" (13) and "according to the rules of a reading in which [Marx] gave us a brilliant lesson in his own reading of classical political economy" (30). But "what is it to read?" is a question of broad and vernacular public interest. If space permitted, I would linger here on the culture-wide debate on reading in the United States. I am not referring mainly to the century-long impact of the linguistic turn, the recognition of language's mediating force across the social field, or of the semiotic nature of the real, nor to the adoption of the rubrics of language or text to think genetic codes or computer programs. I mean literally that questions of reading and reading as an explanatory trope are fully at work in diverse sites across our culture, pervasive in myriad idioms. In a certain respect, we are engaged in precisely the task Althusser set for us in *Reading Capital*. The vernacular theorizations range from the "Read the Bills Act" in the U.S. Congress to "First Read," a feature of the political chat show *The Daily Rundown*, from architectural handbooks—"How to Read New York," "How to Read Houses"—and *New York Times* articles entitled "How to Read Afghanistan" to the ever-increasing popularity of autobiographical accounts of one's reading: of Jane Austen, of Proust, of *Middlemarch*, and so on.[18]

These debates, across disciplines, popular culture, and multiple public spheres, are fascinating in their admixtures of the suspicious and the enchanted, their attention to the other reading, their interrogation of the technologies that "deliver" and constitute texts, their concerns about what (not) reading does to our brains, and their passion for form.[19] The notion that reading, construed as a difficult or demanding practice, is elite or cloistered finds little support in these debates; reading as difficulty is popular, pervasive, and vernacular, as is the insight that to read is to write.[20] Indeed, the question "What is it to read?"

commands the attention of those very publics that some observers suggest have either wearied of the obviousness of critique or learned its lessons all too well. The terrain on which the question "What is it to read?" is contested is not merely academic.

Terrain is Althusser's figure for the problematic. Privileging the question "What is it to read?," he denies reading any essence and shifts attention to the problematic upon which any given reading acts and from which it emerges; he simultaneously registers the way in which readings form new problematics to put texts into motion. For Althusser, a problematic is the structure of pre-suppositions that constitutes a discourse, its enabling conditions, historical and political; the problematic defines the objects within a field, fixes lines of inquiry, and delimits the form of the solutions thinkable within its limits. A discourse "can only pose problems on the terrain and within the horizon of a definite theoretical structure, its problematic, which constitutes its absolute and definite condition of possibility, and hence the absolute determination of *the forms in which all problems must be posed*, at any given moment" (25).[21] The problematic determines forms of inclusion and exclusion, the questions asked and those that go unposed. Every idiom of close reading, as well as suspicious, distant, symptomatic, affective, susceptible, reparative, surface, paranoid, and all other modes of reading, enacts a problematic.

Scholarly discussion associates the Althusserian problematic with ideology critique, thanks in part to "Ideology and Ideological State Apparatuses," his most widely cited work in the American context.[22] *Reading Capital* reorients the problematic of ideology critique by posing the question "What is it to read?" in the course of its reading of Marx's *Capital*, which text is itself both a reading and "A Critique of Political Economy."[23] Althusser and Balibar's book is not entitled *Critiquing Capital* for the excellent reason that it treats Marx not as an inventor of critique but as a theorist of reading and practitioner of readings. Althusser reminds us:

> When we read Marx, we immediately find a reader who reads to us, and out loud. The fact that Marx was a prodigious reader is much less impor-tant for us than the fact that Marx felt the need to fill out his text by reading out loud, not only for the pleasure of quotation, or through scrupulousness in his references . . . not only because of the intellectual honesty which made him always and generously recognize his debts . . . but for reasons deeply rooted in the conditions of his discovery. So Marx reads out loud to us,

not only in the *Theories of Surplus Value* ... but also in *Capital*: he reads Quesnay, he reads Smith, he reads Ricardo, etc. (18)

Althusser here celebrates the discovery of a new theory and practice of reading and writing. He argues: "I dare maintain that only since Marx have we had to begin to suspect what, in theory at least, reading and hence writing *means*" (16). This binding together of reading and writing was once a commonplace of literary studies; but the insight that reading is necessarily writing has been obscured by some of the arguments on behalf of surface reading or thin description or against interpretation.[24] Althusser locates in *Capital* a theory of the meaning of reading and writing and an instantiation of their intertwined practice. "Returning to Marx," Althusser writes, "we note that not only in what he says but in what he does we can grasp the transition from an earlier idea and practice of reading to a new practice of reading and to a theory of history capable of providing us with a new theory of *reading*" (18).

History here has many senses, none of which confuses the problematic with the essence of an epoch or expression of its consciousness, both targets of Althusser's critique. Historicism erases the operation of the problematic in favor of the view that "truth can be read openly in phenomena, if not directly, at least with little difficulty" (124). Althusser dubs this the "historical religion of reading," a "religious myth of *reading*" the real as though it were a "manifest discourse ... in which a voice (the Logos) speaks," the very myth Marx eventually exposes. "The Young Marx of the *1844 Manuscripts* read the human essence at sight, immediately, in the transparency of its alienation," Althusser claims. "*Capital*, on the contrary, exactly measures a distance and an internal dislocation (*décalage*) in the real, inscribed in its *structure*, a distance and a dislocation such as to make their own effects themselves illegible, and the illusion of an immediate reading of them the ultimate apex of their effects: *fetishism*." Rethinking reading and history in a single gesture, Marx opens a chasm "between Logos and Being; between the Great Book that was, in its very being, the World, and the discourse of the knowledge of the world; between the essence of things and its reading" (17). History and reading survive this break, of course, but history is rethought as what Peggy Kamuf calls "historicality," the unpredictable relation of the text, not to its contexts, which will "subsid[e] into archival compost," but "to a future, by which it remains always to some extent incomprehensible by any given present."[25] History is the time of reading and writing.

It Cannot Itself Think Itself

Let us reread our text carefully.

—LOUIS ALTHUSSER

What does Althusser mean when he attributes to Marx a new theory and practice of what it means to read?[26] In *Reading Capital,* he writes: "I am interested in the *play on words* itself [*J'en veux au* jeu de mots *lui-même*]" (41).[27] This comment appears just after he notes that the "perpetual *play on the words* 'real' and 'concrete'" in the early Marx and Feuerbach loosed on the world "a whole series of ambiguities whose delayed effects we are suffering from today." While these effects offer an "extraordinarily rich critical path" (40–41), Althusser swerves away to the problem of the play on words itself where the theory of reading takes form. As we shall see, the work of form entails the play on words, the rendering of form as reading's effect.

Althusser theorizes the "*play on words* itself" as a mobile object of knowledge and a symptom. Reading formalizes this play, and insofar as form can never be discovered but must be actively produced, reading abandons the claims to transparency and immediacy that define fetishism and confesses its (theoretical) guilt: insofar as symptomatic reading proceeds from a shift in the problematic, it cannot progress without a theoretical (theorized) break. As Althusser writes: "Every theory is in essence a problematic . . . a matrix for posing every problem concerning the object of the theory." Symptomatic reading, reading that announces a new play on words, is always "the effect of a new theory . . . the effect of a new problematic" (155). There is no reading that works innocently beyond, before or beneath the theoretical, no reading that can put itself out of play.

The newness of the "new problematic" appears as the formal insight it engenders, for example, in its exposure of "lacunae" in its tutor text, "unasked questions" the text does not utter, but which nonetheless belong to it, silences that the text speaks in "*its own words*" when it answers a question it never asks, providing "*the correct answer to a question that has just one failing: it was never posed*" (22; emphasis in the original). This articulation of the unasked question does not entail a depth model of interpretation; quite the contrary. Althusser presses an unforgiving critique of the "empiricist myth" of reading in which truth is a "kernel" "hidden" within a "husk" or beneath a "veil," "covered and enveloped by the dross of the inessential" (37). He christens this conception of knowledge the "twin brother" of the religious myth of reading in which the world is an open book, its essence to be read at first sight: "The empiricist conception may be thought of as a variant of the conception of vision, with the mere difference that *transparency* is not given from the beginning, but is separated from itself precisely by the *veil*, the dross of impurities, of the inessential which steals the essence from us" (37). Dispelling these myths of innocent reading, "the play on words itself" operates entirely on the surface of the text.

The term *itself* should not mislead us. This play is not singular or unified, obvious or given as such, not given *as itself*. Indeed, "the play on words itself" is never simply "itself," self-identical, indivisible, unified, present. Its lack of self-identity demands the productive process that is reading and the conflict among readers. The trope of "the play on words itself" theorizes the imbrication of the concept and the signifier, the relation between the "written" and "the form of its writing" (69), Althusser argues, and insists in its own form on the impossibility of the "thing itself" as the theoretical object of reading or writing. Althusser captures this "work of reading" in his account of the "inversion" metaphor offered (even by Marx himself) to explain how the Marxian dialectic differs from the Hegelian. He argues that this metaphor "cannot itself think itself" (33);[28] like every figure, it can only be read. The "play on words itself" is never simply *one*, and it does not think itself. To read the play on words itself is to exploit and aggravate its punning, ironic, or oxymoronic character.[29]

Resistance to the presupposition of transparency is thus crucial to everything Althusser teaches us about what it is to read: the "opacity of the immediate" (16) is form in its demand to be read, that is, form as it emerges from the act of reading, the work of form revealed in reading's wake, as reading's encounter. From his call to "abandon the mirror myths of immediate vision and reading, and conceive knowledge as a production" (24) to his rejection of expressive causality and deconstruction of the givenness of the object, Althusser theorizes a dislocating play that excludes the possibility of any conceivable reading that does not bring to bear its own problematic, that merely describes or transcribes. "Guilty" reading, powered and burdened by its problematic, is never a reflection, faithful paraphrase, unveiling, or mimesis of the text. Reading's productivity entails its shift of the problematic, which is historically, theoretically, and politically situated, sometimes antagonistic, and always unfinished and so perpetually reiterating the question of reading.

Displacing the impasse of surface and depth, abstract and concrete, form and content, the play on words itself offers a rejoinder to a range of interpretative projects, including the panoply of historicisms, surface reading and the descriptive turn, and evolutionary or cognitive reading models. Reading symptomatically defetishizes, but exposing the unasked question does not result in a too-knowing paranoia or the gestures of mastery and arrogant negation that Christopher Castiglia dubs "critiquiness."[30] To answer the question "What is it to read?" the symptomatic reader must simultaneously disavow her "innocence." The symptom is not an affliction confined to the textual object or the other reader. What goes around comes around. Every defetishizing reading entails the *production* of a competing problematic—another reading—that in its turn will be read.

Where symptomatic readings harbor unasked questions, the other reader intervenes. Every reading calls up another; symptomatic reading is necessarily *addressed* to another reading, never simply to "the text," and so anticipates its own displacement.[31] Reading "is an activity with a history," Geraldine Friedman argues. "Only when one reading has already taken place or another can still occur do certain moments emerge as discrepant, redundant, or uncertain."[32] The reading effect exposes antagonism and the political impossibility of mastery; making a "break," it formally inscribes its debt to the readings it resists, without which it would have neither significance nor consequence nor a field of play.

Taking Form

The practice of close reading has always been radically cloven: here, on one side, my ambition to master a text, to write *over* its language and refashion it to the cut of my argument, to which it is utterly indifferent; there, on the other, my longing to write *in* this language, to identify and combine with it.

—D. A. MILLER, *Jane Austen, or The Secret of Style*

Althusser takes the figure of the play on words from Marx, who writes of a *Wortspiel* "that is necessarily impenetrable for its author" (24). The notion of Wortspiel is capacious and takes in all kinds of verbal wit, puns, ambiguities, and double entendres, witty uses of words, and word games and puzzles based on linguistic knowledge. Althusser's theoretical interest in this play emerges as he investigates how the conceptual and figural ground shifts under the "unwitting" feet of writing and reading subjects, including Marx.

But Althusser does not simply offer us a *theory* of reading that privileges this Wortspiel. His own text is a rhetorical festival, the play on words in polysemous practice, returning again and again to the critical terms of his reading and rendering the emergence of his problematic at the level of the word, to the letter. His prose is riddled with repetition, italics, doubling, irony, oxymoron, parataxis, citation, translation, metaphor, puns, paradox, and a kind of tongue-twisting play with negation (and the negation of negation). Two examples particularly critical to his intervention capture the latter: "What classical political economy does not see, is not what it does not see, it is *what it sees*; it is not what it lacks, on the contrary, it is *what it does not lack*; it is not what it misses, on the contrary, it is *what it does not miss*. The oversight, then, is not to see what one sees, the oversight no longer concerns the object, but *the sight* itself" (21). The negation of negation stages an encounter, one that eludes readers caught in the myth of reading as first sight. Althusser's many modes of repetition reveal the *necessary* relation of blindness to insight as an effect of rereading, a rereading that must carry out its rewriting literally on the page: "Marx makes us *see* blanks in the text of classical economics' answer; but that is merely to make us see what the classical text itself says while not saying it, does not say while saying it. Hence it is not Marx who says what the classical text does not say, it is not Marx who intervenes to impose from without on the classical text a discourse which reveals its silence—*it is the classical text itself which tells us that it is silent: its* silence *is its own words*" (22). The formal commitment here is complete; the argument turns on the radical resignification of the phrase "its own words" and an equally profound relocation of the word itself.

This commitment is vividly displayed in Althusser's language, especially in the way in which the word itself insists, persists, is reiterated yet displaced, dislocated by the very process of being *read out loud*. The notion of the text *itself* has a long history in twentieth-century literary theory. Althusser places this notion under maximum pressure. Critical puns, paradoxes, ironies, and oxymorons abound: "the non-vision and vision within vision itself" (21), "immobile motion" (142) and "silent voice" (143), the "necessity of contingency" (45), "the inner darkness of exclusion" (26), the "text itself which tells us that it is silent" (22), and of course, the "unuttered *question*" (23) itself. The figure of "the play on words itself" itself appears in ever more duplicitous guises, as the "play on words [that] plays on a difference it kills at the same time [as] it spirits away the corpse," and the "true play of words [that] deceive[s] us" (40). As instances of the unrelenting torrent of Althusserian repetition, consider a passage near the essay's end (67), where *form* appears seventeen times, or, better yet, a "detour" into "empiricist abstraction" (36) where the word *real* appears twenty-seven times. Versions of *read*, *reader*, and *reading* occur twenty-nine times on page 18, offering propositions such as this: "The reading Marx makes of Smith and Ricardo is only lucid for a certain reading of this reading: for an immediate reading that does not question what it reads, but takes the obvious in the text read for hard cash" (18).

The repetition, paradox, and doubling are a powerfully symptomatic feature of Althusser's prose *and* his theory, one that enacts a critical turn in the analysis, staging and restaging the formal encounter with the word that constitutes symptomatic reading. In the current critical context, critique is broadly understood to be both a negative and a "secondary" form, "always a critique *of* something, a commentary on another argument, idea or object," as Rita Felski has pointed out. However, Felski notes that, despite its belatedness, "critique is far from subservient. It seeks to wrest from a text a different account than it gives of itself."[33] In Althusser's text, symptomatic reading is not bound to its text solely by the argument that it discredits or rewrites: it harbors a deeper debt. The *"play on words itself"* makes a formal demand. It depends on repeating the word, to the letter, reinscribing the text we find "in black and white" (192), with all the apparent force that repetition carries as an argument that uncannily needs no elaboration. But that apparent force is forgone: the authority it would claim for its seemingly innocent mode of reading presumes the unity of the word (that is, fetishism) and disavows its own productive operation or play. This model of repetition is anathema to Althusser. Reading the play on words offers a different account of the text than the text gives of itself—in its own words. Repetition itself "inaugurates" an encounter, a "rupture, the reign of a new logic which, far from being a mere development, the 'truth' or 'inversion' of the old [logic], *literally takes its place*" (44; emphasis in the original). Another reading.

Althusser both theorizes this form of ruptural repetition and enacts it. The passage of paratactic negation I cite above—"it is not what it lacks, on the contrary, it is *what it does not lack*; it is not what it misses, on the contrary, it is *what it does not miss*" (20; emphasis in the original)—refers to his most famous example: classical political economy's "unwittin[g] chang[e] of terrain," the blind process in which it "substitute[d] for the value of labour . . . the value of labour power," thus making "a complete change in the terms of [its] original problem" (23), which had been expressed by the old question: what is the value of labor? Classical political economy did this, but without recognizing what it had done, without uttering the question: what is the value of *labor power*? In Althusser's reading, *Capital* provides this unposed question and the theorization of reading that its discovery entailed. It thereby shifts the problematic to reveal the unwitting play on the word-concept labor and gives classical economics the question to which it had unwittingly provided answers it could not explain. In the process, it teaches us what it means to read.

The play on words itself occupies a single plane, a rupture that repeats, condensing discontinuity and continuity. This figural play is a literal displacement; the new problematic emerges by announcing the appearance of the double meaning of a single word. Althusser thus "abolishes . . . the distance between writing and reading, [not] by intensifying the projection of the reader into the work, but by joining them—writing and reading—in a single signifying practice."[34] Reading this shifting terrain requires a patient, retrospective attentiveness to the text's own words, those words now determined, now determining. Althusser's repetitions, italics, doublings, negations, and paradoxes refuse words their proper places, disrupting their "obviousness" and given location. Rereading the word, instigating the play on words, or putting the word into play, is a rewriting that remains necessarily but faithlessly tethered to its text, which it divides against itself. Form is produced as an opacity not to be pierced, penetrated, or described but displaced, refocused (to use the increasingly dead metaphor of vision), and read, played in tandem with the other reading, the work of the other reader, the reader who can always be trusted to surprise.

Althusser thinks this displacement as an encounter or confrontation among readings in the present moment overdetermined by political interests that are incalculable in real time, an encounter from which historicality emerges. The "play on words itself" is a form that is situational, transitive, ultimately incomplete, no more than provisional.[35] But this form appears with a force that is not to be evaded. The reader here is no more the master of her practice than the author whose text silently betrays his unwitting insights. Althusser gives no credit to a "constitutive subject" (27) in his conceptualization of the process by which the terrain shifts: "it is literally no longer the eye (the mind's eye) of a subject which sees what exists in the field defined by a theoretical problematic: it is this field itself which sees itself in the objects or problems it defines" (25). In a new problematic, the object shifts its shape, announcing the subject's unpredictable negotiations with the emerging field; "any object or problem situated on the terrain and within the horizon . . . is visible. We must take these words literally" (25); "the invisible is no more a function of *a subject's sighting* than is the visible: the invisible is the theoretical problematics's non-vision of its non-objects" (26; emphasis in the original). The subject herself takes form as one of symptomatic reading's most unsettling effects.

Surprise Me

At the limit, everyone writing is taken by surprise.

—JACQUES DERRIDA, *Of Grammatology*

The change of terrain comes as a surprise to both the reader and the read. This feature of symptomatic reading often goes missing (is submerged and disavowed) in critique, thus contributing to the latter's reputation for disdainful and hostile suspicions, "knowing above all, and before all."[36] Like the fascination with reading, the valorization of surprise and suspicion of knowingness has grown across cultural fields. Consider the animated film *Ratatouille*. The supercilious food critic, Anton Ego, who learns many lessons (including the unreservedly minor status accorded the critic) over the course of the movie, reveals his complete reformation as a humbler, but happier and indeed more discriminating man by his answer when, in the closing scene of the film, his waiter asks: "What can I get you?" Ego responds: "Surprise me."[37]

Ratatouille has the acuity to play with its Ego—swept into the ecstasy that ultimately frees him to risk surprise—by remaking a homely dish in a luxurious French restaurant. The elegantly sculpted ratatouille (of course) recalls Ego instantly and viscerally to his mother's table: familiarity, unqualified love, repetition, home. The film sees its paradoxical operation clearly, the surprising rupture is also a repetition, ratatouille is ratatouille in a radical new form; the terrain shifts and the (hyper)critical subject falls into an unanticipated relationship to something like what Eve Sedgwick calls "plenitude."[38] Sedgwick theorizes in a profoundly different register from *Rataouille*, and yet, she invokes the reparative as "surplus beauty," "extracting sustenance," and "help[ing] ourselves again and again," terms not so remote from those reorienting the eager diner Ego.[39] Developing her symptomatic reading of paranoid reading's corrosive hegemony, Sedgwick argues that the paranoid reader expresses an "aversion to surprise" born of the conviction that "there must be no bad surprises." Since "learning of the possibility of a bad surprise would itself constitute a bad surprise, paranoia requires that bad news be always already known," the very possibility of surprise lost in the reader's "anticipatory," infinite "exposure" of this "always already known" negativity.[40] But Sedgwick wagers that "to a reparatively positioned reader, it can seem realistic and necessary to experience surprise." She reads, even in the "grimly strong theory" of D. A. Miller's paranoid *The Novel and the Police*, "a wealth of tonal nuance, attitude, worldly observation, performative paradox, aggression, tenderness, wit, inventive reading, obiter dicta, and writerly panache,"[41] that is, surprising readings sheltered beneath Miller's "over-arching" carceral theory. Disclosing the paranoid and the reparative as entwined, Sedgwick stresses Melanie "Klein's insistence that it is not people but mutable positions—or . . . practices—that can be divided between the paranoid and the reparative." Surprise is not strictly speaking an Ego effect: everyone writing (and reading) is *taken* by surprise. Surprise may consequently evolve in the interstices of the avowedly paranoid, unfolding across "shared histories, emergent communities, and the weaving of intertextual discourse."[42] It appears as an unforeseen form with unpredictable force.

Some have argued that surprise figures the very possibilities foreclosed by critique, the prize in whose pursuit postcritical discourses discard procedures that are condemned precisely for imposing an already known template on helplessly inert texts.[43] But Apter and Freedgood express the hope that "susceptible" reading "mean[s] perhaps that we learn more from texts than we teach them; we expect to be surprised."[44] Of course, an expected surprise is an oxymoron, and to engineer the expected surprise of surface reading a daunting task. Given its modest method and refusal of critical agency, celebration of the givenness of the object, and retreat from political possibilities, surface reading cultivates suspicion toward everything as flagrantly artificial as the *pursuit* or expectation of surprise. Given the terms Althusser provides, it cannot recognize itself as a reading at all. No surprises there.

The particular surprise of symptomatic reading has two distinct vectors in Althusser's work: one pertaining to subjectivity and the other to history. He claims that it is not "the eye (the mind's eye) of a subject which sees" the objects in the field, but the field itself. This stricture registers both his anti-humanist unraveling of the subject as consciousness and presence—"the golden rule of materialism is not to judge a being by its self-consciousness"[45]—and the determining force of reading as an actual practice. From this point of view, reading subjects are effects of the intimate break that reading and writing enact. The symptomatic rupture cannot be known in advance or anticipated; neither the unfolding of a presence lying in wait nor a preexisting form, its contingency cannot be eluded: a necessary surprise. It is produced by the work of the text—the play of repetition, doubling, oxymoron, translation, metaphor, parataxis, and so on—as much as by conceptual displacement. The undoing of the reading subject thus always also surprises; the mastery and political "heroics" that figure prominently in the critique of critique are nowhere in evidence. And yet the politics of reading remains.

Barbara Johnson was a reader who often asked, "how can . . . surprise be put to *work* in new ways," and concluded that "the impossible but necessary task of the reader is to set herself up to be surprised."[46] No *method* could sustain innovation indefinitely, but Johnson suggests that one might "be surprised by otherness" provided one risked genuine "ignorance," eschewing the comfort of knowing one's ignorance merely as an oversight, and pursued the reorientation engendered by the unasked question: "If I perceive my ignorance as a gap in knowledge instead of an imperative that changes the very nature of what I think I know, then I do not truly experience my ignorance. The surprise of otherness is that moment when a new form of ignorance is suddenly activated as an imperative." Johnson urges us toward the "surprise encounter with otherness" that will "lay bare some hint of an ignorance one never knew one had," that is, pose a question that reorganizes reading on another terrain and changes "the very nature of what [we] think [we] know."[47] No reader commands this process; she is its symptom, herself a surprising "reading effect" in an encounter with the other reader, one who cannot stay on script.

Étienne Balibar argues that Althusser's account of the epistemological break features the "*constitution* of [a] subject that takes the paradoxically negative form of its *dissolution* in action—one might be tempted to say its 'continuous' dissolution. . . . Not only as empirical, psychological, or substantial subject, but as a function of synthesis, as that gatherer, that owner of itself which modern philosophy has designated by the name of consciousness."[48] In "Lesbian Spectacles: Reading *Sula, Passing, Thelma and Louise*, and *The Accused*," Johnson tracks just such a dissolution of the subject through the "spectacle" of trying "to catch [herself] in the act of reading as a lesbian without having intended to," to "herself read herself." She advances cautiously, wary of political pitfalls of reproducing stereotypes and obviousness: "If I tried to speak 'as a lesbian,' wouldn't I be processing my understanding of myself through media-induced images of what a lesbian is or my own idealization of what a lesbian *should* be?" Seeking to escape these templates, Johnson chooses texts that are not lesbian in content or thematically, falling into conflict with other readers over what does and doesn't "work" as a lesbian novel or film.[49]

Discovering that her attraction to characters who find each other "objects of fascination, ambivalence, and transformation" and wield power "*within* the patriarchal institution" is in fact a disavowed attraction to the "phallic mother," Johnson's first conclusion is rueful: "So much for reading with the unconscious." Encountering "face to face . . . the political incorrectness of [her] own fantasy life," she demonstrates that "it is hard to pin down the origins of a reading-effect."[50] Johnson's identifications and political commitments are dislocated by her *own reading*, whose form leads her to pose a hitherto un-asked question: "If the unconscious is structured by repetition and the political by the desire for change, there is nothing surprising about this. The question, still, would remain one of knowing what the unconscious changes, and what politics repeats."[51] The reading that yields this question is uneven and contingent, marked by discrepancies, repetition, and pleasure; it generates an imperative to think the relation between its (unsurprising) vision and its (disconcerting) non-vision. Johnson's symptomatic reading—by which she differs from herself and desire from politics—proceeds from her ignorance, rather than her insight, establishing new questions that make reading possible *and* political.

This spectacle dislocates the origin of the reading effect in a knowing subject and illuminates the way in which the Althusserian account of surprise proposes a theory of history in tandem with its theory of reading. Althusser argues that Marx reveals the way in which a new problematic "literally takes [the] place" of the old one, rather than "being a mere development, the 'truth' or 'inversion' of the old one." It arrives as surprise, undoing any "linear history of continuous development," as well as "a history of the progressive manifestation or emergence into consciousness of a Reason which is completely present in germ in its origins" (44). Here is where surprise does its greatest damage and richest work. This literal displacement means that "we are thereby obliged to renounce every teleology of reason, and to conceive the historical relations between a result and its conditions of existence as a relation of production and not expression, and therefore as what, in a phrase that clashes with the classical system of categories and demands the replacement of those categories themselves, we can call the *necessity of its contingency*" (45). The necessity of contingency institutes a "paradoxical logic" that discloses "results" as the consequences of a fundamentally unpredictable process, that is, as the effects of symptomatic reading and the play on words itself.

This is the legacy of Marx's revelation of what reading and hence writing means. The play on words engenders a precarious act of reading and taking of form, and it appears as such only after reading has rendered it, belatedly or retrospectively, though not in fact too late. Althusser insists: "We can expect many surprises from this" open-ended textual work. To read symptomatically is "to treat the ideology which constitutes the prehistory of a science, for example, as a real history with its own laws and as the real prehistory whose real confrontation with other technical practices and other ideological or scientific acquisitions was capable, in a specific theoretical conjuncture, of producing the arrival of a science, not as its goal, but as its surprise" (45). Symptomatic readings are constitutively surprise-seeking, taking forms that readers cannot anticipate, evade or guarantee. This is the nature of their historicality and their contemporaneity, and, Althusser tells us, "This is where their *surprise* lies *(there can be no taking-hold without surprise)*."[52]

Coda: A Letter from the Translated

It is hard to pin down the origins of a reading effect.
—BARBARA JOHNSON, "Lesbian Spectacles"

"I am interested in the *play on words* itself" is a translation. Indeed, it is a somewhat puzzling translation, one that seems to make genuine sense only if one reads the word *interested* with a particular inflection, as in, "I am *interested* in how the money we allocated to fix the roof of the daycare center was spent on the city council's fall retreat in Vegas. I am very *interested* in that." This is a familiar but not the most idiomatic English usage. Althusser's French eschews the cognate, *intéresser*, and reads: "*J'en veux au* jeu de mots *lui-même.*"[53] The translation your online dictionary will first provide as you enter *j'en veux* is "I want" or "I want some." But almost immediately you will learn that *j'en veux à [au]* means "I hold it against" or "blame" or even "I have a bone to pick," as in, "I have a bone to pick with you about how the money we allocated to fix the daycare center's roof was spent on the city council's junket to Vegas." When we hold these senses in tension, the puzzling or even slightly misleading translation—given that the English "interested" speaks positive attentiveness and even affirmation, while only secondarily permitting a skeptical inflection—seems brilliant in its capture of the play between the senses of wanting and blaming, and blaming or refusing or even berating, that Althusser's French bears, condenses, and dislocates in the play of words.

The "Glossary" appended to the English translation of *Reading Capital* is itself an importation, transferred, that is, translated, from its origin as the "Glossary" of *For Marx*. It defines dislocation (*décalage*) as a "staggered relation," a relation among elements each with its "own time and rhythm of development."[54] Dislocation is non-coincidence and discontinuity, a disruption of both expressive and empiricist interpretation and of any deterministic account of history, politics, or reading. The "*play on words* itself" is the form *décalage* assumes at the level of the word, a staggered relation that designates the contingent but necessary productivity of reading. The staggered relation between "I have a problem with" and "I want" condensed in *j'en veux au* is a disruptive Althusserian play on words. This relation, disclosed, figured, and thought in the form of the ruptural reading that I have traced in these pages, answers the question "What is it to read?"

But this is perhaps an answer Althusser would have resisted: he might have had a bone to pick with this exorbitant account. I have celebrated the play on words as a form that renders symptomatic reading both distinct from and more potent than critique. But Althusser complains that "the seductive metaphors of the terrain, the horizon and hence the limits of a visible field defined by a given problematic threaten to induce a false idea of the nature of this field, if we think this field literally according to the spatial metaphor" (26). While in my account the shift in terrain that the play on words works is the motor of symptomatic reading, Althusser writes with asperity of the "empiricist conception of knowledge" that makes "a play on the word 'real,'" objecting to this "perpetual play on the words real and concrete" that "plays on a difference it kills; . . . . . spirits away the corpse," and distracts us from the "true play on words," hidden by the "fraudulent unity of the *word* object" (39–40). Ideological mystification works these violent feints and frauds.

Let us reread our text carefully. Warren Montag argues that Althusser believed that "philosophical practice could only ever be understood retrospectively, *après-coup*, and, in his case at least, only through intermediaries."[55] Althusser's insistence on revision, the incomplete, self-criticism, and the guilt of reading extends without question to his own work, and the reading effect of the Althusserian subject is, as Johnson reminds us, hard to pin down. It is especially challenging in relation to the formal productivity of reading and the intimate break it entails. Balibar argues that Althusser's famous "epistemological break" was "an object constantly reworked, in a contradictory process, always torn between its elimination and its reinforcement: as if unbeknownst to him he had 'produced' something other than he 'wanted,' or he 'believed.'"[56] The play on words itself is another such "reworked" object, an object of the break; it instantiates the unposed question as a persistent problem of form, the letter in black and white, and, much as it may long to, it cannot retrieve a space for the literal secure from the seductive and treacherous play on words.

First reading, reading at "first sight," is a reading of consciousness; "destroying" the omissions it exposes in the text, this reading knows in advance where its path innocently leads and what the times demand. By contrast, Althusser's text insistently iterates the "opacity of the immediate," playing the words themselves, and raining them down upon his readers, courting encounters whose future lacks all guarantees. *Reading Capital* ends with Althusser's "Letter to the Translator." He expresses his gratitude to Ben Brewster and his relief that the Glossary's clarifications will protect readers in 1969 from the "snare" into which they "would certainly have 'fallen' if they were allowed to believe that [he had. . . .] *remained in the position* of [his] old articles whereas time has not ceased to pass. . . ." "The author" of those old articles is now the author of "new writings that contain the new definition of philosophy that I now hold." In his final sentence, also *Reading Capital's* last words, Althusser underscores his pleasure that his "corrections and interpolations" (323) to the Glossary's account of his philosophy capture "the *new conception* which I have arrived at (provisionally—but what is not provisional?)" (324). Symptomatic reading is a productive practice that anticipates its undoing, undoing itself, again and again; its transformations of form work its surprising openings to the future. Provisional—but what is not provisional?—it is not concerned to last.

Notes

1   Roland Barthes, "The Structuralist Activity," in *Critical Essays*, trans. Richard Howard (Evanston, IL: Northwestern University Press, 1972), 219. This passage echoes terms from various theorists, including Louis Althusser, Emily Apter and Elaine Freedgood, Stephen Best and Sharon Marcus, Russ Castronovo, Rita Felski, and Stuart Hall.

2   For the disparate analyses in play, see Mark Cooper and John Marx, "Crisis, Crisis, Crisis: Big Media and the Humanities Workforce," *differences* 24, no. 3 (2013): 127–59; Eric Hayot, "I Too Have Dreamed of Another French Messiah," *ELN* 51, no. 2 (2013): 87–94; and Stanley Fish, *Save the World on Your Own Time* (Oxford: Oxford University Press, 2008).

3   STEAM revises STEM: Science Technology Engineering *Arts* Mathematics. There are too many relevant volumes here to begin to cite them adequately; two from the year of this writing are Michael Roth (president of Wesleyan University), *Beyond the University: Why Liberal Education Matters* (New Haven, CT: Yale University Press, 2014), and Fareed Zakaria (host of cable television's GPS), *In Defense of a Liberal Education* (New York: Barnes and Noble, 2014).

4   This rubric appears in *ELN*, qualified in the interrogative as a special issue's title: "After Critique?," special issue, *ELN* 51, no. 2 (fall/winter 2013). Editors Russ Castronovo and David Glimp gloss their pun to indicate their intention "to gauge the current status of critique as a practice central to literary scholarship," observing that "to be 'after critique' is also to pursue it" (1). See Bruno Latour, "Why Has

Critique Run Out of Steam? From Matters of Fact to Matters of Concern," *Critical Inquiry* 30, no. 2 (winter 2004): 225–48; "Dossier: Surface Reading," ed. Jason Potts, special issue, *Mediations* 28, no. 2 (2015); "*Novel* Forum: What Can Reading Do?," ed. Ellen Rooney, special issue, *Novel* 45, no. 1 (2012): 1–29; and Elizabeth Weed, "The Way We Read Now," *History of the Present* 2, no. 1 (2012): 95–106.

5 Lloyd Pratt, "Unfinished Business," introduction to panel at the 2015 MLA convention.

6 Pratt, "Unfinished," 2.

7 Pratt, "Unfinished," 2–3.

8 These phrases originate in Stephen Best and Sharon Marcus ("the way we read now"), ELN ("after critique"), Bruno Latour ("Why Has Critique"), and Elaine Freedgood and Emily Apter ("Afterword"). The rubrics at work in the critique of critique are exceptionally heterogeneous, including the history of the book, affect and thing theory, surface and "just reading," new materialisms, object-oriented ontologies, and the Anthropocene.

9 Althusser speaks of a play on words as early as "Marxism and Humanism," in *For Marx*, trans. Ben Brewster (London: New Left Books, 1977), 235, where he argues that bourgeois "ideology consists of this play on the word freedom." The vicissitudes of play in recent literary theory and philosophy constitute a large topic, in both twentieth-century French and Continental philosophy and the history of European aesthetics, as well as in contemporary work in economics, on probability, on gaming, etc. See Jacques Derrida, "Structure, Sign, and Play," in *Writing and Difference*, trans. Alan Bass (Chicago: University of Chicago Press, 1978), 278–93, for an early and nearly contemporaneous theorization of structure and play.

10 In "Form and Contentment," in *Reading for Form*, ed. Susan Wolfson and Marshall Brown (Seattle: University of Washington Press, 2006), I press this argument in terms of the failure of cultural studies to engage the problematic of form, often explicitly due to its too close association with literary studies and a disdained "textuality." This contribution of literary studies to cultural critique remains crucial, and it has not yet run out of steam.

11 This forgetting has other sources. Scholars have addressed it in the idioms of formalism (see, for example, Ben Burton and Elizabeth Scott-Baumann, *The Work of Form* [Oxford: Oxford University Press, 2014]; Robert Kaufman, "Everybody Hates Kant: Formalism and the Symmetries of Laura Moriarty," MLN 61 [2000]: 131–55; Marjorie Levinson, "What Is New Formalism?," PMLA 112, no. 2 [2007]: 558–69; Caroline Levine, "Strategic Formalism: Toward a New Method in Cultural Studies," *Victorian Studies* 48, no. 4 [2006]: 625–57; Lloyd Pratt, "Introduction: The Nature of Form," in "Forum: Formal Disclosures," special issue, *J19* 1, no. 2 [2013]: 423–31; and Mark David Rasmussen, *Renaissance Literature and Its Formal Engagements* [New York: Palgrave, 2002]) or in related terms such as the aesthetic or style (see Marc Redfield, *The Politics of Aesthetics* [Stanford, CA: Stanford University Press, 2003], and D. A. Miller, *Jane Austen, or The Secret of*

Style [Princeton, NJ: Princeton University Press, 2003], among others). Some adopt the rubric of the "new formalism," though there is no consensus on the term or even on the category of form, as Levinson demonstrates.

12   One rich example is the distinction that opens Michael Warner's "Uncritical Reading," in *Polemic: Critical or Uncritical*, ed. Jane Gallop (New York: Routledge, 2004), between "uncritical reading," which burdens "students who come to [his] literature classes" with impulses to "read in all the ways they aren't supposed to," and what he designates as "critical reading" (13).

13   "Reparative" reading is one form of this attachment. In "Paranoid Reading and Reparative Reading, or, You're So Paranoid, You Probably Think This Essay Is about You," in *Touching Feeling: Affect, Pedagogy, Performativity* (Durham, NC: Duke University Press, 2003), Eve Sedgwick stresses that the reparative "turn[s] to use one's own resources to assemble or 'repair' the murderous part-objects into something like a whole—though I would emphasize, *not necessarily like any pre-existing whole*," which resonates with symptomatic reading's production of a new problematic, also unlike a preexisting whole. Sedgwick seeks to do "justice to the powerful reparative practices that [she is] convinced infuse self-avowedly paranoid critical practices, as well as in the paranoid exigencies that are often necessary for non-paranoid knowing and utterance" (128). Symptomatic reading, neither ideology critique nor "just reading," is such a hybrid.

14   Louis Althusser and Étienne Balibar, *Reading Capital*, trans. Ben Brewster (London: Verso, 1979), 14. Further quotations from this work are cited parenthetically in the text.

15   See Eugenie Brinkema's discussion of the "disciplinary detour" of form in the context of cinema studies and what she brilliantly discloses as "the forms of the affects." While relentlessly defending the criticality of form, Brinkema concedes that "*interpretation is indeed the long way round*." Brinkema, *The Forms of the Affects* (Durham, NC: Duke University Press, 2014), 30.

16   Althusser embraces guilt exuberantly: "This then is the guilt of our philosophical reading of *Capital*: it reads Marx according to the rules of a reading in which he gave us a brilliant lesson in his own reading of classical political economy. Our admission of this crime is deliberate, we shall fetter ourselves to it, anchor ourselves in it, cling fiercely to it as the point which must be hung on to at all costs" (30).

17   Althusser registers his place in critical history, noting that he repeats Marx "by *reading* a text by Marx which is itself a *reading* of a text of classical economics"; citing the "writing and speeches of those who have read [*Capital*] for us, well or ill, both the dead and the living, Engels, Kautsky, Plekhanov, Lenin, Rosa Luxemburg, Trotsky, Stalin, Gramsci, the leaders of the workers' organizations, their supporters and opponents: philosophers, economists, politicians"; and invoking the reader to come (*Reading Capital*, 24, 13–14).

18   On a *Daily Show* episode in March 2015, Jon Stewart berated Senator Harry Reid for the failure of Senate Democrats to have read a bill that they approved in

committee, only to find that they must oppose it on the Senate floor because it contained undiscovered—because it went unread, Reid reported—abortion restrictions. Stewart mocked Reid with the full force of the shameless pun and a thorough understanding of the problem of reading as such.

19 See Keith Oatley and Maja Djikic, "How Reading Transforms Us," *New York Times*, December 19, 2014, http://www.nytimes.com/2014/12/21/opinion/sunday/how-writing-transforms-us.html?_r=0. This is the kind of essay on reading, identity, and the brain one might find in the newspaper on any given Sunday.

20 For example, consider "The Bakersfield Expedition," an episode of CBS's *Big Bang Theory* that analyzes the reading effect in relation to comics and the vehement conflicts and vibrant communities they engender. Of course, these fictional readers are not simply as avatars of readers everywhere. But the episode theorizes reading, illuminating relations between textuality and readerly conflict, concept and play, critique and pleasure.

21 This definition does not render the problematic as homogeneous or predetermined. "In no sense does a problematic impose absolutely identical variations on the thoughts that cross its field: a field can be crossed by quite different paths since it can be approached from many different directions" (*Reading Capital*, 135). Althusser's example is historicism.

22 See Ellen Rooney, "Better Read Than Dead: Althusser and the Fetish of Ideology," *Yale French Studies* 88 (1995): 183–200, and Louis Althusser, "Ideology and Ideological State Apparatuses," in *Lenin and Philosophy*, trans. Ben Brewster (New York: Monthly Review Press, 1971), 127–86, and *On the Reproduction of Capitalism: Ideology and Ideological State Apparatuses*, trans. G. M. Goshgarian (London: Verso, 2014).

23 My analysis focuses on Althusser's lead essay, written after the collection was complete.

24 Literary theory is one example, but the interrogation of the entanglement of reading and writing is an effect of a wider set of discourses, including the challenge to (critique of?) "corelationism," object-oriented ontologies, and some new materialisms. Marcus and Best illustrate "an affirmative version of symptomatic reading [in] Jameson['s insistence] that the 'strong' critic must rewrite narrative in terms of master codes" ("Surface Reading," 5).

25 Peggy Kamuf, *The Division of Literature* (Stanford, CA: Stanford University Press, 1997), 164.

26 Althusser, *Reading Capital*, 33, and "Elle ne peut se penser elle-même," *Lire*, 29.

27 Althusser, *Lire*, 39.

28 See also Rooney, "Form and Contentment."

29 Geraldine Friedman demonstrates the "necessary dependence of Althusser's theoretical project on its figures." Friedman, "The Spectral Legacy of Althusser: The Symptom and Its Return," *Yale French Studies* 88 (1995): 165–82, 168.

30 Christopher Castiglia, "Critiquiness," *ELN* 51, no. 2 (2013): 79.

31 In an extended version of this analysis, I argue that form functions as a mode of address by which symptomatic reading interpellates its readers.

32   Friedman, "Spectral," 169.

33   Rita Felski, "Critique and the Hermeneutics of Suspicion," *M/C* 15, no. 1 (2012): 3.

34   Roland Barthes, *Image/Music/Text*, trans. Stephen Heath (New York: Hill and Wang, 1978), 162.

35   Althusser frequently highlights the tentative, appropriative, and unfinished qualities of his theorizations; acknowledges misgivings that generate revisions; chooses subtitles like "Notes for an Investigation"; and attaches appendixes. *Reading Capital* concedes that the authors haven't "tried to make a *finished* work out of" the essays, which thus remain "incomplete texts, the mere beginnings of a reading." Althusser hopes this incompleteness means "the reader will be able to find in them the new-born experience of a reading; and . . . in turn will be dragged in the wake of this first reading in to a second one which will take·us still further" (*Reading Capital*, 13, 14). See Althusser, *Essays*; Friedman, "Spectral"; Warren Montag, *Althusser and His Contemporaries: Philosophy's Perpetual War* (Durham, NC: Duke University Press, 2013); and Rooney, "Better Read."

36   Emily Apter and Elaine Freedgood, afterword to "The Way We Read Now," ed. Emily Apter, Stephen Best, Elaine Freedgood, and Sharon Marcus, special issue, *Representations* 108, no. 1 (2009): 140.

37   *Ratatouille*, dir. Brad Bird and Jan Pinkava (Pixar Animation Studios, 2007).

38   Sedgwick, "Paranoid Reading and Reparative Reading," 149.

39   Sedgwick, "Paranoid Reading and Reparative Reading," 150. The film and the theorist are perhaps not so very far apart. Sedgwick underlines Silvan Tomkins's view that "there is no distance at all between affect theory in the sense of the important explicit theorizing some scientists and philosophers do around affects, and affect theory in the sense of the largely tacit theorizing all people do in experiencing and trying to deal with their own and others' affects" ("Paranoid Reading and Reparative Reading," 133–34).

40   Sedgwick, "Paranoid Reading and Reparative Reading," 131, 130.

41   Sedgwick, "Paranoid Reading and Reparative Reading," 146, 136.

42   Sedgwick, "Paranoid Reading and Reparative Reading," 150.

43   This is a much longer discussion than I can pursue here. We should recall that there have been theorists who align critique itself with surprise; they have not had the upper hand in the most recent polemics. See Barbara Johnson, "Translator's Introduction," in Jacques Derrida, *Dissemination* (Chicago: University of Chicago Press, 1981), vii–xxxiii, and Wendy Brown, "Untimeliness and Punctuality," in *Edgework: Critical Theory in Dark Times* (Princeton, NJ: Princeton University Press, 2005), 1–16.

44   Apter and Freedgood, afterword, 139.

45   Althusser, *Writings on Psychoanalysis*, trans. Jeffrey Mehlman (New York: Columbia University Press, 1996), 115.

46   Barbara Johnson, "Nothing Fails like Success," in *A World of Difference* (Baltimore: Johns Hopkins University Press, 1987), 11, 15. See Lee Edelman, "Unknowing Barbara," *diacritics* 34, no. 1 (2004): 89–93, and Corey McEleney, "Queer

Theory and the Yale School: Barbara Johnson's Astonishment," GLQ 19, no. 2 (2013): 143–65.

47 Johnson, "Nothing," 16.

48 Étienne Balibar, "Althusser's Object," trans. Margaret Cohen and Bruce Robbins, *Social Text* 39 (1994): 159.

49 Barbara Johnson, "Lesbian Spectacles: Reading *Sula, Passing, Thelma and Louise, and The Accused,*" in *The Feminist Difference: Literature, Psychoanalysis, Race, and Gender* (Cambridge, MA: Harvard University Press, 1998), 157, 159.

50 Johnson, "Spectacles," 162–63.

51 Johnson, "Spectacles," 164.

52 Louis Althusser, *Philosophy of the Encounter: Later Writings, 1978–87*, trans. G. M. Goshgarian, ed. François Matheron and Oliver Corpet (London: Verso, 2006), 196.

53 Althusser, *Lire*, 39.

54 Brewster, "Glossary," 312.

55 Montag, "Contemporaries," 210.

56 Balibar, "Object," 158. See also Montag, who argues that Althusser was "an incomparable reader; to read Althusser is thus to read him reading, sometimes incisively, but just as often struggling to grasp not the meaning of a text or body of work but precisely the contradictions around which it was constituted. . . . Every philosophy is the realization of a contradiction that it necessarily lacks the means to resolve. Thus, it is not enough to read others, that is, to make visible their contradictions; one must constantly attempt after the fact to grasp the conflictuality proper to one's own thought, an attempt that produces new contradictions requiring new interventions ad infinitum" (*Contemporaries*, 7).

6

A Heap of Cliché

C. NAMWALI SERPELL

Criticism is cliché. I mean this in three ways.

One, criticism as a form has always been cliché. Repetition is inherent to the genre of literary criticism, which by necessity entails recapitulation: the summaries and paraphrases of the text under examination, the diligent trotting out of previous critical takes on that text, and so on. A critical essay often repeats itself as well: saying what it's going to say, saying it, then saying what it just said. And literary criticism as such frequently deploys the same argumentative phrases, neverthelesses and howevers, indeeds and to be sures—the worn-out armor and weaponry of scholarly jousting.

Two, criticism has become cliché. By this I mean something more specific than the genre of scholarly writing in the discipline of literary study. Criticism, as a mode of critique, both of which terms come from the Greek *krinein*, "judge, decide," has become an all-too-predictable approach to literature. We might think that to judge the worthiness of literary texts is an old-fashioned model that has long fallen out of favor. But in a sense, critics have merely changed the rubric of value according to which we judge. Even Wayne Booth, unafraid of critical judgment, bemoaned the observable turn toward a new esteem for ambiguity: "We have looked for so long at foggy landscapes reflected in misty mirrors that we have come to *like* fog. Clarity and simplicity are suspect; irony reigns supreme."[1] We continue to critique; we have just swapped out the values that underlie our judgments.

Three, certain forms of criticism are all about cliché. Cliché is the ultimate "usual suspect" for a "hermeneutics of suspicion," Paul Ricoeur's term for an interpretive practice keyed to uncovering the complicities lurking even behind Booth's preferred "clarity and simplicity."[2] Ever since the term *cliché* drifted from print and photography to language in the nineteenth century, Marx-inflected scholarship has tried to unmask cliché as unoriginal, unthinking, and unethical in a critical history I will detail below. Yet to accuse cliché of being superficial, derivative, and ideologically suspect is not just to restate its very nature but, oddly enough, to become susceptible to a set of critical clichés.

I submit that literary cliché requires that we look anew at the clichés of criticism. In what follows, I outline cliché's origins, history, and form in order to understand why it resists our interpretive habits. I then turn to phenomenology—specifically, its manifestations in reader-response criticism and the work of Roland Barthes—as an alternative method that offers tools more suited to the material form of the cliché. Under this method, I consider Jim Thompson's 1952 *The Killer Inside Me*, a campy, pulpy crime fiction novel that deploys cliché in ways we cannot dismiss as ideologically complicit or salutary. My aim is neither simply to debunk nor to praise cliché. As I've suggested, to unmask or judge literary cliché under the auspices of rigorous critique has itself become a cliché. That said, there's no need to eschew the clichés of critique altogether. Indeed, as my unassuming use of critical tropes thus far hints—for example, unpacking a pseudo-controversial statement, enacting argumentative turns, using indeeds and neverthelesses, telegraphing the argument to come—I don't think we ought to undo or do away with clichés, be they literary or critical. To be frank, I don't think we can. Nevertheless, we can apply to cliché a lens *other* than critique or recuperation.[3] As a semantically empty instrument of communication, the cliché draws attention to material aspects of language that literary criticism might do well to acknowledge, especially given how they weigh upon the reading experience.

A Brief History of Cliché

The origin of *cliché* is onomatopoeic. As Daniel Hartley notes, "The word first arose with the advent of stereotype printing. Unlike previous forms of printing, stereotype used type-casts (often made from plaster of Paris) taken from a plate rather than the plate itself . . . 'Cliché' was the word French printworkers coined to imitate the sound of the matrix dropping into the molten metal, and it soon became synonymous with the copies themselves."[4] At the end of the nineteenth century, Lynn Berger explains, "it shed its originally technical connotation and obtained a more pejorative one: that of a phrase that had been reproduced so often it was now trite and hackneyed." The coincidence of burgeoning mass production and a Romantic obsession with artistic uniqueness led, at the turn of the twentieth century, to *cliché*'s now familiar meaning as a lack of originality.[5]

In this origin story, we find several versions of redundancy: sound matches sense; a common synonym for cliché, *stereotype*, derives from the same technology; the process (the machine) becomes indistinguishable from its product (the copy); and the cliché comes to mean a dearth of creativity, its endemic repetitiveness a sign of the "already known." These forms of repetition are definitionally built into the cliché, which is generally a copied piece of language that people reiterate. The cliché's excessive repetitiveness has never been recuperated by theories of the uncanny, the mathematical sublime, or even Baudrillardian simulation, despite the fact that, as Hartley notes, "cliché printing was effectively the copy of a copy; it was originally a simulacrum."[6] Unless defamiliarized by literary technique, cliché has remained relegated to the derivative, and thus to a lack of originality, in both a literal and an artistic sense. Cliché has never quite recovered from this derogation.

The stakes of cliché's defamation have been quite high. We can thank Gustave Flaubert for reinforcing the class biases in how we talk about cliché. His appendix to *Bouvard and Pécuchet* (1881), printed separately since 1931 as *Le dictionnaire des idées reçues*, comprised an alphabetized list of insipid platitudes collected from bourgeois French society.[7] While Jonathan Swift's *Polite Conversations* (1731) deserves credit for the concept, Flaubert's better-known work invented a curiously common genre—the *dictionary* of clichés, which can appear as a mere list or as a comprehensive encyclopedia, and is often laced with class satire.[8] In his castigation of cliché, Flaubert does not just aim at trite or false language; inevitable, ignorant, incoherent, misinformed, prejudicial, and quibbling utterances are equally subject to excoriation. As Jacques Barzun explains in the introduction to his 1954 translation, "From the early 1850s, Flaubert kept writing and talking to his friends about this handbook, this Dictionary, as his beloved work, his great contribution to moral realism. . . . 'To dissect,' he wrote to George Sand, 'is a form of revenge.'"[9] In one letter, Flaubert said that a preface to *Dictionary* would be "so phrased that the reader would not know whether or not his leg was being pulled"; in another, he said that "after reading the book, one would be afraid to talk, for fear of using one of the phrases in it." This ambiguity—inherent to a critique that mimics the object being critiqued—suggests to Barzun that the *Dictionary* denounces not the bourgeoisie, as such, but bourgeois *style*, "in the Nietzschean sense, that is to say, lack of style. . . . lack of passion and imagination."[10]

The rise of propaganda in the First and Second World Wars deepened the political stakes of this disparagement of cliché.[11] In "Enlightenment as Mass Deception," Theodor Adorno and Max Horkheimer inveigh against "ready-made clichés to be slotted in anywhere," not just in formulaic radio and cinema, but also in Fascist mass culture as a whole: "Innumerable people use words and expressions which they have either ceased to understand or employ only because they trigger off conditioned reflexes. . . . In such clichés the last bond between sedimentary experience and language is severed."[12] There is well-established continuity here with Walter Benjamin's thoughts on the artwork's loss of aura in the age of mechanical reproduction, war, and Fascism.[13] In *Minima Moralia*, Adorno again specifically puts cliché in the crosshairs: "A word is seldom banal on its own: in music too the single note is immune to triteness. The most abominable clichés are combinations of words. . . . For in them the brackish stream of stale language swills aimlessly, instead of being dammed up, thrown into relief, by the precision of the writer's expressions."[14] The cliché is dangerous not just because it is banal or trite, imprecise or formulaic, but because it is inexorable—a purposeless flood that threatens to dissolve the divisions between art and the world, language and experience.

Around the same period, George Orwell's "Politics and the English Language" makes the case against cliché's automatism:

> By using stale metaphors, similes, and idioms, you save much mental effort, at the cost of leaving your meaning vague. . . . The sole aim of a metaphor is to call up a visual image. When these images clash—as in *The Fascist octopus has sung its swan song, the jackboot is thrown into the melting pot*—it can be taken as certain that the writer is not seeing a mental image of the objects he is naming; in other words he is not really thinking. . . . This invasion of one's mind by ready-made phrases (*lay the foundations, achieve a radical transformation*) can only be prevented if one is constantly on guard against them, and every such phrase anaesthetizes a portion of one's brain.[15]

Orwell worries that these "ready-made phrases" will "construct your sentences for you—even think your thoughts for you, to a certain extent—and at need they will perform the important service of partially concealing your meaning even from yourself."[16] Fifteen years later, Hannah Arendt's report on the Nazi trials in Jerusalem takes this line of thinking to its logical—that is, ethical—conclusion, noting the striking consistency with which [Adolf] Eichmann, despite his rather bad memory, repeated word for word the same stock phrases and self-invented clichés (when he did succeed in constructing a sentence of his own, he repeated it until it became a cliché) each time he referred to an incident or event of importance to him. Whether writing his memoirs in Argentina or in Jerusalem, whether speaking to the police examiner or to the court, what he said was always the same, expressed in the same words. The longer one listened to him, the more obvious it became that his inability to speak was closely connected to an inability to *think*, namely, to think from the standpoint of somebody else.[17]

Over the course of this short history, cliché becomes coterminous not just with a lack of originality (Flaubert), purposive form (Adorno and Horkheimer), and clarity (Orwell), but also with a lack of thought and empathy (Arendt). Throughout this history, there is a slippage between aesthetic, political, and ethical judgment that is subtended by cliché's blankness, ubiquity, and repetitiousness. We still feel this way about cliché, against which writers and readers, teachers and students, politicians and pundits alike continue to rail.[18] It has become the scapegoat for all language's inevitable tendency toward repetition and calcification.

The Usual Suspect

The trials of cliché from the late nineteenth century through the twentieth present an unacknowledged lineage of the predominance of "ideology critique," "hermeneutics of suspicion," and "symptomatic reading" in literary studies of the recent past. This general critical tendency treats language—including its absences—as a puzzling set of symptoms that are legible only to the right kind of reader. We have seen traces of this reading practice in Flaubert, Adorno, Orwell, and Arendt, who all interpret cliché as a *sign* of unwitting artistic debasement, bourgeois collusion, and complicity with bad politics. By implication, this ideological blindness is discernible to the perspicacious, informed—often Marxist—reader, who dissects the cliché and skewers its source. Cliché, by definition simple enough to be remembered, might seem an unlikely candidate for contemporary ideology critique, which loves to untangle and decipher, to wrangle and rewrite complex figures. But cliché is in fact exactly that quintessentially "blank" and "unwitting," "superficial and deceptive," "secondary," "blind," "collusive," and "thing-like" kind of language to which a hermeneutics of suspicion trains its eye.

In their introduction to a special issue of *Representations*, "The Way We Read Now," Stephen Best and Sharon Marcus locate the origins of this interpretive method that "seeks to unmask hidden meanings" in two more recent sources: Paul Ricoeur's description of Freudian psychoanalysis as a "hermeneutics of suspicion" and the influence of Marxist critic Louis Althusser on literary study: "Althusser unfolded a method of symptomatic reading that he found in Marx and used to read Marx, one that 'divulges the undivulged event in the text it reads, and in the same movement relates it to a different text, present as a necessary absence in the first.' For Althusser, symptomatic reading makes 'lacunae perceptible'; it assumes that texts are shaped by questions they do not themselves pose and contain symptoms that help interpreters articulate those questions, which lie outside texts as their absent causes."[19]

In *Capital*, Marx says, "value does not stalk about with a label describing what it is. It is value, rather, that converts every product into a social hieroglyphic. Later on, we try to decipher the hieroglyphic, to get behind the secret of our own social products."[20] And in *Reading Capital*, Althusser says, "When [Marx] does happen to formulate *an answer without a question*, with a little patience and perspicacity we can find the question itself elsewhere, twenty or one hundred pages further on, with respect to some other object, enveloped in some other matter. . . . there is undoubtedly . . . an answer which Marx only succeeds in formulating on condition of multiplying the images required to render it."[21] In both cases, the mysterious object of analysis—be it a commodity or an answer—hides its relationship to reality through various subterfuges: conversion, delay, diversion, concealment, multiplication.

Sometimes, however, it hides in plain sight. As Althusser describes Marx's analysis of Adam Smith: "[Smith] did not see what was, however, staring him in the face, he did not grasp what was, however, in his hands." Althusser explains that "to see this invisible, to see these 'oversights,' to identify the lacunae in the fullness of this discourse, the blanks in the crowded text, we need something quite different from an acute or attentive gaze; we need an informed gaze, a new gaze." This new gaze becomes the basis for "a reading which might well be called 'symptomatic' (*symptomale*), insofar as it divulges the undivulged event in the text it reads."[22] According to Best and Marcus, Fredric Jameson then applied Althusser's lens to literature: "The interpreter 'rewrite[s] the surface categories of a text in the stronger language of a more fundamental interpretive code.'" In this surface/depth binary, the surface's clarity is what misleads: "The surface is associated with the superficial and deceptive, with what can be perceived without close examination and, implicitly, would turn out to be false upon closer scrutiny."[23]

The Marxist critically reads the passively derivative commodity or the "unwitting" tract on political economy; the Freudian scrutinizes the patient's blind repetition of symptoms.[24] In literary critical practice, the symptomatic method reads the surface symptoms of a text to "unmask" how it capitulates to, and often disguises its complicity with, an ideology. This amounts to what Rita Felski describes as a diagnostic dogmatism that subordinates literature to the secondary status of an object:

> Those critics drawn to the concept of ideology . . . seek to place literature squarely in the social world. . . . Yet this same idea also has the less happy effect of rendering the work of art secondary or supernumerary, a depleted resource deficient in insights that must be supplied by the critic. Whatever definition of ideology is being deployed . . . a text is being diagnosed rather than heard, relegated to the status of a symptom of social structures or political causes. The terms of interpretation are set elsewhere; the work is barred from knowing what the critic knows; it remains blind to its own collusion in oppressive social circumstances.[25]

While it often claims to interpret hieroglyphs, lacunae, decoys, and différance as signs of ideology or complicity, literary critique treats even these textual phenomena as if they were just clichés after all—bits of blind bourgeois banality blundering about, pretending to be art.

As a piece of language that works best—that self-perpetuates—when it goes *unnoticed*, the literary cliché evinces the stubborn invisibility of ideological and psychoanalytic symptoms. Because it is *transparent* in both senses— obvious yet invisible—Ruth Amossy contends that it affords two ways of reading in practice: *passive* (it facilitates, speeds, models, and orients our reading, promoting verisimilitude, identification, and persuasion) or *critical* (we perceive its intertextuality, illusoriness, complicity, and potential for social critique).[26] This distinction maps onto the surface/depth and naive/suspicious binaries of symptomatic reading. If a passive reading of cliché necessarily maintains its hiddenness, a critical reading can also coincide with the object of critique in such a way that it conceals cliché. Althusser explains this radical disguise: "What political economy does not see is not a preexisting object which it could have seen but did not see—but an object which it [political economy] produced itself in its operation of knowledge and which did not preexist it: *precisely the production itself, which is identical with the object.*"[27] The almost Heisenberg-ian distinction here is between something that we miss because it is hidden and something whose hiddenness is caused by our effort to see it. Ideology is not just a blind spot, but also something akin to Oedipus's self-blinding: you bring about the very sightlessness you sought to avoid.

This circularity applies to symptomatic reading now, which is often unwittingly infected by the clichés it always seems to find.[28] While Ellen Rooney critiques Best and Marcus's alternative model of surface reading, she concedes that "modes of ideology critique . . . have, indeed . . . worn their critical edge down to an appalling dullness."[29] Felski too notes how familiar its methods have become: "We know only too well the well-oiled machine of ideology critique, the x-ray gaze of symptomatic reading, the smoothly rehearsed moves that add up to a hermeneutics of suspicion."[30] Critique and cliché may share this dry fate because they are both redundant and communal forms. But cliché, the usual suspect for a "gotcha!" critique, is an especially contagious target. Christopher Ricks claims, "The only way to speak of a cliché is with a cliché. . . . What (as a metaphor) could be more hackneyed than *hackneyed*, more outworn than *outworn*, more tattered than *tattered*?"[31] Even Flaubert bemoaned: "The book I am working on could have as sub-title, Encyclopaedia of Human Stupidity. The undertaking gets me down and my subject becomes part of me."[32] A symptomatic reading that always finds what it seeks—"rediscovering its own gloomy prognosis in every text," as Felski says—devolves into a tautology that has itself become a cliché: "You know it when you see it."[33]

What Is a Cliché?

Cliché both begs for and thwarts literary analysis because it is a repeated, empty, yet rather slippery form of language. Definitionally unoriginal, it is a commonplace that clichés are also meaningless. This can be demonstrated through the coexistence of opposed examples—for example, "The early bird gets the worm" / "Good things come to those who wait"—which is to say, through cliché's sheer plenitude. That there is a cliché for every situation suggests that each one is both self-evidently true and entirely controvertible. Cliché also takes a wide variety of forms, from interjection to aphorism. It can be a concept ("happy ending"); a sentence ("the early bird gets the worm"); a phrase ("the end of time"); a word ("artisanal"); and, in the Internet era, even an acronym ("LOL"). Unlike figurative devices like the simile, rhetorical tropes like paraleipsis, and narrative elements like free indirect discourse, the cliché has no fixed grammar, stylistic marker, or function.

The paradoxes inherent to cliché make it even harder to pin down. While strongly tied to context—characteristic clichés distinctly mark a milieu, a moment, or a medium—clichés as such are cross-cultural, cross-temporal phenomena. Learning about clichés from another place or era is invariably fascinating, but for opposed reasons: we discover the wonders of either universality (everyone has that cliché!) or idiosyncrasy (what a culturally unique cliché!). And although clichés often appear without attribution—origin unknown—an incredible proportion of those we still use in the West come from the same two people, specifically the sixteenth-century writers William Shakespeare and John Heywood. The latter was a relatively unknown playwright and aphorist who coined "Haste maketh waste," "Out of sight out of mind," "Look ere ye leap," "Two heads are better than one," "Beggars should be no choosers," "A penny for your thought," "Rome was not built in one day," and "Better late than never."[34] If we extrapolate that Shakespeare's clichés have withstood the test of time precisely because they are so original, what do we make of unsung Heywood's assortment of aphorisms: can one be a genius of unoriginality? Cliché in a literary context tends to teeter on the edge of this irony, an ambivalence we see not just in Flaubert's style, but also in Arendt's curious reference to Eichmann's "self-invented clichés." This makes it hard to judge tone and intention.

Cliché's rampant, catholic ubiquity also makes it resistant to analysis; indeed, its very popularity seems to preclude analysis, inviting instead the indexical and often accusatory act of "pointing at" clichés that we find in suspicious reading. This makes some sense: it is precisely because a word or phrase can be conveyed and consumed without gloss that it becomes recognizable as a cliché in the first place. Figures for the cliché (fossil, frozen, calcified, stale, worn out) and its transmission (automata, regurgitation, contagion) suggest that we perceive it as a fixed bit of language that moves wholesale into, through, and out of people. In his oft-cited book *On Clichés: The Supersedure of Meaning by Function in Modernity*, Anton Zijderveld says, "This is why it is so hard to change the cliché: like a magic formula, it is unalterable."[35] A cliché's success—its wide recognition and circulation—is paradoxically built both on its failure to signify and on its impermeability to analysis (etymologically, to analyze is "to unloosen"). At its empty core, cliché threatens to expose the groundlessness of all language, flaunting its detachment from originality, meaning, literary form, context, intention, tone. It seems that all we can do is identify it and critique it.

Identification seems easy. Like porn, you indeed know a cliché when you see it. This is why, as Zijderveld notes, the cliché tends toward lists and compilations: "Because of their reified nature, clichés can be collected like stamps or . . . jokes."[36] The so-to-speak exemplarity of cliché—the urge it inspires to offer concrete instances of it—harks back to its origins in photography. Its effect is quasi-indexical, in both the sense of a sign's "pointing" capacity and the effect of actual light particles on photosensitive film. But cliché doesn't always point itself out or make itself noticed in literature because "the familiarity of set expressions virtually insures their transparency."[37] It might be more accurate to say that you know a cliché *only* when you see it. As Althusser observes of ideology's insidious self-evidence, "It is indeed a peculiarity of ideology that it imposes (without appearing to do so, since these are 'obviousnesses') obviousnesses as obviousnesses, which we cannot *fail to recognize* and before which we have the inevitable and natural reaction of crying out (aloud or in the 'still, small voice of conscience'): 'That's obvious! That's right! That's true!' "[38] We repeat truisms, we assume, because they bear some relation, however rustic or antiquated, to the truth.

We can apply to cliché, however, Althusser's brilliant reframing of ideology, which is not a set of true or false ideas *about* reality, but rather a set of practices, rituals, and apparatuses that *constitute* reality. Cliché is in fact often a linguistic operator for ideological interpellation. In Althusser's terms, interpellation entails recognizable, conventional language keyed to certain bodily dispositions—a friend knocking on the door, the policeman hailing the subject of the state, saying hello and shaking someone's hand. Comparing clichés to physical greetings (handshaking, cheek kissing), Zijderveld emphasizes that neither are "to be taken literally. Indeed, they don't mean a thing. They are merely functional in the daily routine."[39] For Zijderveld, their truth value comes from their repetition: "They seem to carry truth—an old and an obvious truth—not because of their semantic content but because of their repetitive use. They are usually not heuristically convincing (that would require a reflective pondering of their meaning), but they are magically convincing, i.e. produce a sort of enchantment (which needs an emotional participation in the general cadence of the words, the sounds and the bodily movements)."[40] Clichés' defining properties emerge not from form or content, then, but from repeated use in physical and social contexts. They carry not truth per se, but rather a certain kind of weight, or if we want to take seriously Zijderveld's description of clichés as "survivals of magic," a kind of *power*.

In this sense, the cliché ought to be the subject par excellence for ordinary language philosophy. As Ludwig Wittgenstein put it: "For a *large* class of cases . . . in which we employ the word 'meaning' it can be defined thus: the meaning of a word is its use in the language."[41] And many of J. L. Austin's *performative utterances*—words that do things, make things happen—are indeed clichés. If we repeat performatives to make them "go," they may over time become fossilized language. In their reading of the uses of cliché in contemporary British poetry, Catherine Bates and Nasser Hussain aver that the reverse is true as well: cliché is often performative—"it is neither true nor false in itself, but it enacts"—and is thus "the language act which reminds us that all language is necessarily something re-used and imitative, not original, but communal."[42] For Zijderveld, this is precisely the point of cliché: "The sociological essence of a cliché consists of the supersedure of original meanings by social functions. This supersedure is caused by repetitive use and enhanced by the avoidance of reflection."[43]

Cliché serves not only as a social regulator, what Zijderveld calls a "microinstitution," but also as a social lubricant, ensuring the workings of communal life: it reassures, soothes, habituates, repairs, and so on.[44] It is thus an important aspect of "the teaching and learning of . . . appropriate emotional reflexes."[45] For Zijderveld, some of cliché's social functions are "emotionally neutral."[46] Clichés like "you know?" or "at any rate" act as *filler*, what Roman Jakobson characterized as the *phatic* function of language: "a profuse exchange of ritualized formulas, by entire dialogues, with the mere purport of prolonging communication."[47] Others are "emotionally expressive," or, in Jakobson's terms, *emotive*: "Oh my God!"[48] While this might seem like just another version of their slipperiness, it is notable that clichés swim in an affective, social sea of communication. Though they may fail to signify meaning, clichés repeat themselves into continued circulation, like coins carrying the warmth of fingers even as their engravings are rubbed smooth by so much handling.

In sum, because the cliché is so tied to context, and use, it is an adamantly *manifest* form of language. It derives from a physical apparatus; its sound and sense are enmeshed; its everyday use is akin to gesture and the exchange of objects; it tends toward lists, dictionaries, and encyclopedias; it fills and moves us. Cliché thus asks us to attend to language's materiality: usages as uses, meaning as matter, affects as effects. This is why some literary critics liken it to detritus: "Cliché is a kind of trash talk—it is devalued, dismissed and degraded language. It is the verbal equivalent to rubbish, trash, garbage, junk ... stuff we expressly do not want to see, or hear. But we only notice it when we do see it."[49] Other literary critics recover cliché from this trash heap by arguing that poetic techniques reframe ordinary language through strange juxtapositions or defamiliarization. This argument is familiar in the analysis of the use of everyday, banal language by modernists like T. S. Eliot and Gertrude Stein, or postmodernists like Thomas Pynchon and Bret Easton Ellis. Art, so the claim goes, turns cliché inside out, breaks it into pieces, makes it wondrous, makes it surreal.[50]

One might say that if symptomatic reading renders ideologically saturated poetic language into mere cliché by way of critique, recuperative readings undo cliché until it is no longer cliché at all—set in a literary frame, it becomes art to the knowing viewer. If symptomatic reading finds cliché kitschy, recuperative reading lends it the gloss of camp; neither takes cliché seriously as a social or textual phenomenon. More than critical analysis or appraisal, I submit that cliché, as a material form, requires a reading practice attuned to phenomenology.

A Phenomenology of the Cliché

My use of the term *phenomenology* does not reach quite so far back into the history of philosophy as to conjure the ghosts of Husserl, Heidegger, Bergson, or Merleau-Ponty. Rather, I want to pick up on more recent literary critical uses of phenomenology and its methods, beginning with reader-response criticism. Early versions of an attention to the reading experience, like Roman Ingarden's *The Cognition of the Literary Work of Art* (1937) and Louise Rosenblatt's *Literature as Exploration* (1938), have their roots in phenomenology and some of its philosophical siblings, functionalism and pragmatism.[51] The titles of two seminal texts of later reader-response criticism speak plainly to this philosophical lineage: Georges Poulet's 1969 "Phenomenology of Reading" and Wolfgang Iser's 1972 "The Reading Process: A Phenomenological Approach." Iser begins: "The phenomenological theory of art lays full stress on the idea that, in considering a literary work, one must take into account not only the actual text but also, and in equal measure, the actions involved in responding to that text."[52] Poulet's claim is even more basic: "Books are objects."[53]

The "actions involved in responding to" the "object" that we call a book of course vary enormously according to the time, motive, skill, and moment of a reading, to say nothing of the reader herself. This approach to literature, like its philosophical forefathers, has also been criticized for being overly opaque and reductive, for its metaphysics of presence, and for abstracting a "subject" and an "experience" out of context. But recent critical turns—to affect, to ethics, to objects, to form—have often entailed a reconsideration of the reading experience, albeit under other names. The methods and emphases of a phenomenology of reading have reemerged explicitly in works like Elaine Scarry's 1999 *Dreaming by the Book*, Felski's 2008 *Uses of Literature* (which she calls a "neophenomenology"), and the essays in both the aforementioned 2009 issue of *Representations* titled "The Way We Read Now" and a "cluster on reading" in the winter 2011 issue of *New Literary History*.[54]

Though there are variously high political and critical stakes of these subtle returns to reader-response criticism, my intent here is not to defend a phenomenology of reading at length. Rather, I wish to express a sense of its utility when it comes to the strange beast under consideration in this essay: the cliché. If, as I hope I have shown, the cliché jams our usual tools for critique, phenomenology offers an alternative method particularly amenable to this adamantly material form of language. Attending to the reading experience—rather than to meaning or beauty or ideology per se—helps illuminate three aspects of cliché we've already glimpsed. To recap, cliché is *a signifier of nonsignification*. Cliché is *a material form of language* that affords cumulative effects. And cliché functions as *a mode of affective exchange* both within the text and across the diegetic line. Cliché thus draws our attention to features of language we might dismiss as obvious or insignificant, like frequency, heft, dimension, sound, and texture. That is, cliché strongly affords a reading attuned to material and experiential qualities. It insists that we read language in *use*, a quality that literary critics insist on in theory—New Historicist context, Bakhtinian dialogism, Austinian performativity, even reader-response experience—but don't always apply in practice.

The exception to this characterization of literary criticism, and the model for the phenomenological reading I will bring to bear on cliché, is the work of Roland Barthes. His oeuvre—from *Mythologies* (1957) to *Empire of Signs* (1970) to *A Lover's Discourse: Fragments* (1972)—could be described as a long, hard look at clichés of many medial and material varieties. Indeed, in *A Lover's Discourse*, Barthes takes on the ultimate cultural repository of cliché: love. He sets himself the near impossible task of grasping the contours of how lovers speak to themselves and each other, and crucially, he does so from the inside. This signaled a striking shift in his method. Barthes's work in semiotics loudly denounced the critic's "personal" experiences of texts, and his eschewal of subjectivity culminated in his pronouncement in 1969 of "The Death of the Author." His early work could be seen as a paragon of what Rita Felski calls poststructuralism's tendency to "stand back," to maintain a critical distance from the text or cultural artifact.[55] *A Lover's Discourse*, however, portended a gradual decrease in this denaturalizing impulse over the last decade of his life.

Perhaps beginning with his biography in 1975, Barthes's personal experiences started to invade his analyses, presenting one path for a return to the phenomenological impulses with which he began his career in the 1950s.[56] By the time he published *Camera Lucida* (1980), Barthes would explicitly invoke a "vague, casual, even cynical phenomenology"—an adaptation of the "Classical phenomenology ... I had known in my adolescence"—as part of his method.[57] In the earlier *A Lover's Discourse*, his prefatory remarks on "how this book is constructed" offer intimations of this transition:

> Everything follows from this principle: that the lover is not to be reduced to a simple symptomal subject, but rather that we hear in his voice what is "unreal," i.e. intractable. Whence the choice of a "dramatic" method which renounces examples and rests on the single action of a primary language (no metalanguage). The description of the lover's discourse has been replaced by its simulation, and to that discourse has been restored its fundamental person, the *I*, in order to stage an utterance, not an analysis. What is proposed, then, is a portrait—but not a psychological portrait; instead, a structural one which offers the reader a discursive site: the site of someone speaking within himself, *amorously*, confronting the other (the loved object), who does not speak.[58]

This method is neither symptomatic nor critical nor merely descriptive. Like Barthes's earlier works, it is a "structural" portrait, a mosaic comprised of fragments; like his later ones, it is a "discursive site" centered by its "fundamental person, the *I*." This first person is not yet Barthes himself mourning his mother, nor is it the abstracted "reader" of his previous method. It is a ghostly medium.

Given this insistent, implicit immersion within the discourse, we might say that *A Lover's Discourse* is *Madame Bovary* as critical theory. Barthes alludes in his preface to another Flaubertian classic: "Amorous *dis-cursus* is not dialectical; it turns like a perpetual calendar, an encyclopedia of affective culture (there is something of Bouvard and Pécuchet in the lover)."[59] *A Lover's Discourse* is a calendar in content—marking the angsty *durée* of the lover's waiting and his spells of relief—but more of an encyclopedia in form. It jumbles order and time; it dilates and contracts fragments of amorous language, which are sorted by an arbitrary alphabet. Barthes never actually uses the word *cliché*, but the "amorous figure" is possessed of its familiarity and self-evidence: "A figure is established if at least someone can say: '*That's so true! I recognize that scene of language*'" (4). Just as for Althusser "*the production [of knowledge] . . . is identical with the object*," so for Barthes the establishment of the figure coincides with its recognition. This again reinforces the radical redundancy and invisibility of the cliché, of which amorous discourse is surely the apogee:

> What do I think of love?—As a matter of fact, I think nothing at all of love. I'd be glad to know *what it is,* but being inside, I see it in existence, not in essence. I want to know (love) is the very substance I employ in order to speak (the lover's discourse) . . . excluded from logic (which supposes languages exterior to each other), I cannot claim to *think properly*. . . . I am in love's *wrong place,* which is its dazzling place: "The darkest place, according to a Chinese proverb, is always underneath the lamp." (59)

Barthes uncovers the extent to which this cliché's contextual embeddedness and semantic tautology—its obscurity even under the brightest light—demands another method of reading.

The self-enclosing, haphazard fragments of *A Lover's Discourse* simulate and stage Barthes's argument that love's figures, which "occur to the lover without any order" (6), "are distributional but not integrative; they always remain on the same level: the lover speaks in bundles of sentences but does not integrate these sentences on a higher level into a work; his is a horizontal discourse" (7). Ranging across love's figures, Barthes's book is a paean to linguistic materiality. I offer here a representative sample of his phenomenological descriptions of language and its effects on speakers, writers, and readers of love: "The lover's discourse is usually a smooth envelope" (28); "Language is a skin: I rub my language against the other. It is as if I had words instead of fingers, or fingers at the tip of my words. . . . I enwrap the other in my words, I caress, brush against, talk up this contact" (73); "A flood of language sweeps me away" (81); "To try to write love is to confront the *muck* of language" (99); "I go on talking, turning my hurdy-gurdy" (161); "My language is not . . . a discard but rather an 'overstock': what is not consumed in the moment . . . and is therefore remaindered" (168); "Language begins its long career as an agitated useless thing" (204); "The scene [of a lovers' quarrel] recalls the Roman style of vomiting: I tickle my uvula (I rouse myself to contestation), I vomit (a flood of wounding arguments), and then, quite calmly, I begin eating again" (207). Language takes on the dimensions and features of the physical world, filling it up rather than serving as a means of communicating aspects of it.

So, for example, instead of defining, exemplifying, or lauding Bakhtinian dialogism—the idea that language emerges in relation to a real or imagined interlocutor—Barthes considers what it amounts to in a material sense. "This is the meaning of what is euphemistically called *dialogue*," he says, "not to listen to each other, but to submit in common to an egalitarian principle of the distribution of language goods" (204). He later reads a lover's quarrel as an inversion of a game of "hunt-the-slipper": "The slipper changes hands throughout the scene, and the victory goes to the player who captures that little creature whose possession assures omnipotence: the last word" (208). The semantic and communicative functions of language are less important than its properties as something distributed and exchanged across time and space. The figure flaunts its materiality, integrity, and shareability: "Figures take shape insofar as we can recognize, in passing discourse, something that has been read, heard, felt. The figure is outlined (like a sign) and memorable (like an image or a tale)" (4).

In *A Lover's Discourse*, the apogee of the amorous figure is of course *je t'aime*, or *I love you*:

> Once the first avowal has been made, *"I love you"* has no meaning whatever; it merely repeats in an enigmatic mode—so blank does it appear—the old message (which may not have been transmitted in these words). I repeat it exclusive of any pertinence; it comes out of the language, it divagates—where?
>
> I could not decompose the expression without laughing. Then there would be "me" on one side, "you" on the other, and in between a joint of *reasonable* (i.e., lexical) affection. Anyone can feel how much such a decomposition, though conforming to linguistic theory, would disfigure what is *flung out* in a single impulse. *To love* does not exist in the infinitive (except by a metalinguistic artifice): the subject and the object come to the word even as it is uttered, and *I-love-you* must be understood (and read here) in the Hungarian fashion, for instance, for Hungarian uses a single word, *szeretlek*, as if French, renouncing its splendid analytical quality, were an agglutinative language (and it is, indeed, agglutination which is in question here). This clump is shattered by the slightest syntactical alteration; it is, so to speak, beyond syntax and yields itself to no structural transformation. (147)

I-love-you is a single, holistic "matrix-sentence," akin to Adorno's "abominable . . . combinations of words" and Zijderveld's "unalterable" "magic formula." Barthes uses the French *agglutination* and *bloc* (Richard Howard translates this last as "clump") to capture the stickiness of this amorous cliché, hyphenating the words to emphasize their inseparability. *I-love-you* is a "holophrase," a childish or economical use of a single word for a complex idea, and it is "extra-lexicographical," "a figure whose definition cannot transcend [its] heading" (148) in a dictionary, an encyclopedia, or even in *A Lover's Discourse*.

Rather than undoing the phrase over the course of his chapter on *je-t'aime*, Barthes simply repeats it, each iteration augmented with brief, fragmentary observations: *je-t'aime* is socially irresponsible; it lacks nuance; it is self-evidently true; it is a performative; it is lonely; it is simple; it is a formula but corresponds to no ritual; it is unclassifiable; it is "irrepressible and unforeseeable"; it is neither strictly an utterance nor an uttering; it is a proffering, a release, the closest analogues to which are music and orgasm (149). As when the repetition of word or phrase eventually makes it sound meaningless or absurd, an effect called semantic saturation, the sheer recurrence of *I-love-you* on Barthes's own pages renders this cliché uncanny. More importantly, it performs the very hollowing out of the phrase's meaning and context that he is describing. That is, repeating the cliché in this form in the work of criticism—a formal choice intensified by Barthes's deployment of fragments and anaphora, commas and semicolons—*enacts* his ideas about cliché. We do not just come to see, we come to *experience* the phenomenological effects of the cliché.

One effect of this agglutination and piling on of adamantly physical language is, oddly enough, to effect a kind of metamateriality. In a chapter of *The Principles of Psychology* (1890), entitled "Habit," William James expresses his concerns about this "enormous fly-wheel of society": "You see the little lines of cleavage running through the character, the tricks of thought, the prejudices, the ways of the 'shop,' in a word, from which the man can by-and-by no more escape than his coat-sleeve can suddenly fall into a new set of folds." But ever-pragmatic James concludes that habit can also allow us to move to higher planes of consciousness: "The more of the details of our daily life we can hand over to the effortless custody of automatism, the more our higher powers of mind will be set free for their own proper work."[60] To put it in the jargon of pseudo-neuroscience, habit affords metacognition. As the most habitual language, cliché too frees up the speaker (or the reader) to concentrate on higher, or at least other, matters. That is, once we are released from seeking meaning in the cliché, we can attend to its other effects.

This is one way we might skirt the seeming pitfalls—naïveté, redundancy—of a phenomenological method that purports merely to stage a discursive experience. When we attend to and repeat a text, we engage in a meta-awareness without necessarily succumbing to a metalanguage.[61] When we read literature phenomenologically, it is as though an experiential track runs above, or alongside, the semantic and narrative ones we're used to. While I will not adapt his critical form exactly, I turn now to apply some of Barthes's phenomenological observations about language to a literary use of cliché that draws our attention to its materiality. I will proceed in three stages. I'll give an interpretation of the novel's clichés through a lens of critique; I'll show the limitations of this approach; and then I'll offer a phenomenological reading that again traces the material and affective affordances of a heap of cliché.[62]

The Effects and Affects of Cliché

The very first scene of Jim Thompson's 1952 noir thriller, *The Killer Inside Me*, seems to lay out a lesson in how to read cliché. The novel begins in a diner. The narrator has just finished his pie and is having a second cup of coffee while exchanging a look with a bum outside the window: "He saw me watching him, and his face faded back into the shadows. But I knew he was still there. I knew he was waiting. The bums always size me up for an easy mark." The scene's immediate atmosphere—its setting, tone, and diction ("size me up for an easy mark")—screams noir, if we hadn't already guessed from the title page. We immediately encounter clichés, or tropes if you prefer, that situate us in a specific genre. In Amossy's terms, we read the rhythms and slang of noir *passively*; they facilitate our entrance into the diegetic world. The possibility of a *critical* reading emerges only when the narrator enters into dialogue:

> I lit a cigar and slid off my stool. The waitress, a new girl from Dallas, watched as I buttoned my coat. "Why, you don't even carry a gun!" she said, as though she was giving me a piece of news.
> "No," I smiled. "No gun, no blackjack, nothing like that. Why should I?"
> "But you're a cop—a deputy sheriff, I mean. What if some crook should try to shoot you?"
> "We don't have many crooks here in Central City, ma'am," I said. "Anyway, people are people, even when they're a little misguided. You don't hurt them, they won't hurt you. They'll listen to reason."
> She shook her head, wide-eyed with awe, and I strolled up to the front.

The waitress seems to stand in for a naive reader. She "shakes her head, wide-eyed with awe," her comment dismissed by the narrator's aside "as though she were giving me a piece of news." These phrases recording the waitress's affects and words, themselves generic clichés, again slide off the reader's eye. But they subtly give the reader pieces of news—the narrator is a deputy sheriff, but doesn't carry a gun; he is intimidating, but easy to talk to. The narrator's hyperaware references to the waitress's reactions introduce a metafictional frame, while her exaggerated naïveté makes her a foil to the discerning reader. This triangulated dramatic irony (narrator-character-reader) opens a gap for a critical reading of cliché to enter. By the middle of the page, then, our passive reading has honed a critical edge, but it is largely still on the narrator's side, directed at the waitress's clichéd behavior.

If we attend to their shared use of clichéd language, we note that the narrator's speech patterns conform to cliché's public, regulatory operations: "People are people, even when they're a little misguided. You don't hurt them, they won't hurt you. They'll listen to reason." These clichés effect authority: they evince wisdom, power, truth. They are characterized by repetition, tautology, and chiasmus, features that make them memorable but vacuous ("people are people"). In Althusser's terms, we might say the narrator is the agent of a repressive state apparatus (deputy sheriff) who uses an ideological state apparatus (language) to wield authority. No need for weapons—"No gun, no blackjack, nothing like that. Why should I?"—when you have words to throw around. Indeed, the cliché soon becomes more than the ideological language to which someone like the awed waitress freely submits; it turns repressive, something to which the deputy sheriff willfully submits others.

This authoritative and purposive use of cliché clarifies when he next exchanges words with the diner's proprietor, whom he has known longer and recently assisted:

He thanked me again for taking his son in hand.

"He's a different boy now, Lou," he said, kind of running his words together like foreigners do. "Stays in nights; gets along fine in school. And always he talks about you—what a good man is Deputy Lou Ford."

"I didn't do anything," I said. "Just talked to him. Showed him a little interest. Anyone else could have done as much."

"Only you," he said. "Because you are good, you make others so." He was all ready to sign off with that, but I wasn't. I leaned an elbow on the counter, crossed one foot behind the other and took a long slow drag on my cigar. I liked the guy—as much as I like most people, anyway—but he was too good to let go. Polite, intelligent: guys like that are my meat.

"Well, I tell you," I drawled. "I tell you the way I look at it, a man doesn't get any more out of life than what he puts into it."

"Umm," he said, fidgeting. "I guess you're right, Lou."

"I was thinking the other day, Max; and all of a sudden I had the dog-gonedest thought. It came to me out of a clear sky—the boy is father to the man. Just like that. The boy is father to the man."

As the third persona in the triangulated narration shifts from naive reader (the new waitress) to knowing reader (the old friend and proprietor), the dramatic irony intensifies. It is no longer that the reader and narrator laugh together at a character; now, the reader understands something about Lou that Max does not understand about his friend. We don't know exactly why Max begins to fidget and demur, nor how he has become Lou's "meat"—given the noir context, the shadow of a previous entanglement hovers over the diction ("life," "father"), making the clichés menacing.

As the scene proceeds, then, cliché goes from producing awe in a subject of the state—the waitress new to Central City—to a personal and psychological intimidation, a matter of feelings between "friends":

The smile on his face was getting strained. I could hear his shoes creak as he squirmed. If there's anything worse than a bore, it's a corny bore. But how can you brush off a nice friendly fellow who'd give you his shirt if you asked for it?

"I reckon I should have been a college professor or something like that," I said. "Even when I'm asleep I'm working out problems. Take that heat wave we had a few weeks ago; a lot of people think it's the heat that makes it so hot. But it's not like that, Max. It's not the heat, but the humidity. I'll bet you didn't know that, did you?"

He cleared his throat and muttered something about being wanted in the kitchen. I pretended like I didn't hear him.

"Another thing about the weather," I said. "Everyone talks about it, but no one does anything. But maybe it's better that way. Every cloud has its silver lining, at least that's the way I figure it. I mean, if we didn't have the rain we wouldn't have the rainbows, now would we?"

"Lou . . ."

"Well," I said, "I guess I'd better shove off. I've got quite a bit of getting around to do, and I don't want to rush. Haste makes waste, in my opinion. I like to look before I leap."

That was dragging 'em in by the feet, but I couldn't hold 'em back. Striking at people that way is almost as good as the other, the real way.[63]

We begin the passage uncertain about Lou's complicity in the use of cliché; by its end, it's clear that the reader, already slotted into alignment with the narrator, is meant to identify with Lou's ironic deployment of cliché rather than with Max's discomfort with it. But only when Lou tells us explicitly that "striking at people that way is almost as good as the other, the real way" do we understand—however incompletely—that this is no coded threat. Lou's use of cliché *as such* is the purposive attack.

As Lou utters his series of unrelated maxims, Max "fidgets," "squirms," "clears his throat," "ums"; "the smile on his face" grows "strained" and he tries to excuse himself back to work. Lou explains the proprietor's reactions by saying, "If there's anything worse than a bore, it's a corny bore." A later instance of cliché overkill, so to speak, has a similar effect, expressed in similar terms: "'In other words,' I said, 'where there's a will there's a way.' She squirmed a little, and then she snickered. 'Oh, Lou, you corny so and so! You slay me!'"[64] Lou is punning here on physical boring and slaying. As Arendt's critique of Eichmann suggests, banal language is often linked to violence (bad puns make us "groan" or "wince"). Thompson collapses this association into an equation: clichés *are* violence.

As Lou's target shifts from the oblivious reader (the waitress) to the mocked reader (the proprietor), the novel seems to offer a hard lesson in how to apply critical thinking to cliché. And the standard reading of *The Killer Inside Me* is that its elision of violence and banality offers an ironic critique from within of the ideological complicities of small-town America.[65] The deputy sheriff turns out to be a serial killer who diagnoses himself as a paranoid schizophrenic. When Zijderveld offers some tentative speculations about the interpersonal psychology of cliché, he posits of the schizophrenic:

He is thus not able to engage in "symbolic interaction," in a true communication, since this requires a mutual identification and internalization of attitudes, as well as a communicability of meaning. Yet, his speech and behavior is quite schematic, demonstrating a kind of reified structure. This indicates that he develops and uses his own, very private clichés—clichés that are only functional in his privately constructed world. . . . Quite understandably, at times he will suddenly resort to violence, because the private "logic" does not seem to work, the private clichés do not seem to yield any results. . . . This leads to an important conclusion: when clichés in which meaning has been superseded by function cannot function (for whatever reason), they may trigger utterly irrational, cruel, bizarre, and violent behavior.[66]

Though it accurately reflects the privacy of Lou's mental world—the novel is a classic of unreliable narration—this analysis does not do justice to his clichés. Unlike the schizophrenic or aphasic's "self-invented clichés," Lou's clichés are expressed, recognized, and felt. Further, if the institutional cover for his murders and his psychological self-diagnosis respectively confirm ideological and psychoanalytic symptomatic readings of his clichés (he is an agent of the state; he is a paranoid schizophrenic), they also obviate them. We once again swim in the ambiguous seas of cliché: is the deputy sheriff a parodic representative (of the state, the human) or an abhorrent deviation?

If we apply a phenomenological lens to its first scene, we can see that the novel in fact troubles from the start a teleology from passive reading to critical reading of cliché. The narrator's use of clichés in the scene initially goes unnoticed by the reader, confirming Amossy's contention that "precisely because of its mechanical nature, [a cliché may be] . . . immediately assimilated before its triteness is even noticed."[67] Because cliché is what makes many texts "go," cliché only registers *as* cliché if it is pointed to or marked as such. Like Barthes, Thompson never outright uses the word *cliché* in his text. Lou's ironic use of cliché doesn't affect his tone or expression, nor does it achieve the relief of a punch line; he is deadpan throughout, whether speaking clichés to the reader, the waitress, or his friend. Without gloss or framing, the initial handful of clichés in the scene do not necessarily portend trouble. For instance, it is Max's phrase, "Because you are good, you make them so," that sets Lou off, but on a first read this cliché is as unnoticeable as Lou's hackneyed speech to the waitress. The scene does not contextualize, explain, defamiliarize, isolate, or poeticize the cliché.

Rather, it is by *gathering* clichés that Lou overwhelms us with the otherwise innocuous linguistic artifact. As in *A Lover's Discourse*, this heaping operation gradually hollows cliché of meaning, while imbuing the reading experience with metamateriality and affective intensity. The scene compounds the semantic saturation we saw in Barthes's repetitions of *I-love-you*. But here neither a repetition of content (the same words) nor a repetition of form (the same grammar or syntax) empties meaning out. Rather, it is the repetition of The Cliché, that is, the repetition of *repetition itself*, its sole identifiable feature, that hollows language out. This evacuation of semantic content is accompanied by an insistent materiality. If Lou pours out clichés until they spill beyond the bounds of communication, believability, and even his own hokey authority, Max's somatic response is equally *de trop*. The scene gradually warps under the pressure of Lou's banal language; the string of clichés goes on too long, so long that the content of the individual clichés matters less than their very profusion, which fills the space between the men, renders it dense with language, smothers Max altogether. By capitalizing on that heaping to which cliché is prone, Thompson shows how language can be felt—can be forceful—though it is semantically negligible. The scene thus undoes Amossy's distinction between passive and critical reading. If we recognize Thompson's prose as a heap of clichés, we do not attend to their content; if we focus on the meaning of each individual cliché, we do not experience the cumulative effects of the heap. Perhaps we read both ways simultaneously, perhaps one way, then the other; in any case, reading is shown to be a layered and variable process irreducible to dichotomies of surface/depth or naïveté/critique.

I want to hypothesize, by way of conclusion, that the material and affective affordances of the heap of clichés enable it to index the unspeakable. Eric Shouse defines affect as "a non-conscious experience of intensity . . . of unformed and unstructured potential."[68] As we have seen, cliché is defined by its ubiquity and availability for affective exchange—we might subsume both under the term *promiscuity*—and by its habitual, if not strictly "non-conscious," use. Cliché thus registers those functions of language Jakobson links to desire: the *phatic* function, used to prolong conversation with nothing words, to keep talking, to stay near, to swing in a hammock of text; and the *emotive* function, the mark of what a person wishes to say or express. So, on one hand, cliché is linked to absence of meaning; to pile up cliché is to accrue nonsignification, mere chat. On the other hand, cliché affords an accumulation of expressivity; to pile up cliché is to insist on the desire to talk. If we put these features together, a heap of cliché registers those desires that exceed language. And it does so by accruing material instances of insufficient (empty, futile) language. We experience a cumulative plenitude of blankness, a vacuum that signifies nothing yet draws affect toward it. While cliché connotes mindlessness, its cumulative effect is to record *willfulness*—the desire to share language's materiality, to throw words at one another.

In Barthes, this desire is loving but also violent: "A specific force impels my language toward the harm I may do to myself" (80); "the lover's discourse stifles the other, who finds no place for his own language beneath this massive utterance" (165); "the difficulties of the amorous relationship originate in his ceaseless desire to appropriate the loved being in one way or another" (232). When, at the close of Thompson's novel, Lou is confronted with a lover he thought he brutally beat to death, their clichéd "lovers' talk" at once disintegrates and proliferates, signaling an unutterable convergence of violence and desire:

> "Two hearts that beat as one," I said. "T-wo—ha, ha, ha,—two—ha, ha, ha, ha, ha, ha, ha—two—J-jesus Chri—ha, ha, ha, ha, ha, ha, ha—two Jesus . . ."
> And I sprang at her. I made for her just like they'd thought I would. Almost. And it was like I'd signaled, the way the smoke suddenly poured up through the floor. And the room exploded with shots and yells, and I seemed to explode with it, yelling and laughing and . . . and . . . Because they hadn't got the point. She'd got that between the ribs and the blade along with it. And they all lived happily ever after, I guess, and I guess—that's—all.[69]

The crooner's cliché, "two hearts beating as one," shatters into "T-wo—ha, ha, ha—two," a maniacal rendering that puts sound ("ha") back into the word ("heart") even as it seems to leave communication behind altogether (how are we to read the word *t-wo?*) in a wake of laughter. While the final cliché, "happily ever after," reduces the linguistic paroxysm to a palatable irony, the double-edged clichés that precede it—"I made for her"; "the point. She'd got that between the ribs"—are disturbing indices of Lou's indivisible intent to harm/love. Incredibly, these puns also participate in the scene's rampant, over-the-top metafiction. You "make" a pun; you "get the point"; the likeliest etymology of pun is the Latin *punctum*, or point, which is also the origin of *punctuation*. The explosion of hyphens, dashes, commas, and ellipses in Lou's staccato speech is as much an assault on the reader as the bullet-fire and yells that follow. The pileup of repeated, fragmented clichés draws metafictional attention to language's material properties (phatic, emotive, sonic, graphic), while sparking a near "non-conscious experience of intensity" and confounding our critical sensibilities.

A Lover's Discourse and *The Killer Inside Me* reveal that we often cannot choose between passive and critical, naive and suspicious, surface and symptomatic readings. Nor, however, do we need to find an altogether novel method of reading. As the book of Ecclesiastes tells us, there is nothing new under the sun. Phenomenology is an old method that directs itself not to the new, but to the *now*. This is why it is so amenable to a study of cliché; despite its association with the past, the cliché is a remarkably *present* and *presentist* linguistic phenomenon. To wit, a cliché never gets fully "worn out"; the minute it does, it loses its recognizability. We might then treat our current clichés as useful rather than used up. Indeed, to take cliché seriously would be pragmatic for several recent critical trends; for one, the proliferative, repetitive nature of online and digital media look quite different if we give credence to cliché's affective and material affordances. More broadly, we ought to open our field of study to the less grandiose ways we use language, rather than doggedly relegating its deceptively simple forms to ideological blindness. As we've seen, a heap of clichés can remind us of the vacuous core and incessant materiality of all language, offer phenomenological description as a metadiscourse, and affectively register the inexpressible union of love and harm. At the very least, cliché, that usual suspect, hidden in plain sight, can force us to take another look at the business as usual that we call critique.

Notes

1 Wayne Booth, *The Rhetoric of Fiction* (Chicago: University of Chicago Press, 1983), 371–72.

2 "Three masters, seemingly mutually exclusive, dominate the school of suspicion: Marx, Nietzsche, and Freud." Paul Ricoeur, *Freud and Philosophy: An Essay on Interpretation* (New Haven, CT: Yale University Press, 1970), 5.

3 Recent work on cliché tends at least to partially acknowledge its usefulness. See Marshall McLuhan, *From Cliché to Archetype* (New York: Viking, 1970); Christopher Ricks, "Clichés," in *The State of the Language*, ed. Leonard Michaels (Berkeley: University of California Press, 1980), 54–63; Orin Hargraves, *It's Been Said Before: A Guide to the Use and Abuse of Clichés* (Oxford: Oxford University Press, 2014). Anton Zijderveld, despite railing against the "tyranny" of clichés, spends much of his book *On Clichés: The Supersedure of Meaning by Function in Modernity* (London: Routledge and Kegan Paul, 1979), dwelling on its uses in a communal and political context and suggesting "strategies to relativize" its power, most of which entail sublimation. Ruth Amossy argues that "instead of condemning the cliché, we should examine the ways it is used within various programmings of reading." "The Cliché in the Reading Process," trans. Terese Lyons, *SubStance* 11, no. 2.35 (1982): 38.

4 Daniel Hartley, "Cliché," *Thinking Blue Guitars* blog, April 27, 2010, https://thinkingblueguitars.wordpress.com/2010/04/27/cliche/.

5 Lynn Berger, "Snapshots, or: Visual Culture's Clichés," *Photographies* 4, no. 2 (September 2011): 15–16.

6 Hartley, "Cliché."

7 Gustave Flaubert, *The Dictionary of Accepted Ideas*, trans. Jacques Barzun (New York: New Directions, 1968).

8   Swift's *A Complete Collection of Genteel and Ingenious Conversation: According to the Most Polite Mode and Method Now Used at Court, and in the Best Companies of England*, in the guise of a how-to reference guide to conversation skills skewered in dialogue form the banal conversations of the eighteenth-century British upper classes. We can include in the canon of "cliché dictionaries" since Flaubert the following books: Gelett Burgess, *Are You a Bromide? or, The Sulphitic Theory* (1907); Ambrose Bierce's *The Cynic's Word Book* (1906), renamed *The Devil's Dictionary* (1911); Eric Partridge's *Dictionary of Clichés* (1940); and James Roger's *Dictionary of Clichés* (1986). Lake Superior State University, the BBC, the *New York Times*, and *Time* publish yearly lists of overused, "banned," or "banished" words and phrases. There are several websites devoted to listing and uncovering the etymologies of clichés, such as Alan Eggleston's Cliché a Day blog July 20, 2016, http://cliche-a-day.blogspot.com.

9   Jacques Barzun, introduction to Flaubert's *The Dictionary of Accepted Ideas*, 2.

10 Quoted in Barzun, introduction, 3, 11.

11 Zijderveld notes, "It stands to reason that clichés have always been instrumental in conveying propaganda. . . . Propaganda bombards individuals widely and repetitively with 'information,' containing the clichés of the propagated ideology" (*On Clichés*, 68).

12 Theodor Adorno and Max Horkheimer, "The Culture Industry: Enlightenment as Mass Deception," *Dialectic of Enlightenment*, trans. John Cumming (London: Verso, 1979), https://www.marxists.org/reference/archive/adorno/1944/culture-industry.htm.

13 "The nature of clichés could easily be described in terms of decline of aura. . . . Clichés are very much the result of reproduction. It is primarily the repetitive use of words, thoughts, emotions and acts which turn these expressions of man into clichés. We have then described the nature of these clichés in terms of the supersedure of meaning by function, of substantial rationality by functional rationality. This supersedure can also be described in terms of a decline of permanence, distance, and uniqueness" (Zijderveld, *On Clichés*, 36). See Zijderveld's discussion of Benjamin in relation to cliché: *On Clichés*, 27–31 passim.

14 Theodor Adorno, *Minima Moralia*, trans. Dennis Redmond (Creative Commons, 2005), https://www.marxists.org/reference/archive/adorno/1951/mm/ch02.htm. July 20, 2016.

15 George Orwell, "Politics and the English Language," in *The Orwell Reader: Fiction, Essays, and Reportage by George Orwell* (New York: Harcourt Brace Jovanovich, 1984), 361.

16 Orwell, "Politics and the English Language," 362.

17 Hannah Arendt, *Eichmann in Jerusalem* (New York: Penguin, 1992), 49.

18 A representative book is Martin Amis's recent collection *The War against Cliché: Essays and Reviews 1971–2000* (New York: Knopf, 2014). A search online yields a variety of pieces, like "5 Cliché Statements That Can Bomb Your Job Search" (*U.S. News and World Report* blog), "10 Most Clichéd Hashtags You're Still Over-

using" (Mashable), and "Top 15 Photography Clichés Everyone Hates" (Fstop-pers). There are dozens of websites devoted to "avoiding cliché," especially in "academic writing," which also seems to be the aim behind Stephen Pinker's new book, *The Sense of Style* (New York: Penguin, 2014).

19 Stephen Best and Sharon Marcus, "Surface Reading," *Representations* 108, no. 1 (2009), 5.

20 Karl Marx, *Capital*, excerpted in *The Norton Anthology of Theory and Criticism*, ed. Vincent Leitch et al. (New York: W. W. Norton, 2010), 778.

21 Louis Althusser and Étienne Balibar, *Reading Capital*, trans. Ben Brewster (London: Verso, 2009), 30.

22 Althusser and Balibar, *Reading Capital*, 19, 28, 29.

23 Best and Marcus, "Surface Reading," 3, 4.

24 "Through the lacunary terms of its new answer political economy produced a new question, but 'unwittingly.' It made 'a complete change in the terms of the "original" problem,' and thereby produced a new problem, but without knowing it" (Althusser, *Reading*, 25).

25 Rita Felski, *Uses of Literature* (New York: Wiley-Blackwell, 2008), 6–7.

26 Amossy, "The Cliché in the Reading Process," 36.

27 Althusser, *Reading*, 25 (my emphasis).

28 This tautological structure characterizes Louis Althusser's insights about ideol-ogy, the elementary effect of which is the "obviousness" that "you and I are sub-jects": "the category of the 'subject' is constitutive of ideology, which only exists by constituting concrete subjects as subjects." "Ideology and Ideological State Apparatuses," *Lenin and Philosophy and Other Essays*, trans. Ben Brewster (New York: Monthly Review Press, 1971), https://www.marxists.org/reference/archive/althusser/1970/ideology.htm, accessed July 20, 2016

29 Ellen Rooney, "Live Free or Describe: The Reading Effect and the Persistence of Form," *differences* 21, no. 3 (2010): 126–27.

30 Felski, *Uses of Literature*, 1.

31 Ricks, "Clichés," 54.

32 Quoted in Barzun, introduction, 9.

33 Felski, *Uses of Literature*, 3.

34 These aphorisms can be found in John Heywood's Wikipedia entry, http://en.wikipedia.org/wiki/John_Heywood, accessed July 20, 2016. They originally appear in *The Proverbs and Epigrams and Miscellanies of John Heywood*, ed. John S. Farmer (London: English Drama Society, 1562). As Zijderveld says, "Shakespeare has always been a rich source of clichés. He formulated many witty and spirited statements about human beings and socio-cultural circumstances which, because of their over-use, have become rather stale and worn-out clichés: 'to be or not to be,' 'method in madness,' 'there is something rotten in the state of—,' etc." (*On Clichés*, 11).

35 Zijderveld, *On Clichés*, 16.

36 Zijderveld, *On Clichés*, 16.

37 Amossy, "The Cliché in the Reading Process," 35.

38 "Ideology and Idological State Apparatuses," *Lenin and Philosophy and Other Essays*, trans. Ben Brewster (New York: Monthly Review Press, 1971), https://www.marxists.org/reference/archive/althusser/1970/ideology.htm, accessed July 20, 2016.

39 Zijderveld, *On Clichés*, 11.

40 Zijderveld, *On Clichés*, 66.

41 Ludwig Wittgenstein, *Philosophical Investigations* (London: Wiley-Blackwell, 1998), 18.

42 Catherine Bates and Nasser Hussain, "Talking Trash/Trashing Talk: Cliché in the Poetry of bpNichol and Christopher Dewdney," in *Trash Culture: Objects and Obsolescence in Cultural Perspective*, ed. Gillian Pye (Bern: Peter Lang, 2010), 167, 173.

43 Zijderveld, *On Clichés*, 10.

44 Zijderveld, *On Clichés*, 17. Among the social and political functions of clichés Zijderveld delineates in *On Clichés*, we find clichés "as the knots of daily communication," "as responses to embarrassment and precariousness," "as survivals of magic," "as propaganda," "as social control," and as forces of "mobilization" for political good or ill, due to their ability to "arouse behavior as in a stimulus-response sequence" (57–65).

45 Zijderveld, *On Clichés*, 16. "Clichés . . . bring people unobtrusively into a certain mood" (13).

46 Zijderveld, *On Clichés*, 14.

47 Roman Jakobson, *Linguistics and Poetics*, excerpted in *The Norton Anthology of Theory and Criticism*, ed. Vincent Leitch et al. (New York: W. W. Norton, 2010), 1263.

48 Jakobson, *Linguistics and Poetics*, 1261.

49 Bates and Hussain, "Talking Trash/Trashing Talk," 173.

50 Through readings of the art of cliché in Geoffrey Hill and Bob Dylan, Christopher Ricks makes a case for what he calls the "artistic gracing of clichés, or their imaginative redemption": "Instead of banishing or shunning clichés as malign, haven't we got to meet them imaginatively, to create benign possibilities for and with them?" (Ricks, "Clichés," 58, 55). Ricks quotes McLuhan—who lauds cliché as "an active, structuring, probing feature of our awareness"—to similar effect: "The Theater of the Absurd has shown us some of the creative contemporary uses of cliché" (McLuhan, *From Cliché to Archetype*, 55). This can be semi- or unintentional. McLuhan cites this anecdote: "A teacher asked her class to use a familiar word in a new way. One boy read: 'The boy returned home with a cliché on his face.' Asked to explain his phrase, he said, 'The dictionary defines cliché as a worn-out expression'" (McLuhan, *From Cliché to Archetype*, 54). Ricks notes that the unlikely juxtaposition of examples in the midst of Orwell's pillory of cliché produces a kind of poetry: "For what is most alive in that sentence is not the sequence where Orwell consciously put his polemical energy. . . . but rather the sombre glints lurking in the sequence of scorned clichés themselves: the way in which, even while he was saying they were useless phrases, Orwell used them so as to create a bizarre vitality of poetry" (Ricks, "Clichés," 55). Indeed, many have delighted in Orwell's example of a mixed metaphor made of two clichés, "the Fascist oc-

topus has sung its swansong." Zijderveld (*On Clichés*) considers two forms of sublimation—aesthetic and comic—that might help "relativize" the cliché.

51 "The special meaning, and more particularly, the submerged associations that these words and images have for the individual reader will largely determine what the work communicates to him. The reader brings to the work personality traits, memories of past events, present needs and preoccupations, a particular mood of the moment, and a particular physical condition. These and many other elements in a never-to-be-duplicated combination determine his response to the peculiar contribution of the text" (Louise Rosenblatt, *Literature as Exploration* [New York: Noble and Noble, 1968], 30–31). Rosenblatt adapted her "transactional theory of the literary work" from William James, John Dewey, Charles Peirce, and Arthur F. Bentley. See also Louise Rosenblatt, *The Reader, the Text, the Poem: The Transactional Theory of the Literary Work* (Carbondale: Southern Illinois University Press, 1992).

52 Wolfgang Iser, "The Reading Process: A Phenomenological Approach," *New Literary History* 3, no. 2 (winter 1972): 279.

53 Georges Poulet, "New and Old History," *New Literary History* 1, no. 1 (October 1969): 53–68.

54 *Representations* 108 (fall 2009). See, for example, Paul B. Armstrong's argument that we rethink "the experience of reading as . . . a dynamic, mutually constituting relation where the encounter is shaped by both sides . . . reading is simultaneously both subjective and objective." "In Defense of Reading," *New Literary History* 42, no. 1 (winter 2011): 102.

55 For Felski, "this anti-naturalism is not just a matter of content or argument but of style, attitude, and tone. It is expressed not only in what is said but in how it is said; the espousal of a quizzical, impassive, or ironic gaze; the ruthless weeding out of an expressive or emotionally tinged vocabulary; the avoidance of any words that might seem to sanction a commitment to norms or values; the deadpan citation of commonplace phrases in such a way as to lay bare their sheer hollowness and hypocrisy. In the act of distancing herself from the assumptions and attitudes of her fellow human beings, the critic models an exemplary self-consciousness and a heightened aesthetic sensibility. An early and powerful salvo in this line of thought was [Barthes's] Mythologies." Felski, "Digging Down and Standing Back," ELN 51, no. 2 (fall/winter 2013): 16.

56 Like other poststructuralists, the young Barthes was deeply engaged with Sartrean phenomenology and in his early work, as Seán Burke has noted, this "took the form of championing the nouveau roman, a loosely phenomenological genre which privileged narratorial consciousness." *The Death and Return of the Author: Criticism and Subjectivity in Barthes, Foucault, and Derrida* (Edinburgh: Edinburgh University Press, 1998), 12.

57 Roland Barthes, *Camera Lucida: Reflections on Photography* (New York: Hill and Wang, 1980), 20–21.

58 Roland Barthes, *A Lover's Discourse: Fragments* (New York: Farrar, Straus and Giroux, 1978).

59 Roland Barthes, *A Lover's Discourse: Fragments*, trans. Richard Howard (New York: Hill and Wang, 2001), 3. Further quotations from this work are cited parenthetically in the text.

60 William James, *The Principles of Psychology*, vol. 1 (New York: Cosimo Classics, 2007), 121, 122.

61 This resonates with what Best and Marcus have to say about "attention to surface as a practice of critical description": "This focus assumes that texts can reveal their own truths because texts mediate themselves; what we think theory brings to texts (form, structure, meaning) is already present in them. Description sees no need to translate the text into a theoretical or historical metalanguage in order to make the text meaningful" ("Surface Reading," 11).

62 I would distinguish my use of "heap" from Sianne Ngai's description of "stuplime" modernist heaps, which have more to do with "breakdown" and "fragmentation" than with the plenitude of empty but self-contained forms I'm interested in. There is some affinity to our arguments about how affective responses to literature delineate what cannot be represented: "The stuplime points to the limits of our representational capabilities, not through the limitlessness or infinity of concepts, but through a no less exhaustive confrontation with the discrete and finite in repetition." Sianne Ngai, "Stuplimity: Shock and Boredom in Twentieth-Century Aesthetics," *Postmodern Culture* 10, no. 2 (2000): paragraph 16, http://muse.jhu.edu.ezp1.harvard.edu/journals/pmc/v010/10.2ngai.html.

63 Jim Thompson, *The Killer Inside Me* (New York: Vintage: 1991), 3–5.

64 Thompson, *The Killer Inside Me*, 4, 5, 15.

65 See Dorothy G. Clark's assessment of critical investigations of Thompson's work: "Thompson's narrators do become 'a source of pure menace,' turned into 'a source of disorder and danger,' and they certainly point to hypocrisy within the 'national myth' and 'small-town America.' *The Killer Inside Me*, one of Thompson's most disturbing works, is central to these analyses; yet even more than 'moral indistinguishability,' it demonstrates the representation of evil and the dismantling of a still-existent Enlightenment faith in reason." "Being's Wound: (Un)Explaining Evil in Jim Thompson's *The Killer Inside Me*," *Journal of Popular Culture* 42, no. 1 (February 2009): 49.

66 Zijderveld, *On Clichés*, 59.

67 Amossy, "The Cliché in the Reading Process," 35.

68 Eric Shouse, "Feeling, Emotion, Affect," M/C 8, no. 6 (December 2005): paragraph 5, http://journal.media-culture.org.au/0512/03-shouse.php. Shouse draws this definition of prepersonal affect—in distinction to both public emotion and personal feeling—from Brian Massumi's *Parables for the Virtual* (Durham, NC: Duke University Press, 2002), which garners them from a strong reading of his own translation of Gilles Deleuze and Félix Guattari, *A Thousand Plateaus: Capitalism and Schizophrenia*, trans. Brian Massumi (Minneapolis: University of Minnesota Press, 1987).

69 Thompson, *The Killer Inside Me*, 244.

7

Why We Love Coetzee; or, *The Childhood of Jesus* and the Funhouse of Critique

ELIZABETH S. ANKER

Few living writers can claim the kind of cult following enjoyed by J. M. Coetzee. Coetzee's writing has inspired outpourings of commentary, even relative to other highly acclaimed authors. Himself a frequent critic, his celebrity has often seemed fueled by his evasiveness, whether about his own biography or matters of authorial intent. Coetzee can be notoriously withholding: stories abound of his perplexing refusal to reply to queries even during public events or readings. This perception of Coetzee's reticence has ironically been exacerbated by his autobiographies, *Boyhood* (1998), *Youth* (2002), and *Summertime* (2010), which masquerade as memoirs only to deliberately confuse fact with fiction. A related blurring of generic boundaries informs Coetzee's frequent incorporation of philosophy into his novels. Many, including *The Childhood of Jesus* (2013), contain extended philosophical dialogues that overtake their plots, subordinating narrative to those often metafictional ruminations while raising complicated questions about the cross-contaminations of contemporary literature and theory.[1]

The role of theory, and in particular certain kinds of *critique*, in both Coetzee's writing and Coetzee's criticism is the focus of this essay. In a recent discussion of *The Childhood of Jesus*, Gayatri Chakravorty Spivak describes Coetzee in instructive terms. For Spivak, Coetzee's writing is noteworthy in how he "draws the reader in" to "learning how to 'read,'" a tactic that ultimately renders him "a creative writer of theory."[2] There is little doubt that the many thought experiments unfolded in Coetzee's novels both conduct a form of theory and prompt its application, and that invitation to theorize is one reason why so many critics have been drawn to Coetzee. But an observation like Spivak's nonetheless begs the questions: what modes and styles of theory does Coetzee elicit? What theoretical paradigms are rewarded in his writing? And what does Coetzee's "creative theory" reveal about the state and stakes of interpretation: what does it tell us about how we read, and why? As I'll argue, the many factors that have contributed to Coetzee's popularity can also be taken as a referendum on "theory now," especially the current reevaluation of critique. For while Coetzee's prolific and frequently self-reflexive theorizing has motivated intense devotion from many readers, that very attribute of his fiction has for others—including me—been cause for reluctance, if not outright frustration. These competing responses to Coetzee, I'll maintain, are worth taking stock of, since they capture a broader mood of ambivalence over the sort of relationship to theory that would have, not too long ago, been touted as theory's (and Coetzee's) basic mystique.

Over the years, Coetzee's novels have engendered a wide range of interpretations, from a multitude of perspectives. When postmodernism was in high fashion, they were understood to evince a quintessentially posthistorical, fragmentary consciousness. Coterminous with the rise of postcolonial studies, his oeuvre dramatizes many of that field's central themes: the quagmire of complicity, the codependence of imperial power, the politics of language, and the gendered, eroticized dynamics of conquest and mastery. Relatedly, Coetzee's novels are frequently read as staging grounds for deconstructive ethics, as this essay will consider. Yet whether refracted through Marxist, Foucauldian, postcolonial, or psychoanalytic thought, Coetzee's writing has been seen to verify a motley assortment of literary criticism and theory's most influential interpretive schools and approaches. If Coetzee thus "writes theory," as Spivak claims, his theory is a promiscuous one that courts an array of diverse methodological investments.

A study of Coetzee's oeuvre and reception accordingly provides an ideal forum for assessing a number of characteristic features, moves, and styles of critique—insofar as critique has represented *a,* if not *the,* dominant approach within literary theory over the past few decades. As a term of art, *critique,* of course, carries conflicting resonances and derives from a vast and complex genealogy that can be traced to sources as different as Kant, biblical exegesis, and Platonic dialogue—the latter of which many Coetzee novels self-consciously mimic. Within literary and cultural studies, critique is usually associated with a hermeneutic that submits the text to interrogation, debunking, and exposure, whether because it is seen as a container for ideology or a puzzle to be decoded or a vehicle for other kinds of unconcealment. The prevalence of such modes of reading has been widely remarked and scrutinized of late, perhaps most notably through the work of Stephen Best and Sharon Marcus, Eve Sedgwick, Rita Felski, and Bruno Latour.[3] It is thus not surprising that Coetzee's theoretically minded readers would bring critique-based methods of interpretation to bear upon his novels. In addition, his writing itself exhibits a range of qualities that can themselves be explained as hallmarks of critique. Not only did Coetzee rise to fame during the ascendency of poststructuralist thought in the Anglo-American academy, but his fiction is itself steeped in the habits of theorizing that academic criticism has naturalized. To make such observations is therefore partly to echo Spivak's diagnosis. But whereas Spivak celebrates Coetzee's distinct brand of creatively profuse theory, Coetzee's writing can also act as a screen reflecting back the insights we as critics are preconditioned to see. Coetzee's theorizing, that is, can feel primed to gratify whatever explanatory paradigms we seek out and already inhabit.

This essay accordingly looks to *The Childhood of Jesus* to sketch a partial portrait of critique, in the process wrestling with different concerns about critique-inflected genres of analysis. At the same time as Coetzee's playfully theoretical fiction has inspired a loyal following among academic readers, it persistently writes back to the same frameworks it solicits, enacting limits and blind spots within those interpretive perspectives. In effect, Coetzee's fiction can appear to conduct self-aware dialogue with the very theoretical models that his critics have most commonly employed to decipher his enigmatic writing. While exemplifying the seductions of theory, his fiction thus equally problematizes a particular, narrow kind of reliance on it.

The Childhood of Jesus is one of Coetzee's more unnerving, perplexing novels— and in an oeuvre filled with haunting and frequently distressing subject matter. In classic fashion for Coetzee, its plot unfolds in an unnamed location at an unspecified historical time, although clues suggest after a large-scale, apocalyptic societal collapse. It follows the misadventures of Simón and the orphaned child David as they arrive in "Novilla," a fledgling state implied to be composed entirely of other displaced persons. Yet what initially resembles a Kafka-esque parable concerning the plight of the refugee soon shifts into a meditation on the ill effects of centralized state planning: Novilla is a near classless society that has eliminated virtually all economic and other competition. Also typical in Coetzee's novels, significant portions of the narrative find Simón and other characters in quasi-philosophical dialogues debating the merits of life in Novilla: its economic structure, its peculiar educational system, its approach to health and safety, and even the ontological status of different bodily functions like "poo." Almost every aspect of Novillan society feels contrived to provoke philosophical questioning and contemplation.

Yet if *The Childhood of Jesus* is a difficult, confounding novel, much of that difficulty surrounds the problem of how it should be read. Indeed, the matter of its own interpretation is, in many ways, what the novel is about. From the outset, even Coetzee's title introduces the quandary of method. As Coetzee explained before a reading in Cape Town in 2012, he had wanted to leave the cover and title page blank, withholding the title until the final page. However, his publisher insisted otherwise, and that ambiguous frame contextualizes and, in turn, complicates *The Childhood of Jesus*'s entire narrative.[4] Deferred or not, what the title does is to flag the dilemma of the novel's interpretation, and through what hermeneutic or theoretical lens(es). As the narrative progresses, both the title's expected correspondence with Coetzee's subject matter and its explanatory relevance are increasingly eroded. Although the plot follows a strange, gifted child named David and is replete with Judeo-Christian allusions, it contains no overt Christ figure. While on the one hand these religious references might affirm the title's salience, on the other the apparent disconnect between title and content activates suspicion over whether it represents a calculated decoy or ploy—or a form of game playing on Coetzee's part. This indeterminacy calls attention to the choices that govern how we read. The title proposes one optic for deciphering the novel's odd plot—an optic that might direct us to biblical exegesis and allegorical styles of reading. However, the text's lack of overall thematic unity raises the question of whether that (Judeo-Christian) label is a red herring. Also presumably arousing a certain discomfort in Coetzee's secular academic readers, this refusal of an organic nexus linking title to plot highlights as well as interrogates the role genre coding can play in predetermining interpretive method. Is Coetzee in fact instructing his readers to treat the novel as a quasi-religious parable or allegory? Is the title (and by extension novel as a whole) to be analyzed as an instance of symbolic language—in other words, as a nonmimetic story that necessarily requires decryption and elucidation? In essence, *The Childhood of Jesus* summons the application of theory even before the reader commences the actual narrative.

Just as the novel's perplexing title problematizes its analysis, pivotal moments in the narrative metafictionally comment on related interpretive dilemmas. When Simón and David first arrive in Novilla, they are assigned to a temporary room in a dormitory for the night. However, the administrator who processes their registration cannot locate either the key to the room or the supervisor who might have it. In an attempt to resolve their predicament, Simón inquires about the existence of a *"llave universal,"* only to be corrected: *"Llave maestra.* There is no such thing as a llave universal. If we had a llave universal all our troubles would be over" (4). No doubt, this dialogue similarly begs for a metaphorical or allegorical reading. Although the administrator chides Simón's desire for a transcendental, universally relevant key, her response acknowledges his yearning and the prospect that a global cipher might in fact exist. This metaphor of a llave universal or llave maestra captures the role of theory for many readers of Coetzee. Like the title, these appeals rouse the reader to quest for a key or code capable of cracking the text's many conundrums. They goad the critic to pursue a methodological (and, arguably, metaphysical) heuristic that can explain the novel's otherworldly, disconcerting elements, which again can appear calculated to elicit near-philosophical speculation. For many, Coetzee's writing has functioned as exactly something to be unraveled, debunked, and deconstructed—in other words, as a prime occasion for critique. One initial explanation for this impulse clearly extends from the philosophical complexity of his thought experiments and their density of citations (to Voltaire, Plato, Goethe, Dante, Kafka, among others in *The Childhood of Jesus*). To fully engage Coetzee's writing one must be a student of not only the Western literary canon but also Jacques Lacan, Jacques Derrida, Emmanuel Levinas, Michel Foucault, and many others.

But while devices like the metaphor of the llave maestra actively court theorization, other features of *The Childhood of Jesus* instead rebuke such a reliance on theory. Over its course, the novel requests a truly diverse range of theories and theorists—although only to complicate and subvert their explanatory relevance. At first blush, its plot encourages the application of various analytics already well familiar within Coetzee criticism. For instance, the scenario of statelessness and exile might prompt the enlistment of Hannah Arendt or Giorgio Agamben's thought. That plot motif, however, quickly fades into the background and is subordinated to other facets of Novillan life. Novillan society is founded on a proto-Marxist creed of unalienated labor and classless coexistence, details that might instead inspire Marxist analysis. But here, too, whatever insight Marxist thought might offer is undercut by other aspects of life in Novilla, like its residents' anemic diets and utter indifference to health and physical safety. Many Novillans occupy their spare time by enrolling in free courses at the local "Institute." Organized around subjects like "Life Drawing," "Weaving," and "Philosophy and Everyday Life," that curriculum might instead evoke recent debates over the value of the humanities (121).

But likewise, such a theoretical vantage point would encounter a dead end, as the Institute's pedagogy doesn't add up to a coherent philosophy of education or humanistic inquiry—at least not in terms that mesh with established scholarly debates.

By no means last, a similarly vexed relationship to theory emerges in the narrative's philosophical digressions, which often voice Simón's rejoinders to the Novillan worldview. Simón complains that its lifestyle is "bloodless" and devoid of "substance" and "weight" (3, 65), and those objections motivate ardent defenses of materiality and embodiment. Simón's philosophical materialism, moreover, seems confirmed by a number of allegorically charged incidents, such as when the character Inés seeks help with a stopped toilet apparently clogged with a sanitary napkin. This bodily obstruction in Novilla's infrastructure incites passionate ruminations by Simón over the ontological status of "poo," with "poo" operating as a suggestive metaphor for larger ideological blockages in Novilla's idealized, sanitized worldview (132–35). However, in the end, Simón's glaring character flaws undermine his principled materialism, in another example of the narrative's destabilization of whatever theoretical llave maestra might appear to unlock its riddle-like details. Recurrently, the novel summons a particular interpretive framework or theoretical conversation only to refuse to deliver on it.

In sum, *The Childhood of Jesus* contains a wealth of what at first appear freighted, instructive signs and allusions holding out the promise of a master theory; yet the narrative consistently refutes the expectation that any given theory or theorist could possibly resolve or explain anything. Precisely this theoretical versatility has been one signature of Coetzee's writing across his oeuvre. His novels frequently give the impression of being crafted in anticipation of their own Norton Critical Editions, equally catered to entries on "psychoanalysis" and "feminist interpretation" and "the novelist and apartheid." Cynically speaking, one reason for Coetzee's acclaim lies precisely with how his writing thus indulges a superabundance of interpretations. This bounty and inexhaustibility has, without question, informed my own pleasure in Coetzee; I feel like I discover something new and unexpected every time I study or teach about him. Coetzee's writing can feel like a bottomless archive of infinite hermeneutic lessons and layers, appeasing the expertise of the critic while productively unsettling it. As an ongoing adventure in learning, unlearning, and relearning, this writing fosters and confirms the plentiful, limitless enterprise of criticism. There is little doubt that Coetzee's cult status has been motored by this never-ending receptivity to theory, or by how his writing both excites and gratifies the hermeneutic impulse. Coetzee's fiction, again and again, demonstrates why we need literary criticism.

However, this theoretical largesse can carry troubling side effects. On one level, it can shore up our faith in theory, and especially in the singular wisdom of particular schools and approaches, whether psychoanalysis, postcolonial theory, or deconstructive accounts of alterity and Otherness. When Coetzee's creative theory mollifies a given metric, it can appear to corroborate it: to affirm its status as a hermeneutic master key. Best and Marcus have raised such questions about the dominance of readings that delve for depth, hiddenness, and repressions within a text,[5] and precisely such modes of analyzing Coetzee's fiction have been widespread. However, the insights thereby divulged can function to consolidate the critic's belief that the hermeneutic tools facilitating that process of decryption are the best, superior, or savvier ones. In other words, the conceit of decoding and demystification seems especially prone to methodological didacticism. As Tim Dean has observed of Slavoj Žižek's thought, such modalities of analysis have the tendency to become "universalizing" lenses that map onto almost anything, setting the critic up to see what she wants to or believes she will see.[6]

On another level, the sheer range and variety of theorizations elicited by Coetzee's fiction alert us to another by-product of critique within literary and cultural studies. The smorgasbord of hermeneutic recipes available to analyze a writer like Coetzee, that is, can turn interpretation into an intellectual exercise or entertainment. Coetzee's writing satisfies a truly eclectic array of theoretical tastes and choices, across the gamut; whatever one's favored theory, Coetzee's writing is almost certain to accommodate if not vindicate it. However, there are real questions about what that profligacy does to the critic's relationship to theory. What happens when the application of theory starts to feel like a game, and a game with predictable outcomes guaranteeing that a given theory will win? Interpretation, it seems, can become too easy, or a fail-safe formula for having one's intellectual predispositions pandered to and ratified. And it can also cultivate self-certainty: an overconfidence in whatever methods a critic might tout as authoritative.

So on the one hand, Coetzee's writing has, for me at least, often felt like an overly responsive and generous sounding board geared to test and, to varying degrees, to confirm whatever chosen theory I bounce off of it. Coetzee's novels, in other words, mirror back my preexisting preoccupations. But on the other hand, Coetzee's writing can itself appear to perform characteristic attributes of much popular theory, especially poststructuralist thought. For while Coetzee's writing appeases the impulse to theorize, it can simultaneously function as something of a hermeneutical hall of smoke and mirrors. Coetzee's creative theorizing can act as a type of decoy or hook: the allure of a master key that won't actually open any worthwhile or meaningful doors. In this respect, one might conclude that Coetzee's fiction simulates or mimics a style otherwise associated with Lacan, or Derrida, or Walter Benjamin (or Spivak's own writing, for that matter) in its refusal of pat, conclusive answers and stable truths. Coetzee's imaginative experiments can follow a "hide the ball" pattern. Precisely when one suspects they've located the master decoder, Coetzee's novels thwart that elusive promise—a refusal that Coetzee criticism frequently explains in terms of ethics. Likewise, while Coetzee's novels indulge an expansive scope of theoretical perspectives, rarely do those perspectives cohere or purvey either clarity or resolution. Inherently self-complicating, almost every Coetzee novel (including *The Childhood of Jesus*) thus concludes on a notoriously indeterminate note. Indeed, for some critics it is precisely this impossibility of closure that both renders interpretation permanent or unending and implicates the reader within that process, transmuting critique into autocritique.

For such reasons is Coetzee a forerunner within a growing corps of twenty-first-century novelists ushering in varied yet arguably Coetzee-esque innovations in the novel. Scholarly discussions of contemporary fiction have been shaped if not dominated by this breed of writer who, like Coetzee, is often self-consciously in dialogue with academic criticism and theory. This recent proliferation of novels, plays, and poems that undertake creative theory akin to Coetzee's represents another manifestation of the prevalence and dominance of what this essay describes as critique-based ways of reading. Building on Mark McGurl's work, that fertile cross-pollination between fiction and theory might be viewed as a natural outcome of the institutionalization and frequent housing of creative writing programs within literature departments.[7] Yet the enthusiasm and playful self-awareness with which many contemporary novelists announce their debts to theory is nonetheless striking. Whether Tom McCarthy, Zadie Smith, Percival Everett, Colson Whitehead, Junot Diaz, Rachel Kushner, Kazuo Ishiguro, China Miéville, or multiple others, these authors conduct vocal and often pointed conversations with their academic commentators. We can think of Smith's barbed rejoinder at the end of *NW* to James Wood's ill-chosen characterization of Smith's writing as "hysterical realism"; McCarthy's knowing nod with *Remainder*'s title to the publishing industry's anxieties about book sales; or how Everett's *Erasure* carries out the very obliteration of black subjectivity that its academic narrator-protagonist rails against. These texts, again like Coetzee's, flout and assail generic barriers in the same move as they enter the realm of theory, here whether via the footnotes accompanying Diaz's *The Brief Wondrous Life of Oscar Wao; Remainder*'s speculative materialism, of which McCarthy is also a philosophical proponent; or the multiple discursive and aesthetic registers of Claudia Rankine's 2014 *Citizen: An American Lyric*. The imprint of theory on these widely discussed texts raises much broader questions about how the theory era has molded and transformed the evolution of the contemporary novel.

In many such critically self-aware texts does the absorption with theory find central expression in allegory. Whitehead's *The Intuitionist* and *Zone One* are often cited for their allegorical resonances; Everett's *Erasure* concludes with a parable-like condemnation of the inability of both popular culture and academe to actualize black consciousness; and the aftereffects of *Remainder*'s unnamed narrator's brain injury find analogues in a range of contemporary phenomena, whether the global financial industry or technology in general. Frequently self-parodying, what allegory also achieves is the implication of the reader. Precisely those plots elements that function allegorically and thus demand analysis enmesh the reader within their problematics, as the activity of interpretation itself works to stage the reader's complicity and, as such, seamlessly mutates into a form of autocritique. Returning to *The Childhood of Jesus*, the entire novel in key ways holds itself out as allegory. In addition to its title, a number of plot devices typically associated with allegory create the impression that it is a fable-like, mythical thought experiment. Its refusal of geographical and historical specificity most immediately has this effect. Coetzee depicts characters with Judeo-Christian names trapped on a type of pilgrimage in a strange land. That land, moreover, is governed by polarized conceptions of the good. Whereas for Simón the odd Novillan worldview begets philosophy, his speculative digressions are adjudicated by specific narrative events that equally gesture toward allegory.

As this volume's introduction also argues, allegorical reading is in many ways itself characteristic of critique as a genre. In turn, some recent attempts to rethink method have focused on allegory, in effect taking allegorical analysis to exemplify larger tendencies within literary theory. For instance, Best and Marcus's defense of surface reading begins with an extended discussion of Fredric Jameson's thought, wherein Jameson comes to embody both the opportunities and shortcomings of symptomatic reading.[8] Within postcolonial studies (the main categorization of Coetzee's writing), the modalities of allegorical interpretation naturalized by Jameson have incited particular contention. Indeed, Coetzee himself was famously castigated by fellow Nobel Prize–winner Nadine Gordimer for relying on allegory. For Gordimer, not only do Coetzee's allegories mask historical context in depoliticizing ways, but they also divert attention from the "daily, grubby tragic consequences" of events.[9] In a 1987 essay in *Social Text*, Aijaz Ahmad notoriously attacked Jameson's use of allegory along analogous lines; for Ahmad, this approach both homogenizes geographic specificity and absolutizes difference as Otherness.[10] Relatedly, postcolonial theorists have complained that allegorical criticism imposes reductive, totalizing understandings on the underlying sociopolitical realities being depicted that, in the process, reinforce the myopia and self-reference of the Westernized critic's gaze.[11] As allegorical reading subsumes a text or texts within a single explanatory grid, it can thereby furnish the illusion of interpretative mastery.

For such reasons can the spirit of allegory within Coetzee's fiction help us contend with its larger workings within literary criticism and theory. As I've suggested, in *The Childhood of Jesus* Coetzee's deployment of allegory (along with related devices, namely metaphor) both solicits theory and permits the copious theorization for which Coetzee's corpus is renowned. If Coetzee's allegories are rich and compelling, it is because they are sufficiently open-ended yet complex to reward a miscellaneous mix of theoretical perspectives. They resist being pinned down or wedded to a finite, readily discernible set of meanings or heuristics—which is one reason studying Coetzee can feel like an endless odyssey of discovery. This versatility has been celebrated as the basic essence of modern allegory. However, the implications of Coetzee's allegories, akin to the metafictional play of other contemporary authors, can be doubled and ambivalent. Like his creative theory overall, Coetzee's allegories often work to destabilize or trouble whatever insights they initially afford, complicating allegorical styles of reading even as they requisition them. Here again, the figure of the llave maestra is instructive: as a metaphor, it invites the allegorical mode while simultaneously rebuffing it. That very duality, to be sure, has itself been prized as valuable, as for some readers allegory ultimately offers a lesson in the indeterminacies and "impossibility of reading," to evoke Paul de Man's terms.[12]

Nonetheless, the prevalence of what resemble allegories within Coetzee's writing also alert us to the limits of such an analytic. On one level, the markers of allegory provoke readings that pursue enigmas or deeper truths ripe for decipherment, opening up, and adumbration, as Coetzee's dense allusions and philosophy-driven thought experiments similarly motivate. But on another level (and as others have remarked), such interpretive agendas not only can fuel desires for interpretive mastery (implicating the critic within a colonizing project akin to the one Coetzee's novels otherwise deconstruct) but also can sanction a blinkered analytic focus. After all, any choice of method privileges certain properties and energies of literature while demoting and downplaying others. The question, then, is whether Coetzee's creative theory (like that of other contemporary writers) encourages such circumscribing, narrowing effects, and of what nature. By prompting modes of analysis aimed at decoding and demystification, does the impulse toward allegory overshadow other dimensions of literary form, aesthetics, and experience? Does the allegorical mode facilitate certain kinds of insight and engagement while foreclosing others?

Moreover, Coetzee's plentiful allegories can risk transforming the hermeneutic enterprise into a kind of game. As with the oddities of Novillan life, Coetzee's allegories can seem readymade or staged, contrived to interface with highly specific debates and preoccupations within theory. Some of the enjoyment of reading Coetzee, no doubt, extends from this sense of assembling a puzzle, or of successfully matching interpretive model with underlying pattern, structure, or scheme. I've already questioned whether such an approach to theory can become self-confirmatory, validating whatever paradigms a critic already espouses or is primed to discover. The irony of Coetzee's ostensible theoretical eclecticism, then, is that it has produced not merely an unusual volume of Coetzee criticism (even relative to other widely acclaimed contemporary writers) but a series of rather predictable, routinized interpretations—of which deconstructive ethics remains perhaps the most prevalent. Coetzee's popularity thus illustrates how and why critique-based styles of reading are just as likely to consolidate as to unsettle a critic's preformed methodological goals and expectations, even while the labor of exposure and unmasking purveys the impression of both hermeneutic revelation and self-scrutiny.

This is all to say that *The Childhood of Jesus* is itself an allegory of reading, although one that simultaneously problematizes such methods of analysis. Related allegories of reading and writing alike suffuse Coetzee's oeuvre, often offering self-reflexive commentaries on the stakes of authorship as well as criticism. These metafictional episodes frequently occasion the autocritique that has become de rigueur, chastening the critic for complicity with the very structures of domination and exploitation that Coetzee's novels interrogate.

To recall an earlier text, a highly memorable crucible of this type occurs in Coetzee's 1980 *Waiting for the Barbarians*. In an unnerving scene, the novel's protagonist, an unnamed Magistrate, meticulously examines the naked body of a tortured "barbarian" girl, as he strives in vain to comprehend her abuse.[13] The fact that the Magistrate is a representative of law only renders his scrutiny all the more invasive. Moreover, his act of reading and interpretation conspicuously revisits the torturer's violence, indicting the law's collusion with those wrongs as his treatment of the girl replays her original victimization.[14] But as the Magistrate reads the girl's body—like a text—for the signs and markers of torture, *Waiting for the Barbarians* parallels the critic's act of reading with his actions, incriminating the critic within the Magistrate's dubious desires. The novel thus sets the reader up, like the Magistrate, to quest for clues to decipher and decode. At once, however, it impugns that impulse, exposing it to be not so distant from the enabling logic of imperial violence. *Waiting for the Barbarians*, of course, deals with the extreme case of literature aspiring to lend aesthetic representation to torture. Nonetheless, the scene's implicit cautionary tale raises troubling questions about allegorical habits of reading in general.

This insistence on the ideological and other compromises that color the activity of criticism has been especially pronounced within postcolonial studies. Spivak's entire corpus, in a way, conducts an extended negotiation of the many snares of complicity, as they play out within politics, one's own methodological commitments, and a deconstructive awareness of the basic slipperiness and unpredictability of linguistic reference and meaning. For such reasons is postcolonial theory itself, for Spivak, both necessarily dependent on and forged in protracted self-examination.[15] However, one set of recent objections to the dominance of critique decries this emphasis on shame and guilt. As Jacques Rancière observes, shame becomes compulsory, not only rendering auto- or self-critique an inexhaustible mandate but also inadvertently valorizing self-recrimination as a form of therapy.[16] The identification of one's own complicity, in other words, becomes enshrined as a crucial step in the interpretive process—a step that has been particularly compulsory in readings of Coetzee.

Many of the foregoing dynamics become especially vivid when *The Childhood of Jesus* is approached through deconstructive ethics: that is to say, a form of ethical analysis shaped by wariness of norms, stable truths, and formalized moral systems and often closely allied with the thought of Derrida, Levinas, Lyotard, and Bataille, among others. Spivak's focus on complicity likewise derives from her investment in a deconstructive ethics. While as a theoretical approach ethics might not seem to be targeted at critique, it, too, claims such a lineage. Typically in ethics-oriented readings, the critic mines the text for signs of radical Otherness or alterity excluded from the dominant legal, political, or symbolic order. The value of such alterity lies in fulfilling multiple functions: it interrogates a text's representational exclusions and foreclosures, implicitly critiquing those limits; in the process, it discloses more totalizing structures of oppression; it subverts the subject position of the reader/critic, exposing his or her unwitting complicity with those structures; and it forecasts ethical renewal, while underscoring both the impossibility and necessary deferral of any and all such resolution. The ethical encounter accordingly becomes one of both rupture and disclosure, but without finality. Within Coetzee's novels, the emergence of alterity (whether embodied in *Waiting for the Barbarian*'s tortured barbarian girl or the titular character of *Life and Times of Michael K* or the lame dog in *Disgrace*) is frequently staged through the perspective of proxies whose blindnesses and complicities, as we've seen with the Magistrate, mirror those of the reader/critic. Like Simón in *The Childhood of Jesus*, the narrative's focalization through a conspicuously compromised, flawed character reinforces these parallels.

Seeing as it gestures toward hope and promise, a deconstructive ethics has often been actively opposed to suspicious or critique-based hermeneutics, especially when employed in the service of Marxist or Foucauldian thought. However, I want to argue that there are nonetheless key features of deconstructive brands of ethics that both inherit and emulate the logic of critique. Even though the ethical event is pregnant with redemptive potential, it is overshadowed with some of the fatalism of a purely negative, oppositional hermeneutic. The goal of unconcealment, for instance, typically gains value because of how it subverts and by extension interrogates the existing sociopolitical or symbolic order, requiring a stance of suspicion toward the status quo. As a vector for ethics, what constitutes Otherness is likewise its antagonism with the rule, norm, and dominant. What this means, however, is that alterity is never an inherent property of something but dependent on particular histories and contexts that cry out for ethical alternatives. In turn, radical alterity will exist only when there are exclusionary background circumstances that its arrival can expose and disrupt: domination, totalization, and oppression represent baseline realities necessary to engender ethical disclosure.[17] As a consequence, deconstructive ethics can follow a pattern of reasoning that Robyn Wiegman attributes to critique more generally. For Wiegman, critique is frequently hamstrung by "the sheer incongruity of trying to dislodge the authority of an object while training one's attention on it";[18] the basic argumentative logic of critique necessitates the very realities or situations it denounces as unjust or oppressive. A version of Wiegman's concern pertains to much theory in the vein of deconstructive ethics. Frequently, alterity paradoxically acquires its essential and resistant properties vis-à-vis the underlying "objects" it promises to "dislodge," although only to concentrate the critical gaze on those unethical conditions all the more intently and, in the process, to reify them.

Another common feature of a deconstructive ethics involves the view that the ultimate payoff of the ethical encounter, despite its provisional illumination, must remain deferred or adjourned until an unnamed future. Some have therefore characterized deconstructive ethics as a weak messianism or negative theology. If we consider what I've described as the inherently oppositional, subversive qualities of Otherness, we can see why this would be the case: incorporating Otherness into the established terms of the existing sociopolitical order— thereby normalizing it—would divest Otherness of its capacities for resistance, subversion, and unconcealment. Hence, Otherness must be, in Derrida's idiom, "impossible," "incalculable," "untranslatable," and "aporetic," just as for Derrida it carries the aura of a secret or crypt.[19] These qualities inscribe Otherness and ethics within a futuristic or messianic temporality, as is captured by Derrida's notion of the "democracy-to-come." In order to preserve its ethical status, Otherness must constitutively defy not only practical realization in the here-and-now but also full linguistic and other symbolization. Along with ethics, Derrida understands justice, hospitality, forgiveness, testimony, and democracy in analogous terms. Yet as variants of what Eve Sedgwick referred to as "dramas of exposure,"[20] ethical readings have cultivated their own fixation on limits, impossibilities, foreclosures, and exclusions—given how the divulgence of those limits is pivotal to the ethical encounter.

From a political vantage point, there are other reasons many formulations of ethics should give pause. I've argued that the ethical promise of illumination is typically undercut by deep negativity and even fatalism. Even more, work on ethics can seem to undertake critique only to guarantee that it be devoid of real-world, normative outcomes. The futuristic, deferred temporality of a deconstructive ethics strategically short-circuits any attempt to enlist Otherness to mete out concrete, instrumental, or pragmatic goals or effects. The cordons of the "impossible," "incalculable," and "untranslatable" can thus have the effect of enclosing ethics within the imaginative domain of theory and aesthetics. To be sure, there are important justifications (historical and philosophical) for this quarantine of ethics, and those justifications further speak to vital characteristics of both justice and literary-aesthetic experience alike, which often do proceed through meaningful kinds of rupture and unconcealment. Nonetheless, there remain troubling concerns about whether these metrics can render critique little more than an imaginative exercise. While ethical readings often navigate eminently political questions, those problematics and their insights can feel strangely confined to the realm of the text. We can similarly observe this tendency in the frequent emphasis on singularity. That insistence on the exemplary, exceptional nature of the ethical encounter creates a separation between ethics/justice and the familiar, commonplace, habitual, and day-to-day. A deconstructive ethics, as a result, can implicitly deny ordinary actors in routine situations the capacity for ethical action (recalling Gordimer's critique of Coetzee's allegories). Ethics can thus appear to reside within a strikingly privileged, rarefied sphere, antiseptically cut off from the messiness of real-world action and decision making. Lauded for its radicalness, the core qualities of ethics (singularity, deferral, impossibility, untranslability) can come worrisomely close to providing rationales for withdrawal or inertia.

Importantly, most variants of deconstructive ethics extend from semiotic or language-based analysis and are therefore grounded in specific theories of representation. This connection further raises questions about the legacy of the linguistic turn,[21] and we can look to Derrida's intertwined theories of politics and language to grasp certain of those implications. In his classic "Force of Law" (1990), a text often credited with inaugurating the "political turn" in deconstructive theory, Derrida explicitly models ethics on the chains of signification that comprise a written text. Derrida claims not only that matters of justice are the "most proper place" for "studies of deconstructive style" but also that deconstruction has always already been about justice.[22] This nexus is one that his late writings frequently revisit. For instance, in *Rogues: Two Essays on Reason* (2005), a democracy-to-come is defined equivalently: "This renvoi of democracy is thus still very much related to différance. Or if you prefer, this democracy as the sending off of the putting off, as the emission of remission [*envoi du renvoi*], sends us or refers us back [*renvoie*] to différance. But not only to différance as deferral, as the turn of a detour [*tour du détour*], as a path that is turned aside [*voie détournée*], as adjournment in the economy of the same."[23] Derrida thus links his vision of democracy-to-come to the slippages and infinite, unpredictable mediations that govern writing, which defy the "logocentrism" of "metaphysics of presence" and self-same, immanent, and transparent meaning. In so doing, Derrida defines democracy, along with other relatedly ethical precepts, as regulated by analogous dynamics as those that structure a text, further highlighting the negativity latent within a deconstructive ethics. Just as deconstructive theories of textual reference set out to complicate and dispel ideas about the unity, transcendence, and self-evidence of textual meaning and "truth," so, too, does ethics-oriented criticism deconstruct views about the natural, essential, organic, and self-evident. We can thus again discern the central part played by critique within a deconstructive ethics. Despite the pretext of messianic hope stimulating the ethical encounter, it is almost invariably colored by a mood of suspicion that, furthermore, can culminate with a sense of either impossibility or failure.

There are other disturbing ways that the scene of ethics can replay the colonial encounter—returning us to the Magistrate's treatment of the barbarian girl. Insofar as Otherness is defined by its refusal of normalization or assimilation, those oppositional qualities can have the effect of further focusing the critical gaze on the Other, intensifying whatever fascination that figure may elicit. In essence, the "romance of singularity and negativity" that Jose Muñoz described as motoring much theory can endow alterity with a tantalizingly foreign aura.[24] Relatedly, the category of Otherness can become inflected with what Anne Cheng calls the continued "critical sway of the ethnographic imagination."[25] The basic properties of ethics—impossibility, untranslatability, indeterminacy, exemplarity—inadvertently become projected onto those lives seen to epitomize Otherness, rather than being confined to the ethical event per se. In turn, the premise that Otherness inherently resists incorporation is worrisome: it can smuggle in assumptions reminiscent of other colonialist and paternalistic prejudices and stereotypes. A hermeneutic preoccupation with unknowability and difference can consequently inculcate not only a fetishization of those traits but also the perception that cultural difference and exclusion are innate and insurmountable. In other words, the very "economies of the same" that demand deconstruction to begin with can become reintroduced through the interpretive categories brought to bear upon them.

Before returning to Coetzee's novel, many deconstructive formulations of ethics privilege literature, art, and aesthetics. Although the ethical demand may be triggered by real world scenarios, ethics is often hallowed as the special provenance of the literary—or what Derek Attridge calls the "singularity of literature."[26] Attridge defines ethics as *the* overriding goal of art; the very essence of literature is to "[hold] out the possibility of a repeated encounter with alterity."[27] Often, this emphasis on the literary mounts a defense of literature's divergence from and superiority over other registers of discourse (law, politics, science, economics, and so forth). Whereas positivist, truth-oriented systems of thought reinforce stable, universal, normative, and authoritative principles and rules, the recognitions furnished by literature are irreducibly multiple, mutable, fragmentary, and inconclusive (like Coetzee's allegories). While other disciplines and their rhetorics fortify totalizing, unitary, and hence oppressive knowledge systems, the literariness celebrated by deconstructionists like Attridge is heralded for suspending views about the natural and essential, undermining legalities, resisting instrumentalism, and flouting nonconstructivist conceptions of truth. Here again, literature is singular in part because it enacts critique. But such accounts of the ethics of literature rely on a rather deceptive binary. Literature and ethics are functionally immunized against or insulated from the inevitable errors tainting political life—precisely because literary texts dramatize their own failures, limitations, aporias, and lack of guarantees. In Coetzee's novels, the many parables of complicity that populate them are thus commonly explained as inoculating the literary against the dual threats of rationalism and instrumentalism. However, this equation secures the ethical value of literature and art against the backdrop of oppressive structural conditions and through the perceived danger of those modes of reasoning and discourse understood to shore such conditions up. Many such justifications for literature accordingly exhibit a degree of idealism, marshaling their own conceptions of the relative autonomy of the work of art.

In *The Childhood of Jesus*, young David invites interpretation as a figure for the Other often central to a deconstructive ethics. As the narrative progresses, David's developmental woes dominate the other plot threads. He is highly resistant to Novilla's normalizing educational system and repeatedly misbehaves in school, eventually inciting a state attempt to take over his parenting. After he is temporarily interned in a reform school and a state custodial battle, Simón and Inés enter a truce predicated on a type of collaborative stewardship over him. To avoid David's confinement, they collectively flee into exile beyond the borders of Novillan society, an odyssey deemed to found the "family of David" (260). However, Simón and Inés's devotion to David is depicted as exceeding the customary bounds of parentage and instead inspired by David's unusual traits and gifts. Plot incidents show David to be both a charismatic leader and a potentially rebellious outcast—much like radical accounts of the biblical Christ. What's more, Simón and Inés repeatedly debate their allegiance to David in the language of faith and belief. As Inés chides Simón: "You don't really believe in the child. You don't know what it means to believe" (232).

Of even greater significance, David's genius seems to derive from his extraordinary relationship to signs, texts, and interpretation. He mysteriously learns to read and write without instruction, apart from catechistic repetitions of *Don Quixote* (another of his literary forebears) with Simón, and, like Simón, he conflates figural with literal meanings. A deeply philosophical thinker, David recurrently wrestles with quasi-metaphysical dilemmas, many of which ensue from his confusion of factual or realistic statements with metaphor and allegory. At one point, he is distressed that he might "fall through a crack in the paving" (35), and he later frets about what happens "when the numbers open up and you fall" (226). David's refusal to take signs at face value thus defies customary, normative ways of reading and seeing, rendering him a compelling spokesperson for the inseparably interruptive and transformative capacities of art and literature.

While David masks his talents, even his punitive teacher seizes on his peculiar relationship to signs, although wrongly attributing it to a "specific deficit linked to symbolic activities" (205). As a disciplinary test, his teacher instructs him to write the phrase "I must tell the truth" over and over again on the blackboard; however, David substitutes it with the assertion "*Yo soy la verdad*, I am the truth" (225). This gesture recalls countless other passages in *The Childhood of Jesus* that exploit slippages between factual versus figural or metaphorical statements. Akin to the allegorical resonances of motifs like the llave universal or "poo," David's claim creates, for Coetzee's readers, an explicitly hermeneutic or interpretive dilemma. On the one hand, we're inclined to be suspicious of David's grandiosity, just as his behavior cements his expulsion from school. Even while David's symbolically loaded claim might seem to transport the narrative into the realm of allegory, its sheer preposterousness and narcissism forestall such a reading. Coetzee almost seems to taunt his academic readers: "I dare you to imbue David's claim with larger figural meaning and content."

But on the other hand, David's assertion does capture the basic essence of what literature and art do, which is to deal in symbols, figures, metaphors, and other imaginative experiments that test the boundaries of the true and the real. So David's behavior, in a way, crystallizes larger interpretive premises that inform how we read. One natural response is to view David's pronouncement with skepticism: to doubt his adoptive parents' belief, to dismiss him as a mere fib-telling child, and perhaps to feel irritation with Coetzee for once again baiting us to vest the novel's tritely religious, ethnocentric title with serious explanatory weight. David's statement almost feels designed to trigger academic recoil. However, the reader's quandary simultaneously extends from that fact that sustaining such a response would implicitly permit the novel's imaginative experiment to collapse. In other words, pure hermeneutic suspicion would mean giving up faith not only in David and Coetzee but also in the world-altering, visionary capacities of art and literature.

Precisely this dilemma, then, returns us to the status of critique: to both its opportunities and its limits. One frequent complaint has been that an overreliance on critique can shut down, constrain, or impoverish the kinds of interpretations facilitated by engagement with a text. However, to enlist the lens of critique also means to harness one's discontent with merely literalist, referential analysis—burgeoning and multiplying the meanings that lie below surface or transparent levels of signification. Paul Ricoeur described what he referred to as the "two poles" of interpretation. One is the school of suspicion, which he famously explained as dominated by "three masters": Marx, Nietzsche, and Freud. This pole aims at "demystification" or the "reduction of illusions"—hence, it is the pole that would view David's exorbitant assertion skeptically. For Ricoeur, the other pole approaches the logic of double meanings very differently: interpretation instead represents a call to listen in ways aimed at either a manifestation or restoration of meaning.[28] On first blush, David's strange hermeneutics seems to thus polarize: to face the reader with a stark choice between either suspicious dismissal or a quest for symbolic plenitude. But precisely that polarity seems to be what is broken down within the novel. David's unusual relationship to signs and symbols instead necessitates the equal and simultaneous reliance on—or straddling of—what Ricoeur explained as two competing hermeneutic modes. No doubt, this is exactly what many deconstructive accounts of ethics do, and where much of their value lies: they carry out a balancing act, critiquing while yet preserving faith in the near-theological capacities of signs to infinitely proliferate unexpected significance. Because giving up on David also entails giving up on literature, *The Childhood of Jesus* seems to test, more than anything, the bounds of how far we're willing to go to safeguard and maintain that faith. It may feel like Coetzee is playing games with us, but he has a point: what if consent to David's naive, self-indulgent claim is also the prerequisite for gaining entrance into the life of the imagination?

In short, it is understandable that readers (including this one) would approach David as yet another figure for the Otherness that has provided fodder for so many ethical readings of Coetzee's novels. The impossible, untranslatable belief that he inspires, as well as the singular, exemplary truth he claims to incarnate, certainly do appear perfectly constructed to elicit such a reading. Yet I'd like to argue that *The Childhood of Jesus*'s relationship to a deconstructive ethics—in key ways *the* "chosen" metric for reading Coetzee—is far more conflictual and ambivalent. In fact, the novel culminates with a cautionary tale that more accurately forewarns against the styles of reading we might associate with ethics. The novel's conclusion accordingly provides another, arguably even more barbed and pointed example of the vexed role of theory in Coetzee's writing: his seeming tendency to solicit the application of a given framework only to refute or undermine it. To such ends is the title's messianic promise simultaneously actualized and thwarted by way of the novel's concluding incident—an incident, not coincidentally, involving another manifestation of David's uncanny approach to interpreting signs.

In its own mini-allegory of sorts, this incident finds David's metaphorical thinking getting him into serious trouble. As a parting gift from a friend, David receives a "magic cloak of invisibility" alleged to cause "the earthly body [to] vanish into the mirror leaving only the traceless spirit behind." Accompanied by a letter, the present instructs him to set a white powder on fire in order to activate the transformative process (266). This gift, however, is exposed as a cruel trick when the powder erupts in an explosion that literally blinds David. However, instead of shrouding David in darkness, that injury produces magnificent visions of "green light" and "cascades of stars" that "enthrall" him. David at first thinks that he is "inside the mirror" and later believes that he "can see the whole world" (267–69). Here, David's usual mode of reading is inverted: a text that should have been purely figural and imaginary produces material, physical results that outright wound him. But this injury simultaneously represents an extreme materialization of a condition that has afflicted David all along. As Simón informs the doctor, his son "can't see properly" (271); from the outset David has refused to blithely "see" the world in the normative, socially mandated, incurious ways prescribed by Novillan society. Precisely this improper vision is why David begs to be read as a proponent of the singular, exemplary, and metaphomorphic energies of literature.

Yet David's predicament is, not surprisingly by now, far more complex. Through his injury, the traffic between the literal and the metaphorical at stake in symbolic language is not only reversed but tragically so, laying bare hazards of David's (and the critic's) overly indulgent relationship to metaphor and allegory. Regardless of our conclusions about how to interpret David's character, the implication is that he and his parents take figures and symbols too far and aren't suspicious enough: their faith in David and his visionary capacities (as well as in the trustworthiness of their gift-giving friend) backfires. Ironically, it is David's penchant for allegory that proves perilous; at once, that very outcome itself invites allegorization—presumably, as still another allegory of reading. Or, we might say, as an allegory of the perils and pitfalls of allegorical analysis. So what, then, should we make of David's violent wounding?

For one, the "enthralling" visions conjured by David's free play with metaphor lure him into a state of isolation and self-reference, sanctioning his retreat into the self-sustaining operations of the mind (or, in the text's terms, into the safety of what's "inside the mirror"). His enchantment with the figural powers of signs cuts him off from the world, even inuring him to his own bodily suffering. David's injury produces a kind of idealism that is not only antimaterialist but also egoistical and self-certain, since he further believes that he can "see" the entirety of existence. David, that is, begins to sound a lot like Novilla's malnourished philosophers. Paradoxically unchastened by the accident, he is increasingly confident in the singularity of his insight, such as when he attempts to "save" his treating physician by recruiting the doctor to join the family's exodus. David's revelatory visions, in short, attune him neither to other people's needs nor to his own vulnerability.

Some recent critiques of critique have argued that an overinvestment in critique-based analysis can result in exactly such cognitivist neglect of embodiment, or what Adam Frank and Eve Sedgwick described as an "automatic antibiologism" that, I'll suggest, parallels David's.[29] Here, it is not accidental that David's injury stems from a scene of interpretation and reading, given how a related complaint about critique as a method arraigns its textualist derivation from semiotic analysis, as for deconstruction.[30] Language-based models of critique, critics argue, are rooted in antimaterialist, bloodless conceptions of human subjectivity and consciousness that "blind" them (like David) to the self-present experiential realities of the body.[31] As Sara Ahmed puts it, a "fetishism of figures" can divert attention from material "histories of determination" and context.[32] Ahmed therefore calls for a focus on "*inter-embodiment, whereby the lived experience of embodiment is always already the social experience of dwelling with other bodies.*"[33] Routing David's blindness through these theoretical debates, of course, far from either diagnoses his condition or resolves those debates' ultimate merits. Nonetheless, it's tempting to explain David's isolation and self-enclosure at the novel's end as a warning against the very schools of theory that have fueled Coetzee's academic acclaim and popularity.

Likewise, it's hard to escape the fact that David's insights result from—and hence actively require—his violent injury. That violence, perhaps more than anything, enacts a pointed challenge to the title's (and Coetzee's) promise of messianic redemption and illumination. The spiritual pilgrimages evoked by *The Childhood of Jesus*'s title typically culminate with such spiritual plenitude, as does the usual denouement of the disclosure at stake within a deconstructive ethics. However, those expected endpoints are—once again—pointedly refused, just as any yearning for closure is sorely rebuked. We must note, furthermore, that David's enchanting visions are forged in a relay of blindness and insight that itself "mirrors" the methodology of much theory, including much theory grounded in critique. It's certainly appealing to extol that blindness as the enabling condition for David's enhanced awareness, which would also serve to congratulate our labor of negative exposure as literary theorists. Such a move, however, comes dangerously close to justifying—if not outright glorifying—the underlying violence of David's wounded and wounding circumstances.

This essay has attempted to raise analogous concerns about critique, particularly those variants at issue in a deconstructive ethics. Above all, the worry is that such theoretical metrics can inadvertently valorize the very baseline realities that they define themselves against. In *The Childhood of Jesus*, blindness and insight are not opposed but intimately dependent on one another; they are coconstitutive and mutually formative. Critique similarly requires something negative, unjust, oppressive, or unknowing to critique, or it loses its basic mission and raison d'être. Without forms of relative blindness to diagnose, demystify, dismantle, and deconstruct, critique has no purpose. The problem is not that this renders theory a secondary, derivative, or reactionary activity, although it can and sometimes does. The problem is likewise not that critique is a contradictory undertaking: an activity that relies on the very phenomena it resists. Rather, the fear is that negativity and negation are almost uniformly predicates to and spurs for our labors as critics, and training our attention on those adverse qualities can both naturalize and acclimate us to them. Or even worse, it can unwittingly entrench and enshrine the very things we aim to protest.

This, in essence, is why David's blindness throws a wrench in our theory. The novel invites us to endow his wounds with some kind of hermeneutic significance or deeper symbolic import—just as I'm doing now. But as theorists, how do we begin either to fathom or to explain David's injury without reifying or romanticizing it? How do we avoid transposing his literal and figural blindness onto actual, material realities in ways that cause them to appear somehow unavoidable or incurable or even necessary, deciphering his blindness as a symptom of larger, institutionalized structures of Othering and failed representation? How do we avoid rationalizing David's fate as an inevitable or potentially fruitful step in the impossible labor of justice and ethics? In short, can we account for what we do as critics and theorists in terms that don't somehow need or begin with conditions of blindness akin to David's?

There are many reasons for Coetzee's enormous popularity as a combined writer-critic-theorist, and his novels' dialogue with theory certainly represents one. As what Spivak dubs "a creative writer of theory," Coetzee and his oeuvre have donned many of the different guises and garbs of critique, in the process likewise illustrating how the theory era has shaped developments in the evolution of the novel. Coetzee's fiction, I've argued, encourages us to look to theory as something of a llave maestra: a cipher capable of decrypting the many allegories, allusions, and hermeneutic puzzles staged within his novels. This impulse to decode is one hallmark of a critique-based hermeneutic, hence a common method within contemporary literary criticism. However, Coetzee's abundant incorporation of theory into his fiction can, at times, make the call to theorize feel like a game: a game that ultimately makes sport of Coetzee's readers. Within *The Childhood of Jesus*, Coetzee's writing solicits the application of theory only to confound theorization. This is especially true of the novel's frequent invitations to read allegorically, or to refract particular plot incidents and details through a metaphorical or allegorical lens. Yet the novel requisitions allegory only to expose the explanatory errors and blockages (whether those blockages resemble "poo" or something less noxious) that constrain such modes of interpretation. Just as the many philosophical digressions in Coetzee's novels turn out, more often than not, to be dead ends, so, too, can the various theoretical approaches that his fiction courts come to appear as diversions or false leads.

One might therefore conclude that Coetzee provokes theory only to dramatize the stranglehold any given metric can exert on the limitless possibilities of interpretation. Yet the sheer panoply of analytics summoned by Coetzee's writing is separately instructive, since they can appear to vie with one another for authority. That theoretical playfulness and prodigality is itself one clear factor informing academic devotion to Coetzee, given how his promiscuous enlistment of theory can be, as for me, a source of boundless pleasure. At the same time, however, this onus to theorize can cajole our expertise only to leave us embattled. For Coetzee creatively theorizes in ways that put intractable pressure on the methodological assumptions that guide how and why we read. Coetzee's novels, that is, can resemble a hall of mirrors that at first verify whatever theories we expect to see although only to reflect them back to us warped and perverted.

For such reasons can the funhouse of Coetzee's creative theory tell us a lot about the current climate of methodological rethinking and recalibration, which this volume takes stock of. For Coetzee's seeming eclecticism can ultimately leave one feeling ambivalent. On the one hand, Coetzee's theoretically dense and allusive writing gratifies the academic critic in ways that are delicious and enthralling. No doubt, this is why so many love Coetzee. But on the other hand, chasing his narratives' innumerable false leads can become fatiguing. Theorizing Coetzee can feel like an infinite journey through endless detours around strategic decoys, a journey that many, I expect, would cite as exactly the point. But when does that degree of gamesmanship turn criticism into a parade of gimmicks and ploys? When all is said and done, is Coetzee setting us up? Whatever weariness Coetzee (and Coetzee criticism) induces thus seems to echo a more pervasive mood within theory—a mood that equally responds to disappointments, roadblocks, and dead ends.

A range of explanations has recently been offered for why critique is running out of steam, to invoke Latour's much-cited formulation. The character David also embodies this crisis of faith in theory. The nature of the theory era was likewise to inspire frequently exorbitant confidence and belief. For the past few decades, the profession has experienced overwhelming faith in theory: faith, like David, that theory can "save" us as well as allow us to "see the whole world." The question, then, is whether and when that faith became excessive. We can all remember our self-identifications in graduate school, when being a "card-carrying [Marxist] or [Lacanian] or [Coetzee person] or [what have you]" was what we prided ourselves on. But we've also witnessed doctrinaire allegiances to particular schools of theory (or to the latest political cause célèbre) serve as grounds for policing, whether in hiring, scholarship, or promotion. Allegiance to theory has motivated some of the academy's most puritanical and zealous attacks. Our faith in theory, in other words, has too often masqueraded as a privileged claim to truth, or at least a favored ground for demystifying it. It's no wonder that such certitude in theory would become tiring or tedious: something itself in want of unmasking. Especially when—as for David—theory blinds us not only to the people around us but also to the challenges of existing in the real world.

Notes

1   J. M. Coetzee, *The Childhood of Jesus* (New York: Penguin, 2014). Further quotations from this work will be cited parenthetically in the text.

2   Gayatri Spivak, "Lie Down in the Karoo: An Antidote to the Anthropocene," *Public Books*, June 1, 2014.

3   Stephen Best and Sharon Marcus, "Surface Reading: An Introduction," *Representations* 108, no. 1 (fall 2009): 1–21; Rita Felski, *The Limits of Critique* (Chicago: Chicago University Press, 2015); Bruno Latour, "Has Critique Run Out of Steam? From Matters of Fact to Matters of Concern," *Critical Inquiry* 30, no. 2 (winter 2004): 225–48; Adam Frank and Eve Kosofsky Sedgwick, "Shame in the Cybernetic Fold: Reading Silvan Tomkins," *Critical Inquiry* 21, no. 2 (winter 1995): 496–522; Eve Kosofsky Sedgwick, *Touching Feeling: Affect, Pedagogy, Performativity* (Durham, NC: Duke University Press, 2003).

4   Jason Farago, "J. M. Coetzee's Stunning New Novel Shows What Happens When a Nobel Winner Gets Really Weird," *New Republic*, September 14, 2013.

5   For example, see Best and Marcus, "Surface Reading."

6   See "Art as Symptom: Žižek and the Ethics of Psychoanalytic Criticism," *diacritics* 32, no. 2 (2002): 22. See also Frank and Sedgwick, "Shame in the Cybernetic Fold," 512; Ruth Leys, "The Turn to Affect: A Critique," *Critical Inquiry* 37 (spring 2011).

7   Mark McGurl, *The Program Era: Postwar Fiction and the Rise of Creative Writing* (Cambridge, MA: Harvard University Press, 2009).

8   See Best and Marcus, "Surface Reading," 5.

9   Nadine Gordimer, "The Idea of Gardening," *New York Review of Books*, February 2, 1984, 3, 6; for such a critique of Coetzee, see also Abdul R. JanMohamed, "The Economy of Manichean Allegory: The Function of Racial Difference in Colonialist Literature," *Critical Inquiry* 12, no. 1 (1985): 73.

10 Aijaz Ahmad, "Jameson's Rhetoric of Otherness and the 'National Allegory,'" *Social Text* 17 (autumn 1987): 3–25, 10.

11 For the former, see Gayatri Spivak, *Critique of Postcolonial Reason: Toward a History of the Vanishing Present* (Cambridge, MA: Harvard University Press, 1999). See also JanMohamed, "The Economy of Manichean Allegory."

12 Paul de Man, *Allegories of Reading: Figural Language in Rousseau, Nietzsche, Rilke, and Proust* (New Haven, CT: Yale University Press, 2002), 205.

13 Some Coetzee scholars have disputed that such a passage should be read allegorically. See Derek Attridge, *J. M. Coetzee and the Ethics of Reading: Literature in the Event* (Chicago: University of Chicago Press, 2004).

14 Work on trauma has widely contended with how legal procedures can retraumatize a victim in their efforts to master and contain past suffering. See Shoshana Felman, *The Juridical Unconscious: Trials and Traumas in the Twentieth Century* (Cambridge, MA: Harvard University Press, 2002).

15 See Spivak, *A Critique of Postcolonial Reason*, preface and 112.

16 See Jacques Rancière, *The Emancipated Spectator* (London: Verso, 2009), 40.

17 Ian Hunter describes this relay as a type of "negative theology." "Scenes from the History of Poststructuralism: Davos, Freiburg, Baltimore, Leipzig," *New Literary History* 41, no. 3 (summer 2010): 491–516.

18 Robyn Wiegman, "The Ends of New Americanism," *New Literary History* 42, no. 3 (2011): 385–407, 391.

19 Jacques Derrida, *Sovereignties in Question: The Poetics of Paul Celan* (New York: Fordham University Press, 2005), 87.

20 Eve Sedgwick, "Paranoid Reading and Reparative Reading, or, You're So Paranoid, You Probably Think This Essay Is about You," in *Touching Feeling*, 7.

21 For other theorists who associate the retraction of critique with a rethinking of the linguistic turn, see Heather Love, "Close Reading and Thin Description," *Public Culture* 25, no. 3 (2013); Frank and Sedgwick, "Shame in the Cybernetic Fold."

22 Jacques Derrida, "Force of Law," *Cardozo Law Review* 11 (1989–90): 929.

23 Jacques Derrida, *Rogues: Two Essays on Reason*, trans. Pascale-Anne Brault (Stanford, CA: Stanford University Press, 2005), 38.

24 Jose Estaban Muñoz, *Cruising Utopia: The Then and There of Queer Futurity* (New York: New York University Press, 2009), 292, 327.

25 Anne Cheng, "Psychoanalysis without Symptoms," *differences* 20, no. 1 (2009): 90.

26 Derek Attridge, *The Singularity of Literature* (New York: Routledge, 2004), 29. See also *J. M. Coetzee and the Ethics of Reading*.

27 Attridge, *The Singularity of Literature*, 28.

28 Paul Ricoeur, *Freud and Philosophy: An Essay on Interpretation*, trans. Denis Savage (New Haven, CT: Yale University Press, 1970), 27, 32.

29 Frank and Sedgwick, "Shame in the Cybernetic Fold," 512.

30 For example, Heather Love locates her defense of "thin description" within a larger reaction against "the antifoundationalist claims and textual orientation of poststructuralism." See "Close Reading," 402.

31 This extends from what M. C. Dillion has termed a "semiological reductionism." See *Semiological Reductionism: A Critique of the Deconstructive Movement in Postmodern Thought* (Albany: State University of New York Press, 1995).

32 Sara Ahmed, *Strange Encounters: Embodied Others in Post-Coloniality* (New York: Routledge, 2000), 5.

33 Ahmed, *Strange Encounters*, 47. See also Jane Bennett, *Vibrant Matter: A Political Ecology of Things* (Durham, NC: Duke University Press, 2010); Charles Hirschkind, *The Ethical Soundscape: Cassette Sermons and Islamic Counterpublics* (New York: Columbia University Press, 2006).

PART III. AFFECTS, POLITICS, INSTITUTIONS

8

Hope for Critique?

CHRISTOPHER CASTIGLIA

The growing popularity of the term *postcritique* signals what may prove the most important dispositional change in literary studies since the advent of New Historicism four decades ago. As the "post-" suggests, the term has mostly, to this point, been defined oppositionally, a repudiating break with what Paul Ricoeur called the hermeneutics of suspicion, what Eve Sedgwick called paranoid reading, or what Stephen Best and Sharon Marcus more recently have called symptomatic reading: the assumption that texts conceal beneath their surface an abstract agency, sinister and ubiquitous, to be unearthed by astute and usually indignant critics whose empirical location of that agency "in the text" safeguards their own unimplicated status.[1] Through suspicion, critics become truth-tellers or, more accurately, naysayers, imagining themselves among the so-called radicals who, according to Rebecca Solnit, have poisoned the Left "with the sense of personal superiority that comes from pleasure denied."[2] The working premise of that radicality, Solnit contends, is "The powers that be are not telling you the whole truth." But Solnit points out that those who reveal that the *real* truth is "pure bad news" and who "appoint themselves the deliverers of it, and keep telling it over and over," substitute one untruth for another.[3] Given critiques of critical suspicion like Solnit's, it's understandable that some today would like to leave critique in the past.

Such characterizations, however, being caricatures, are neither fair nor full. Very little is gained, I believe, by understanding "post-" in an oppositional sense or in the name of avant-gardism. And yet such caricatures suggest that *something* is wrong, which may require not that we rush "postcritique" but rather that we think constructively about how critique might be revitalized for a new critical era. What has made critique seem sour—in the sense both of unpleasantly dour and past its prime—is, I will argue, the orientations implied by words like *suspicious, paranoid,* or *superior.* The "something" that is wrong with critique, I believe, is not its desire to criticize social injustice, but its disposition, the *attitude* with which critique is approached. It may not be "critique" that has outlived its usefulness, in other words, but the dispositions that have become customary, even mandatory, to carry it out. Dispositions have their corollary in methodology, however, so as part of suggesting an alternative disposition for criticism—hopefulness—I will argue that the introduction of two concepts—idealism and imagination—can revitalize critique. Although those terms seem old-fashioned and perhaps naive, as ways of thinking they contribute centrally to efforts to move *postcritique.*

Before advocating for hope as a vigorous form of critique, I want first to set forth the limitations of the dispositions that currently characterize critique. To that end, I make two interrelated arguments. First, that our understanding of critique as *only* ideological analysis has kept us from exploring a fuller and more socially relevant role for criticism, namely, its capacity for articulating and opening for deliberation and refinement ideals that would make criticism a site for imagining more just presents and futures. The function of critique need not be only the articulations of "bad news," in other words; it might also encourage the risky speculations that would make critics active participants in making the kinds of social relations we nominally seek but rarely "find" (because we can't imagine them ourselves) "in" literature. Right now, that kind of critical idealism is almost unimaginable largely because, when it appears, it is dismissed as subjective, unrealistic, presentist, or naive, all of which excuse critics from rethinking our superiority to our objects of study and our detachment from the "real world," where ideologies operate unseen (as they never do, apparently, in our criticism or in the institutions that support it). My first goal, then, is to resist that dismissal, and to advocate for the value of the unreal world of imaginative idealism, or what I will call hope, as a reinvigorated critical practice.

My second argument has less to do with a practice than with the dispositions with which a hopeful criticism is carried out. The shifting from one concept of critique to another, from denunciation to reconstruction, requires not only a change in critical content or methodology; it involves an adjustment of critical disposition. The attitudes that have become synonymous with critique are more than irritating; they protect critics from risk and responsibility, and define "politics" in limited, disempowering, and critically self-serving ways. Given the gravity assigned to critique by its practitioners, disposition might seem like an insignificant way to approach the movements "postcritique." I would argue, however, that the apparent insignificance of dispositions is the result of how deeply habituated they have become, and that habituation, the hallmark of any naturalized ideological system, including academic doxa, is precisely what makes the analysis of dispositions necessary. Without an investigation of disposition, that is, there is very little chance of understanding why, in Bruno Latour's phrases, critique has run out of steam or how, in its exhausted state, critique can take on a new and reinvigorating social role.

Dispositions, as I use the term here, are neither inborn character traits nor simple matters of circumstances (neither "He's just born happy" nor "Sure, if I had what he had I'd be happy too"), but a cultivated frame of mind, an orientation toward the text, less self-conscious than method and more sustained than mood. Dispositions are what make certain epistemologies feel *right* to us, and the fact that we can change our minds about what feels right and that large numbers of academics change their minds simultaneously suggests that dispositions are both historically grounded and subject to deliberate practices that transform our relation to literature more radically than do changes in interpretive methodologies. The same methodology approached from different dispositions will produce dramatically different results. I want to begin, then, by outlining some of the dispositional traits currently associated with "critique" and the obstacles that make their abandonment difficult.

First, to call attention to dispositions is to challenge critical objectivity conceived as a transcendent and unimplicated position that allows the critic to make truth claims about a text's "meaning" while simultaneously denying the validity of truth claims, placing the critic in a privileged position of discernment above the ideological dynamics she or he describes. One result, intentional or not, of locating ideology in texts is the removal of critics from the act of making meaning, thereby absolving them from the responsibility for *explicit* ethical positions in relation to the time or place they study as well as their own. The transcendent critic, in other words, has responsibility only to reveal, not to articulate alternative ethical, social, and political standards in ways that make the critic an active participant in the production of "meaning" and of its lived consequences, particularly when such standards are relevant less for what they say about "there" and "then" than for what they imply about here and now.

The second, and more vexed, challenge is to the common practice of assuming a necessary congruence between dispositions and politics, in ways that prevent us from criticizing the dispositional *tone* of critiques. An attitude, a tone—in short, a disposition—has become associated with ideology critique in ways that make the two indistinguishable so that the former can substitute for the latter. If the attitude in which critique is undertaken is "correct," the politics underlying that critique need not be rationalized or investigated. One need not articulate one's political commitments—thereby risking one's stance as transcendent empiricist—because political engagement is signified through dispositions. In this system, to suggest changing dispositions is mistakenly—and self-servingly—taken as either an abandonment of any political role for criticism whatsoever or, worse, a conservative advocacy for the unquestionable continuation of social inequality.

Dispositions thus occupy a contradictory position in much contemporary critique. On the one hand, critical disposition plays no acknowledged role, the critic being detached and hence his or her orientation toward the studied text being irrelevant; on the other hand, disposition is all important, becoming a stand-in for critical intervention. The problem with this paradox is not only that the immunity of critique's disposition to analysis polices what counts as "politics" or that it risks evacuating critical politics beyond their performance as tone, but that it precludes the development of other critical dispositions that might involve a different conception of the political role of literary and cultural studies.

When critics label critique "suspicious" or "paranoid" they implicitly place disposition at its core. Yet neither term quite names the dispositional orientation of much contemporary critique. I want to suggest instead a combination of mistrust, indignation, ungenerosity, and self-congratulation I'm calling, with a nod to Stephen Colbert, *critiquiness*.[4] Colbert coined the term *truthiness* to describe the *sound* of truthfulness without appeal to logic or fact, based solely on what a speaker (usually, for Colbert, a politician) and his audience wish to be true. Critiquiness similarly names the appearance of critique, of textual politics, that reinforces a cycle of expectation about the way the world—and the text—works without acknowledging the existence of experiences that vary from or defy those expectations. Like truthiness, with its sanctimonious assertions of facts that seem to prove the ideology that generated them, critiquiness speaks with self-satisfaction about an agency locatable in a text's "depth" that is actually a phantasmatic location of the critic's own beliefs. And like truthiness, critiquiness hides that projection behind assertions of fact, even as those assertions substitute for the work properly done by the root term (*truth* or *critique*). Critiquiness is the *sound* of critique without the ethical positioning, the explicit statement of ideals, and the imaginative presentation of alternatives based on those ideals that, I believe, critique devoid of critiquiness might involve. To put this another way: critiquiness shrinks the imaginative and political possibilities of criticism to the narrow performance of dispositions, and a scandalously small range of compulsory and compulsive dispositions at that.

Such dispositional constriction, as much as the particular dispositions it permits, is a result of the same Cold War politics that generated the political divisiveness Colbert parodies with his term *truthiness*, although in the case of critiquiness any self-parody is unintentional. The Cold War represented a dangerous transformation of the responsibilities of citizenship, in which civic involvement, limited though it was, became an orientation *toward* such involvement, a disposition substituting for participation. If the activities undertaken by citizens during World War II—rationing, knitting, or factory work, for instance—were productions of patriotic exceptionalism, even they disappeared in the Cold War, replaced by a narrow repertoire of affective orientations that made dispositions feel like participation. Along with suspicion, citizens were encouraged to feel indignation, anxiety, and self-satisfaction in relation to the Soviet Union and its hidden domestic agents, an enemy that, shifting location continually, might be located anywhere and everywhere.[5] Perpetually pulling citizens between confidence and fear, exhilaration and anxiety, resentment and inspiration, without any opportunities for civic action as outlets for—or reality checks on—these dispositions, the Cold War, as historian John Lewis Gaddis has argued, became a war of orientations.[6] By the end of the Cold War, then, the manipulation of dispositions felt like civic participation, politics becoming recognizable not by what governments asked citizens to do but by what dispositions they encouraged them to adopt.

Like the ever-wary Cold War citizen, critics operating within the hermeneutics of suspicion treat the text's surface as a deceptive cover below which they discover and reveal dangerous ideological complicities in which critics themselves are unimplicated. One reason critique appears to have run its course, as I've observed elsewhere, is its unacknowledged belatedness, its melancholy maintenance, however unconscious, of the state's imperative and totalizing explanatory powers that were rendered obsolete by the Cold War's end with the 1989 Malta Summit.[7] That the same dispositions that characterized the Cold War's state operations—indignation, suspicion, complacency—are also constitutive of critiquiness should give us pause. Even more dangerous than its perpetuation of particular dispositions, however, critique as it is most often currently practiced makes dispositions feel like participation, the critic's tone substituting for self-implicated and imaginatively reparative investments in the discourses the critic discerns but rarely participates in (re)shaping.

It may be hard, after four decades of the Cold War, to imagine—much less enact—alternatives to dispositional politics, especially if, as Donald Pease has argued, the Cold War did not end with the fall of the Berlin Wall.[8] In *The New American Exceptionalism,* Pease persuasively argues that the U.S. government replaced one abstract enemy (communism) with another (terrorism). Pease's analysis suggests why the politics of disposition still feels so compelling nearly forty years after the Cold War's nominal end. The goal of the "War on Terror" is not the spread of democracy, but the securing of "safety," which leaves citizens today, like those living in the Cold War, anxiously suspicious. The denationalizing of terror allows the state to multiply suspicious dispositions (as exemplified by announcements ubiquitous in airports, subways, and other public spaces: "If you observe anything suspicious, report it to the authorities"). This denationalizing may also explain why critics can direct state-sponsored epistemologies at the nation-state itself. If that is the case, the echo of Cold War dispositions in contemporary critique may be mimetic rather than melancholic. In either case, the continued presence of dispositional state epistemologies in contemporary critique (ironically, especially when those critiques are directed *against* state epistemologies) makes it even more vital that we examine the sources and operations of critical dispositions, especially critiquiness.

The purpose of that examination is not to dismiss critique, however, but to revitalize it through a new critical orientation. If critiquiness is the echo of Cold War state epistemologies, it's important to remember that even during the Cold War, when the state encouraged suspicion of everything except its own dispositional imperatives, antiwar protestors, civil rights and prolabor activists, and feminists, among others, *did* turn suspicion against the state but, even more importantly, developed alternative critical orientations that made critique more than simple denunciation. They coupled their critiques with an explicit and shameless idealism that led to civic action: in naming their ideals, they implicitly critiqued the conditions that made hope necessary; in offering critiques, they measured the present or the past against the imagined alternatives generated from an often radically insufficient *now.* It is that combination of critique and imaginative idealism that, in what follows, I call *hopefulness,* and that I will offer as an alternative disposition for a "postcritique" criticism.[9] What the antiwar and civil rights movements show is that critique and hopefulness are not mutually exclusive. They are profoundly intertwined in any genuinely activist impulse. The problem with critiquiness is that, by disavowing the critic's hopefulness, it defuses its most powerful critical force, leaving criticism in the domain of state-sponsored Cold War dispositions, even when the *content* of critique echoes the liberation movements of the 1960s, as the work of the best baby boomer critics did and does. I am not dismissing the political power of critique, therefore, but reclaiming the dispositional capaciousness also evident in its Cold War origins.

Here it is worth stressing the essential simultaneity not only of idealism and critique but also of critique and *imagination* as a critical refusal of presentations of phantasms as realities, a presentation underlying the wars on both communism and terrorism. From Martin Luther King Jr.'s evocation of his dream to the psychedelic visions of 1960s hippie culture, from feminist consciousness raising to gatherings of radical fairies, one of the crucial aspects of Cold War activism was its denial of imperative versions of "reality" in favor of more inventive and experientially diverse versions of the possible. Those imaginative states simultaneously served as an implicit critique of what the state presented as necessary truth and as an aspirational articulation of an ideal substitute, critique and imagination working as a single force. In proposing hopefulness as an alternative to Cold War critiquiness, I propose a similar combination of idealism and imagination that generates other versions of what constitutes reality and provides other metrics by which to evaluate and challenge a truthiness passing as truth.

Understood this way, hopefulness is not the opposite of critique but its lifeblood. Hopefulness shows that critique does not require suspicion. When critique and critiquiness are taken as synonymous, the hope at the heart of the former is overcome by the latter, articulated explicitly only at the risk of dismissal as naive, conservative, or unknowing. But the dismissal of imaginative idealism in favor of suspicion is no more dangerous than its dismissal in the name of *anti*suspiciousness, especially when the latter takes the form of calls for a criticism rooted more firmly in facts. Stephen Best and Sharon Marcus, for example, argue for practices of "surface reading" that will return us to "what has almost become taboo in literary studies: objectivity, validity, truth." Using the same language as the symptomatic readings they criticize, Best and Marcus assert that after decades of ideology critique "we now have to reveal the real objective and incontrovertible facts hidden behind the *illusion* of prejudices."[10] In "Why Has Critique Run Out of Steam?" Bruno Latour similarly claims, "The question was never to get *away* from facts but *closer* to them."[11] The imaginative idealism that constitutes dispositional hopefulness counters not only the critiquiness of symptomatic reading, therefore, but the neoempiricism of postcritique theories as well.

In claiming imagination as a crucial aspect of hopefulness and hence of an activist politics, I want to suggest that literature serves otherwise than as a cover for ideological operations that shape the *were* and *are*—the *realities*—of social injustice. Literature is a training ground in the unreal, and hence a powerful partner in the work of critique aimed not *at* the text but alongside it. Imagination, as I mean it here, is akin to what Ralph Waldo Emerson endorsed as a belief in "the Unattainable, the flying Perfect,"[12] which he found most available through literature. For Emerson, literature is the force creating circles without end, "a point outside of our hodiernal circle through which a new one may be described. The use of literature," Emerson contends, "is to afford us a platform whence we may command a view of our present life, a purchase by which we may move it."[13] Criticism, too, can be an imaginative space coexisting with and perpetually troubling the imperative here and now within which new ideals, new versions of the real, can be envisioned. If we see literature not only as the object of criticism but as its best model, we might again have a critique in the service of living value, a self-transforming and adaptable willingness to hold vision above necessity. Dispositional hopefulness is therefore an alternative to critiquiness and is, in Newton Arvin's words, "accessible as always to those who wish not merely to 'interpret the world variously' (in Marx's phrase) but to change it."[14]

If such hopeful criticism has rarely existed after the Cold War, it did exist, ironically, during it. Midcentury critics are often disparaged today as defenders of the conservative nationalist values known as "the Cold War consensus." In some ways that is a fair account of their work, which often invokes "the American imagination" and "our" literary tradition. But, as I have argued elsewhere, these critics also opposed the development of nuclear weapons, strict social normativity, and the indiscriminate skepticism of Cold War America.[15] If they supported national exceptionalism, they also criticized the United States of their time as exceptionally destructive. As important as their denunciations, however, is their hopefulness, their faith in an imaginative idealism they drew from the romantic writers to whom they most frequently turned, not with suspicion, but with a critical intelligence that was, as Richard Chase put it, open-minded and capacious as well as skeptical.[16] These critics forged from romanticism a notion of imagination as a conceptual space where ideals could be developed and given allegorical structure. Taking up literary "myth and symbols," they expected to stir debate, turning idealism into an occasion for public deliberations in the ways the Cold War consensus sought to foreclose. They did so not simply by critiquing what was but by proposing, explicitly, what might be, in ways that brought hopefulness to the forefront of critique. Whether it was Arvin celebrating the "strong intuition of human solidarity as a priceless good" and countering the "brutality of indiscriminate skepticism," Richard Poirier describing "consciousness momentarily set free" and becoming "a law unto himself," ignoring "all outward allegiance, whether to nature or society," Lewis Mumford extolling the virtue of potential affiliations made between "outcasts, recluses, exiles," C. L. R. James's dream of a "world civilization" confronting "a state of hopelessness" with the free association of "mass movements, uprisings of the people, and unofficial individuals," or Richard Chase's promotion of the "blissful, idyllic, erotic attachment to life and to one's comrades, which is the only promise of happiness," midcentury critics were often shameless idealists.[17] Phrases restrained by scare quotes in suspicious critique—humanism, solidarity, betterment, liberalism, justice, moral distinctions, values—were alive to these critics, animating their hopeful challenges to the uncritical conformity and coerced consent of middle-class American life in the 1950s and 1960s. As we move postcritique and the critiquiness it has often adopted from Cold War state epistemologies, then, one viable model for a new critical disposition might come, ironically, from the hopefulness of critics who wrote during, but were not fully *of*, the Cold War.

It's difficult to advocate for critical hopefulness, much less to locate it in a discredited lot like the myth and symbol critics, without a certain embarrassment. Hope, in the evaluative norms of academic criticism today, seems naive, risibly optimistic, or insufficiently rigorous, willfully blind to the conditions that make a socially engaged criticism necessary, in short, a- or even antipolitical. Scholars engaged in positing alternatives to "symptomatic reading" are aware of such charges and have been quick to assert the political efficacy of alternative methodologies. Surface reading, for example, in Best and Marcus's words, "might easily be dismissed as politically quietist, too willing to accept things as they are."[18] That "hope" lies at the core of so much bland political rhetoric—from Ronald Reagan's "New Day in America," through Bill Clinton's self-promotion as the "Man from Hope," to Barack Obama's "Audacity of Hope"—contributes to the embarrassment attendant on offering it as a serious critical disposition. But the fact that "hope" in political rhetoric has enticed citizens in the United States to concede their social imaginations to a government that gestures toward inclusion but more typically generates estrangement does not mean the term must be surrendered to those uses. Critical hopeful-ness is an opportunity to enact a counterdiscursive occupation of an evacu-ated disposition in order to turn it *against* the alienated nonparticipation that critiquiness can also cause. Best and Marcus insist that "immersion in texts (without paranoia or suspicion about their merit or value)" can result in an "attentiveness to the artwork as itself a kind of freedom."[19] As Best and Marcus affirm, "In relinquishing the freedom dream that accompanies the work of demystification, we might be groping toward some equally valuable, if less glamorous, states of mind."[20] If moving "post" critique means changing dis-positions without changing the political commitments that animate the best work of the last decades, then the central question is: what forms of social engagement are possible without suspicion? In the remainder of this essay, I show how hopefulness as a dispositional combination of imagination and ide-alism has functioned in social theory, and how it might, therefore, constitute "another kind of freedom."

Social theory has often revealed its romantic sympathies when it locates transformation in the *not-yetness* that challenges inevitable versions of reality. Judith Butler, for example, defines the real as "an installation and foreclosure of fantasy, a phantasmatic construction which receives a certain legitimation after which it is called the real and disavowed as the phantasmatic."[21] This construction of reality, Butler argues, relies on a "set of exclusionary and con-stitutive principles" that amount to a simple pointing at an external world that presumably represents reality's referent.[22] Efforts to sanction and police alternative versions of the real, Butler contends, necessarily produce "cer-tain forms of exclusion that return, like insistent ghosts, to undermine those very efforts."[23] While fantasy "postures *as* the real," establishing "through a repeated and insistent posturing" its empirically verifiable status, the fantastic origins of the real persist as "the possibility of suspending and interrogating the ontological claim itself, of reviewing its own production, as it were, and contesting their claim to the real."[24] As a result, "fantasy is not equated with what is not real, but rather with what is not *yet* real, what is possible or futural, or what belongs to a different version of the real."[25]

Ideology critique comprises a series of disavowed identifications and reifica-tions akin to what Butler describes as powerful representations of the "real," giv-ing phantasms an apparent ontological stability. When the critic "discovers" an ideology "behind" or "beneath" a text, she or he "reveals" something that, too often, moves quickly from being a complex discursive exchange to operating as an abstract, organized, and empirical force that gives the feel of realness to what might otherwise be a questionable projection of what the critic needs to "find" "there." Not only does this create an oppositional stability from a largely indeterminate nexus of agencies and social positions, an ontology necessary to give form to an "object" of discovery, it also permits an identification that occludes both the privileged status of the critic and the largely amorphous nature of the phantasmatic beings with whom one identifies. The act of discovery, in other words, is a fantasy in the sense put forward by Jean Laplanche, in which the entire mise-en-scène of fantasy—both the existence of ideology and its "discovery"—represents the consciousness of the critic.[26] The objects of ideology function, then, for the purposes of critical identification, through which the "resistance" of a phantasmatic object allows the critic the appearance of heroic reversals of power in the act of discovery, while the identification with victimization disavows the critic's own position within institutional privilege. That privilege reasserts itself, however, in the ability of those engaged in critique not only to determine which political struggles count as real but to dismiss other political visions as illogical, naive, self-indulgent, impractical, or unproductive. Calling other critical dispositions and critical beliefs *apolitical* becomes an academic version of the social infliction of what Erving Goffman calls "stigma." In denying the political status of the unreal, in other words, critique risks reproducing the social genesis of nonsubjects, noncitizens, or what Butler calls *abjects*.[27] Abjects are those who refuse to surrender fantasy to what is deemed real, and who, I would add, maintain idealism in the face of an ideological suspicion that becomes synonymous with the gravitas of the paradoxically hidden actual.

In response to the disavowed phantasms of critique and the stigmatizations it allows, Gilles Deleuze calls for a different form of disavowal that, in "radically contesting the validity of that which is," potentially "suspends belief in and neutralizes the given in such a way that a new horizon opens up beyond the given and in place of it."[28] Such a disavowal, Deleuze contends, "does not believe in negating or destroying the world" but operates "to disavow and thus to suspend it, in order to secure an ideal which itself is suspended in fantasy." Deleuze challenges, in other words, "the validity of existing reality in order to create a pure ideal reality" that Deleuze identifies as "a state of mystical contemplation."[29] Deleuze's mysticism is kin to what Michael Taussig calls "the half-awake world" in which "free-floating attention" generates hope.[30] Emerging from such states does not mean, for Taussig, "awakening from a period of inertia to one of action," a formulation that makes hope the opposite of politics, but rather engaging an imaginative "demystification and re-enchantment" of the real that gives hope "an electrifying role to play."[31] Similar dynamics of demystification arise from what Gayatri Spivak calls "a *site of hope*," which she locates in "that moment which you cannot plan for." Those moments, for Spivak, force "something inherited" to "jump into something other, and fix onto something that is opposed."[32] Freeing us momentarily from what Butler identifies as the regulatory regime of the real, the unexpected—what I am identifying as imaginative idealism—involves what, for Spivak, "is not the leap of faith, which hope brings *into* crisis, but rather the leap of hope."[33] Spivak's "leap of hope" becomes socially active when taken up by Rebecca Solnit, who claims that the common feature of most important moments of social transformation in America "is that they begin in the imagination, in hope," which, Solnit believes, "calls for action; action is impossible without hope."[34] Political action, for Solnit, springs from the belief that "another world might be possible, not promised, not guaranteed,"[35] but generating, in Ernst Bloch's words, an "'informed discontent which belongs to hope, because they both arise out of the No to deprivation.'"[36]

The social efficacy of hope comes in large part from what would seem to make it most dubious as a model for political action: its "informed discontent" or what we might think of as the unceasing deferral of hope. That deferral might seem to make hope a motivation for activism rather than an agenda in itself, a disposition for criticism rather than a methodological program. But in its commitment to the perennial not-yetness of idealism, hope is necessarily imminent and never fully satisfied. Hope attached to a specific object—a hope *for*—becomes *want*, a surrender of the self-perpetuating drive toward betterment in favor of a rearrangement of already-existing conditions. A generalized hope, by contrast, is the itch that refuses to be soothed, an ongoing discontent that is not reducible to the dead end of suspicion.[37] The continual drive inspired by imminent hope is what keeps struggles with the regimes of the real from becoming programmatic, making dissatisfaction— both a critique of the present and an imaginative ideal of a not-yetness—a social and critical disposition in the here-and-now.

To examine how the demystifying and reenchanting dynamic of what Deleuze calls "idealism," Solnit calls "imagination," and Spivak and Taussig call "hope" becomes, as it does for all these theorists, an efficacious social force, we might turn to Jacques Rancière's concept of political agency as invested in "an abstract supplement in relation to any actual (ac)count of the parts of the population, of their qualifications for partaking in the community and of the common shares that they are due by virtue of these qualifications."[38] The partitioning off of this supplement from social accounts involves more than stigmatization; it forces its banishment to the space of the invisible and the inarticulable. "If there is someone you do not wish to recognize as a political being," Rancière writes, "you begin by not seeing him as the bearer of signs of politicity, by not understanding what he says, by not hearing what issues from his mouth as discourse."[39] The constitution of social reality, in other words, requires a rendering of "what 'is not,'" a paradoxical absent presence that I would identify with hope.[40]

The relationship between those who are and are not counted is not the conventional opposition between defined groups, one with power and the other without (the oppressive and the subversive agents of much critique). For Rancière, such formulations of political opposition are "the reduction of the people to the sum of the parts of the social body and of the political community to the relations between the interests and aspirations of these different parts."[41] Accounts of the opposition between the subjects and objects of power, for Rancière, do not constitute "politics" at all but a "normal state of things—the non-existence of politics" that he names *policing*. In the logic of policing the disempowered have the *potential* to assume the qualities to rule, and therefore operate within a hierarchical relationship (ruler/ruled, oppressor/oppressed) that, because it is built on a common metric of values, is open to reversal without changing the fundamental logic of the opposition.[42] That reversal may well be painful, violent, or slow. The point for Rancière is that, within a common set of criteria, reversal is *conceivable*. Reducing "politics" to a single opposition between the empowered and the disempowered, an oversimplified version of critique again betrays its roots in the Cold War, when conflicts over geopolitical "influence" took rhetorical shape as a single determinant dispute between the United States and the Soviet Union, an opposition that, as Donald Pease observes, absorbed "everyday life into a 'battlefield' arena" in which "the complications, doubts, and conflicts of modern existence get a single opposition that then clears up the whole mess and puts everybody back to work."[43] The problem with policing passing as politics is not simply that the former relies on "a single opposition," reducing complicated networks to abstract and unified agencies, but that the opposition subsumes *other* "complications, doubts and conflicts within modern existence" that might disrupt the version of reality policed by the critic, and therefore disrupt the transcendent acuity signified by vigilant revealings of what lies behind or beneath a text. That Pease identifies such gestures as the function of national exceptionalism arising from the Cold War state should again give us pause when considering the political claims of contemporary critique.

The doubts and contradictions Pease refers to are not, however, neutralized by being subsumed by a central, totalizing opposition. Rather, they arguably become the stuff of Rancière's unseen supplement. Politics, for Rancière, is a clash not between two entities but between "two partitions of the sensible."[44] While one partition allows for political resolution by means of the circulation of different groups through a common language of empowerment, sovereignty, self-determination, rights, normativity, and so on, the second comprises what Rancière variously calls a gap, a vacancy, or a supplement that insistently troubles social (ac)counts without becoming a social constituency itself. In order to have politics, in other words, there must be an unseen force that doesn't contest its exclusion but "disjoins the population from itself, by suspending all logics of legitimate domination" and "separat[ing] the community out from the sum of the parts of the social body."[45] The unseen and unheard are never *outside* the circle of the social, then, but are, paradoxically, the unsettling "*presence of two worlds in one*," revealing "a society in its difference to itself."[46] That unsettling absent presence that disrupts the social real—even the real understood in terms of ideological opposition—in order to initiate the political departitioning of the seen and unseen I would call imaginative idealism, or hope.

We can roll our eyes at the political agency of the "unseen," just as we can dismiss the proposal that literature's hopefulness generates from the not-yetness of imagination an ideal vision of the socially possible as politically efficacious as our suspicious critiques *of* literature. Critiquiness requires such eye-rolling. Despite our smirks, however, I think many critics today are already hopeful. Our ideals are implicit in our critiques, creating standards of the possible against which the merely actual or probable seem lacking. In so doing they are, of course, part of yet another opposition that Rancière would attribute to dead politics: suspicion versus hope. But ideals are more than that. Unlike critiquiness, which congratulates itself on finding the "real" meaning beneath a text's obfuscating surface, the idealism of hopefulness, being imaginative and speculative, is always its own undoing, and productively so, since its necessarily unfinished business is what keeps the real in an ongoing state of un- and remaking. Ironically, the seedbed of our hopefulness is what we, in our critiquiness, are most likely to brush aside. I'm talking about the hopefulness of literature, which shows us how the social supplement becomes a disruptive force, refusing social logics of the real. Just as importantly, literature is also a springboard, turning the unreal into a source of hopeful world-making. Rather than viewing literature suspiciously, therefore, we might take it as an opportunity to imagine and acknowledge the idealism that already animates—without acknowledgment—what is best about literature and about critique.

And here we can turn to the archenemy of critique, Bruno Latour, who, like Rancière, believes that "any given interaction seems to *overflow* with elements which are already in the situation coming from some other time, some other place, and generated by some other agency."[47] That "other place" and "other agency" Latour calls *plasma*, that which is "not yet formatted, not yet measured, not yet socialized, not yet engaged in metrological chains, and not yet covered, surveyed, mobilized, or subjectified" (244). For Latour, the "potential lying in wait" (246) is in literature, which, he fears, "has been explained to nothingness by the social factors 'hidden behind' them" (236). What concerns Latour in the deadening of literature is the loss of "the diversity of the worlds of fiction invested on paper," a diversity that "allow[s] enquirers to gain as much plausibility and range as those they have to study in the real world. It is only through some continuous familiarity with literature," Latour urges, that critics "might become less wooden, less rigid, less stiff in their definition of what sort of agencies populate the world" (55). Literature has been done in, I would argue, not by critique, as Latour claims, but by critiquiness.

Literature is, we might say, the supplemental world that persists within the predictability of critiquiness, continually inspiring "the irruption into the normal course of action of strange, exotic, archaic, or mysterious implements" (80). The ficticity of literature, for Latour, represents the liberatory impulse of politics: "We have to let out of their cages entities which had been strictly forbidden to enter the scene until now and allow them to roam in the world again. What name could I give them? Entities, beings, objects, things, perhaps refer to them as invisibles" (239). In conceiving the "invisibles" as political agents, Latour makes literature the home of Rancière's "unseen" and Butler's "abjects." Fictional imagination, in this sense, is not so much the opposite of reality but an expression of an imminent gap in the logic of precedent and plausibility, of what *is* and what *might be,* the hopeful potential of the "not-yet real." As Latour insists, "When everything else has failed, the resource of fiction can bring . . . the solid objects of today into the fluid states where their connections with humans"—and, I would add, *between* humans—"may make sense" (82).

I endorse Latour's understanding of literature's power, but I would argue that what is true of literature is just as true of criticism. As critics we do more than let literature instill its magic in us, a formulation that makes texts as animate and critics as passive as does critiquiness. Without understanding the active potential of critical hopefulness, we may, even in moving away from critiquiness, fall prey to what R. W. B. Lewis called "the sheer dullness of unconscious repetition."[48] The opposition of critique and postcritique, as it has been articulated so far, would seem to leave us three options: the suspiciousness of critique, the empiricism of surfaces, or the giddy receptiveness of "mystical" but ultimately inactive critics. But as critics, we have access to what Latour calls "the vast outside to which every course of action has to appeal in order to be carried out" (244). When Jane Bennett claims that imagination has led "certain writers to devise literary strategies to combat the everyday," she might include critics among those writers.[49] I don't believe, as Latour does, that critique has run out of steam, although I think critiquiness has. Some dispositional change is necessary for critique to get a second wind, to bring to the surface the imaginative idealism that has always been criticism's greatest strength and best hope. In *The Promise of Happiness*, Sara Ahmed writes, "In imagining what is possible, in imagining what does not yet exist, we say yes to . . . the possibility of things not staying as they are, or being as they stay. Revolutionaries must dream; if their imaginations dwell on the injustice of how things stay, they do not simply dwell in what stays."[50] More than simply dreaming, critics must develop new dispositions, which, as Bennett claims, are as "crucial to ethics as principles, reasons, and their assemblage into a moral code."[51] With a different disposition—and hopefulness, I am arguing, may prove among the most viable—critique may actively contribute to the ethics of the possible, speaking to "the public" not as smug debunkers of but as imaginative defenders of the imaginatively ideal unreality of literature, not as melancholic dwellers in the Cold War but, like our critical progenitors, as its staunch critics in our hopes as well as in our denunciations. The "potential lying in wait" that Latour speaks of is available to us, finally, not postcritique but postcritiquiness.

Notes

For generous feedback on versions of this essay and for invitations to try material out at their institutions, I am grateful to David Alworth, Elizabeth Anker, Jonathan Arac, Michael Bérubé, Robert Caserio, Amanda Claybaugh, Paul Erickson, Rita Felski, Eric Hayot, Eve Keller, Robert S. Levine, Anne McCarthy, Donald Pease, Joseph Rezek, Ben Schreier, Jordan Stein, anonymous readers for Duke University Press, and, most of all, Chris Reed.

1 Paul Ricoeur, *Freud and Philosophy: An Essay on Interpretation* (New Haven, CT: Yale University Press, 1977); Eve Kosofsky Sedgwick, *Touching Feeling: Affect, Pedagogy, Performativity* (Durham, NC: Duke University Press, 2003); Stephen Best and Sharon Marcus, "Surface Reading: An Introduction," *Representations* 108, no. 1. See also Rita Felski, "Context Stinks!," *New Literary History* 42, no. 4; and Heather Love, "Close but Not Deep: Literary Ethics and the Descriptive Turn," *New Literary History* 41, no. 2 (spring 2010): 371–91.

2 Rebecca Solnit, *Hope in the Dark: Untold Histories, Wild Possibilities* (New York: Nation Books, 2005), 15.

3 Solnit, *Hope in the Dark.*

4 This essay draws on, and substantially develops, ideas that appeared in an earlier essay. See my "Critiquiness," ELN 51, no. 2 (2013): 79.

5 See my "Melville's Cold War Allegories and the Politics of Criticism," in *The Cambridge Companion to Herman Melville*, ed. Robert S. Levine (New York: Cambridge University Press, 2014).

6 John Lewis Gaddis, *The Cold War: A New History* (New York: Penguin, 2006), 32.

7 Castiglia, "Melville's Cold War Allegories."

8 Donald E. Pease, *The New American Exceptionalism* (Minneapolis: University of Minnesota Press, 2009).

9 This essay is in conversation with a number of philosophers, political theorists, and literary scholars who have expanded our concept of hope, including Jane Bennett, *The Enchantment of Modern Life: Attachments, Crossings, and Ethics* (Princeton, NJ: Princeton University Press, 2001); Richard Rorty, *Philosophy and Social Hope* (New York: Penguin, 2000); Solnit, *Hope in the Dark*; Tzvetan Todorov, *Hope and Memory: Lessons from the Twentieth Century* (Princeton, NJ: Princeton University Press, 2003). For a fuller discussion of these writers, see my "Melville's Cold War Allegories." My thinking has been most influenced by the wonderful essays contained in Mary Zournazi, *Hope: New Philosophies for Change* (New York: Routledge, 2003), and by the work of Ernst Bloch, especially *The Spirit of Utopia* (Stanford, CA: Stanford University Press, 2000) and *The Principles of Hope* (Cambridge, MA: MIT Press, 1995).

10 Best and Marcus, "Surface Reading," 18.

11 Bruno Latour, "Why Has Critique Run Out of Steam? From Matters of Fact to Matters of Concern," *Critical Inquiry* 30, no. 2 (winter 2004): 225–48, 231.

12 Ralph Waldo Emerson, "Circles," in *Selected Essays*, ed. Larzer Ziff (New York: Viking, 1982), 225.

13 Emerson, "Circles," 232.

14 Newton Arvin, *American Pantheon* (New York: Delacorte, 1966), 14.

15 See my "Melville's Cold War Allegories."

16 Richard Chase, *Herman Melville: A Critical Study* (New York: Hafner, 1971; first published 1949), vi.

17 Arvin, *American Pantheon*, 518; Richard Poirier, *A World Elsewhere: The Place of Style in American Literature* (New York: Oxford University Press, 1966), 7;

Lewis Mumford, *The Golden Day: A Study in American Literature and Culture* (Boston: Beacon Hill, 1955), xix; C. L. R. James, *American Civilization* (Oxford: Blackwell, 1992), 38, 30, 36; Richard Chase, *The American Novel and Its Tradition* (Baltimore: Johns Hopkins University Press, 1957), 107.

18 Best and Marcus, "Surface Reading," 16.

19 Best and Marcus, "Surface Reading."

20 Best and Marcus, "Surface Reading," 17.

21 Judith Butler, "The Force of Fantasy: Mapplethorpe, Feminism, and Discursive Excess," in *The Judith Butler Reader*, ed. Sara Salih (Oxford: Blackwell, 1990), 186.

22 Butler, "The Force of Fantasy."

23 Butler, "The Force of Fantasy," 187.

24 Butler, "The Force of Fantasy."

25 Butler, "The Force of Fantasy," 185.

26 Building on Laplanche, Judith Butler writes, "Fantasy is self-reflexive in its structure, no matter how much it enacts a longing for that which is outside its reach. Yet the subject cannot be collapsed into the subject-position of that fantasy; all positions are the subject, even as this subject has proliferated beyond recognition. In a sense, despite its apparent referentiality, fantasy is always and only its own object of desire." Butler, "The Force of Fantasy," 189.

27 Erving Goffman, *Stigma: Notes on the Management of Spoiled Identity* (New York: Simon and Schuster, 1963). Butler writes of the form of oppression that works "not merely through acts of overt prohibition, but covertly, through the constitution of viable subjects and through the corollary constitution of a domain of unviable (un)subjects—abjects, we might call them—who are neither named nor prohibited within the economy of the law." Judith Butler, "Imitation and Gender Insubordination," in *The Judith Butler Reader*, ed. Sara Salih (Oxford: Blackwell, 1990), 126.

28 Gilles Deleuze, *Masochism: Coldness and Cruelty* (New York: Zone Books, 1991), 31.

29 Deleuze, *Masochism*, 32–33.

30 Michael Taussig, "A Carnival of the Senses: A Conversation with Michael Taussig," in *Hope: New Philosophies for Change*, ed. Mary Zournazi (New York: Routledge, 2003), 54.

31 Taussig, "A Carnival of the Senses."

32 Gayatri Spivak, "The Rest of the World: A Conversation with Gayatri Spivak," in Zournazi, *Hope*, 173.

33 Spivak, "The Rest of the World."

34 Solnit, *Hope in the Dark*, 4–5. In his discussion of the "postrace" novel, Ramón Saldívar offers a superb example of both the possibilities and limitations of the intermixings of the imaginary and the real, the ideal and the experiential, that I am describing as hopefulness. Describing what he calls the "postrace" novel, Saldívar writes, "Instead, these novels perform the critical work of symbolic action, denoting the public work of the private imagination, but only after routing it through the pathway of fantasy in the service of the profoundly unsymbolic ra-

cialized imagination. That is, what matters is that historical fantasy is not merely phantasmal depiction of deep ideological mystifications. Rather, it works also as a basis for recognizing and understanding the construction of the new political destinies we may witness taking shape among diasporic groups in the US today." Ramón Saldívar, "Historical Fantasy, Speculative Realism, and Postrace Aesthetics in Contemporary American Fiction," *American Literary History* 23, no. 3 (fall 2011): 595.

35 Solnit, *Hope in the Dark*, 5.

36 Solnit, *Hope in the Dark*, 13.

37 In setting forth this account of hopefulness as the basis of social critique, I draw on Ernst Bloch, who describes the combination of heritage and invention as an "anticipatory illumination," a glimmer of what will become conscious but is only glimpsed within the terms of the present. Anticipatory illuminations—which Bloch likened to daydreams—thus represent "that which has not yet become, that which has still not been accomplished, but which has not been thwarted in existence." Bloch, *Utopian Function of Art and Literature* (Cambridge, MA: MIT Press, 1989), 50.

38 Jacques Rancière, *Dissensus: On Politics and Aesthetics* (London: Continuum International, 2010), 33.

39 Rancière, *Dissensus*, 38.

40 Rancière, *Dissensus*, 117.

41 Rancière, *Dissensus*, 42.

42 Rancière, *Dissensus*, 43.

43 Donald E. Pease, "Moby-Dick and the Cold War," in *The American Renaissance Reconsidered*, ed. Walter Benn Michaels and Donald E. Pease (Baltimore: Johns Hopkins University Press, 1985), 155.

44 Rancière, *Dissensus*, 39.

45 Rancière, *Dissensus*, 33.

46 Rancière, *Dissensus*, 37, 42.

47 Bruno Latour, *Reassembling the Social: An Introduction to Actor-Network Theory* (New York: Oxford University Press, 2007), 166. Further quotations from this work are cited parenthetically in the text.

48 R. W. B. Lewis, *American Adam: Innocence, Tragedy, and Tradition in the Nineteenth Century* (Chicago: University of Chicago Press, 1955), 9–10.

49 Bennett, *Enchantment*, 76.

50 Sara Ahmed, *The Promise of Happiness* (Durham, NC: Duke University Press, 2010), 197.

51 Bennett, *Enchantment*, 144.

9

What Are the Politics of Critique?

The Function of Criticism at a Different Time

RUSS CASTRONOVO

Sticks and Stones

Perhaps no single image better captures the much-debated and often-vexed relationship between criticism and politics than a photograph of Edward Said, professor of literature at Columbia University and author of the influential books *Orientalism* and *Culture and Imperialism*, hurling a stone across the Lebanese border toward an Israeli guardhouse in 2000. Media and academic controversy ensued almost immediately.[1]

For his part, Said called his rock throwing "a symbolic gesture of joy," and observed that "the guardhouse was at least half a mile away," well beyond the range of most critics.[2] Others viewed the matter differently, contending that the gesture was really an action that violated core humanist values associated with the function of criticism. Whether symbolic or actual, Said's stone throwing exposed how the proximity—or is it the distance?—of academic criticism to political intervention leads to fraught questions about the status of intellectual work with respect to the realities of conflict and struggle. Whether politics is understood strictly as "the science or study of government and the state" or is taken in a looser sense that indicates a concern with the ways in which power underlies activities and attitudes (*OED*), the photograph illustrates the brouhaha that erupts when practitioners of critique stake a political claim. The shifting definitions of politics only deepen this uncertainty and intensify the debate over the proper purview of interpretation, analysis, and any number of other critical functions.

The first sense of politics emerges from the historical specifics of Said's vocal opposition to the state of Israel's occupation of and military operations in southern Lebanon. Said's stance, in fact, has become a prominent aspect of professional identity for many humanities scholars. For organizations of critics such as the American Studies Association (ASA) and the Modern Language Association, the policies of the Israeli government with respect to Palestinians have continued to provide an occasion for linking academic work to politics in the strict sense of states and rights. Not without controversy, the membership of the ASA in 2013 approved a measure to endorse a boycott of Israeli academic institutions. The resolution, made in the name of "social justice" and "committed to . . . the struggle against all forms of racism, including antisemitism, discrimination, and xenophobia," links critique to politics in ways that are overt, direct, and urgent.[3] Overall, the common thread here is consistent with Max Weber's famous understanding of politics as the legitimization of state violence and other forms of domination.[4]

The second, looser sense of politics is not wrapped up in specific governmental policies but comes into play at a broader level where critique is seen as unmasking cultural formations of power, exposing the unquestioned assumptions behind entrenched beliefs, and resisting knowledge that is simply taken for granted. In this vein, critics often start by homing in on the representation of social structures and institutions in literary texts and move on to using novels, poems, and other forms of aesthetic expression to provide a critical vantage point on social conditions, historical as well as contemporary. A politically inclined critic might begin by examining the representation of gender and social class in Jane Austen's *Emma* as the first step toward understanding how the novel itself provides a critique of gender norms and class politics more broadly. Overall, the common thread here is an understanding of "textual politics" as the practice of discourse analysis that sets out a "radical rhetorical posture" with revolutionary ambitions.[5]

Yet this neat distinction between critiquing Realpolitik and the cultural politics of literature and other aesthetic forms has never been hard and fast. Theodor Adorno's anecdote about Picasso exemplifies this point: "An officer of the Nazi occupation forces visited the painter in his studio and, pointing to *Guernica*, asked: 'Did you do that?' Picasso reputedly answered, 'No, you did.'"[6] Picasso's deft response highlights how cultural politics and the real politics of state can become indistinguishable from one another. University activism in both the United States and Europe vividly demonstrated that cultural issues involving race, feminism, and sexuality were real-world problems even though their impacts might be felt in zones other than those governed by the state and its policies. If anything, as groups such as the Third World Liberation

Movement perceived, enough continuity existed between the cultural mission of public education and state policing for the critique of academic disciplines to acquire political urgency.[7] Still, the impression persists that the intellectual activity associated with humanities disciplines and cultural critique is somehow less practical and less weighty. Ironically, such dismissive arguments about the inconsequential nature of textual politics depend on cultural assumptions about gender and sexuality: as opposed to the "hard" sciences, the "soft" (read: "feminine") matters of aesthetic criticism lack both the rigor and temerity to confront real injustice or inequality in its most immediate and pure forms.

An unmistakable note of urgency ties the concreteness of politics to the insistent demands of the present. Real intervention in the world means acting now. This prescription can be a sore spot for critics seeking to justify their professional existence. Critique often makes only negligible claims on the present and instead seems better suited to the prospective temporality of the future. Talk of imminent social transformation, impending upheavals in human consciousness, and the promised teleology of revolution have been so captivating as to place critique in a position of constant anticipation. From Tom Paine's announcement that "the birthday of a new world is at hand" to W. E. B. Du Bois's promise that black art is "going to be" so beautiful as to one day "compell recognition" and from Gil Scott-Heron's faith that black people will soon "be in the street looking for a brighter day" to the messianic strains discernible in the work of intellectuals writing after Marx such as Walter Benjamin, the future has long been a part of the horizon when, keeping with the tenor of these examples, it comes to critiques of colonialism, racism, art, and capitalism.[8]

The subtitle of this chapter alludes to this temporal orientation without caving in to the "reproductive futurism" that Lee Edelman has diagnosed so powerfully: building on both Edward Said's and Matthew Arnold's separate statements about "the function of criticism at the present time," I seek to place criticism at a *different time* than the now.[9] More varied than the future, a different time seeks to be receptive to immanent moments that suggest temporalities other than those implied by planning and outcome, cost and benefit, means and end, or sacrifice and progress. By decoupling critique from the demand and desire that it be immediately relevant, we can gain a wider sense of politics that is not limited to specific solutions or pegged to quantifiable results. Indeed, we might say that this freedom from having to be relevant is exactly what makes the critic's task so meaningful in an age of benchmarks and assessment.

Appropriately enough, getting started on this task can be difficult, especially since the definitional confusion about the two senses of politics outlined above is augmented by uncertainty over whether there's a difference between "critique" and "criticism" and how that difference might matter to an understanding of politics. Critique at times is indistinguishable from criticism, while at other moments the two practices seem to register different aims and ambitions. Critique often implies a comprehensive, even aggressive, perspective for taking on an entire system of thought or belief. The broad aims of Kant's critiques of pure reason, practical reason, and judgment or Marx's *Contribution to the Critique of Political Economy* are not inconsistent with contemporary projects that endeavor to understand, for instance, the systemic nature of heteronormativity or whiteness. Criticism, by contrast, can often seem to have more modest goals that fit with its colloquial usage. My criticism of the film version of *Emma* is not the same as my critique. Leaving the movie theater, I might criticize Gwyneth Paltrow's accent or the costume designer's take on Regency style. Were I to generate a critique, however, I might be inclined to target the ways in which contemporary films inspired by British novels make the history of class hierarchy and gender conventions into a decorative effect. But, like the competing senses of politics, this opposition also crumbles, not the least because there's no corresponding career choice for critique as there is for criticism. People readily identify as critics, but no one calls herself a critiquer. Nevertheless, criticism and critique are often used interchangeably. For its part, this essay will try to remain attentive to the differences between the comprehensive nature of critique and the finely grained aspects of criticism by following the lead of critics' understanding of their own projects.

With these unstable distinctions in mind, we can proceed cautiously to pose a few questions. Is there any necessary correlation between critical views of state practices and critical readings of literary texts? Or, might the linkage between critique and politics be better understood as a disjunction in which an interpretative reading of a poem or novel, no matter its cleverness or explanatory power, offers no special insight or aptitude for understanding the world outside the text? To put the matter in terms of my opening example, throwing a rock from occupied territory does not have the same political value or force as examining a novel's connection to imperialism.[10] From one perspective, literary interpretation and cultural analysis hardly seem as concrete or as insistent as tossing stones. Then again, each entails a reckoning of power that confronts a larger determining structure. In the first instance that governing structure is the Israeli state, and in the second it is the novel and the system of geopolitical representation that it enshrines. Rock throwing may be no more real than critical reading; after all, Said called his act at the border a "symbolic gesture."

These twists and turns leave literary and other critics in an impossible place, denounced, on the one hand, for jumping over an invisible fence between the heady intellectual work performed on campus and the gritty political engagement undertaken in the real world and, on the other, dismissed for trafficking only in words and not being genuinely political. Viewers disturbed by the photograph of Said at the Lebanese border asked why a literary critic, distinguished for his readings of Joseph Conrad, Jane Austen, and William Butler Yeats, was making a gesture that seemed more violent than symbolic. To this question, the rejoinder might be offered that Said's central role in placing comparative literature into conversation with postcolonial studies made it both entirely appropriate and necessary for him to direct his critique at this particular instantiation of colonial power. Despite the conflict between these estimations of Said's political and intellectual work, each position nonetheless accepts prima facie the notion that critique can extend outward, beyond the journal article or monograph, to intervene in configurations of power. Where they differ is whether this sort of critical intervention is legitimate. There is still another position that rejects this notion tout court. Both within and outside the academy, skeptics such as Daphne Patai, Will Corral, and Richard Levin have asked whether the political positions claimed by the professoriate—a social group that seems to have become more and more irrelevant to the public sphere with each passing decade—add up to a politics that by any stretch of the imagination might be recognizable in ways that actually matter. To this rather snide suggestion, the counterpoint might be made that it is shortsighted to define politics so narrowly by curtailing it to a thin slice of empirical reality.

These competing claims suggest that the political tenor of critique is at an impasse worthy of Goldilocks: this critique is "too political," while that critique is "not political enough." The likelihood of finding some equilibrium where the balance between these extremes is "just right" seems remote. Accordingly, this essay does not seek a middle ground. The first section proceeds by examining how and why intellectuals have invested critique with a political function. This function is frequently imbued with progressive tendencies, although the correlation between critique and leftist politics has also been hotly contested. The second section thus examines how and why academic critique is conceived as having liberal-to-leftist tendencies. But the sparring over the presumably progressive valence of critique is only half the battle, since many commentators, including the practitioners of radical critique themselves, question whether critique can be equated to a politics at all. A brief coda suggests that, instead of seeing critique as political, as not political enough, or as a false politics, it may be more productive to understand critique as the impossible pursuit of political relevance and meaning, one that anticipates but is destined never to achieve its exigent ends.

Political Functions

Years before he ever stood at the Lebanese border and threw a rock into Israeli territory, Said had staked out a position for contemporary criticism that placed literary texts into the world of historical conflict. "Secular Criticism," the opening essay in his *The World, the Text, and the Critic* (1983), explicitly challenges the notion that the critic's "expertise is based upon noninterference" in political affairs, especially those having an international dimension.[11] Only recently has literary theory been divorced from the secular world, according to Said. A quick glance at Freud, Nietzsche, Marx, and other thinkers reveals to Said that modern critical interpretation begins with "insurrectionary" ambitions that destabilized traditional ideas about human identity.[12] An acute appreciation for the particular conditions of the 1980s deepened Said's conviction that critique had—or should have—an undeniable political core. His reasoning on this point is as powerful as it is counterintuitive. Literary theory, in Said's account, becomes political in inverse correlation to the degree that its practitioners advocate for a style of critique that is disengaged and insular. A critical practice that hovers above the messy world of politics is itself the result of political pressures that are deeply rooted in cultural policing and social governance. A view of critique as an endeavor that is removed from historical and social context is in reality the afterimage of an already-fought battle to make intellectuals consent to "the depoliticization of the citizenry."[13] The fact that literary theory in the 1980s has been confined to "pure textuality"—what Marx in an earlier moment derided as "theoretical bubble-blowing"—is an effect of worldly matters, particularly the rise of reactionary attitudes toward culture that have been ascendant since the days of Matthew Arnold.[14] What are the pressures coming from the geopolitical world that mandate the critic's self-involved fascination with "pure textuality" but not the crises of a wider reality? The "ascendancy of Reaganism"—a phrase that Said uses twice in the essay—accounts for the cultural shift that has relegated literary theory to the sidelines of civil society.[15]

Rather than accept such irrelevance, Said calls for a mode of critique whose politics exceed the single-mindedness of countering 1980s conservatism and encompasses a horizon wider than the face-off between Right and Left. His position is a curious one, since it is motivated at the outset by frustration with the reactionary tone of U.S. governmental policy that would intensify with Reagan's second term and the election of George H. W. Bush. Nevertheless, the idea of "secular criticism" ends up in a very different place from where it began by eschewing the traditional labels provided by the contemporary political spectrum and opting instead for an orientation that conjures up an older humanist vocabulary. "Criticism must think of itself as life-enhancing and constitutively opposed to every form of tyranny, domination, and abuse; its social goals are noncoercive knowledge produced in the interests of human freedom," writes Said, blending Enlightenment concepts and the aims of Third World liberation movements.[16] By rejecting political orientations of the moment, including 1980s conservatism as well as unreflective versions of Marxism and liberalism, "secular criticism" seeks to remain open to the debate and uncertainty that characterizes democracy. The result is an intellectual disposition that invites criticism of its own views, ideas, and solutions. This prospect of an intellectual orientation that surpasses petty and entrenched political identifications constitutes for Said the "function of criticism at the present time."[17]

Unmistakable echoes to Matthew Arnold's 1864 essay "The Function of Criticism at the Present Time" resound through Said's formulation, just as the title of Said's *Culture and Imperialism* (1993) simultaneously alludes to and departs from Arnold's *Culture and Anarchy* (1869). This convergence between a nineteenth-century liberal who sought to defend Western civilization from working-class radicalism and upper-class degeneracy and a postcolonial critic who sought to show how the idea of Western civilization has relied on "the *interpellation* of culture by empire" no doubt seems odd.[18] Even odder is the claim here that the two share a profound awareness that the function of criticism is, by and large, political.

Stung by the charge that criticism is a second-order discourse that takes a backseat to creative work, Arnold rejects the conventional wisdom that criticism has a negligible social effect or that critics themselves lack inventiveness. This gambit represents one of the earliest refusals to accept the idea that criticism is or should be confined to a cloistered domain, sheltered from the rude clamor of the everyday world. Far from being a self-enclosed avocation, criticism functions to inject new energies into society by throwing out antiquated knowledge and ushering in innovative ideas. As Arnold glanced around midcentury Britain (a task he would do more thoroughly a few years later in *Culture and Anarchy*), he took stock of, on the one hand, a burgeoning middle class that thought only about its gut and its wallet and, on the other, an enervated elite that cared only about foxhunting and sport. Arnold's appraisal of this socially stratified landscape suggested an urgent need for cultural renewal. The critical faculty, by virtue of a comparative method that trains us to judge that *this* is better than *that*, "displaces" ideas that have outlived their usefulness, effectively pruning cultural traditions of excess so that only "the best that is known and thought in the world" remains, according to Arnold.[19] You're welcome, says the Arnoldian scourge to the nation that has been reinvigorated by the harshness of his assessments. The function of criticism in the present time requires opening the narrow ranks of culture to foreign influences and news ways of thinking. In this respect, Arnold's view of criticism is as worldly as Said's: tired of the stale precepts endemic to British social hierarchy, he seeks to "*establish* a current of fresh and true ideas."[20]

The correlation between criticism and the act of establishing is key to discerning Arnold's politics. Even though he seems ready to sweep out the dusty drawing rooms of upper-class barbarians and unclutter the dens of middle-class philistines of gimcracks and other commodities, the intellectual's mission to "establish" lasting monuments of cultural tradition offsets this progressive tendency and brings criticism into line with what in the late 1960s came to be known as The Establishment. In other words: better not go too fast in connecting ideas about art and literature to the social and political world; ease up on the accelerator of cultural critique that encourages people to push ideas to the next extreme and "transport them abruptly into the world of politics and practice" and "violently to revolutionize this world to their bidding."[21] The specter here is the French Revolution, which, in Arnold's reading, witnessed an entire nation carried away by the criticism of Voltaire and Rousseau. It's all well and good to shine a light on the abuses of the church or the excesses of the ancien régime, but it's quite another to "transport" those critiques to the "world of politics and practice" when politics and practice have been fused at the guillotine. "This was the grand error of the French Revolution," Arnold states, "and its movement of ideas, by quitting the intellectual sphere and rushing furiously into the political sphere," was a fatal misstep that not only failed to bear any "intellectual fruit" but also fueled a backlash that effectively swung thought to the right, where it became narrow, suspicious, and doctrinaire.[22] From Arnold's perspective, that of a British liberal in the mid-nineteenth century, the goal of sharpening criticism with a revolutionary political edge had set the Enlightenment project of disseminating liberty and rationality back by decades. His reasoning reveals a bit of sophistry: revolutionary thought actually engendered conservatism by being so radical as to sow the seeds of reaction. The political aspect of criticism thus proves to be itself the undoing of a functional criticism.

Bringing Arnold, whose name during the "culture wars" of the 1980s became synonymous with conservative and falsely apolitical approaches to humanities education and research, into a discussion about the politics of critique no doubt seems a conversation stopper. But Arnold's plan to outline "the function of criticism at the present time"—a task, ironically, which anxiously reverts to the social upheaval of the previous century—is tragic proof of the fact that criticism can have "an immediate and political and practical application."[23] His assertions that ideas should not be political are an admission that criticism is already political. The question therefore is not whether criticism is political or not, since for Arnold the convergence of criticism and radical politics is a foregone—and regrettable—conclusion.

From Said's perspective at the close of the twentieth century, literary theory has blunted the revolutionary political edge of critique. As he updates the Arnoldian chore of writing about the "function of criticism at the present time," Said contends that while critique should engage with and intervene in worldly affairs, it currently abstains from doing so. Where Arnold believed that overzealous thinkers had interfered with matters beyond the intellectual sphere, Said regrets that "literary theory now explicitly accepts the principle of noninterference."[24] In essence, Said takes up what Arnold rejects—yet beneath this opposition is a shared belief that critical work, perhaps most especially when it is surrounded by calls that it not engage, intervene, or interfere with worldly matters, is necessarily political in nature.

Moving Left and Right

If the function of criticism at the present time is political, it remains important to figure out what sort of politics it seeks to enact. On the correlation between critique and a certain political orientation, there is broad agreement. As Rita Felski observes, "Critique is a term associated with a progressively-oriented politics."[25] Because critique seeks to dismantle ossified structures of knowledge that are standing in the way of everything from social equality to individual liberation, its practitioners regularly seem aligned with the cultural and political Left. "Critique's fundamental quality is that of 'againstness,'" writes Felski, observing how animus within the academy is directed outward against prevailing myths, ideologies, inequalities, and other cultural constructs.[26] Arnold no doubt felt that this oppositional stance had gone too far, since his age seemed hell-bent on according the citizen the "right to do what he likes; his right to march where he likes, meet where he likes, enter where he likes, hoot as he likes, threaten as he likes, *smash* as he likes."[27] As opposed to the prospect of a nineteenth-century criticism that would "establish" lasting values, contemporary academic critique seems more ready to disestablish the assumptions behind class hierarchy, racism, and heteronormativity.

Nevertheless, reservations about the "againstness" of critique persist. Has there been too much smashing by those using critique only as a blunt instrument? "With a hammer (or a sledge hammer) in hand you can do a lot of things: break down walls, destroy idols, ridicule prejudices, but you cannot repair, take care, assemble, reassemble, stitch together," writes Bruno Latour, as a part of a broader inquiry into whether smashing has proceeded so far apace that critique can now be put to perverse uses such as disputing established scientific facts.[28] Not unlike Arnold, Latour seeks to balance destructive critique and creative composition—and he's led to do so because of political considerations that also recall Arnold's reaction to the migration of ideas into the secular world of action.[29] But unlike Arnold, who fretted over the transit of radical ideas to radical revolutionary practices, Latour wonders if radical ideas have been taken up by conservatives who, it seems, find more than enough encouragement for surveillance in the work of Michel Foucault and willingly deploy the moves of hermeneutic skepticism to argue that the evidence and "truths" about climate change remain up for debate.

Despite Latour's wondering if folks over at the National Security Administration are making *Discipline and Punish* "their bedtime reading," the concern more commonly is that critique is directed against any and all types of social order and administration.[30] Critique seems immanently hostile to politically conservative interests, a suspicion that goes a long way toward explaining why "conservative critics charge that American higher education has become the playpen of radical faculty who seek to spread their antireligious, big-government, liberal ideas to their young undergraduate charges."[31] When critique adopts political aims and profane accents, it seemingly participates in rock throwing, smashing, and hammer-striking, causing consternation that varies in direct proportion to its social thrust and worldly overtones. As James

English notes, when academics associated with interdisciplinary concentrations such as postcolonial studies, cultural studies, queer studies, and New Historicism engage literary texts, they do so by pointedly referencing "the social forces of their production, the social meanings of their formal particulars, and the social effects of their circulation and reception."[32] In other words, these practitioners have read their Karl Marx, having found their way to the nexus of sociology and literature via Antonio Gramsci and the Birmingham Centre for Contemporary Cultural Studies. The prevalence of the social thoroughly thrusts critique into the material world.

Even detractors who are convinced that the reign of sociology has made literature little more than a dependent vassal in "theory's empire" acknowledge that the worldly thrust of critique is political and almost always to the left. Contributors to the seven-hundred-page volume *Theory's Empire: An Anthology of Dissent* gravitate around the perspective that the predominance of social categories such as race, class, gender, and sexuality in literary studies constitutes a new political orthodoxy, which, not unlike totalitarian renditions of orthodox Marxism, leaves little room for the disagreement or the nuances of interpretation. The long shadow of the Cold War rhetoric is operative in this sort of narrative, since what has transpired under "theory's empire" is hardly different from "the reduction of art to politics" that occurs under "the totalitarian state."[33] Just as Arnold's stance against transporting intellectual ideas to the public sphere represents an implicit acknowledgment that politics are already infected with the ferment of a criticism that smashes, so too this desire for hard-and-fast divisions between aesthetics and the social world that is evident in *Theory's Empire* confirms like nothing else that the cross-migrations of critique and leftist politics are a fait accompli.

From this perspective, it is easy to describe the history of post-1960s critique as a battle for intellectual territory: "The rhetoric of Theory has been successful in gaining the moral and political high ground," the editors of *Theory's Empire* lament, "and those who question it do so at their peril."[34] This intellectual summit, so the charge goes, affords no quarter to those who dissent from the presumed party line, leaving more conservatively inclined readers out in the cold. Although the handwringing about politically driven critique, as I have suggested, extends back at least as far as Arnold, the perception arose in the 1980s that this activist engagement is of a more recent vintage. In this rendering, the politicization of critique represents the misshapen fruit of second-wave feminism, Black Power, gay liberation, antiwar protests, and other social movements that found refuge in the academy. As the social fervor of the 1960s waned, "professors trained primarily in literature began to claim for themselves a commanding position from which to comment importantly on any and all aspects of cultural and political life," write Daphne Patai and Will Corral.[35] One unremarked irony of such assessments is, of course, that the elevation of theory, which supposedly gave academics a soapbox, actually corresponded to the marginalization of intellectuals in the public sphere during the era of the "culture wars" and shrinking investments in higher education. Another is that the implicit nostalgia for intellectual work that would study literature strictly in its own right apart from any sociological or political considerations is, in fact, a faux Arnoldian position. Simply to speak of the "function of criticism at the present time," as Arnold first knew and as Said later echoed, is to imbue critique with a relevance and utility that befits political commitments.

Overstepping and *Understepping*

Yet for every assertion that critique supplies a politics, skepticism remains about whether the critic's various acts of comparing, decoding, deconstructing, describing, and unmasking count as politics at all. The unstable definitions of politics noted at the beginning of this essay—is it a broader concern about how power operates and is distributed in society, or is it a more precise endeavor to study state and governmental matters?—lie at the core of this doubt. Teachers and students in the academy regularly confuse these senses of politics, approaching a text or other aesthetic object with one sense of politics in mind and exiting with another in hand. Critiquing the state's monopoly on legitimate force and showing how a text offers a critique of incarceration and surveillance are deeply intertwined activities. But they are not the same activity. Even though Terry Eagleton at the outset of *Marxism and Literary Criticism* reminds us that "there is nothing academic" about "the struggles of men and women to free themselves from certain forms of exploitation and oppression," politics and critical practice always seem on the verge of parting ways.[36] There is plenty that is academic about the contexts of critique, not the least of which are the research protocols of the contemporary corporate university, reliance on adjunct labor,[37] and pressures of professionalization and publishing, that often make interpretative practices inconsistent with political commitments. No matter how delightfully reassuring it would be to transform Eagleton's dictum and assert that "there is everything political about using texts to critique certain forms of exploitation and oppression," academic critique is frequently subject to complaints that it yields a watered-down version of the political.

Even worse, it is not subject to these complaints at all, since professors and students regularly read, write, and critique without ever realizing or acknowledging that intellectual work is much better for contemplating politics in a loose sense than for intervening in insistently concrete issues such as widening economic inequality, militarization, and environmental catastrophe.

This disconnect does not necessarily mean that critique falls short of politics in either of its two senses. After all, Said's rock missed an Israeli guardhouse by a country mile even as *Orientalism* fixes its sights so exactly on the history of Western misrepresentation that the book has become synonymous with reshaping the ways in which people write and think about the Middle East, Asia, and Africa. Critique in the humanities expands well beyond narrowly defined targets by addressing problems associated with the history of capitalism, globalization, and climate change that have been centuries in the making. The point of critique is not to dazzle by outlining "an alternative technique for interpreting *Paradise Lost* or *Middlemarch*," writes Eagleton. Instead, critique, specifically Marxist reading practices, belongs in any toolbox that is devoted to "our liberation from oppression."[38] This appreciation for critique as a mode of intellectual engagement that allows for an expansive social intervention is not solely the property of Marxist readers. Not unlike Eagleton, Said calls for readings that promote "alternative acts and alternative intentions" to imagine interpretative practices whose concerns are as wide as humanity itself. The result is "life-enhancing" critique that serves "the interests of human freedom."[39] Even Arnold, who no doubt held very different ideas about human freedom and the liberation from oppression, felt that the political slant of criticism should open onto an ample social vista. What would be the point of criticism, he wondered in *Culture and Anarchy*, whose ambit was limited to debating specific proposals such as ones that would make it lawful to marry your dead wife's sister?[40] To be sure, such criticism would have a point, but it often seems to be making too fine of a point to restrict critics to political questions of the moment. Just as Adorno scorned authors who relegated their art to narrow causes by writing "propagandist plays against syphilis, duels, abortion laws or borstals," pundits and other observers routinely skewer intellectuals who are seen as condescending from the ivory tower to weigh in on political matters.[41] Expertise in John Milton or George Eliot, to return to the locale of Eagleton's examples, does not necessarily make the literary critic an expert on blindness and tenant farming any more than on venereal disease or detention centers.

The issue here is not only that scholars of the epic or the British novel are wary about overstepping their literary expertise by secularizing what might otherwise be viewed as purely textual matters. More pointedly, it is also the case that intellectuals routinely wonder whether they are *under*stepping their authority by not fully embracing critique as a type of political activity in its own right. Rather than feel that they need to abandon their areas of specialization in order to make a political intervention, critics instead have claimed that their field is itself political. Robyn Wiegman has argued that this conflation of critique as politics has become particularly acute in American studies. Despite her focus on this one interdisciplinary field, she suggests that the conflation of critical agency and political agency is symptomatic of other academic discourses as well. In a trenchant reading, Wiegman argues that American studies scholars tend to see transformative power in their academic practices. For Americanists, "the ascription of political agency to critical inquiry" appears "as a generative, indeed foundational aspect of the field's disciplinary demand."[42] Because of the notion that unmasking, debunking, and other acts of intellectual smashing "are now thoroughly institutionalized in American studies, no less than across the humanities and interpretative social sciences as a whole, the claim to 'progressive political critique' is not exterior to disciplinarity but a constitutive agency of its professional authority."[43] And there's nothing more that American studies scholars like to smash than the entanglements with state power, nationalism, and geopolitical might that go hand in hand with the field itself. Practitioners of American studies, it seems, willingly cloak themselves with a hair-shirt logic that makes their own penance about American nationalism a prerequisite for progressive critique.[44]

This posture of self-abnegation can prove pleasurable. By expressing ambivalence and even opposition toward their object of study, Americanists seek an exteriority that supports a stance that seems permanently on the vanguard. As Wiegman asserts, "Casting the critical act as a form of political transgression against the state" has an "effect for the practitioner that must be understood as deeply comforting."[45] In the face of worries that critique has been co-opted by state-sponsored fields of study and the institutions of the corporate university, the feeling of being always at odds with one's academic discipline provides intellectuals with an identity that seems innately committed to and assured of being on the right side of history. I should hasten to add that these feelings have often been my own. Whether my focus has been the paternalist aspects of national memory, the constraints of state citizenship, or the clampdown on the more vibrant aspects of democracy, my career has encouraged me to see intellectual work as political work. Wiegman concludes on a similar note, acknowledging that her critique, both within and of American studies, has sought to connect hermeneutic practices with social transformation. What proves so "seductive" and "gratifying," to use Wiegman's terms, about this "disciplinary disposition" is that it makes academic critique a matter of political urgency.[46]

Although Wiegman is careful not to trot out the complaint that interpretation remains too esoteric to amount to politics in any meaningful sense, other commentators are not so scrupulous. Theory is "a displacement of or surrogate for real political activity"; it represents an inflated "arena for waging ersatz politics"; it is steeped in "political pretensions" that do little more than allow professors and students to pretend that their classrooms and syllabi have some political gravitas.[47] It is an accusation that dates back to misreadings of Marx's eleventh thesis on Feuerbach: "The philosophers have only *interpreted* the world, in various ways; the point, however, is to *change* it."[48] As Marx very well understood, an interpretation of the world is already a transformation of that world. From Marx's perspective, the problem was that philosophers of the day had been using their intellectual prowess to keep the world as it is. But from the perspective of those who see politically minded professors as poseurs, critique should know its place just as literary and academic critics should not imagine that they are somehow positioned at the barricades.

Make no mistake, however: the place of a critique is frequently an entitled one. Plenty of incisive social and political thinkers have enjoyed relative privilege, but this position should not be treated reductively in ways that invalidate their insights. After all, one of American democracy's foremost critics, Alexis de Tocqueville, boasted an ancient aristocratic lineage. Wealth and status do not necessarily disable critical acumen, just as these entitlements do not require the beholder to side with conservatives and reactionaries. Still, as Ian Hunter observes, the subject whose vocation is critique cultivates a disciplinary identity that comports with the ethos of modern biopolitics. Insofar as theory stakes political commitments, "we can also ask whether the political salience of theory might arise less from its unmasking of power than from . . . [its] redeployment of aesthetic education as a governmental pedagogy."[49] In Hunter's incisive account, critique enables its practitioners not to intervene in the realm of politics but to work on the self. What literary theory ultimately reveals are not the inner contradictions of the text but the mysteries of the subject. Critique prepares entry into a "civic elite" by legitimizing a class of intellectuals who decipher all that is usually only seen through a glass darkly. In place of the desires for social transformation that Wiegman sees motivating American studies scholars, Hunter's literary theorists work on "a practice of self-transformation."[50]

Work conducted at the crossings of political and aesthetic representation would seem to confirm this suspicion that critique can lead to the internal world of the subject, not the outer geopolitical world that begins to come into focus with Said's mentions of Reaganism and Vietnam. The author of *Aesthetic Democracy*, for instance, hypothesizes that democracy is an engine of self-transformation, a conclusion that seems to gut democracy of much of its social energy and historical content.[51] In this way, the argument of *Aesthetic Democracy* confirms Hunter's judgment that critique rendered as literary theory actually devolves into "counterpolitics." The reversal is complete: critique that starts out with political intentions winds up abandoning politics altogether. In fact, as Hunter contends, this turn away from the secular world is consistent with Christian hermeneutics that underpin the genealogy of modern literary theory.[52] But what is perhaps most surprising is that Hunter includes none other than Said, author of "Secular Criticism," among those critics who have confused and conflated self-consciousness with political consciousness.

Said's misstep, according to Hunter, is that his work on imperialism and the novel "converts a political situation into an occasion for hermeneutic self-clarification."[53] Although Said's declaration in *Culture and Imperialism* that "we are at a point in our work when we can no longer ignore empires and the imperial contest in our studies" speaks of urgency, Hunter feels that this conviction is misplaced, since Said's interpretations of the European novel become fixated upon matters that in the end seem more metaphysical than political.[54] In the simplest terms, reading a novel, for Hunter, is not the same thing as exercising critical citizenship. Or, with a bit more nuance, reading a novel in order to map the geopolitical contradictions where aesthetic representation can go no further permits and even encourages readers to focus on the dramas of their own intellectual processes. For Hunter, Said's position is emblematic of all who mistake criticism for politics. "When it comes to their roles as citizens, then, it is important for literary theorists not to take their work home with them," Hunter concludes in the final sentence of his essay.[55] Given this scolding, one might also wonder if critics should also not take their work with them when they travel, say, to the border between Israel and Lebanon, where stones—and reasons for throwing them—abound.

The incommensurability between the sheltered world of critics and the broader world of political conflict means that critique is destined to always fall short of its targets. Said's stone is never going to hit the guardhouse, just as a poststructuralist reading of allegory is unlikely to pinpoint the social and institutional structures that maintain hierarchy and inequality. For Hunter, such imprecision is damning, indicative of critique's quasi-theological insularity that stymies meaningful engagement with the world. But what if being off target is the condition of emancipatory politics? What if coming up short and perennially missing the mark are the very characteristics that make critique political?

Missing the Critical Mark

Coming up short resounds with the failure. It suggests a missed target, a squandered opportunity, an incomplete engagement. But it also contains the faint promise that there will be renewed attempts, future trials, and continued struggle. Walter Benjamin described this sense of critique's flitting and undetermined possibility as a "*weak* Messianic power."[56] Critique in this sense does not purify by fire. It does not usher in a revolutionary transformation of the world. As opposed to the steadfast faith that the Messiah will come and intervene in the secular world so as to redeem it, this weak critical force barely leaves a scratch on the hard surface of politics. Even for a critic who traffics in the concrete—Benjamin invokes the "historical materialist," and today we might enlarge that category to refer readers who deal with all sorts of vibrant matter[57]—intellectual engagement might only ever amount to a form of politics that barely registers. Like the "secret heliotropism" that turns flowers almost imperceptibly toward the sun, the "historical materialist must be aware of this most inconspicuous of all transformations," writes Benjamin.[58] So weak, imperceptible, and unremarkable are the politics of this critique that they likely do not even register as political.

For an essay that takes seriously the understanding of politics as grounded activity, it must seem like a turnabout to ally the political capacity of critique with the ever-receding horizon of messianic deferral. Perhaps so. One effect of this irony is to detach our methods of reading and interpretation from any certain trajectory. Even the most compelling critics are hesitant about saying that reading or interpreting a text produces a discernible change in the social world, let alone our understanding of that world. To be sure, many critics, myself included, operate with the sad knowledge that our readings and interpretations, no matter how dazzling, will not change how others read even the texts that are our object of study. What a messianic disposition does change, however, is the temporality of critique so that it falls out of step with the straightforward telos of the political. Or, better yet, it expands "political redemption beyond the language of secularity" so that instead of adhering to the liberal faith in progress, critique opens itself to the time before politics ever takes final shape.[59]

The time before the political properly congeals may be only a moment's duration, but such moments can also last longer than a lifetime. For Jacques Derrida, a weak messianic power "obliges us to think, from there, another space for democracy. For democracy-to-come and thus for justice."[60] Critique in this sense leaves us poised on the brink of political decision, but always hesitating, uncertain about what is to come next. It does not predict a course of action or point in any one direction, especially one whose arrow-like vector is aimed at some notion of "progress." Instead, messianic criticism resounds with an elusive temporal richness that promotes the indeterminacy of ever-present possibility. "Every second of time was the strait gate through which the Messiah might pass," writes Benjamin.[61] At any moment, critique might help to generate a broad political insight or a specific political stance; then again, as is more often the case, such moments might just as well pass by unrealized. In terms of both space ("the strait gate") and time ("every second"), critique is always just outside the political realm. It may be poised on the threshold, ready to enter, yet it is never here now. This is the function of criticism at a different time.

Adorno's remarks on politicized art provide a vital reminder about why critique must always fall short of its destination. Although Adorno's focus in "Commitment" is postwar aesthetics, his comments can be usefully adapted to the matter of critique. As we have seen, Adorno expressed deep reservations about literature that has a specific axe to grind, whether it is pointed at sexually transmitted diseases or modern forms of punishment. "Bad politics becomes bad art, and vice-versa," he contends.[62] Art with defined political intentions lacks nuance and flexibility, which in turn encourages a political outlook lacking these qualities as well. He instead prefers artistic forms that "point to practice from which they abstain: the creation of a just life."[63] There is salvation, but we will never get there by way of art or critique. The theological dimension of this statement entails awareness that a messiah, like Moses, can see a promised land off in the distance but never enter it. "The very idea of the messianic," writes Fredric Jameson, "then brings the feeling of dashed hopes and impossibility along with it."[64] Yet if the messiah has not yet arrived, there nonetheless remains the incalculable possibility that he or she will arrive in the very next moment. As the weak messianic power of critique alternately fades from and comes into partial view, it never resolves into a fully actualized politics, but it does indicate the spaces and times where politics might emerge. In short, although neither criticism nor critique is identical to politics, each does produce the conditions for politics to be imagined differently from both what has come before and what seems certain to come in the future.

Such anticipation, whether it takes shape as "democracy-to-come" or the narrow gate through which a redeemed world might one day be glimpsed, imbues critical work with its political potential. It is an expectation tinged with scant hope and more than enough despair. When Matthew Arnold concluded his comments on "the function of criticism at the present time," he acknowledged that any certainty about this functionality would be best put off until another time: "There is the promised land, towards which criticism can only beckon. That promised land it will not be ours to enter, and we shall die in the wilderness: but to have desired to enter it, to have saluted it from afar, is already, perhaps, the best distinction among contemporaries."[65] Arnold may not have much in common with a German-Jewish leftist intellectual of the twentieth century, but, like Benjamin, he invested critique with a messianic power that recognizes how the very desire to engage the world invariably sets critique apart from that world. The upshot, appropriately enough, is a contradiction worthy of untangling: only by miscalculating, mistaking, and just plain missing out on the political in its varying senses does critique acquire political possibility.

Notes

1 The photograph of Edward Said throwing a stone has been much publicized and debated. It is readily available on the web and can be viewed, among other places, at http://constructionlitmag.com/culture/books/the-charisma-of-edward-said/.

2 Dinitia Smith, "A Stone's Throw Is a Freudian Slip," *New York Times*, March 10, 2001, http://www.nytimes.com/2001/03/10/arts/a-stone-s-throw-is-a-freudian-slip .html?scp=1&sq=%22edward+said%22&st=nyt.

3 American Studies Association, "Council Resolution on Boycott of Israeli Academic Institutions," December 4, 2014, http://www.theasa.net/american_studies _association_resolution_on_academic_boycott_of_israel.

4 See Max Weber, "Politics as Vocation," http://anthropos-lab.net/wp/wp-content /uploads/2011/12/Weber-Politics-as-a-Vocation.pdf, accessed November 21, 2014.

5 Michael Sprinker, "Textual Politics: Foucault and Derrida," *boundary* 2 8, no. 3 (spring 1980): 76.

6 Theodor Adorno, "Commitment," in *Aesthetics and Politics* (London: New Left Books, 1977), 189–90.

7 See Russ Castronovo, "Within the Veil of Interdisciplinary Knowledge? Jefferson, Du Bois, and the Negation of Politics," *New Literary History* 31 (2000): 781–82.

8 Thomas Paine, *Common Sense*, in *The Thomas Paine Reader*, ed. Michael Foot and Isaac Kramnick (New York: Penguin, 1987), 109; W. E. B. Du Bois, "Crite-

ria of Negro Art," in *The Norton Anthology of African American Literature*, ed. Henry Louis Gates Jr. and Nellie Y. McKay (New York: W. W. Norton, 1997), 759; Gil Scott-Heron, "The Revolution Will Not Be Televised," https://play.google .com/music/preview/Tuaqbvo36fr5a7dnmbgntgoegoi?lyrics=1&utm_source =google&utm_medium=search&utm_campaign=lyrics&pcampaignid=kp -lyrics, accessed February 24, 2015.

9   Lee Edelman, *No Future: Queer Theory and the Death Drive* (Durham, NC: Duke University Press, 2004), 2.

10   The prime example is Said's *Culture and Imperialism* (New York: Knopf, 1993).

11   Edward Said, "Introduction: Secular Criticism," in *The World, the Text, and the Critic* (Cambridge, MA: Harvard University Press, 1983), 2. As Said later developed this idea in *Culture and Imperialism*, "Culture conceived in this way can become a protective enclosure: check your politics at the door" (xiv).

12   Said, "Secular Criticism," 3.

13   Said, "Secular Criticism," 25.

14   Said, "Secular Criticism," 4; Karl Marx, "The German Ideology," in *The Marx-Engels Reader*, 2nd ed. (New York: W. W. Norton, 1978), 166.

15   Said, "Secular Criticism," 4, 25.

16   Said, "Secular Criticism," 29.

17   Said, "Secular Criticism," 5.

18   Said, *Culture and Imperialism*, 61.

19   Matthew Arnold's "The Function of Criticism at the Present Time" was first published in the *National Review* in November 1864. It is online at *Fortnightly Review*, http://fortnightlyreview.co.uk/the-function-of-criticism-at-the-present -time/, accessed September 16, 2014.

20   Arnold, "The Function of Criticism" (my emphasis).

21   Arnold, "The Function of Criticism."

22   Arnold, "The Function of Criticism." Note how his formulation presumes a separation between "intellectual" and "political" spheres.

23   Arnold, "The Function of Criticism." Elsewhere in the essay he states that the ideas associated with the "French Revolution took a political, practical character," condensing politics and praxis.

24   Said, "Secular Criticism," 3.

25   Rita Felski, *The Limits of Critique* (Chicago: University of Chicago Press, 2015) 140.

26   Felski, *The Limits of Critique*, 129.

27   Arnold, *Culture and Anarchy* (New York: Oxford University Press, 2006), 57 (my emphasis).

28   Bruno Latour, "An Attempt at a 'Compositionist Manifesto,'" *New Literary History* 41 (2010): 475. See also his "Why Has Critique Run Out of Steam? From Matters of Fact to Matters of Concern," *Critical Inquiry* 30, no. 2 (winter 2004): 225–48.

29   For more on this point, see Russ Castronovo and David Glimp, "Introduction: After Critique?" ELN 51, no. 2 (fall/winter 2013): 2.

30   Latour, "Why Has Critique," 228.

31 Amy J. Binder and Kate Wood, *Becoming Right: How Campuses Shape Young Conservatives* (Princeton, NJ: Princeton University Press, 2013), ix.

32 James F. English, "Everywhere and Nowhere: The Sociology of Literature after 'the Sociology of Literature,'" *New Literary History* 41, no. 2 (spring 2010): viii.

33 Harold Fromm, "Oppositional Opposition," in *Theory's Empire: An Anthology of Dissent*, ed. Daphne Patai and Will H. Corral (New York: Columbia University Press, 2005), 455.

34 Daphne Patai and Will H. Corral, introduction to *Theory's Empire*, 3. Their capitalization of "Theory" has the effect of making critique appear to be an ideologically consistent and monolithic entity.

35 Patai and Corral, introduction to *Theory's Empire*, 8.

36 Terry Eagleton, *Marxism and Literary Criticism* (Berkeley: University of California Press, 1976), vii.

37 For more on the vexed intersection between critique and the contemporary "crisis" of the humanities, especially with respect to issues involving graduate students, debt, and adjunct labor, see Bennett Carpenter, Laura Goldblatt, Lenora Hansen, Anna Vitale, Karim Wissa, and Andrew Yale, "Feces on the Philosophy of History! A Manifesto on the MLA Subconference," *Pedagogy: Critical Approaches to Teaching Literature, Language, Composition, and Culture* 14, no. 3 (fall 2014): 381–93.

38 Eagleton, *Marxism and Literary Criticism*, 76.

39 Said, "Secular Criticism," 29–30.

40 "The believer in machinery may think that to get a Government to abolish Church-rates or to legalise marriage with a deceased wife's sister is to exert a moral and ennobling influence upon Government," writes Arnold (*Culture and Anarchy*, 10).

41 Adorno, "Commitment," 180.

42 Robyn Wiegman, "The Ends of New Americanism," *New Literary History* 42, no. 3 (summer 2011): 393.

43 Wiegman, "The Ends of New Americanism," 394.

44 For more on the "hair-shirt logic" of American studies, see Russ Castronovo and Susan Gillman, "Introduction: The Study of the American Problems," in *States of Emergency: The Object of American Studies* (Chapel Hill: University of North Carolina Press, 2009), 19.

45 Wiegman, "The Ends of New Americanism," 398.

46 Wiegman, "The Ends of New Americanism," 398. See also her final paragraph, which explains that her intent is not to debunk, belittle, blame, or find impossibly new and utopian forms of critical agency but to thoroughly "understand the stakes" of the political investments of American studies (403).

47 Richard Levin, "Silence Is Consent, or Curse Ye Morez!," in Patai and Corral, *Theory's Empire*, 470; Patai and Corral, introduction to *Theory's Empire*, 13; back cover of *Theory's Empire*.

48 Karl Marx, "Theses on Feuerbach," in *The Marx-Engels Reader*, 2nd ed., ed. Robert C. Tucker (New York: W. W. Norton, 1978), 145.

49 Ian Hunter, "Literary Theory in Civil Life," *South Atlantic Quarterly* 95, no. 4 (fall 1996): 1103–4.

50 Hunter, "Literary Theory in Civil Life," 1107.

51 Thomas Docherty writes, "Democracy can be characterized not only as an event, but more precisely as an event that is predicated upon beauty and as an event that signals a predicament in representation. Further, this event, insofar as it is democratic, signals not the identification of the self, not the consolidation of a preexisting and predetermining identity, but rather the altering of the self, such that the self that exists after the event must of necessity differ from the self that inaugurated it." Docherty, *Aesthetic Democracy* (Stanford, CA: Stanford University Press, 2006), 158.

52 Thus Hunter: "Let us formulate a relation between the early Christian and the modern literary hermeneutics of the self as follows: In deploying ethical writings in the space of hermeneutic self-problematization—that is, by tying hidden meaning of the text to the opacity of the reader's ethical being—modern literary theory emerges as a historical improvisation on the hermeneutic exercises associated with the Christian pursuit of holiness" ("Literary Theory in Civil Life," 1110).

53 Hunter, "Literary Theory in Civil Life," 1124.

54 Said, *Culture and Imperialism*, 6.

55 Hunter, "Literary Theory in Civil Life," 1130.

56 Walter Benjamin, "Theses on the Philosophy of History," in *Illuminations*, ed. Hannah Arendt (New York: Schocken, 1968), 254.

57 Jane Bennett, *Vibrant Matter: A Political Economy of Things* (Durham, NC: Duke University Press, 2010).

58 Benjamin, "Theses on the Philosophy of History," 255.

59 Avery Slater, "American Afterlife: Benjaminian Messianism and Technological Redemption in Muriel Rukeyser's *The Book of the Dead*," *American Literature* 86, no. 4 (December 2014): 770.

60 Jacques Derrida, *Specters of Marx*, trans. Peggy Kamuf (New York: Routledge, 1994), 169. On Benjamin's and Derrida's different shadings of messianism, see Owen Ware, "Dialectic of the Past/Disjuncture of the Future: Derrida and Benjamin on the Concept of Messianism," *Journal for Cultural and Religious Theory* 5, no. 2 (April 2004): 99–114.

61 Benjamin, "Theses on the Philosophy of History," 264.

62 Adorno, "Commitment," 187.

63 Adorno, "Commitment," 194.

64 Fredric Jameson, "Marx's Purloined Letter," in *Ghostly Demarcations: A Symposium on Jacques Derrida's Specters of Marx*, ed. Michael Sprinker (New York: Verso, 1999), 62.

65 Arnold, "Function of Criticism."

10

Tragedy and Translation

A Future for Critique in a Secular Age

JOHN MICHAEL

Post-Enlightenment Secularism and the End of Comic Romance

The humanities seem, at least in the United States, increasingly marginalized and subjected to attacks from all quarters for a certain hubristic politicization, on the one hand, and what is often described as a corresponding diminished relevance to students and the world, on the other. These contrasting pressures suggest that something has gone awry. In this context, it is worth reevaluating the place and practice of critique, for since the Renaissance practices of close reading and textual analysis that subtend critique have been identified with humanistic scholarship. As Michael Warner reminds us, techniques of close reading are rooted in ancient textual practices, in the invention of the codex, and in Renaissance and Reformation biblical exegesis that become associated with the ascendency of modernity and the emergence of literature at the end of the eighteenth century.[1] These practices of close reading or depth analysis remain critique's basic method and ground its fundamental claims. *Critique* can seem a confusingly capacious term and is usually applied without much reflection to a range of textual strategies or hermeneutical approaches common in a variety of literary and cultural studies domains. Critical camps that seem quite opposite claim a stake in this term. These might include both critical theory as it derives from the Frankfurt School and poststructuralist or deconstructive reading as it follows from early works by Derrida, Lyotard, and others. It may also include both versions of New Critical close reading and New Historicist attacks on formalism's putatively apolitical aestheticism. As different as they may be, all of these approaches share a marked family resemblance. In its resistance to commonsense versions of intentionality or meaning in literary texts, even New Criticism has affinities with what Paul Ricoeur long ago called the hermeneutics of suspicion.[2] Each of these varied approaches relies on techniques of deep or close reading meant to uncover the networks of power and the designs of obfuscation, or the tensions and lapses in structures of signification, or the linguistic patterning of ironies and paradoxes, or the institutional imbrications of complicity or co-optation that constitute the real meaning or actual significance of a text, a meaning or significance that awaits within the text for the critic, the master interpreter, to decipher and reveal it. In one way or another, despite their differences in vocabulary and purpose, each of these approaches subscribes to a sense of textuality that Derrida himself characterized in the opening sentence of "Plato's Pharmacy," one of deconstruction's founding texts, "A text is not a text unless it hides from the first comer, from the first glance, the law of its composition and the rules of its game."[3] The text's truth hides within the text, and the task of critique is to bring it to light, to decode or uncover it, even if the truth be, as Derrida would have it, that there is no final truth available except the play of textuality itself. This sense of textuality and the practice of critique it enables still predominate in literary and cultural studies.[4] Indeed, critique may be said to have long defined the humanities as an academic enterprise. It is this version of critique that seems increasingly questionable today, as the humanities find themselves beset by a faltering sense of purpose on the one hand and increasingly skeptical public scrutiny on the other.

Much of what follows here specifically addresses those forms of critique associated with academic leftism, especially since the 1970s. Here critique has effectively focused on the textual and institutional imbrications of gender, race, and class, of nation and empire. These forms of critique attracted many of us precisely because we wanted to make our work as textual interpreters, as humanists trained as close readers, relevant. Critique seemed a powerful tool. It promised to help overcome the obfuscations of the world by those powerful forces of the government and the economy interested in controlling the discourses, means, and materials of culture and representation and to reveal the real relationships of power and oppression encoded within or subtending the cultural artifacts we studied. Through critical analysis of these phenomena, we hoped to contribute to the emancipation of subjects and societies. Often this required us to adopt postures as supposedly knowing subjects, saddled with the necessary but essentially belligerent task of explaining the realities of the world to our less enlightened audiences. Today, however, we continue to perform this work in a world that no longer provides an easily discernible platform for the staging of these critical performances, however important they may sometimes be.

Critique, despite its roots in religious exegetical traditions, assumes that suspicious hermeneutics plays an important part in the drama of Enlightenment and emancipation that Kant and Hegel identified with the evolution of the Western mind.[5] Marx's refurbishing of Hegelian dialectic as material historicism and the demystification of bourgeois ideology that he made critical theory's legacy was, in an important sense, a continuation of this project to further the human subject's "emergence from [its] . . . self-incurred immaturity," bringing it out of the "barbarism" of superstition into the light of reason through critical thinking.[6] The Euro- and ethnocentric imbrications of the precritical link between Enlightenment and emancipation are no longer immediately credible for most of us, and this is one important reason that the traditional role of critique as a secular demystification that inculcates a universal rationality has itself been discredited by our suspicious scrutiny. The necessary tension between the critic as missionary of enlightenment and the audience in its darkness now sometimes seems just another antagonism among the many contending beliefs of a secular world.

If we equate modernity and secularization, then critique finds itself undermined by the very modernity it helps to establish. Recently, the traditional understanding of secularism itself has altered. The familiar opposition between secular reason and uncritical belief, material reality and ideological mystification that has long grounded the critical project threatens to collapse. It is not so much that the hosts of fundamentalisms, including evangelical Christianity, political Islam, and religious Zionism, confront and threaten secular reason. It is rather that, given the uneven heterogeneities of the globalized public sphere and political world in which we have all for some time lived, the understanding of what secularism itself is has changed. The proliferation of beliefs, even fundamentalisms, is itself one sign of a secular age. As Charles Taylor argues, secularism can no longer be understood as the rejection of parochial beliefs and superstitions in favor of catholicisms of science and rationality. In this age, any belief, including the belief in science and rationality, emerges within a context teeming with heterogeneities of contradictory and competing beliefs that do not preclude commitment but disrupt its immediacy, its untroubled possession of its own groundedness. Disenchantment or demystification do not adequately describe the experience of secularization thus understood. Belief, even the belief in reason and science and the critical thinking that characterizes both, remains desperately important—indeed arguably inevitable—for everyone. Life and thinking seem unimaginable other-wise. But naive belief, belief without awareness of multitudinous and challeng-ing others, has become very rare if not impossible. In "our civilization," as Taylor puts it, "we have largely eroded . . . forms of immediate certainty," including an immediate certainty in the virtues of reason, science, and progress.[7] In this sense, what Taylor calls "our civilization" is truly global. Evangelical Chris-tians, Wahabi Muslims, religious Zionists, ethnic absolutists, and critical the-orists all work within the confines of the same secular civilization, in which the fervor of one's beliefs often seems, to the critically minded, to be a reaction formation and a defense against competing beliefs that threaten to undermine one's faith and even one's way of life.[8] What part can critique play in a world where a belief in rational discourse as a contribution to progress, enlighten-ment, and emancipation has ceased to be a belief that the secular critic can naively hold, or simply believe that her audience shares?

This is not merely an alteration of the conditions in which leftist critics work. It is a fundamental change in the nature of what they can aspire to do. Indeed, the meaningfulness of words like *progress*, *enlightenment*, and *emancipation* has itself become increasingly doubtful, as has the overarching narrative understanding of the world that gave these terms historical heft and material density. This may be understood as the secularization of nonreligious beliefs. It is now over thirty years since contemporary critical theorists began describing postmo-dernity as the waning of naive belief in grand historical narratives—especially the narratives of enlightenment, progress, justice, and equality associated with Kant, with Hegel, and above all with Marx. We remain confused, perhaps necessarily so, about what difference all this makes for critical practice and the worldly or political hopes attached to it.

Kant, Hegel, and Marx in their different ways manifested a philosophical and historical optimism that today seems difficult to maintain. As David Scott has recently observed, "we live in tragic times," and we have failed sufficiently to note the implications of our world-historical tragedy. Scott continues, "This . . . is not merely because our world is assailed by one moral and social catastrophe after another. It is rather because, in Hamlet's memorable phrase, our time is 'out of joint.' The old languages of moral-political vision and hope are not in sync with the world they were meant to describe and normatively criticize."[9] Scott understands the inadequacy of contemporary critical practice to be the result of a continuing fascination with a form of critical narrative that can no longer capture the contemporary historical moment.[10] The moral and social catastrophes of the world increasingly resist narrative enchainment as part of a romantic comedic plot that culminates in enlightenment and emancipation. The "horizon of possible futures," as Scott puts it, that allowed C. L. R. James, for example, to interrogate culture, history, and literature with an optimistic eye toward a happy ending in revolution, justice, and freedom is no longer simply "ours to imagine."

Critics who seek to engage today's world (and what would critique without such engagement be?) must confront both the enormity of the contemporary material and moral catastrophe and the paucity of the political-moral imaginary and discourse available to meet it. As Scott puts it: "Today nation and socialism do not name visionary horizons of new beginnings any of us can look toward as though they were fresh thresholds of aspiration and achievement to be fought for and progressively arrived at; to the contrary, they name forms of existing social and political reality whose normative limits we now live as the tangible ruins of our present, the congealing context of our postcolonial time."[11] Today we live in a world where democracy—appeals to which often give socialism and the nation their moral force—has become a nearly universal and compulsory term at the same time that a ubiquitous neoliberal state capitalism deprives the popular will of real meaning. This is one reason that political hope today seems so circumscribed. It is one reason that today history, that great adventure of progressive liberty, seems to have ended.

Of course, such a tragic vision of the world is hardly new. In 1956 Adorno and Horkheimer wrote, "For the first time we live in a world in which we can no longer imagine a better one."[12] This is not quite right, however, because many critics today believe they can imagine a better, a more just and humane world. "The problem," as Simon During notes, "is not imagining a better society, the problem is realizing it." "In effect," he continues, "democratic state capitalism ends history prematurely. Or rather: it propels us toward living without strong historical hope."[13] In fact, if an essentially philosophical project like deconstruction, with its radical skepticism regarding any utopian teleology, can be said to have had a political implication, it is that it drew our attention to this absence of strong historical hope that had already come to define our critical horizon. Critique, as traditionally understood, no longer seems an adequate tool to assist us in realizing the better society many of us can still imagine. It too finds itself undermined by the doubts that characterize a secular age. Without strong historical hope, a naive belief in the Enlightenment narrative, and an essentially comedic and romantic sense of history, critical thought lacks grounds and leverage.[14] Yet this cannot be the end of the story. However stern a taskmaster critique may be, however fixed it may become on the ways in which enlightenment fails to emancipate through reason, critique remains wedded to indispensable desires for a wiser world, an increase in justice, a decrease in war, an amelioration of suffering. The belief that there is light at the end of this dark tunnel is what gives critical theory—and arguably life itself—meaning.[15]

In fact, the real achievements of critique, especially in the humanistic disciplines, do furnish some bright spots. David Holliger, writing in the *Chronicle of Higher Education*, even argues—against those who would dismiss the importance of humanistic studies today in favor of what have come to be called the STEM disciplines—that the achievements in African and African American studies, in women's studies, in LGBT and postcolonial studies are critical evidence for the continued importance of the humanities today, an importance that economic crises and technocratic euphoria have made many doubt:

> The humanities deserve support not because they always get things right— often they do not—but because they are the great risk takers in the tradition of the Enlightenment. Nothing could be further from the uncritical preservation of traditional culture so often advanced by nonacademics under the sign of the humanities. . . . The academic humanities and social sciences in the United States have long constituted a major apparatus for bringing evidence and reasoning to domains where the rules of evidence are strongly contested and the power of reason often doubted. These domains, on the periphery of an increasingly natural-science-centered academic enterprise, embrace the messy, risk-intensive issues left aside by the methodologically narrower, largely quantitative, rigor-displaying disciplines. The human sciences are at the borderlands between Wissenschaft and opinion, between scholarship and ideology. Here, in the borderlands, the demographic and cognitive boundaries of the entire academic enterprise have been the least certain; here it is the greater challenge to act on the great Kantian imperative to dare to know, to have the courage to actually use one's understanding instead of running from all that messiness back to less risky inquiries.[16]

No one who believes in the continued importance of liberal or humanistic education should hastily dismiss what Holliger says, nor should we passively accept the popular denigration of these projects and achievements, the audiences that have been won over to share these more humane and enlightened beliefs, as merely political and hence a betrayal of the universal principles that the humanities, and especially the arts, supposedly serve. These are profoundly ethical and moral achievements, and in a secular world they are as close to universal values as we may hope to find.

Yet these achievements may not be an adequate vision for criticism's future. In the absence of a powerfully transformative vision of history, the real and admirable conceptual and practical gains made, in part, by critical thinking can seem like adjustments in a large, oppressive, neoliberal economic and social order rather than a challenge to it. Global capitalism, and its watchword *democracy*, often come to support gender and racial equality, because these forces of modernity open new markets and remove barriers to the free flow of goods and services and information.[17] This may dim the luster of these critical achievements, but they remain admirable and essential nonetheless.

The corrosive effects of globalized state capitalism are as large a problem for leftist critics as they are for many religious traditionalists. Both seek to preserve and protect an idea of community grounded in common beliefs from the decadence and injustices of contemporary commodity culture. Critical intellectuals' strongest work traditionally involves unmasking the hard, material truths obfuscated by the ideological blandishments of bourgeois false consciousness, values, and ideals. The urgency of this critical project can seem doubtful. In the nineteenth century, the newly hegemonic bourgeoisie believed social order and civilization to be ideologically grounded on what Marx called the holy trinity of family, church, and state. In *The Eighteenth Brumaire of Louis Napoleon,* Marx analyzed the savage brutality and systematic violence that these bourgeois pieties masked and which the state's violent reaction against the proletarian revolutions of 1848 exposed.[18] This book, along with *The Communist Manifesto,* exemplifies the transformative work of demystification that criticism can do in a society that still believes its material reproduction requires a large degree of ideological conformity. The belief in the fundamental importance of ideology in nineteenth-century bourgeois social orders furnishes Marx the leverage that enabled him to upset the existing order. Today intellectuals find their leverage lessened as commodity capitalism, neoliberal economics, and empty pieties about the nominatively democratic orders that serve both, achieve near universal dominion. As Scott says, what defines the tragedy of our times is that both national emancipation and socialist justice—the great ideological and political projects of the twentieth century—seem to be the ruins among which we live rather than the end of history toward which we might aspire.

Zygmunt Bauman, writing twenty years ago and summing up several decades of sociological analysis, observed that ideological conformity no longer seems so crucial to capitalism's material reproduction.[19] The ideological pillars of religion, nation, and family have all developed major cracks in the uniformity of their ideological façades, and the result has had little discernible effect on the spread of capitalism to every corner of the globe. Capitalism and secularization go very well together. As Bauman noted, given "the altered setting within which the Western intellectual tradition developed and took place"—given, that is to say, the erosion of the intellectual's naive belief in "reason," "universal truth," and "the universal progress of mankind"— the fundamental nature of intellectual work alters as well.[20] No longer can intellectuals credibly believe themselves to be the adjudicators of liberating universal truth in a world of mass deceptions. As capitalism, globally, runs up against its own contradictions, it is most likely the local failures of neoliberal economic policies and practices more than alternative universal ideologies or utopian visions that will provide pressure for change. More important, it is deeply uncertain what direction those changes will take, as the example of Islamist and Christian evangelical reactions against modernity makes clear. For the moment critical intellectuals must assess what it means to function in a world where a universalized economic order seems completely capable of tolerating—indeed, of celebrating—a large degree of ideological heterogeneity. This heterogeneity itself poses a distinct problem for intellectuals, who, in Bauman's formulation, must understand themselves to be "interpreters" of difference across the boundaries of belief rather than legislators of universal truths.[21] This is the tragic knowledge critics must absorb going forward. But the end of historical optimism is not the same thing as the end of political hope or a role for critique in a secular world.

The Place of Critique, the End of Art, and After

Tragic knowledge, as critics since Aristotle have known, involves knowing not only who one is but what conduct—what ambitions and aspirations—are proper to one's place. Tragic knowledge, that is to say, is, in its positive dimension, the positive and negative realization of one's proper place, its limitations and possibilities. For literary, film, and cultural critics whose work in the world importantly involves considerations of art, the wisdom of knowing one's place is essential and entails assessing the place of art as well. Intent on uncovering the implication of our texts in the establishment of social hierarchies or the maintenance of ideological hegemonies, we sometimes forget how mediated and even marginal the place of art and, therefore, our own place as critics of art can be. By the time Shelley wrote in his "Defense of Poetry" that poets are the "institutors of laws and founders of civil society," he was already indulging in a bit of vainglorious boasting.[22] By the beginning of the nineteenth century, the forces of expanding colonial and commercial empires and the consolidation of capitalism and the democratic bourgeois social order were altering the historical place of art and its role in Western society. All forms of art were rapidly becoming for the first time commodities, or potential commodities, addressed to a mass audience that, in an increasingly utilitarian social order, could not be counted on to know or care much about art. Thus, the stress in Shelley's famous last sentence ("Poets are the unacknowledged legislators of the world") should fall on the word *unacknowledged*.[23] As Walter Benjamin, still among the most sensitive critics of modernity's crises, describes the situation: "The crowd—no subject was more entitled to the attention of nineteenth-century writers. It was getting ready to take shape as a public in broad strata who had acquired facility in reading. It became a customer."[24] The modern crowd, heterogeneous and conflicted as it is, becomes the occasion for art's commodification and makes modern art significantly different from the popular arts and the art of the court and church that had preceded it.

In these remarks, as in his better-known analysis of auratic decay in "The Work of Art in the Age of Mechanical Reproduction," Benjamin gives a materialist interpretation of what Hegel called the end of art.[25] Hegel wrote,

> It is certainly the case that art no longer affords that satisfaction of spiritual wants which earlier epochs and people have sought therein, and have found therein only; a satisfaction which, at all events on the religious side, was most intimately and profoundly connected with art. . . . Therefore our present in its universal condition is not favourable to art. . . . In all these respects art is and remains for us, on the side of its highest destiny, a thing of the past.[26]

Hegel, of course, does not mean that art ceases or will cease to be made. But art's traditional association with revelation, with the progress of truth and the self-realization of spirit, its transcendent relationship to meaning and existence, its coincidence with history's unfolding, can no longer be assumed. As Arthur Danto puts it, "The energies of history" and "the energies of art" no longer coincide.[27] This distance of art from the motors of history and the subjectivities of its audience is one more aspect of that tragic knowledge with which contemporary critics must contend.

In another critical idiolect, one could say that art ceases to be a primary inculcator of ideological conformity at the same time that ideological conformity begins to lose its crucial function as a guarantor of social and economic reproduction. In Europe, a marked divergence between the ends of art and the interests of the state, the family, and the church is already noticeable in the nineteenth century. Perhaps inevitably, as writers confronted the discipline of the market and the inanities of the bourgeois state and the indignities of their part in both, their mood progressively soured. It does not seem an exaggeration to say that for many artists the ability to believe in the comedy of progress ended by the middle of the century. Edgar Allan Poe, who rejected any relationship of art to truth, was an early harbinger of this development. Another manifestation occurs in the obscenity trials of Flaubert and Baudelaire, both influenced by Poe, in Louis Napoleon's France, for what Dominique La Capra rightly labels "ideological crimes" against the pieties of the bourgeois state.[28] These trials were contemporary with Marx's *Eighteenth Brumaire*. Taken together, these texts mark a high point in the belief, among social and political elites, that the arts and criticism play an important role on the world-historical stage. But as the modern era continues, such prosecutions in Western democracies become increasingly rare as the bourgeois state learns how little difference such ideological deviations usually make. (It takes communist authorities far longer to learn this lesson, if they ever do; but that is another story.) For a literary critic devoted to a hermeneutics of suspicion, dedicated to uncovering the implication of art in the maintenance of an unjust social order or to celebrating the subversive potentials of artistic expression, this is tragic knowledge indeed. But it may also have a positive dimension. Like art, and indeed like the nation, and perhaps like history itself, critique continues after it has, in Hegel's sense, ended. In fact, after the end of art, the possibilities of both artistic and critical practice proliferate like other forms of belief and modes of life under the sign of secular modernity.[29]

In our own secular, post-Hegelian moment, a naive belief in Geist or progress is as difficult to maintain as any other belief. The teleological quest of the Western spirit, the unfolding of human progress as Hegel understood it, has gone astray. And here, paradoxically, one rediscovers a crucial and continued importance of art in the modern era. It both maps and performs this errancy of existence. This is, in part, because the genius of art is that it can involve its readers not primarily in the transmission of meaning but in the materiality of the sign, in the limits of meaning's transmissibility. Art depends on but works against ideas of communication that foreground meaning. It depends on an ideal of mutual comprehension that it often frustrates. Art can focus our attention—the attention of critics and audiences—on the dense particularities and opacities of existence at a moment when universals no longer seem available and neoliberal principles threaten to abstract more of life into the rigors and disciplines of the cash nexus. These dense particularities, after all, are a major part of our everyday experience as modern subjects in a secular world where homogeneities of belief and immanences of human presence can no longer be assumed as a basis of community.[30] These particularities are, in an important sense, what we literary and cultural critics have to think with and about when we think about art and politics, not as objects to be known but as alterities to be respected. I take Stathis Gourgouris to mean something like this when he describes the *poien* of literature and "history in the making" to be linked "precisely as shaping matter into a form in such a way that the form itself becomes the cipher for the utterly elusive meaning of its own (trans)formation."[31] A transformation of form that engages but also takes its distance from meaning suggests the work of translation, and as we will see, translation may describe both art and the work of criticism in a secular age.[32]

Whitman, or Modern Poetry as Translation

As modernity disrupts traditional linkages between art and belief, literature and meaning, the function of art and critique alters as well. Yet, in a secular age, when the grounds of belief and meaning always seem vulnerable because so many contending beliefs and contradictory meanings welter around any subject, the end of art that Hegel described might actually be a new beginning. A consideration of how art—literary art in particular—adjusts in the aftermath of its ending as a vehicle for truth will suggest what role the criticism of art beyond critique (the discursive mode particularly dedicated to discerning or deciphering meaning) might play. Critique as a hermeneutics of suspicion committed itself to unveiling truths and to furthering progress toward history's happy ending. If a naive belief in history as comedy—as progressing toward that happy ending—no longer seems possible, then what work should criticism take it upon itself to do? Practitioners of the hermeneutics of suspicion are, by necessity, unlikely to admit that an artistic text effectively anticipates their concerns. On the eve of the U.S. Civil War, Walt Whitman self-consciously embraced the teeming, dangerous heterogeneities of the masses that define democratic modernity. Doing so, he acknowledged a redefined role of art in a democratic and secular age. For literary critics who remain interested in critique, Whitman offers some indications of a possible future.

Few poets have been more subject to the rigors of ideology critique—usually reserved for novelists—than the self-proclaimed voice of the nation and of democracy, Walt Whitman.[33] But it may be that Whitman's undeniable investments in the idea of the nation, the individual, and democracy are, today, the least interesting aspects of his poetry. More than just the poet of democracy, I take Whitman to be the poet of poetry's altered place in a secular age. He may claim to "give the sign of democracy," but he also refrains from declaring what that sign might mean.[34] He is a very different poet from the unacknowledged legislator Shelley imagined. He is also unlike those more popular poets writing in the mid-nineteenth century who offered truths of life and consolations for loss, like William Cullen Bryant, whose "Thanatopsis" promised a good death to those who fulfilled well the duties of life. Rather, his poetry works to refocus his reader's attention on the incalculable materiality and sometimes overwhelmingly unruly energy of the life and lives around them. Any ultimate meaning or final purpose that might be assigned to his poetry is secondary to the ways in which, at its best, it revels in sheer being, in existence as an embodied and incalculable experience. He presents himself not as sovereign arbiter of truth but as a maker of provisional meanings, responding to and refiguring the teeming masses he imagines as his audience, whose lives involve the same provisional, contested, and partial acts of meaning making as the poet.

Whitman, perhaps more than any other poet, represents both his readers and the act of reading within his poems, making them central to the poetry's structure and significance. From the very first lines he published in 1855, beginning *Leaves of Grass* with the poem that would he would later entitle "Song of Myself," he links the poet's "I" to the reader's "you": "I celebrate myself; / And what I assume you shall assume; / For every atom belonging to me as good belongs to you" (27). In these opening lines, the material consubstantiality takes precedence over the assumed accord and actually defines its limits. The poem presents no single meaning, but a welter of meanings among which the poet moves and chooses without ultimate arbitration. Not many lines later, he introduces a figure of reading in the person of a wondering child who asks the poet what the grass, the metaphorical frame and ground of his entire project, filling the boy's hands might mean. "How could I answer the child?" the poet responds, "I do not know what it is any more than he" (31). There is nothing coy about this statement. The grass may be a uniform hieroglyph, as the poet suggests, but who can say what its meaning might be? Who can "translate" it? No one and anyone, for the poet here appears less as the purveyor of ultimate truths than as another translating interpreter of the uttering tongues that surround him. "I wish I could translate," the poet says near the section's end, but that wish remains unfulfilled. In this world, there is no single univocal truth that can declare itself transcendent. There are contradictory and conflicting interpretations that must contend for space and authority in the reader's estimation.

"I wish," the poet says, "I could translate the hints about the dead young men and women, / And the hints about the old men and mothers, and the offspring taken soon out of their laps" (32). His wish to translate these "hints" marks his poem as a site where the babbling tongues of the dead and of the living might be made articulate, but translating these "hints" also suggests a desire not to add or subtract significance, not to unify in a singular meaning, but to remain faithful to their babble, all the while knowing that any act of translation reforms as much as it transmits the meaning of its original. Anyone who has translated a literary text knows that the meaning of the text quickly becomes involved in a series of compromises as the translator attempts the impossible, to preserve or re-create the source text's particularity.[35] Translation, here and elsewhere in Whitman's poems, which are often self-reflexively about poetry, figures his ideal poetic strategy, which combines a nearly manic sense of erotic engagement with the world's manifold details and a tragic—though resolutely affirmative—sense of human limitation in the face of life's extremes and the impossibility of fixing life's meaning.

In the final analysis, Whitman's poetry is not so much about conveying meanings as it is about modeling experience—especially the experiences of making meaning and of failing to make meaning—and by doing so recalling to the reader the power and the limitations of existence in a secular world.[36] Whitman frequently enacts the gestures of interpretation as the translation of experience, and he often makes this activity appear not as the attempt to represent life but as an expression of life's protean force and its ultimately inexplicable heterogeneities:

> Through me many long dumb voices,
> Voices of the interminable generations of prisoners and slaves,
> Voices of the diseas'd and despairing and of thieves and dwarfs,
> Voices of cycles of preparation and accretion,
> And of the threads that connect the stars, and of wombs and of
>   the father stuff,

And of the rights of them the others are down upon,
Of the deform'd, trivial, flat, foolish, despised,
Fog in the air, beetles rolling balls of dung.

Through me forbidden voices,
Voices of sexes and lusts, voices veil'd and I remove the veil,
Voices indecent by me clarified and transfigured. . . .

Copulation is no more rank to me than death is. (211)

To ask what such a metonymically enchained catalogue might mean—what ideology on which it might depend—seems to be exactly the wrong question, a question that might belong to those Whitman elsewhere dismisses as "linguists and contenders." "I exist as I am," he writes, "that is enough" (207). His project is not to convey familiar meanings, but to take the "pains of hell" and "translate" them "into a new tongue" (207) where meaning through translation remains a negotiable process. This is, in essence, what literature in the modern era often is, a translation of life's tragic dimensions, of limitation itself into something that surprisingly joins the peculiarities of a self to the demands of an audience, something invigorating and potentially active in both individual life and social engagement but the meaning of which remains difficult if not impossible to specify.

Whitman was not dismayed by art's inability to assign meanings or achieve transcendence. He modeled the materially grounded, conflictual heterogeneity of modern secular reality in a poetry aimed at revealing the physically concrete specifications of existence and resisting their abstraction into meanings, morals, or dogmas removed from the contexts of his poetry's immediate engagement with them. Whitman's best poetry demands interpretation of the welter of signifiers he produces and simultaneously resists the pull of meaning toward abstraction, the lure of the signified as fixed significance. He bundles and inventories his perceptions and the objects of the world and leaves them for the reader to see.

As an ethics, in a nation mired in slavery, committed to violent expansion, and moving swiftly toward a cataclysmic war, this may seem woefully inadequate—as any literary ethics in the face of atrocity likely does. Despite, indeed because of, the generous openness of Whitman's poetic performance, he can be blamed for a tendency to reproduce the political and ideological commitments of his era that contributed to the oppression of Africans, Native Americans, and women. But Whitman is finally not an apologist for injustice, for that itself would be a fixture of meaning he seems intent to resist. The purposes of art in a secular age, he stands to remind us, may usefully differ from the ends of those contenders for truth who otherwise occupy the public sphere. He remains a tragic-minded analyst of the ethics of open-ended engagement, of engagement in a world of uncertain and contested meanings, where the translation and transformation of meaning rather than any transcendental significance is the crucial ground of social life, ethics, and politics, whatever shape those might finally take. As Michael Moon has said, while Whitman may reflect the dominant ideological commitments of his age, at its best, his poetry also "provides the means for making a critique of these [his era's ideological] commitments," in part by indiscriminately embracing otherness while realizing that that otherness will always be less than fully understood.[37] In other words, Whitman's poetry will yield to a critique of its ideology, but such a critique will miss what is most potent and prescient in it—even if one remains interested in his poetry's engagement with ideology. At his best, Whitman troubles some of the most profound assumptions of his era concerning spirituality, personal identity, sex, and death, because he troubles the belief in belief itself. "What is this blurt about virtue and vice?" he asks, "Evil propels me and reform of evil propels me, I stand indifferent" (209). This pose of indifference before good and evil may be difficult to accept, but it recognizes an ethical principle that fundamentally unsettles all others, in the absence of presumed agreement each must finally affect to choose. Art may not make that choice for its audience, but it can refresh its sense of the conditions in which choices must be made and lives lived or sacrificed.

"To die," as he says earlier in "Song of Myself," "is different from what anyone supposed, and luckier." This defamiliarization of his culture's fundamental sentiments and most cherished beliefs is intimately linked to his poetics, his foregrounding in his verse of sheer metonymy and the proliferation of signifiers, his attempt to dwell at the limits of meaning, and his belief in the transformative power of literature as translation, as an imperfect but open-ended engagement with what he calls "Reality," "Materialism first and last imbuing" (210). Death here becomes materialized, associated through metonymy, through sheer juxtaposition and not through metaphoric illumination or elevation, with the endless erotic impulses and sexual minglings of life. It becomes one more of those impulses—"Agonies," Whitman had written, "are one of my changes of garments" (225). When Whitman's poet, near the end of his poem, becomes a preacher ("Do you see O my brothers and sisters? / It is not chaos or death—it is form, union, plan—it is eternal life—it is Happiness"), he un-names each of these terms and breaks the vessel of its commonly comprehended meaning.

It is the broken vessels of sacralized meaning, the open question of life's ultimate meaninglessness, that opens in turn onto the poetic question of democracy and the practical questions of democratic ethics, an open-ended and formal commitment to otherness and to negotiation ("what I assume you shall assume" may be less statement than appeal) to which he so often returns in the poems he wrote between 1855 and the beginning of the Civil War. To a dedicated reformer, Whitman's poetry inevitably disappoints (compared with John Greenleaf Whittier, for example, whom Frederick Douglass called "the slave's poet"). But art has seldom worked efficiently to further the interests of specific reform. For leftist critics, the shortcomings of tendentious literature have longed been a commonplace. For a critic interested in the critical future of a secular age, Whitman's poems furnish material for meditation on the tragic limitations of democratic ethics and the force of translation as an opportunity for engagement with the world that might, in some way, offer hope for improvements. That was Whitman's hope. In a secular age, this limited, imperfect but crucial hope may be all the hope in which we can believe and all we have to work with and for.

Criticism in a Secular Age

The rise of the modern crowd, paradoxically heterogeneous and massified at the same time, constituted a new audience for art, one lacking expertise in art, and it was accompanied in the nineteenth century by the rise of a new figure in the world of art, the figure of the critic as master of meaning and sovereign of judgment. In retrospect, this development seems inevitable. The modern critic, the hermeneutical genius, is related to another new figure on the literary scene that Poe, that pioneer of literary modernity, is often credited with inventing. The private detective as a master of forensic hermeneutics becomes a dominant figure in the popular press at the same time as the critic. Both are figures of explication and both embody fantasies of managed anxiety, a way to reduce the welter of possible and contradictory meanings in the world or the text and to produce a single coherent narrative line or univocal evaluation revealed with the air of incontrovertible truth. But as belief in final truths becomes more difficult to maintain, the power of explication becomes less credible. This has long been evident in crime fiction where more turbulent modes of engagement have long since supplanted the cool analytical reasoning of Auguste Dupin or Sherlock Holmes.

The adjustment of critique to these secular pressures has been uneven. Critique no longer seems credible as the masterful deciphering of codes or uncovering of preexisting meanings for an audience in need of enlightenment. Critique should see its role as something else, something like translation, as Whitman, for example, models it, something that is less a restatement or revelation of meaning and more a performance of meaning making, one that acts in the awareness of the provisional nature and final inadequacy of any meaning made. This is one sense in which criticism becomes a tragic performance, one suited to a tragic sense of modernity as entailing at least as much loss as gain. In the preface to *Is Critique Secular?*, the authors—Talal Asad, Wendy Brown, Judith Butler, and Saba Mahmood—offer the following description of translation as a contemporary modality of critique in a secular age where Western rationalism still seeks to maintain its commitments to enlightenment and progress. In a world where the opposition between reason and faith breaks down, critique begins to seem less like an imposition of universal reason on specific particularities than a confrontation between or among different modes of belief that requires continuous acts of careful translation if any progress toward understanding is to be made. But as they point out, translation poses problems as well and, like critique, must struggle to remain aware of its own limitations:

> Translation can be a form of assimilation, but also a mode of "giving over" to a countervailing perspective in an emphatic vein. A different alternative for translation emerges, however, when we are compelled to identify and sustain sites of untranslatability. In effect, letting the untranslatable situation stand sometimes opens up another field of understanding that serves at least two different purposes: the first is to map incommensurable world views without seeking to reconcile them; the second is to see how these very incommensurable domains constitute, inflect, and even suffuse one another without projecting a broader dialectical unity to which they ultimately tend.[38]

This is one manner in which critique may conceive itself as functioning within the limits of a secular world—not simply or always as the bringer of enlightenment that divulges the truth and demystifies the world, but as a performance, always aware of its own limitations and keeping an eye on the particular purposes it might serve, always "marked by the encounter with the untranslatable," always mindful, as the authors of *Is Critique Secular?* put it, that even for Kant critique "is everywhere concerned with the limits of what can be known" and with "the epistemic limits on the knowable imposed by secularism itself."[39] Such an awareness of limitations—essentially a tragic awareness of our common mortality—may be the precondition of ethical action in a secular age. Exploring the dimensionality of these limitations is one function critique may hope to claim.

What I'm suggesting is not so much a wholly altered as an expanded and perhaps more generous sense of what critique, especially in the realm of literary studies, may hope to achieve. This entails an increased mindfulness of the range of purposes—including aesthetic delight (not a value critique has often endorsed) as well as political contestation—that art can and does serve. Meaning, which remains critical theory's traditional and perhaps indispensable obsession, does not end contingency or ever arrive at the finality of absolute or theoretical truth. Critical meaning, contingent truth, grows out of various and conflicted lived situations that furnish opportunities for and limitations to critical action, which action can refashion common beliefs and resharpen dulled sensibilities. All this might remind us that our loss of confidence in the ability of critique to discern the happy culmination of history points toward a heightened ethical and political awareness, as tragic knowledge tends to do. Critique remains necessary in the contemporary attempt to negotiate the limits of human wisdom and power. This tragic knowledge is not the grounding of despair or quietism, but it is the likely precondition for ethical action and effective political engagement in the secular world.

But engagement founded on tragic knowledge may require a disavowal of the hubris that sometimes mars critique's relationships to its audiences and objects. The task of critique has often seemed to be the disruption of the audience's pleasure in the object in the interests of a heightened sense of the artwork's obfuscated complicity in practices and ideologies of oppression. This task is often well motivated. There is, of course, a relationship—variable but frequently discernible—between the conventions that shape the forms and aspirations of imaginative art and the ideologies (another word for conventions or rules of representation) that shape—as Althusser helped us to see—the ways in which we understand ourselves and our places in the world and our relationships with each other.

It is the illusion of mastery that so often attends critical feats of deciphering that we must question. Literature and its reception remain privileged sites for the sharpening of the ethical sense as tragic awareness. Critique cannot pretend to escape the tragedies of its age. The ethical exempla, including the political failures, in even the most canonical works represent more than another turn of the ideological screw that requires the critic's demystifying reversal or denunciation. Often the text can be as smart or smarter—politically, ethically—than we are, or better yet, it can become the occasion of our own education. Sometimes our texts can be good to think with—rather than to think against or resist. As Rita Felski puts it, literature, and by implication art more generally, should be recognized as more than "objects of knowledge," for they can be "sources of knowledge as well."[40] And sometimes they offer a pleasurable alternative to the world as it is, and sometimes that pleasure itself has a great value. All of these alternatives involve critique and its audience in the contexts and choices of concrete aesthetics, the experience of otherness, and the practical politics of our shared lives. The value or valences of any of these alternatives cannot reliably be prejudged by critics pretending to possess sovereign mastery over meaning and implication. Each kind of intervention entails the critic's self-realization through a critical performance that meets, and sometimes contends with, an audience with understandings of its own.

The Ends of Art and Criticism after Critique

A critic does well to remember that art has little directly to do with truth, as philosophers understand truth. For art and criticism, the object is usually not simply truth nor is it simply meaning—criticism, like art, cannot be limited to hermeneutics or decipherment. Both criticism and art work in a theater of rhetorical and aesthetic engagement, which, at least since the eighteenth century in the West, has been the scene of confrontations between principles that aspire to universality and the equitable requirements of particular judgments. This is one important but shifting ground of the political aspirations that often attend critical work in a secular age. Criticism functions in the realm of opinions, not truth, which is the realm of democratic politics as well. Plato's antipathy to democracy, based on Athens's tragic experience of democratic self-government, leads him to dream of excluding rhetoric and art, opinion and democracy from *The Republic*. This is not a critical dream progressive critics can afford to share, though at moments of frustration with democracy's foibles it can appear to have its attractions.

One important function for critique might be not to arbitrate meaning or to serve truth (at least not always) but to exemplify how problems of understanding and otherness, problems, that is, of translation, might be and already are being lived, how, indeed, in a secular world living with and through these problems of otherness has no alternative but violence. *Translation* is a better word than *interpretation* or *hermeneutics* for the work of critique because the end of translation cannot be reduced to the realization of truth. Translation is the activity of reconstituting, redescribing, and recontextualizing meanings and experiences in forms more useful or pleasurable, moving them from one immediate cultural and linguistic context to another. There can be no general or transcendental theory of translation, though the practical fact of translation evokes the transcendent by its very existence. As Benjamin understands it, each act of translation into a particular language affirms the participation of the text in a universal language, a transcendent form of literariness as he describes it, even as it moves the text from one specific context to another. The implication of the unrealizable universal language entails the possibility that we might, at least for a moment, close gaps in our understanding of each other and the world, arriving for a moment at something that can for a moment illuminate a world.[41]

Translation, rather than decipherment, as a figure for the critic's task, precludes too close a fixation on suspicions about hidden truths that await revelation and refocuses attention and labor on the imbrications of ethics and the materiality of signs, on the inevitable slippages of signification between a text and an audience that are the grounds and limits of understanding and the field of play through which whatever truths that may be realized may emerge. For the translator, there can be no pretense of sovereign hermeneutical power, since debt and obligation—to the original and to the audience— are fundamental to the work. As Gayatri Spivak says about translation and debt: "One attempts to repay what cannot be repaid, and should not be thought of as repayable."[42] Truth plays a role here, but it has more do with the manifold and frequently political truths of textuality than with the absolute truth of revealed significance. Translation is itself a form of close reading and careful interpretation, but one that must remain attentive to the specificity of the text's signifiers, the materiality of its signs, the exigencies of an audience.

Finally, critique may have to unlearn, or at least must learn at times to bracket, the critical truth that aesthetic pleasure often becomes a mask that hides realities of human pain. In many ways, this has been critique's founding assumption since the Frankfurt School's early work.[43] The translation of real-life pain into aesthetic pleasure may not always serve the interests of obfuscation. If it becomes an occasion for a poignant recollection of the mutual tragedies of mortal existence, it may contain within itself, as tragedy sometimes does, a kernel of what Adorno himself called a philosophical standpoint of redemption, a redemption of the value of human experience in the face of reifying economic and social pressures, which truth alone cannot do:

> The only philosophy which can be responsibly practiced in the face of despair is the attempt to contemplate all things as they would present themselves from the standpoint of redemption. Knowledge has no light but that shed on the world by redemption: all else is reconstruction, mere technique. Perspectives must be fashioned that displace and estrange the world, reveal it to be, with its rifts and crevices, as indigent and distorted as it will appear one day in messianic light. To gain such perspectives without velleity or violence, entirely from the felt contact with its objects—this alone is the task of thought. It is the simplest of all things, because the situation calls imperatively for such knowledge, indeed because consummate negativity, once squarely faced, delineates the mirror-image of its opposite. But it is also the utterly impossible thing.[44]

Between this simplest of all things, which is at the same time necessary and impossible, between a messianic time to come in which we can no longer really believe and a desire for redemption we cannot do without imagining, is the tragic world in which translation and critique (the latter itself a form of the former) find themselves.[45]

Oddly, these limitations seem to me to increase the importance of the critic's task. Within these limits, in the absence of what David Scott has called strong hope, the critical stories we humanists tell and the truths we sometimes realize find their use value as translations of experience, sometimes with an eye toward the future, sometimes in honor of the past, sometimes in the service of simple truths, sometimes as an act of sustaining imagination, sometimes as the critical debunking of collective delusions or corporate lies that seek to convince us of our freedom even as they work to constrain our lives by obfuscating the real conditions of our existence. We try to discern or guide the meaning of these and our own actions, but we know that these will emerge only in negotiations with specific audiences at specific times and for particular ends. That critical truth alone furnishes us sufficient place and importance in the world, or at least it should.

Finally, if translation describes critique, or includes critique among the critical practices translation describes, then remembering the work of translation also reminds us that critique is an eminently practical and pragmatic activity, not to be mastered by theoretical directives or reduced to methodological procedures. Instead, translation focuses our attention, or should, on issues of ethos in the practice of critique and cautions us against the critical hubris that might delude us into believing that we have mastered our texts, the world, or our audience when we really seek to serve in whatever way seems most appropriate to a given moment and context. Translation as a description of critique should renew and focus our awareness of the situational and context-bound importance of critique's potential contribution, an importance that shifts and alters as the nature and goals of the specific interpretive and communicative task of reading and translation at hand prescribe. These are the tasks at which a secular critic and translator may credibly work, through the art and artifacts of her culture, to redeem artistic and critical acts of displacement and defamiliarization that can revivify our relationship to the world. As translators and interpreters our work will often seek to further rather than contest the aesthetic effects and cognitive impact of a work of art or cultural artifact, for these often have implicit or explicit critical engagements of their own. A good translation can often bring these to the surface. Critique, like art itself, can help restore and renew capacities for feeling contact with the objects and, most importantly, with the others who constitute the world. It can also become an occasion for reflection on what those felt encounters might mean or imply about the state of this world and our place in it. This may be the highest goal of art and critique in a secular age, and it may be the highest use to which the humanities can be put.

Notes

1   Michael Warner, "Uncritical Reading," in *Polemic: Critical or Uncritical*, ed. Jane Gallop (New York: New York University Press, 2004), 13–37.

2   Paul Ricoeur, *Freud and Philosophy*, trans. D. Savage (New Haven, CT: Yale University Press, 1970), 32–33.

3   Jacques Derrida, *Dissemination*, trans. Barbara Johnson (Chicago: University of Chicago Press, 1981), 63.

4   This remains true despite more recent calls for distant or surface readings driven by big data analyses or the abandonment of the search for hidden or elided meanings in favor of a renewed commitment to aesthetics and presence. For a summary of positions in what may eventually amount to a generational shift away from critique in literary and cultural studies, see Jeffrey J. Williams, "The New Modesty in Literary Criticism," *Chronicle Review*, January 5, 2015; for the argument against meaning, see, for example, Hans Ulrich Gumbrecht, *Production of Presence: What Meaning Cannot Convey* (Stanford, CA: Stanford Univer-

sity Press, 2004). As I hope will be apparent in what follows, I am far from ready to abandon critique and the close reading on which it depends, though I am interested in altering the ethos of the practice.

5   Talal Asad, assessing the opposition between Western ideals of free speech and Islamic reactions to blasphemy, refers to Edward Said's claims for "Secular Criticism," in *The World, the Text, and the Critic* (Cambridge, MA: Harvard University Press, 1983), 1–30, to make the point that the genealogy of critique in the West, despite Said's claims for secularism, is deeply imbricated with the history of Christian skepticism and credulity (cf. Bayle) and Protestant models of rational belief. Talal Asad, "Free Speech, Blasphemy, and Secular Criticism," in Talal Asad, Wendy Brown, Judith Butler, and Saba Mahmood, *Is Critique Secular? Blasphemy, Injury, and Free Speech* (New York: Fordham University Press, 2013), 14–57, 42–45. See also Michel Foucault, "What Is Critique?," trans. Kevin Paul Geiman, in *What Is Enlightenment? Eighteenth-Century Answers and Twentieth-Century Questions*, ed. James Schmidt (Berkeley: University of California Press, 1966).

6   Immanuel Kant, "What Is Enlightenment?," in *Kant: Political Writings*, trans. H. S. Nisbet (Cambridge: Cambridge University Press, 1991), 54–63, 54, 59.

7   Charles Taylor, *A Secular Age* (Cambridge, MA: Harvard University Press, 2007), 12–13.

8   On the inadequacy of understanding the confrontation of the West with Islam as a confrontation between secular rationalism and theocratic superstition, see Tariq Ali, *The Clash of Fundamentalisms: Crusades, Jihads, and Modernity* (London: Verso, 2002); Talal Asad, *Formations of the Secular: Christianity, Islam, Modernity* (Palo Alto, CA: Stanford University Press, 2003); and the symposium recorded in Asad et al., *Is Critique Secular?*, esp. Asad's contribution, "Free Speech, Blasphemy, and Secular Criticism," 14–57.

9   David Scott, *Conscripts of Modernity: The Tragedy of Colonial Enlightenment* (Durham, NC: Duke University Press, 2004), 2.

10 Hayden White, of course, borrowing from the traditions of formalist criticism, has long argued for the determinant influence of narrative form on cognitive content. See, among others, *Metahistory: The Historical Imagination in Nineteenth-Century Europe* (Baltimore: Johns Hopkins University Press, 1973), and *The Content of the Form: Narrative Discourse and Historical Representation* (Baltimore: Johns Hopkins University Press, 1987).

11 Scott, *Conscripts of Modernity*, 29.

12 Theodor Adorno and Max Horkheimer, "Toward a New Manifesto," *New Left Review* 65 (September–October 2010): 33–63, 61.

13 Simon During, *Against Democracy: Literary Experience in the Era of Emancipations* (New York: Fordham University Press, 2012), 4–5.

14 The persistence of Enlightenment beliefs as necessary grounds for any political analysis or action is separate from the availability of naive, unquestioning and untroubled, forms of those beliefs. Deconstruction's skepticism is itself a legacy of the enlightenment, especially in its earliest forms.

15 Fredric Jameson's long and generous review of the essays in *Cultural Studies*, ed. Lawrence Grossberg, Cary Nelson, and Paul Treichler (New York: Routledge, 1992), makes an excellent analytical case for the difficulty of imagining any political articulation for cultural work that does not involve a narrative telos with a utopian element, despite the postmodern aversion to grand narratives. See "On 'Cultural Studies,'" *Social Text* 34 (1993): 17–52, esp. 28–33.

16 David Holliger, "The Wedge Driving Academe's Two Families Apart: Can STEM and the Humanities Get Along?," *Chronicle Review*, October 14, 2013, http://chronicle.com/article/Why-Cant-the-Sciencesthe/142239/.

17 See, for example, David Harvey, *The New Imperialism* (Oxford: Oxford University Press, 2005), and Paul Smith, *Primitive America: The Ideology of Capitalist Democracy* (Minneapolis: University of Minnesota Press, 2007).

18 Karl Marx, *The Eighteenth Brumaire of Louis Napoleon* (New York: International, 1994).

19 Zygmunt Bauman, *Legislators and Interpreters: On Modernity, Post-modernity, and Intellectuals* (Oxford: Basil Blackwood, 1987). Of course, much of the best work in cultural studies in the last several decades has focused on the thick meanings of objects in the world and especially on the social and ideological significance of commodities as the point where global circulations and local appropriations meet. As Arjun Appadurai notes, "Consumption is now the social practice through which persons are drawn into the work of fantasy" that forms the personal narratives that give shape and meaning to their personal and collective lives. Appadurai also notes that while this makes reading commodities of great interest to those of us interested in parsing the life worlds of global modernity, one should not make the mistake of assuming that commodities have become the "driving force of industrial society." See *Modernity at Large: Cultural Dimensions of Globalization* (Minneapolis: University of Minnesota Press, 1996), 82–83.

20 Bauman, *Legislators and Interpreters*, 146.

21 For an analysis of the role communities of belief play in contemporary intellectual discourse see John Michael, *Anxious Intellects: Academic Professionals, Public Intellectuals, and Enlightenment Values* (Durham, NC: Duke University Press, 2000), 64–107.

22 Percy Bysshe Shelley, "A Defense of Poetry," *Shelley's Poetry and Prose*, ed. Donald H. Reiman and Neil Fraistat (New York: W. W. Norton, 2002), 512.

23 Shelley, "A Defense of Poetry," 535.

24 Walter Benjamin, "On Some Motifs in Baudelaire," in *Illuminations: Essays and Reflections*, trans. Harry Zohn, ed. Hannah Arendt (New York: Schocken, 1969), 155–56, 166.

25 See Walter Benjamin, "The Work of Art in the Age of Mechanical Reproduction," in *Illuminations*, 217–51.

26 Georg Wilhelm Friedrich Hegel, *Introductory Lectures on Aesthetics* (New York: Penguin, 1993), 12–13.

27 See Arthur C. Danto, "The End of Art," in *The Philosophical Disenfranchisement of Art* (New York: Columbia University Press, 1986), 81–115, 83.

28 See Eileen Ka-May Cheng, *The Plain and Noble Garb of Truth: Nationalism and Impartiality in American Historical Writing, 1784–1860* (Athens: University of Georgia Press, 2008), and Dominick La Capra, *Madame Bovary on Trial* (Ithaca, NY: Cornell University Press, 1982).

29 For a fascinating account of the afterlife of art and of the thesis about art's end see Eva Geulen, *The End of Art: Readings in a Rumor after Hegel*, trans. James McFarland (Palo Alto, CA: Stanford University Pres, 2006), esp. 1–40, 65–89. Geulen aptly discusses Hegel's "thesis" of the end of art less as a theoretical statement and more as rumor, one that his own work—indeed the very introduction to his lectures on aesthetics (transcribed by a member of the audience)—belies (10–13). Yet the sense that art was at an end or in crisis is, not for the first time in world history, notable in the nineteenth century and closely linked to ideas about modernity and secularization and therefore of great use to us here, for our epoch—like the nineteenth century—unfolds itself under the sign of art's end even if that sign has no very precise referent.

Though Charles Taylor cites the secession of elite art forms from popular culture as one of the harbingers of secularization and dates it from the late Renaissance (*A Secular Age*, 87–88), the historical collapse of art into commodity and the interpenetration of high and low forms unfolds in the shadow of art's aftermath (in the Hegelian sense) during the nineteenth century. The politics of the avant-garde, for example, depends on the availability of art not to fulfill but to oppose the dominant expression of the age in the bourgeois state—a project related to the market differentiation between high and low art, as Andreas Huyssen has investigated in detail in *After the Great Divide: Modernism, Mass Culture, Postmodernism* (Bloomington: Indiana University Press, 1986). "The irony of course is that art's aspirations to autonomy, its uncoupling from church and state, became possible only when literature, painting and music were first organized according to the principles of a market economy. From its beginnings the autonomy of art has been related dialectically to the commodity form" (17).

30 See Jean-Luc Nancy, *The Inoperable Community*, ed. Peter Connor, trans. Peter Connor, Lisa Garbus, Michael Holland, and Simona Sawhney (Minneapolis: University of Minnesota Press, 1991); Maurice Blanchot, *The Unavowable Community*, trans. Pierre Joris (Barrytown, NY: Staton Hill, 1988); Giorgio Agamben, *The Coming Community*, trans. Michael Hardt (Minneapolis: University of Minnesota Press, 1993).

31 Stathis Gourgouris, *Lessons in Secular Criticism* (New York: Fordham University Press, 2013), 10–11.

32 For Thomas McFarland, "all cultural activity is a kind of translation" and both impossible and unavoidable in all spheres of human endeavor. *Shapes of Culture* (Iowa City: University of Iowa Press, 1987), 82.

33 Critics have generally been glad to take him at his word. See, to look at just a few examples, Betsy Erkkila's *Whitman: The Political Poet* (Oxford: Oxford University Press, 1989); Kerry Larson's *Whitman's Drama of Consensus* (Chicago: University

of Chicago Press, 1988); George Kateb, *The Inner Ocean: Individualism and Democratic Culture* (Ithaca, NY: Cornell University Press, 1992), 152–71, 240–66; Philip Fisher, "Democratic Social Space: Whitman, Melville, and the Promise of American Transparency," in *The New American Studies: Essays from "Representations,"* ed. Philip Fisher (Berkeley: University of California Press, 1991), 70–11.

34 Walt Whitman, *Poetry and Prose*, ed. Justin Kaplan (New York: Library of America, 1996), 211. All quotations from Whitman's poetry, except where otherwise noted, are from this edition and are cited parenthetically in the text.

35 The theoretical reflections of working translators often engage these issues, which ultimately engage the ethics of alterity. The violence translation does to the original has been, of course, the worry of translators and of translation studies at least since Schleiermacher's "On the Different Modes of Translating" (1813) brought the issue into modern focus. This text is available in *The Translation Studies Reader*, 2nd ed., ed. Lawrence Venuti (New York: Routledge, 2004), 43–63. As Emily Apter describes this aspect of translation, it entails "the traumatic loss of native language," of the specificity of the other, but in that trauma she sees, as Walter Benjamin did, the perpetuation of literature and alterity both— see Apter, *The Translation Zone: A New Comparative Literature* (Princeton, NJ: Princeton University Press, 2006), xi, 88–93; Walter Benjamin, "The Task of the Translator," in *Illuminations*, 69–82.

36 "Literature," as it comes to be defined as a category in the nineteenth century, becomes increasingly identified with such critical and sometimes corrosive stagings of meaning making. See, for example, Jacques Derrida's comments in "This Strange Institution Called Literature," in *Acts of Literature*, ed. Derek Attridge (London: Routledge, 1992), 33–75; see also Derek Attridge, *The Singularity of Literature* (London: Routledge, 2004), esp. 1–35, and Stathis Gourgouris, *Lessons in Secular Criticism* (New York: Fordham University Press, 2013), esp. 1–27. Derrida, as Elissa Marder remarks, makes translation a central figure in his rendering of philosophical discourse, responsible for the materiality of the sign or the body of the word in his many texts on translation, including "Des tours de Babel," in *Psyche: Inventions of the Other*, vol. 1, ed. Peggy Kamuf and Elizabeth Rottenberg (Stanford, CA: Stanford University Press, 2006), 191–225; "What Is a 'Relevant' Translation?," trans. Lawrence Venuti, in *The Translation Studies Reader*, ed. Lawrence Venuti (New York: Routledge, 2000), 423–26. For a powerful account of these works and of the crucial place of translation in global ethics and literary studies see Elissa Marder, "Force and Translation or the Polymorphous Body of Language," in *Philosophia* 3, no. 1 (winter 2013): 1–18. I am grateful to Professor Marder for having shared a manuscript copy of this article with me as I was beginning to formulate these ideas.

37 Michael Moon, *Disseminating Whitman: Revision and Corporeality in "Leaves of Grass"* (Cambridge, MA: Harvard University Press, 1991), 82. As Moon says, "The text can serve to empower others—genuine others, that is, women and nonwhite men, not just homotypes of the (male) poet—to assert their own respective difference or 'untranslateability' " (83).

38 Asad et al., *Is Critique Secular?*, xvi.

39 Asad et al., *Is Critique Secular?*, xvi.

40 Rita Felski, introduction to *The Uses of Literature* (Malden, MA: Wiley-Blackwell, 2008), 7.

41 Walter Benjamin's sense of the translator's task has affinities with Seyla Benhabib's idea of the critic's work as an "interactive universalism." Seyla Benhabib, "Interactive Universalism: Fragile Hope for a Radically Democratic Conversational Model," *Qualitative Inquiry* 8 (August 2002): 463–88.

42 Gayatri Spivak, "Translation as Culture," in *An Aesthetic Education in the Era of Globalization* (Cambridge, MA: Harvard University Press, 2012), 244.

43 Eve Kosofsky Sedgwick, *Touching Feeling: Affect, Pedagogy, Performativity* (Durham, NC: Duke University Press, 2003), interrogates this critical suspicion of pain and has inspired a renewed interest in pleasure and in other forms of affect. Nonetheless, I am not suggesting abandoning the position Horkheimer and Adorno defined in their work on the culture industry.

44 Theodor Adorno, *Minima Moralia: Reflections from Damaged Life*, trans. E. F. N. Jephcott (London: Verso, 2005), 247.

45 I am indebted here to Michael Levine's generous rereading of Benjamin, Derrida, and Celan in light of "weak messianic power" to which Benjamin refers in his theses on history. See *A Weak Messianic Power: Figures of Time to Come in Benjamin, Derrida, and Celan* (New York: Fordham University Press, 2013).

11

Then and Now

ERIC HAYOT

How did we get to the end of critique? At this point in the book, the story hardly needs to be re-rehearsed; the actors have made their stand, and the play is ready, finally, to be staged. What we know is that something has been lost, that literary criticism, today, floats adrift on an open, darkling sea, while the sailors search desperately for new compasses. Something has changed.

What is the nature of that change? It appears, first of all, under the name of the "death of Theory." To understand the death of Theory, you have to understand what Theory was, what it meant in the American literary academy, such that it could be conceived of as having a death. Because to have a death means, of course, having had a life.

Let's begin, then, with the life of Theory. It has multiple beginnings, and many possible parents. We might point to the impetus to literary criticism provided by the work of the scholars later known as the Russian formalists, beginning in the 1910s. Or we could say that Theory began in the 1920s, with I. A. Richards's experiments, in England, in the teaching and interpretation of poetry, or in Vienna in that same period, with the revolution in psychology and psychoanalysis that began with Sigmund Freud. We can identify another origin in the between-the-wars work of Marxist scholars like Georg Lukács, Bertolt Brecht, Ernst Bloch, Hannah Arendt, Mikhail Bakhtin, or Walter Benjamin, work that flourished after the war in the new Marxism of the Frankfurt School (emblematized by the writing of Theodor Adorno). Another major starting point could be the work of the so-called New Critics (Cleanth Brooks, John Crowe Ransom, W. K. Wimsatt, and others), who before and after World War II trained a generation of scholars in a new and more scientific understanding of the literary. Or we could say that Theory got its start in the Parisian university classrooms of the 1950s and 1960s, when the scholars who would write the major works of the Theory era taught or plied their trade: Louis Althusser, Jacques Lacan, Claude Lévi-Strauss, Georges Canguillhem, Michel Foucault, Pierre Bourdieu, Jacques Derrida, Hélène Cixous, Luce Irigaray, Roland Barthes, Julia Kristeva.

Theory began in all of these places, and in others still, but we cannot say that Theory existed at any of these moments. It was only when these influences and others came together in the American university in the 1970s and 1980s that something called "Theory" could begin to be talked about as a single movement. The Theory era swept through the entire American university system, affecting not only literature departments but units across the humanities and social sciences, changing patterns and practices of teaching not only in the liberal arts but also in schools of education (producing, from there, carryover effects to the K–12 classroom), colleges of communication and media (thereby making its way into newspapers, television), programs in art, architecture, and art history (thereby affecting the understanding of the aesthetic and the making of works from novels to paintings to skyscrapers). It also affected the structure of the university itself, not only within departments, but across them: most programs in ethnic studies, women's or gender or queer studies, or science and technology studies (as well as a host of other interdisciplinary centers, summer programs in criticism, and so on) originate in the Theory era, and owe something to its influence. From the United States this thing called "Theory" bounced back and forth to Europe, filed up and down the Americas, went out to Africa, South Asia, East Asia, and returned from those places (in the form of books, people, or ideas) with new insights and new ways of seeing and understanding the world.

We thus live today in a post-Theory era, in the sense that the entire intellectual and social lifeworld of the planet has been affected by the intellectual debates and insights that took place under the broad banner of Theory.

Theory's diversity was its strength. It could be described, in its heyday, as an uneasy congeries of approaches. In the late 1980s these were largely mappable under the banners of Marxism, structuralism, deconstruction, psychoanalysis, feminism, and ethnic studies; a decade later you might, noting the disappearance of structuralism and the decline of Marxism, add to the list schools of thought organized around New Historicism, cultural studies, cultural materialism, sociology of literature, and queer theory, while observing the glimmering births of groups oriented toward disability studies or affect studies. Some of these approaches overlapped heavily—psychoanalysis and feminism, structuralism and Marxism, for instance—and others seemed deeply incompatible.

A book like Michael Ryan's *Marxism and Deconstruction*, published in 1984, or the endless debates about Marxism and feminism, testify to the kinds of tensions produced when major schools of Theory, each with a strong picture of the world, encountered one another in practice. The 1980s also saw tensions arise between ethnic studies and various poststructuralist approaches, with bell hooks noting that it was ironic for white men to discover that the subject didn't exist at just the moment when black folks seemed to be acquiring social power; you might have read, alongside hooks, a book like Henry Louis Gates Jr.'s *The Signifying Monkey* (1989) as an attempt to reconcile deconstructive critique with the African American experience by locating the former in the material and lived practice of the latter. The intensity of the debates between and among schools, and the various attempts to reconcile them, were features not only of institutional but also intellectual life; the questions they raised went straight to the heart of the basic questions of knowing and being.[1]

None of this academic summary quite captures, however, what it was like for me to go to college (1989–93) and graduate school (1994–99) in those Theoretical years. It was *exciting*. My classmates and I, reading these amazing books and unlearning everything we thought we'd known, felt like we were on the verge of making a significant difference, not just in school, but on the planet: a difference in the field of political economy and social power, in relations between men and women and the possibilities inherent in the production and performance of sexuality (and the possibility of a significant politics therein), in the radical undermining of the kinds of truth that had, until then, given us an all-too-imperfect world. We had, I think, a sense of ourselves as belonging very much to rival schools, of not only being interested in "topics" but of holding critical positions that governed our approaches not only to literature but our teaching, our politics, our relationships, indeed all aspects of our everyday lives. We were in fact trained to think this way: a class I took as a college senior asked us, in the name of understanding and inhabiting those changes, to occupy for the entire semester a position borrowed from one of Theory's major schools: we were only to speak in class *as* either a Marxist, a feminist, a psychoanalytic critic, or a deconstructive one. We were taught to imagine that one thought, and spoke, from a specific intellectual position, and to connect that position to a school of thought that encompassed not only modes of reading, but also personal and public politics, everyday habits, and modes of talk and dress. We were, in a word, *acculturated*.

Like many of the people who teach in universities today, I read as part of my introduction to Theory Terry Eagleton's *Literary Theory: An Introduction,* whose 1983 first edition was the stuff of a thousand college courses. You get some sense of the scope of the change we hoped for in the book's final sentences, which followed a Marxist-tinged historical overview of all the major currents of Theory from 1917 to the present, and capped it with an allegory whose meanings were by that point all too clear: "*We* know that the lion is stronger than the lion-tamer, and so does the lion-tamer. The problem is that the lion does not know it. It is not out of the question that the death of literature may help the lion to awaken."[2] Reading those lines in the fall of 1989, and hearing what I now understand as their echo of the rhetoric of Marxist revolutionary awakening that appears in *The Communist Manifesto* (1848), I swear to you I thought they were true.

It is in the nature of idealisms to disappoint. You start out planning to change the world; you end up teaching in a university, changing one small thing or another in yourself, your students, or the curriculum, while the world goes on without you. Or you end up changing quite a lot—perhaps as one small soldier in the giant army of what used to be called lesbian and gay studies, and is now queer theory, an army that helped make possible the stunning national and international transformations in the political status of homosexual, transsexual, and transgendered men and women, and in the civic recognition and legitimation of their sex and their love. Or perhaps as a teacher of teachers who have rewritten high school and university curricula in the United States to include engagement with the bleak, inspiring history of ethnic struggle, or with the fight for women's rights, and with the art and the literature of those battles, a change that seems radical and huge to someone who in his American high school English classes never read a single book written by a woman, or a person of color.

In the long run, though, those changes haven't felt like enough, in the face of all the things that haven't changed. In 1984 a white New Yorker named Bernard Goetz shot and wounded four black men on the subway; charged with attempted murder, assault, and reckless endangerment, he was acquitted on all but one charge (carrying an unlicensed firearm) by an all-white jury. I remember thinking at the time, well, this is at least a start; at least a white man was charged with a crime, and this is the beginning of change. In 1992 the white police officers who beat a defenseless Rodney King were acquitted, again by an all-white jury. I wrote my senior thesis on media coverage of the trial and the riots that followed the verdict. Twenty years later, Trayvon Martin, a seventeen-year-old black boy walking home to the house of his father's fiancée, was shot and killed by a neighborhood watch volunteer named George

Zimmerman; Zimmerman, who claimed he fired in self-defense, was not charged with a crime. Two years after that, in 2014, a man named Michael Brown was shot and killed by a white police officer in Ferguson, Missouri; a grand jury voted not to indict.

The disasters accumulate. The rise of the surveillance state, aptly analyzed and even predicted by theorists like Louis Althusser or Michel Foucault; the mobilization of populations for endless war, and the destruction of civil liberties in the name of freedom, so clearly described by Hannah Arendt or Giorgio Agamben; the absurd extension of imperialist violence by the United States and its allies in the Middle East and elsewhere, which repeated so precisely the historical situations described radically and for the first time by scholars like Frantz Fanon, Edward Said, or Gayatri Spivak; the seemingly unstoppable force of rape culture, and the intensification since the 1980s of restrictions on women's reproductive freedom: all of these feel like endless and exhausting extensions of forms of social violence and phallic stupidity that I, at least, in 1992, felt like we were on the verge of ameliorating, if not getting rid of forever. Back then, the 1992 election of Bill Clinton (after twelve years of Republican leadership), the overwhelming victory of the Labour Party in the UK elections of 1997, and, honestly, even the rise of grunge and hip-hop, seemed to presage a large-scale change of the entire field of cultural belonging and an opening toward a new century.

That century never came. And that is, for me, where so much of the disappointment in Theory, and the crisis in criticism, comes from.

If my explanation is more personal than those you will have read so far, it is because I believe that part of what we are describing, when we describe the crisis in critique, has to do with changes that are not completely *inside* the problem of critique, but belong rather to other areas of human culture: biological patterns involving relations to aging (you will note that the "crisis" is being described largely by professors in their forties and fifties), patterns of institutional development involving the ways that ideas become dominant and then fade, and, more broadly, global patterns of intellectual, economic, and political development that overwhelm, and *aim* to overwhelm, by their sheer scale, the possibilities of individual and social resistance to capitalism and violence. In what follows I'll be exploring a number of these arenas as I attempt to understand what it means to believe one is "after critique," and to think about the ways one might come to think so.

First, the personal. Already in the second edition of *Literary Theory*, published in 1996, you can hear Eagleton, at this point a decidedly middle-aged

Marxist (he was fifty-three), beginning to wonder about the effectiveness of the Theory revolution and to remark on the ways in which the institutionalization and popularity of Theory had begun to chip away at its radical potential. The edition featured an "afterword," which followed immediately on the allegory of the lion and the lion tamer that had so rousingly concluded the book's 1983 first edition.

Eagleton is three decades older than me, and his description of the pattern of hope and failed idealism moves back accordingly. The 1970s, he writes, "or at least the first half of them, were a decade of social hope, political militancy, and high Theory" (190). The defeat of the political forces of the 1960s and 1970s that had motivated that hope and Theory, and their overcoming the Reagan and Thatcher revolutions in the United States and United Kingdom, respectively, had left Theory, he says, somewhat adrift. Faced with that defeat, scholars turned away from the great grand narratives, the forms of overarching, total possibility that had governed the ambitions of those earlier decades, looking instead toward interior realms of experience and smaller, more unimpressive projects. Eagleton:

> Since state power had proved too strong to dismantle, so-called micropolitics were now the order of the day. Totalizing theories and organized mass politics were increasingly associated with the dominative reason of patriarchy or Enlightenment. And if all Theory was, as some suspected, inherently totalizing, then the new styles of Theory had to be a species of anti-Theory: local, sectoral, subjective, anecdotal, aestheticized, autobiographical, rather than objectivist and all-knowing. Theory, it seemed, having deconstructed just about everything else, had now finally succeeded in deconstructing itself. (195)

You will note in Eagleton's description of "styles of Theory" a contempt for the remaking of politics as aesthetics, of (objective) commitment as (subjective) mood, that governs many of the critiques of the Theory of the 1980s and 1990s. And you can of course agree with him, or argue instead that the postdeconstructive, subjective Theory that Eagleton in his melancholic mode decries (and associates consistently, by the way, with feminism) was in fact fantastic, inspiring, revolutionary, and as oriented toward social change as any Marxist program of a decade earlier. Either way, what I want you to notice here is the historical structure of the argument, the way in which its disappointed hope corresponds to the ways in which two somewhat disparate forces—the force of institutionalization and the force of political history and class struggle—combine to unravel the youthful dreams of the disappointed critic.[3]

What are these two forces? How do we understand them in relation to the current crisis in critique? First we must recognize that, as forces, they have histories and rhythms of development that belong properly to them—that they are, that is, not simply the fields of play in which the action of intellectual life reveals itself, but rather competing structures in the making of complex history. What do I mean? Well, first, that institutions, and institutionalizations, have, like political struggle, lives of their own. They operate, that is, not merely as reflections of existing historical activity and human biological time, but rather with temporalities particular to their social forms of embeddedness (and self-embeddedness). To take the case of universities in particular, we might say that they operate on a temporality that is in some respects incompatible with the temporality of ordinary human life, that they simply move more slowly than people through processes of change, and that this is the normal "biological" pattern of university development. You might think, then, of a concept like "university-years," which would function more or less like dog-years in reverse, in which universities are to humans what humans are to dogs: they live on a slower scale.[4] And so how frustrating, for those of us living in human time, to watch the seven years go by that it takes a university to change. And how much more frustrating to wait out the long decades it takes a whole society to change! Of course universities or societies sometimes change even more slowly, or more quickly than this; the point of this example is to allow you to imagine that the *human* reaction to the crisis in criticism, or the death of Theory, results partly from the fact that humans live in human-years, whereas things like Theory or indeed processes like institutionalization, never mind political struggle, happen in radically other temporalities. And I think that's what you see so clearly in Eagleton's 1993 "afterword": an analysis that is after all that not exactly incorrect, but which cannot see that the relation between the personal temporality of Eagleton's own life and work and the very different temporality of class struggle, and because it cannot see that relation, or imagine it, reads the critical situation of the 1990s as a kind of exhaustion or betrayal of the 1960s and 1970s of Eagleton's youth.

I am not saying—no one could reasonably say—that Eagleton's analysis of the situation in 1993 stemmed *exclusively* from his generational disappointment. I am saying two related things: first, that history happens at the intersection of multiple competing temporalities; it is not merely a day-to-day, year-to-year process driven by the successive unfolding of various cause-effect relations.

Cause-effect relations also unfold in formal structures that may reflect normative biological imperatives (the gap between human generations, for instance), larger socioeconomic rhythms (the business cycle, or Kondratieff patterns), or even geological or climatic shifts operating at either the microlevel (leaded gasoline affecting crime rates) or the macrolevel (the little Ice Age). Second, I am saying that the way we *perceive* and *understand* history, especially the history in which we are currently living, passes through our own personal relations to that history, which are partly biological. That youthful idealism gives way to midlife disappointment is a cliché of bourgeois psychodevelopment. For precisely this reason, scholars who find themselves, in midlife, disappointed by the empty promises of the methods and ideas that so inspired them as young people ought to be profoundly suspicious of themselves. They ought to ask whether it is possible that their own psycho-biological position is governing their sense of the history of ideas, or of the political world more generally.

But the personal or psycho-biographical is not, as I have been saying, the only kind of temporality that interferes with a sense of what the present means, and what it needs. What if, for instance, patterns of theoretical change correspond to an internal formal temporality of rises and falls, what one might think of, quite generally, as the temporality of intellectual fashion? We see Eagleton hinting as much with his language of "styles," though, somewhat predictably, the Theory he likes is not a style but the real thing, and the arrival of a fashion in theories the mark of the market's capturing of real Theory's revolutionary power. In any case, the temporality of intellectual fashion would not be identical with the temporality of fashion in clothing, or in architecture, to be sure, but it would share with those forms of temporality some relation both to the institutional context in which it emerges and to the market that governs it. So, for instance, shifts in intellectual fashion would among other things be subject, at least in the U.S. context, to the production of PhD students, the granting of tenure, the rate of change in university curricula, timelines to book publication, and so on; though the rhythm of change would be therefore slower than that of the clothing industry, its general shape and pattern might be similar. Here then we need to consider how the entire sweep of our contemporary history of ideas conceals both larger and smaller patterns of conceptual fashion, visible for instance in the shifts from structuralism to poststructuralism, second-wave to third-wave feminism, Derrida to Foucault, or the rise of postcolonial studies, each of these internal to a potentially much larger structural pattern governing the entire arc of Theory itself.

Something like this awareness has already been grasped when someone imagines the Theory era (or the era of critique) as a single thing. Such a maneuver produces intellectual power by identifying a structural-historical pattern larger than the one that governs our habitual critical practice. Tying the birth of critique to the 1981 publication of Fredric Jameson's *The Political Unconscious*, the critique of critique opens up a scale (of about thirty years) that is longer than the normal scale at which literary scholars describe their own critical position and innovation (which I am going to put at about a decade).[5] It is by narrating the nature of an entire thirty-year span *as* a single period, and thus by seeing a number of smaller movements that we might have thought of previously as opposed as elements in the same larger pattern, that the critique of critique acquires much of its rhetorical and hermeneutic force, and seems to break out of a pattern of historical development that had ground to an ineffectual halt.

Seeing the Theory era as a single period, then, feels like a major step forward—but it is not. That's because the historical logics previously internal to Theory (in which one school follows another school, in a parody of revolutionary change) are simply, in this more generalizing conception, elevated to principles for the Theory era as a whole. The "end of critique," even as it demarcates and reframes the small-scale succession of schools under a larger historical umbrella, adopts once more the logic of succession and decline that characterized those schools in the first place. In this way what a certain vision of the end of critique seeks is in fact a *return to critique under another name*, a reproduction of the very historical pattern from which it sees itself as having escaped. We need to do better.

Let's step back a bit. One of the singular features of the Theoretical revolution in the American academy was that it was organized, as I noted a few pages ago, around a series of schools. Though these schools did on occasion confront one another, face to face, as part of a larger synchronic system of options, they also quite consistently organized themselves as forms of *succession*—forms, that is, that followed upon one another in a sequence of moments that, marketized in both the academic professoriate and in the publishing industry, operated very much like a fashion system. Here one need only think of the way that Foucault succeeded Derrida, Bourdieu Foucault, Badiou Bourdieu, Rancière Badiou, and so on, to think about the ways in which Theory as an era in intellectual history constituted itself around a succession of novelties articulated as progress. The mining of various authors or critical modes (deconstruction, New Historicism, feminism, queer theory) to the point of exhaustion, followed by the rapid opening up of a new field whose resources would be the next to be fully extracted and explored, was one of the singular rhythms of the Theory era. And the decreasing half-life of each new French philosopher in these sequences suggested, I think, something of the desperation of an entire scholarly field to reproduce the thrill and power of the 1980s, and the modes of influence-generation that it produced and allowed, as well as the unconscious awareness (if a field can be said to have such a thing) of the actual and potential exhaustion implicit in such a pattern of "development."

I am suggesting, therefore, that the rhythms of the early Theory period (from the mid-1970s through the mid-1990s, more or less) essentially *taught* a couple of generations of academics a pattern of intellectual historicity, a pattern, that is, of what "normal" intellectual development looks like, and ought to look like. The crisis caused by the so-called death of Theory, then, would have to be read partly as a historical crisis in two senses: as a crisis, first, in the history of the American university and its overall organization (about which more shortly), and, second, as a crisis in the very theories of historicity that permitted us to understand the university and the ways it developed in the first place. The first crisis is admittedly complicated. But the second crisis is not. It can be partly resolved by refusing to take the historicity of Theory as a *model* for all intellectual development. We might recognize Theory's historicity instead as a particular, historically situated instance of development under certain intense intellectual and political conditions. No law of history obliges the patterns of intellectual life under which several generations of scholars have grown up, from the 1970s through the early 2000s, to repeat themselves forever. History does not exist to make people comfortable. Rather than imagining the disappearance of the historical pattern or cliché in which the literary academy follows an endlessly self-renewing succession of academic stars as a crisis and a disaster—rather than imagining that such a pattern needs to be renewed via the continued production of new neologisms and new schools—we might imagine what it would look like if intellectual history proceeded otherwise. And to wonder whether we need that succession of stars to feel whole, comfortable, or secure. We might, that is, think about how our own comfort with a certain developmental model (one, by the way, that we both imagined into being, and through our actions reproduced) keeps us from seeing history otherwise, and thus pushes us toward the frantic representation of elegy and crisis.

It is in this sense that I find myself very much on the side of the "beyond" critique argument—the argument, that is, that we must move (or already in fact have moved) beyond the intellectual demands of the Theory era, defined as the product of a hermeneutics of suspicious reading, driven always to over-master the text by locating it within a historical context that it itself could not have grasped or managed as such, a style of reading, it is worth noting, that also defined itself strongly in opposition to what one might think of as "ordinary" or "amateur" reading, as Rita Felski has argued.[6] Where I side with the argument, it is because I agree most strongly with its historical perspective, which gathers together the variegated histories and methods of the Theory era together into a single unit; this recognition of the multiple scales at which history takes place is healthy and good. Where I break from it, however, is in believing that "after critique" does not let go of the Theory era *enough*. Even as it seeks to move beyond the intellectual ethos and reading modes of the period it disdains, "after critique" remains trapped, I am saying, by the basic historical presumptions of the very period it wishes to abandon. That is why it must imagine itself in the mode of the "after" or the "beyond," and present itself, as it does in the various models for surface reading, new formalism, distant reading, and so on, as a new messiah who will reconstitute the very structures of faith and belief that the death of Theory destroyed in the first place.

This doesn't mean that one cannot move beyond critique, or change one's ideas! But it might mean that we ought to understand this movement or these changes as themselves part of a general pattern of development—and see that from the perspective of a constant flux and flow of institutional change the desire to change, to appear within the star-succession model, is not in fact a desire to *change* at all, but rather a desire to *continue* a pattern of emergence, dominance, and decline that typifies the general development and institutionalization of ideas in the last forty years. Among other things, this would suggest that the movement forward need not, as it seems to now, so strongly organize itself around an oppositional mode. To declare instead that the old ways are tired, and new ones are needed, is a gesture of the most profound historical provincialism, and a failure of the historical imagination. The truly radical thing, the truly insane gesture, would be to imagine ourselves a relation to the disappointing past that would be essentially *continuous*. At which point the terms of the disappointment would surely also have to be reimagined and rewritten.

Let me give you an example of the way in which a certain historical perspective on the present has shaped the conceptualization of the historical necessity of "beyond" critique. Consider the role the George W. Bush administration plays in two of the major essays that launch us beyond critique. Bruno Latour opens "Why Has Critique Run Out of Steam?" (2004) with an extended

metaphor involving critics as generals that makes clear reference to the proliferation of American-led wars; he offers as an instance of the misuse of critique
the use of anthropological work on scientific certainty by Republican strate-
gist Frank Luntz, in order to support the manufactured "doubt" of climate
change deniers. Stephen Best and Sharon Marcus observe, on the second page
of "Surface Reading: An Introduction" (2009), that "eight years of the Bush
regime may have hammered home the point that not all situations require the
subtle ingenuity associated with symptomatic reading," and they follow up by
noting that the "disasters and triumphs of the last decade" (they mention the
war in Iraq, the torture of prisoners at Abu Ghraib, and Hurricane Katrina—
no real triumph among them) "have shown that literary criticism alone is not
sufficient to effect change."

All this is true enough. You can see why in the middle of the Bush administration the sudden realization that one wanted to be, after all the relativism
and the deconstruction, on the side of the "facts" would come as something of
a shock.[7] And at some level the novelty of that historical situation is useful if
it presents a test that our epistemological and rhetorical assumptions fail; this
is in fact part of what history is for.

One might ask, nonetheless: what concept of historical activity governs the
claims made here about the move beyond critique? What theory of historical
presentness allows the extended anecdotal example of an eight-year presidency
of the United States to justify arguments about philosophical method? At some
level, the most "natural" one of all, that of a simple concept of biological, social
time, in which one's own emotional and professional development parallels
the lived rhythm of American politics (which are themselves, with their eight-
year cycles, no "natural" marker of historicity). But why should that be the
best historical context through which to think about the history of criticism,
or even the history of the Bush years? One could, for instance, broaden one's
perspective, placing those eight years within a historical context that they do
not and cannot themselves dominate. What kinds of theories of criticism do
we develop if we imagine ourselves in a longer or shorter *durée*? Which *durée*,
you ask? Well, of course, that's an important epistemological choice. The
choice of the Bush presidency (or the post-9/11 period) as the "relevant" present is an epistemological choice. What does it mean for a theory (of what to
do about the end of Theory) to justify itself within and through this context?
How does that context shape the theory?

We can get some purchase on that question by looking at another significant historical context for the contemporary crisis, this one substantially

closer to home. I am speaking of the global threat to higher education posed by the twin forces of neoliberal capital and conservative politics. One no longer needs the Marx of *The German Ideology* or even Althusser theorizing the ideological state apparatus to understand that conservatives in the United States want to destroy not only the humanities but indeed the entire apparatus of scientific knowledge, and that this desire stems not only from a political resentment (of, e.g., research on climate change) but from an understanding that such a project would allow for the creation of a more vulnerable and hence more pliable class of worker-citizens. When the Republican governor of Georgia suggests that students majoring in women's studies should not receive state scholarship funds, or the Republican legislature of North Carolina considers a bill to require all university-system professors to teach eight courses a year, we require no advanced courses in interpretation to understand the stakes of the situation.

For some of my friends this institutional crisis, itself produced by the enormous cuts in state funding for higher education over the last decades, counts as further evidence for the failure of critique—after all that work, it turns out critique couldn't even protect the site of its own emergence. What's more, the argument goes, it was precisely the turning inward of Theory toward itself, the rise of academic jargon and the separation of the field of professional reading from amateur practice, that made the literary academy increasingly self-absorbed and thus increasingly irrelevant, not only inside the university but to the society at large. The road back to relevance would thus involve a turn away from scholarly publishing, a movement toward belle-lettrism, novel-writing, and other forms of public scholarship and digital engagement, all this amounting to a general undoing of the Theory mistake and a renewed relationship to activism, outreach, and engaged criticism.

Whether or not those solutions will save us is a topic for another place. For now I simply want to note that the feeling of threat and malaise engendered by the coordinated attacks on the university combines with the despair about the state of world politics and world economics to create an especially ugly situation for the vast majority of university professors in literary fields.[8] Together these two contexts, one more global, the other more local, constitute the historical framework within which any question about the state of the contemporary will be asked. And, as I am suggesting here, this entire contextual framing has as much to do with our understanding of the scope of the "contemporary" as a historical category. Imagine what things would look like if "contemporary" meant fifty or even one hundred years.

It is now possible to bring these various features together. The current historical moment "after critique" is, then, I am arguing, being produced by a series of interlocking historical structures, structures whose own historical partiality both engenders and is engendered by our existing theories of historicity, or historical periodicity (beginning, as I have just suggested, with the idea of the "contemporary"). I have identified five of these:

the history of *global politics* and economics since the early 1990s, when a series of steps forward for liberal social democracy seemed to presage the arrival of a new, less violent socialism, a history that would have fulfilled the more general Enlightenment faith in the eventual bending of the arc of history, as Martin Luther King Jr. once said, toward justice, all of this now ruined by the post-9/11 political climate, increasing income inequality nationally and globally, Obama's failure to close the prison at Guantanamo Bay, and so on;

the history of *the university* since roughly the 1970s, when the first explicit conservative plans to destroy the liberal elements of that institution were laid; these plans have come now to their fullest fruition;

the *psycho-biographical* development of various members of the Theory and post-Theory generations, who find themselves bored or disappointed in relation to the theoretical and intellectual situation of their relative youth, and in relation to the work they have already done under Theory's aegis;

the generic possibility that the currents of *intellectual fashion* move at rhythms substantially different from those of ordinary human time, and thus that the rise and fall of Theory constitutes, not a disaster or a surprise, but an ordinary event in the general swirling of prestige and new thought in the institutional context, which would have to be considered in relation to a much wider variety of interlocking historical rhythms, from the quotidian to the geological, that affect the various social forms that organize the institution as such; and,

the *idea of historicity* as succession-of-novelty-and-progress that typified the Theory era, and the historical imagination that takes that particular historical run as a general model for intellectual development whose stalling or failure signals the presence of a much larger crisis.

The themes cannot be disaggregated. It is not simply a question of figuring out what kinds of historical structures are getting in the way, and ignoring them so that we can focus on the real problem, of adjusting our ideological blinders so as to think without thinking through any of these important patterns. Rather, it is a question of including these structures in our understanding of what the contemporary moment means, ideally before we decide to announce that we are (or must go) "after" or "beyond" critique, ideally before we theorize our way into the present by adopting too readily historical models (and models of affective relation to history) that determine in advance our understanding.

Part of what I'm suggesting, then, is that any declaration that literary criticism needs to move beyond critique must take into account both the histories that govern the more general structure of feeling operating beneath or around the entire act of theorization in the first place, and, second, to account in complex ways for its own theory of history, a theory of history that, while generated by an implicit understanding of the nature of the past, gestures also toward the possibility of a new future—and contains, therefore, a concept of futurity itself, of the kind of future that can exist, and a theory of how one gets there (via, that is, a "break" of the type announced in the "after" and "beyond"). That the arguments against critique so often begin by describing the exhaustion or failure of critique exacerbates this historicism by positing a developmental parabola in which critique moves from early success to total institutional dominance to contemporary senescence. That parabola aligns, implicitly and explicitly, with larger understandings of the history of politics (e.g., the Iraq War) and of academia (e.g., the university in ruins), framing a narrative of total decline that suggests either directly or by association, as we have seen, that Theory has failed because it did too little to stop the disasters from forming.[9] To this knot we must add the psycho-biographical dimension, which, as it is never explicitly addressed, counts as the truest blind spot of this entire network of ideas, a fact that renders it also, paradoxically, the least clearly ideological of its facets.

Let me speak, finally, to that blind spot, which can also be, like the sad, bovine eye at the beginning of the famous Dalí film, a tender, open wound.[10] I have felt disappointed by critique, have felt bored by critique, have wondered if I will ever recapture the sense of faith and belief I had in college and in graduate school. I have been afraid that I have put my life into something I don't believe in anymore. I have wondered whether it make sense to teach others to be excited about the things that used to (and can still) excite me, whether in connecting students to Theory, to critique, I am not also connecting them to an empty, broken practice and introducing them to the miseries of disappointed hope. All these things are true.

And yet in the face of those feelings I want—I want, in a gesture that for me is pretheoretical, and whose desire has not yet been fully understood—to be suspicious of that disappointment, to be wary of its conservatism and its self-indulgence, to remember the Gramscian lesson of the optimism of the will. And to be suspicious, more intellectually, of the too-rapid abandonment of ideas that, in my reading, my writing, and my teaching, still have the power to create hope, to alter relations to the world, to be suspicious also of the ways in which we do not challenge ourselves enough to rethink the basic historical presumptions that we allow to govern us, many of which can be subsumed under the general rubric of the then and the now. This latter is only one of the major tropes in the imaginative production of history, and we know this, because we have taught it to ourselves, because we have learned it, through Theory. Here are some others: a progressive relation to the future, in which the then projects forward in time against the now, and whose naïveté has as often been a source of triumph and positive change as of stupidity and error; the notion of a circle or cycle, in which the then and the now typologically repeat themselves, and reverberate with a more general rhythm of the cosmos, which escapes the domination of the classically modern causal continua; and something like the Benjaminian *Jetztzeit,* the time that explodes "out of the continuum" of history to punctuate it with the nearly sublime presentness of connection and change.[11] Each of these would unwrite the present as "crisis," would help us shed our addiction to crisis, and to the need to manage a given situation by positing it as in desperate need of an after or a beyond. Beyond critique: to let go of the desire for the beyond as the only beyond, to see the beyond as one choice among many in the vast plains of historical conceptualization, and to remember that our claims about what's old, what's new, and what might happen next can be driven—and are driven—by forces that the history of Theory has taught us, better than anyone, to be able to understand.

Notes

1 For two far better, and more interesting, histories of Theory than the one you have here, see D. N. Rodowick's *Elegy for Theory* (Cambridge, MA: Harvard University Press, 2014) and François Cusset's *French Theory: How Foucault, Derrida, Deleuze, & Co. Transformed the Intellectual Life of the United States*, trans. Jeff Fort (Minneapolis: University of Minnesota Press, 2008).

2 Eagleton, *Literary Theory: An Introduction,* 2nd ed. (Oxford: Blackwell, 1996), 189. There is also an anniversary edition of 2008. Further quotations from this work are cited parenthetically in the text.

3 No one is blaming the death of Theory, this time around, on feminists and their subjectivist ways. Progress!

4   We say casually that seven years of a dog's life is equivalent to one year of a human's life, so that a ten-year-old dog is like a seventy-year-old human, and so on. I have no idea whether this is true, but it doesn't matter.

5   Think here of the ways in which an average essay or conference talk positions itself in relation to the critical history that precedes it. In the common "they say, I say" structure that governs those moments of self-positioning, the "they" in question tend to be scholars and critics who have written on the issues in the last decade or so (and frequently only in the last few years). To position oneself in an antagonistic relation not just to work in a subfield, but to work in Theory or critique in general, produces immediately a substantive distance between the speaker/writer and the history she describes, as though the talk were being delivered from an extraordinarily high vantage point, from which the variegated landscapes of the ordinary thinker would appear as a series of smooth and mappable surfaces. The impressiveness of the vantage point testifies, naturally, to the intellectual capacities of the scholar able to produce it.

6   See the introduction to Rita Felski, *The Uses of Literature* (New York: Wiley-Blackwell, 2008).

7   To revert to facts would be, however, a mistake (as Latour suggests in both the steam essay and his compositionist manifesto)—it is not a question of returning to the facts and the Enlightenment but of inventing new concepts that do not require the fact/fiction distinction.

8   It would be possible to make some specific arguments against this more general feeling of despair, suggesting as I have above that the incredible changes in the status of gays, lesbians, and the transgendered, or the rise of the anti–World Trade Organization and anti-Davos movements, count as two of the many successes of the Theory era, and noting that the relentless, naked attacks on the university come from the conservative movement's correct apprehension of those successes, and ought to be understood therefore as counterattacks. The satisfactions of knowing that one is being threatened for the right reasons do little, however, to mitigate the feeling that one remains steadily under threat.

9   This position gives too much credit to philosophy as a historical force in general, to be sure (consider that the world has yet to fulfill the long-awaited promise of the Enlightenment). But it draws its force from the fact that so often the claims made for Theory (by Theory and by the teachers and learners of Theory) promised just that kind of difference.

10 The film, *Un chien andalou* (1929), is a surrealist collaboration between Salvador Dalí and the director Luis Buñuel.

11 See Walter Benjamin, "Theses on the Philosophy of History," in *Illuminations*, ed. Hannah Arendt (New York: Schocken, 1968).

BIBLIOGRAPHY

Adorno, Theodor. *Aesthetics and Politics*. London: New Left Books, 1977.

———. *Minima Moralia*. Translated by Dennis Redmond. Creative Commons, 2005. https://www.marxists.org/reference/archive/adorno/1951/mm/ch02.htm.

Adorno, Theodor, and Max Horkheimer. *Dialectic of Enlightenment*. Translated by John Cumming. London: Verso, 1979.

———. "Towards a New Manifesto?" *New Left Review* 65 (September–October 2010): 33–63.

Agamben, Giorgio. *The Coming Community*. Translated by Michael Hardt. Minneapolis: University of Minnesota Press, 1993.

Ahmad, Aijaz. "Jameson's Rhetoric of Otherness and the 'National Allegory.'" *Social Text* 17 (1987): 3–25.

Ahmed, Sara. *The Cultural Politics of Emotion*. New York: Routledge, 2014.

———. *The Promise of Happiness*. Durham, NC: Duke University Press, 2010.

———. *Queer Phenomenology: Orientations, Objects, Others*. Durham, NC: Duke University Press, 2006.

———. *Strange Encounters: Embodied Others in Post-Coloniality*. New York: Routledge, 2000.

Ali, Tariq. *The Clash of Fundamentalisms: Crusades, Jihads, and Modernity*. London: Verso, 2002.

Althusser, Louis. *Essays in Self-Criticism*. Translated by Grahame Lock. London: Verso, 1976.

———. *For Marx*. Translated by Ben Brewster. London: New Left Books, 1977.

———. "From Capital to Marx's Philosophy." In *Reading Capital*, by Louis Althusser and Étienne Balibar, translated by Ben Brewster, 13–69. London: Verso, 1979.

———. "Ideology and Ideological State Apparatuses." In *Lenin and Philosophy and Other Essays*, translated by Ben Brewster, 127–86. New York: Monthly Review, 1971.

———. *On the Reproduction of Capitalism: Ideology and Ideological State Apparatuses*. Translated by G. M. Goshgarian. London: Verso, 2014.

———. *Philosophy of the Encounter: Later Writings, 1978–87*. Edited by François Matheron and Oliver Corpet, translated by G. M. Goshgarian. London: Verso, 2006.

———. *Writings on Psychoanalysis*. Translated by Jeffrey Mehlman. New York: Columbia University Press, 1996.

Althusser, Louis, and Étienne Balibar. *Reading Capital*. Translated by Ben Brewster. London: Verso, 1979.

Amis, Martin. *The War against Cliché: Essays and Reviews 1971–2000*. New York: Vintage, 2014.

Amossy, Ruth. "The Cliché in the Reading Process." Translated by Terese Lyons. *SubStance* 11, no. 2.35 (1982): 34–45.

Andrews, Malcolm. *The Search for the Picturesque: Landscape Aesthetics and Tourism in Britain, 1760–1800*. Stanford, CA: Stanford University Press, 1989.

Appadurai, Arjun. *Modernity at Large: Cultural Dimensions of Globalization*. Minneapolis: University of Minnesota Press, 1996.

Apter, Emily. *The Translation Zone: A New Comparative Literature*. Princeton, NJ: Princeton University Press, 2006.

Apter, Emily, Stephen Best, Elaine Freedgood, and Sharon Marcus, eds. "The Way We Read Now." Special issue, *Representations* 108, no. 1 (fall 2009).

Apter, Emily, and Elaine Freedgood. Afterword to "The Way We Read Now," edited by Emily Apter, Stephen Best, Elaine Freedgood, and Sharon Marcus, special issue, *Representations* 108, no. 1 (fall 2009): 139–46.

Arendt, Hannah. *Eichmann in Jerusalem*. New York: Penguin, 1992.

Armstrong, Paul B. *How Literature Plays with the Brain: The Neuroscience of Reading and Art*. Baltimore: Johns Hopkins University Press, 2013.

Arnold, Matthew. *Culture and Anarchy*. New York: Oxford University Press, 2006.

———. "The Function of Criticism at the Present Time." *Fortnightly Review*. Republished from *The National Review*, November 1864. http://fortnightlyreview.co.uk/the-function-of-criticism-at-the-present-time/.

Arvin, Newton. *American Pantheon*. New York: Delacorte, 1966.

Asad, Talal. *Formations of the Secular: Christianity, Islam, Modernity*. Palo Alto, CA: Stanford University Press, 2003.

Asad, Talal, Wendy Brown, Judith Butler, and Saba Mahmood. *Is Critique Secular? Blasphemy, Injury, and Free Speech*. New York: Oxford University Press, 2013.

Attridge, Derek. *J. M. Coetzee and the Ethics of Reading: Literature in the Event*. Chicago: University of Chicago Press, 2004.

———. *The Singularity of Literature*. New York: Routledge, 2004.

Balakrishnan, Gopal. "The Abolitionist—1." *New Left Review* 90 (2014): 101–38.

Balibar, Étienne. "Althusser's Object." Translated by Margaret Cohen and Bruce Robbins. *Social Text* 39 (1994): 157–88.

Barthes, Roland. *Image/Music/Text*. Translated by Stephen Heath. New York: Hill and Wang, 1978.

———. *A Lover's Discourse: Fragments*. Translated by Richard Howard. New York: Hill and Wang, 2001.

———. "The Structuralist Activity." In *Critical Essays*, translated by Richard Howard, 212–20. Evanston, IL: Northwestern University Press, 1972.

Bartolovich, Crystal. "Humanities of Scale: Marxism, Surface Reading—and Milton." *PMLA* 127, no. 1 (2012): 115–21.

Barzun, Jacques. Introduction to Gustave Flaubert, *The Dictionary of Accepted Ideas*. Translated by Jacques Barzun. New York: New Directions, 1968.

Bates, Catherine, and Nasser Hussain. "Talking Trash/Trashing Talk: Cliché in the Poetry of bpNichol and Christopher Dewdney." In *Trash Culture: Objects and Obsolescence in Cultural Perspective,* edited by Gillian Pye. Bern: Peter Lang, 2010.

Bauman, Zygmunt. *Legislators and Interpreters: On Modernity, Post-modernity, and Intellectuals.* Oxford: Basil Blackwood, 1987.

Beauvoir, Simone de. *The Second Sex.* Translated by Constance Borde and Sheila Malovany-Chevallier. New York: Knopf, 2010.

Benhabib, Seyla. "Interactive Universalism: Fragile Hope for a Radically Democratic Conversational Model." *Qualitative Inquiry* 8 (August 2002): 463–88.

Benjamin, Walter. *Illuminations.* Edited by Hannah Arendt. New York: Schocken, 1968.

Bennett, Jane. *The Enchantment of Modern Life: Attachments, Crossings, and Ethics.* Princeton, NJ: Princeton University Press, 2001.

———. *Vibrant Matter: A Political Ecology of Things.* Durham, NC: Duke University Press, 2010.

Berger, Lynn. "Snapshots: or, Visual Culture's Clichés." *Photographies* 4, no. 2 (September 2011): 15–16.

Berlant, Lauren. *Cruel Optimism.* Durham, NC: Duke University Press, 2011.

Berlin, Isaiah. *The Roots of Romanticism.* Princeton, NJ: Princeton University Press, 2001.

Best, Stephen. "Well, That Was Obvious." *Representations* 125 (winter 2014). Accessed August 14, 2016. http://www.representations.org/responses/.

Best, Stephen, and Sharon Marcus. "Surface Reading: An Introduction." *Representations* 108 (2009): 1–21.

Bewes, Timothy. "Reading with the Grain: A New World in Literary Criticism." *differences* 21, no. 3 (2010): 1–33.

Bhabha, Homi. *The Location of Culture.* New York: Routledge, 1994.

Binder, Amy J., and Kate Wood. *Becoming Right: How Campuses Shape Young Conservatives.* Princeton, NJ: Princeton University Press, 2013.

Blanchot, Maurice. *The Unavowable Community.* Translated by Pierre Joris. Barrytown, NY: Staton Hill, 1988.

Bloch, Ernst. *The Principles of Hope.* Cambridge, MA: MIT Press, 1995.

———. *The Spirit of Utopia.* Stanford, CA: Stanford University Press, 2000.

———. *Utopian Function of Art and Literature.* Cambridge, MA: MIT Press, 1989.

Boltanski, Luc, and Laurent Thevenot. *On Justification: Economies of Worth.* Translated by Catherine Porter. Princeton, NJ: Princeton University Press, 2006.

Booth, Wayne. *The Rhetoric of Fiction.* Chicago: University of Chicago Press, 1983.

Brewster, Ben. "Glossary." In Louis Althusser and Étienne Balibar, *Reading Capital,* translated by Ben Brewster, 307–24. London: Verso, 1979.

Brinkema, Eugenie. *The Forms of the Affects.* Durham, NC: Duke University Press, 2014.

Brown, John. *A Dissertation on the Rise, Union, and Power, the Progressions, Separations, and Corruptions of Poetry and Music.* London: L. Davis and C. Reymers, 1763.

———. *An Estimate of the Manners and Principles of the Times by the Author of Essays on Characteristics, &c.* London: L. Davis and C. Reymer, 1757.

Brown, Marshall. *Preromanticism*. Stanford, CA: Stanford University Press, 1993.

Bryant, Levi, Nick Srnicek, and Graham Harman, eds. *The Speculative Turn: Continental Materialism and Realism*. Melbourne: re:Press, 2011.

Burke, Seán. *The Death and Return of the Author: Criticism and Subjectivity in Barthes, Foucault, and Derrida*. Edinburgh: Edinburgh University Press, 1998.

Burton, Ben, and Elizabeth Scott-Baumann, eds. *The Work of Form*. Oxford: Oxford University Press, 2014.

Butler, Judith. "The Force of Fantasy: Mapplethorpe, Feminism, and Discursive Excess." In *The Judith Butler Reader*, edited by Sara Salih. Oxford: Blackwell, 1990.

———. *Gender Trouble: Feminism and the Subversion of Identity*. 10th anniv. ed. New York: Routledge, 1999.

———. "Imitation and Gender Insubordination." In *The Judith Butler Reader*, edited by Sara Salih. Oxford: Blackwell, 1990.

Candea, Matei, ed. *The Social after Gabriel Tarde: Debates and Assessments*. New York: Routledge, 2012.

Capra, Dominick La. *Madame Bovary on Trial*. Ithaca, NY: Cornell University Press, 1982.

Carbonell, Curtis D. "A Consilient Science and Humanities in Ian McEwan's *Enduring Love*." CLCweb: *Comparative Literature and Culture* 12, no. 3 (2010). Accessed August 14, 2016. http://docs.lib.purdue.edu/cgi/viewcontent.cgi?article=1425&context=clcweb.

Carpenter, Bennett, Laura Goldblatt, Lenora Hansen, Anna Vitale, Karim Wissa, and Andrew Yale. "Feces on the Philosophy of History! A Manifesto on the MLA Subconference." *Pedagogy: Critical Approaches to Teaching Literature, Language, Composition, and Culture* 14, no. 3 (fall 2014): 381–93.

Castiglia, Christopher. "Critiquiness." *ELN* 51, no. 2 (2013): 79–86.

———. "Melville's Cold War Allegories and the Politics of Criticism." In *The Cambridge Companion to Herman Melville*, edited by Robert S. Levine. New York: Cambridge University Press, 2014.

Castronovo, Russ. "Within the Veil of Interdisciplinary Knowledge? Jefferson, Du Bois, and the Negation of Politics." *New Literary History* 31 (autumn 2000): 781–804.

Castronovo, Russ, and Susan Gillman. "Introduction: The Study of the American Problems." In *States of Emergency: The Object of American Studies*. Chapel Hill: University of North Carolina Press, 2009.

Castronovo, Russ, and David Glimp, eds. "Introduction: After Critique?" In "After Critique?," special issue, *ELN* 51, no. 2 (2013): 1–6.

Cavell, Stanley. *The Claim of Reason: Wittgenstein, Skepticism, Morality, and Tragedy*. New York: Oxford University Press, 1999.

———. *In Quest of the Ordinary: Lines of Skepticism and Romanticism*. Chicago: University of Chicago Press, 1994.

———. *Must We Mean What We Say?* Cambridge: Cambridge University Press, 2002.

———. *The Senses of Walden*. Chicago: University of Chicago Press, 1981.

Chakrabarty, Dipesh. *Provincializing Europe: Postcolonial Thought and Historical Difference*. Princeton, NJ: Princeton University Press, 2000.

Chase, Richard. *The American Novel and Its Tradition*. Baltimore: Johns Hopkins University Press, 1957.

———. *Herman Melville: A Critical Study*. New York: Hafner, 1971. First published 1949.

Cheng, Anne Anlin. "Psychoanalysis without Symptoms." *differences* 20, no. 1 (2009): 87–101.

Cheng, Eileen Ka-May. *The Plain and Noble Garb of Truth: Nationalism and Impartiality in American Historical Writing, 1784–1860*. Athens: University of Georgia Press, 2008.

Childs, Peter, ed. *Ian McEwan's "Enduring Love."* London: Routledge, 2007.

Clark, Dorothy G. "Being's Wound: (Un)Explaining Evil in Jim Thompson's *The Killer inside Me*." *Journal of Popular Culture* 42, no. 1 (February 2009): 49–66.

Condren, Conal, Stephen Gaukroger, and Ian Hunter, eds. *The Philosopher in Early Modern Europe: The Nature of a Contested Identity*. Cambridge: Cambridge University Press, 2006.

Cooper, Mark Garrett, and John Marx, "Crisis, Crisis, Crisis: Big Media and the Humanities Workforce." *differences* 24, no. 3 (2013): 127–59.

Culler, Jonathan. *Literary Theory: A Very Short Introduction*. Oxford: Oxford University Press, 2011.

Cvetkovich, Ann. *Depression: A Public Feeling*. Durham, NC: Duke University Press, 2012.

Danto, Arthur C. "The End of Art." In *The Philosophical Disenfranchisement of Art*, 81–115. New York: Columbia University Press, 1986.

Dean, Tim. "Art as Symptom: Žižek and the Ethics of Psychoanalytic Criticism." *diacritics* 32, no. 2 (2002): 20–41.

Deleuze, Gilles. *Masochism: Coldness and Cruelty*. New York: Zone, 1991.

Deleuze, Gilles, and Félix Guattari. *A Thousand Plateaus: Capitalism and Schizophrenia*. Translated by Brian Massumi. Minneapolis: University of Minnesota Press, 1987.

de Man, Paul. *Allegories of Reading: Figural Language in Rousseau, Nietzsche, Rilke, and Proust*. New Haven, CT: Yale University Press, 1982.

Derrida, Jacques. *Dissemination*. Translated by Barbara Johnson. Chicago: University of Chicago Press, 1981.

———. "Force of Law." *Cardozo Law Review* 11 (1989–90): 920–1045.

———. *Of Grammatology*. Translated by Gayatri Chakravorty Spivak. Baltimore: Johns Hopkins University Press, 1976.

———. *Psyche: Inventions of the Other*. Vol. 1. Edited by Peggy Kamuf and Elizabeth Rottenberg. Stanford, CA: Stanford University Press, 2006.

———. *Rogues: Two Essays on Reason*. Translated by Pascale-Anne Brault. Stanford, CA: Stanford University Press, 2005.

———. *Sovereignties in Question: The Poetics of Paul Celan*. New York: Fordham University Press, 2005.

———. *Specters of Marx*. Translated by Peggy Kamuf. New York: Routledge, 1994.

———. "Structure, Sign, and Play." In *Writing and Difference*. Translated by Alan Bass. Chicago: University of Chicago Press, 1978.

Dillion, M. C. *Semiological Reductionism: A Critique of the Deconstructive Movement in Postmodern Thought*. Albany: State University of New York Press, 1995.

Docherty, Thomas. *Aesthetic Democracy*. Stanford, CA: Stanford University Press, 2006.

Du Bois, W. E. B. "Criteria of Negro Art." In *The Norton Anthology of African American Literature*, edited by Henry Louis Gates Jr. and Nellie Y. McKay. New York: W. W. Norton, 1997.

Dudley, Donald R. *A History of Cynicism from Diogenes to the 6th Century A.D.* Cambridge: Cambridge University Press, 1937.

During, Simon. *Against Democracy: Literary Experience in the Era of Emancipations*. New York: Fordham University Press, 2012.

Eagleton, Terry. "The Death of Universities." *The Guardian*, December 17, 2010.

———. *Literary Theory: An Introduction*. 2nd ed. Oxford: Blackwell, 1996.

———. *Marxism and Literary Criticism*. Berkeley: University of California Press, 1976.

Edelman, Lee. *No Future: Queer Theory and the Death Drive*. Durham, NC: Duke University Press, 2004.

———. "Unknowing Barbara." *diacritics* 34, no. 1 (2004): 89–93.

Emerson, Ralph Waldo. "Circles." In *Selected Essays*, edited by Larzer Ziff. New York: Viking, 1982.

English, James F. "Everywhere and Nowhere: The Sociology of Literature after 'the Sociology of Literature.'" *New Literary History* 41, no. 2 (spring 2010), v–xxiii.

Farago, Jason. "J. M. Coetzee's Stunning New Novel Shows What Happens When a Nobel Winner Gets Really Weird." *New Republic*, September 14, 2013.

Felman, Shoshana. *The Juridical Unconscious: Trials and Traumas in the Twentieth Century*. Cambridge, MA: Harvard University Press, 2002.

Felski, Rita. "After Suspicion." *Profession* (2009): 28–35.

———. "Context Stinks!" *New Literary History* 42, no. 4 (Autumn 2011): 573–91.

———. "Critique and the Hermeneutics of Suspicion." *M/C* 15, no. 1 (2012), http://journal.media-culture.org.au/index.php/mcjournal/article/view/431.

———. "Digging Down and Standing Back." *ELN* 51, no. 2 (fall/winter 2013), 7–23.

———. *The Limits of Critique*. Chicago: University of Chicago Press, 2016.

———. "Modernist Studies and Cultural Studies: Reflections on Method." *Modernism/Modernity* 10, no. 3 (2003): 501–18.

———. *Uses of Literature*. New York: Wiley-Blackwell, 2008.

Fetterley, Judith. *The Resisting Reader: A Feminist Approach to American Fiction*. Bloomington: Indiana University Press, 1981.

Fish, Stanley. *Save the World on Your Own Time*. Oxford: Oxford University Press, 2008.

Flaubert, Gustave. *The Dictionary of Accepted Ideas*. Translated by Jacques Barzun. New York: New Directions, 1968.

Foster, Hal. "Post-Critical." *October* 139 (winter 2012): 3–8.

Foucault, Michel. *The Courage of Truth*. Translated by Graham Burchell. London: Palgrave, 2011.

———. "What Is Critique?" Translated by Kevin Paul Geiman. In *What Is Enlightenment? Eighteenth-Century Answers and Twentieth-Century Questions*, edited by James Schmidt. Berkeley: University of California Press, 1966.

Fowler, Alastair. *Kinds of Literature: An Introduction to the Theory of Genres and Modes*. Cambridge, MA: Harvard University Press, 1985.

François, Anne-Lise. *Open Secrets: The Literature of Uncounted Experience*. Stanford, CA: Stanford University Press, 2007.

Frank, Adam, and Eve Kosofsky Sedgwick. "Shame in the Cybernetic Fold: Reading Silvan Tomkins." *Critical Inquiry* 21, no. 2 (winter 1995): 496–522.

Freedgood, Elaine, and Cannon Schmitt. "Denotatively, Technically, Literally." *Representations* 125, no. 1 (2014): 1–14.

Freud, Sigmund. "Fragment of an Analysis of Case of Hysteria ["Dora"]." 1905. In *The Standard Edition of the Complete Psychological Works*, edited and translated by James Strachey. 24 vols. London: Hogarth, 1953–74.

———. "The Method of Interpreting Dreams: An Analysis of a Specimen Dream." In *The Interpretation of Dreams* (1900). *Standard Edition*, vol. 4.

Friedman, Geraldine. "The Spectral Legacy of Althusser: The Symptom and Its Return." *Yale French Studies* 88 (1995): 165–82.

Fromm, Harold. "Oppositional Opposition." In *Theory's Empire: An Anthology of Dissent*, edited by Daphne Patai and Will H. Corral. New York: Columbia University Press, 2005.

Gaddis, John Lewis. *The Cold War: A New History*. New York: Penguin, 2006.

Galloway, Alexander. "Plastic Reading." In "A *Novel* Forum: What Can Reading Do?" *Novel* 45, no. 1 (2012): 10–12.

Gaskill, Nicholas, and A. J. Nocek. *The Lure of Whitehead*. Minneapolis: University of Minnesota Press, 2014.

Gazari, Vanessa M. "How to Read Afghanistan." *New York Times*, August 10, 2013.

Geertz, Clifford. *The Interpretation of Cultures*. New York: Perseus, 1973.

Geulen, Eva. *The End of Art: Readings in a Rumor after Hegel*. Translated by James McFarland. Palo Alto, CA: Stanford University Press, 2006.

Geuss, Raymond. *The Idea of a Critical Theory: Habermas and the Frankfurt School*. Cambridge: Cambridge University Press, 1981.

Ginzburg, Carlo. "Clues: Roots of an Evidential Paradigm." Translated by Anne C. Tedeschi and John Tedeschi. In *Clues, Myths, and the Historical Method*, 3–30. Baltimore: Johns Hopkins University Press, 1992.

Giroux, Henri. *Neoliberalism's War on Higher Education*. Chicago: Haymarket, 2014.

Goffman, Erving. *Stigma: Notes on the Management of Spoiled Identity*. New York: Simon and Schuster, 1963.

Goodlad, Lauren M. E., and Andrew Sartori. "The Ends of History: Introduction." *Victorian Studies* 55, no. 4 (summer 2013): 591–614.

Gordimer, Nadine. "The Idea of Gardening." *New York Review of Books*, February 2, 1984.

Gourgouris, Stathis. *Lessons in Secular Criticism*. New York: Fordham University Press, 2013.

Grossberg, Lawrence. *Bringing It All Back Home: Essays in Cultural Studies*. Durham, NC: Duke University Press, 1997.

Gumbrecht, Hans Ulrich. *Production of Presence: What Meaning Cannot Convey*. Stanford, CA: Stanford University Press, 2004.

Hadley, Elaine. "On a Darkling Plain: Victorian Liberalism and the Fantasy of Agency." *Victorian Studies* 48, no. 1 (Autumn 2005): 92–102.

Hall, Stuart. "The Problem of Ideology—Marxism without Guarantees." *Journal of Communication Inquiry* 10, no. 2 (1986): 28–44.

Haraway, Donna. "Modest_Witness@Second_Millennium." In *Modest_Witness@Second_Millennium.FemaleMan©_Meets_OncoMouse™*. New York: Routledge, 1997.

———. "Situated Knowledges: The Science Question in Feminism and the Privilege of Partial Perspective." *Feminist Studies* 14, no. 3 (fall 1988): 575–99.

Harding, Sandra. "Rethinking Standpoint Epistemology: What Is 'Strong Objectivity?'" In *Feminist Epistemologies*, edited by Linda Alcoff and Elizabeth Potter, 49–82. New York: Rutgers University Press, 1993.

Hardt, Michael. "The Militancy of Theory." *South Atlantic Quarterly* 110, no. 1 (winter 2011): 3–28.

Harney, Stefano, and Fred Moten. *The Undercommons: Fugitive Planning and Black Study*. New York: Autonomedia, 2013.

Hartley, Daniel. "Cliché." *Thinking Blue Guitars* blog. April 27, 2010. http://thinking blueguitars.wordpress.com/2010/04/27/cliché.

Harvey, David. *The New Imperialism*. Oxford: Oxford University Press, 2005.

Hayot, Eric. "I Too Have Dreamed of Another French Messiah." *ELN* 51, no. 2 (2013): 87–94.

Hegel, Georg Wilhelm Friedrich. *Introductory Lectures on Aesthetics*. New York: Penguin, 1993.

Hemmings, Clare. "The Materials of Reparation." *Feminist Theory* 15, no. 1 (2014): 27–30.

Hennion, Antoine. "Pragmatics of Taste." In *The Blackwell Companion to the Sociology of Culture*, edited by Mark D. Jacobs and Nancy Weiss Hanrahan. Oxford: Blackwell, 2005.

Hensley, Nathan K. "Curatorial Reading and Endless War." *Victorian Studies* 56, no. 1 (Autumn 2013): 59–83.

Hirschkind, Charles. *The Ethical Soundscape: Cassette Sermons and Islamic Counterpublics*. New York: Columbia University Press, 2006.

Hollinger, David. "The Wedge Driving Academe's Two Families Apart: Can STEM and the Humanities Get Along?" *Chronicle Review,* October 14, 2013, http://chronicle .com/article/Why-Cant-the-Sciencesthe/142239/.

Hume, David. "My Own Life." In *Essays: Moral, Political and Literary*, edited by Eugene F. Miller. Indianapolis: Liberty Classics, 1987.

Hunter, Ian. "Literary Theory in Civil Life." *South Atlantic Quarterly* 95, no. 4 (fall 1996): 1099–1134.

———. "Scenes from the History of Poststructuralism: Davos, Freiburg, Baltimore, Leipzig." *New Literary History* 41, no. 3 (summer 2010): 491–516.

Hurd, Richard. *An Introduction to the Study of the Prophecies in Twelve Sermons.* London: T. Cadell, 1772.

Huyssen, Andreas. *After the Great Divide: Modernism, Mass Culture, Postmodernism.* Bloomington: Indiana University Press, 1986.

Iser, Wolfgang. "The Reading Process: A Phenomenological Approach." *New Literary History* 3, no. 2 (winter 1972): 279–99.

Jakobson, Roman. *Linguistics and Poetics.* Excerpted in *The Norton Anthology of Theory and Criticism,* edited by Vincent Leitch et al. New York: W. W. Norton, 2010.

James, C. L. R. *American Civilization.* Oxford: Blackwell, 1992.

James, William. *The Principles of Psychology.* Vol. 1. New York: Cosimo Classics, 2007.

Jameson, Fredric. "Marx's Purloined Letter." In *Ghostly Demarcations: A Symposium on Jacques Derrida's* Specters of Marx," edited by Michael Sprinker. New York: Verso, 1999.

———. "On 'Cultural Studies.'" *Social Text* 34 (1993): 17–52.

———. *The Political Unconscious: Narrative as a Socially Symbolic Act.* Ithaca, NY: Cornell University Press, 1981.

———. "Third-World Literature in the Age of Multinational Capitalism." *Social Text* 15 (1986): 65–88.

JanMohamed, Abdul R. "The Economy of Manichean Allegory: The Function of Racial Difference in Colonialist Literature." *Critical Inquiry* 12, no. 1 (1985): 59–87.

Johnson, Barbara. "Lesbian Spectacles: Reading *Sula, Passing, Thelma and Louise,* and *The Accused.*" In *The Feminist Difference: Literature, Psychoanalysis, Race, and Gender,* 157–64. Cambridge, MA: Harvard University Press, 1998.

———. "Nothing Fails like Success." In *A World of Difference,* 11–16. Baltimore: Johns Hopkins University Press, 1987.

———. "Translator's Introduction." In Jacques Derrida, *Dissemination,* vii–xxxiii. Chicago: University of Chicago Press, 1981.

Kamuf, Peggy. *The Division of Literature.* Stanford, CA: Stanford University Press, 1997.

Kant, Immanuel. "What Is Enlightenment?" In *Kant: Political Writings,* translated by H. S. Nisbet, 54–63. Cambridge: Cambridge University Press, 1991.

Keen, Suzane. *Empathy and the Novel.* New York: Oxford University Press, 2010.

Kierkegaard, Søren. *Fear and Trembling. Repetition,* edited and translated by Howard V. Hong and Edna H. Hong. Princeton, NJ: Princeton University Press, 1983.

Knights, Mark. *Representation and Misrepresentation in Later Stuart Britain: Partisanship and Political Culture.* Oxford: Oxford University Press, 2005.

Koselleck, Reinhard. *Critique and Crisis: Enlightenment and the Pathogenesis of Modern Society.* Cambridge, MA: MIT Press, 1988.

Kramnick, Jonathan. "Against Literary Darwinism." *Critical Inquiry* 37, no. 2 (2011): 315–47.

Latour, Bruno. "The Compositionist Manifesto." *New Literary History* 41, no. 3 (2010): 471–90.

————. *An Inquiry into the Modes of Existence: An Anthropology of the Moderns.* Translated by Catherine Porter. Cambridge, MA: Harvard University Press, 2013.

————. *Pandora's Hope: Essays on the Reality of Science Studies.* Cambridge, MA: Harvard University Press, 1999.

————. *Reassembling the Social: An Introduction to Actor-Network Theory.* Oxford: Oxford University Press, 2007.

————. *Rejoicing: or, The Torments of Religious Speech.* Translated by Julie Rose. Cambridge: Polity, 2013.

————. *We Have Never Been Modern.* Translated by Catherine Porter. Cambridge, MA: Harvard University Press, 1993.

————. "Why Has Critique Run Out of Steam? From Matters of Fact to Matters of Concern." *Critical Inquiry* 30 (winter 2004): 225–48.

Latour, Bruno, and Vincent Antonin Lepinay. *The Science of Passionate Interests: An Introduction to Gabriel Tarde's Economic Anthropology.* Chicago: Prickly Paradigm, 2010.

Lazarus, Neil. "The Politics of Postcolonial Modernism." In *Postcolonial Studies and Beyond*, edited by Ania Loomba, Suvir Kaul, Matti Bunzl, Antoinette Burton, and Jed Esty, 423–38. Durham, NC: Duke University Press, 2005.

Lear, Jonathan. *Radical Hope: Ethics in the Face of Cultural Devastation.* Cambridge, MA: Harvard University Press, 2008.

Lemke, Thomas. "The Risks of Security: Liberalism, Biopolitics and Fear." In *The Government of Life: Foucault, Biopolitics, and Neoliberalism*, edited by Vanessa Lemm and Miguel Vatter. New York: Fordham University Press, 2014.

Lesjak, Carolyn. "Reading Dialectically." *Criticism* 55, no. 2 (2013): 233–77.

Levin, Richard. "Silence Is Consent, or Curse Ye Morez!" In *Theory's Empire: An Anthology of Dissent*, edited by Daphne Patai and Will H. Corral. New York: Columbia University Press, 2005.

Levine, Caroline. "Strategic Formalism: Toward a New Method in Cultural Studies." *Victorian Studies* 48, no. 4 (2006): 625–57.

Levine, Joseph. *The Battle of the Books: History and Literature in the Augustan Age.* Ithaca, NY: Cornell University Press, 1991.

Levine, Michael. *A Weak Messianic Power: Figures of Time to Come in Benjamin, Derrida, and Celan.* New York: Fordham University Press, 2013.

Levitin, Dimitri. *Ancient Wisdom in the Age of the New Science: Histories of Philosophy in England, c. 1640–1700.* Cambridge: Cambridge University Press.

Lewis, R. W. B. *American Adam: Innocence, Tragedy, and Tradition in the Nineteenth Century.* Chicago: University of Chicago Press, 1955.

Leys, Ruth. "The Turn to Affect: A Critique." *Critical Inquiry* 37 (spring 2011): 434–72.

Locke, John. *Two Treatises of Government.* Edited by Peter Laslett. Cambridge: Cambridge University Press, 1988.

Love, Heather. "Close but Not Deep: Literary Ethics and the Descriptive Turn." *New Literary History* 41, no. 2 (2010): 371–91.

————. "Close Reading and Thin Description." *Public Culture* 25, no. 3 (2013): 401–34.

———. "Truth and Consequences: On Paranoid Reading and Reparative Reading." *Criticism* 52, no. 2 (spring 2010): 235–41.

Löwy, Frederick, and Robert Sayre. *Romanticism against the Tide of Modernity*. Translated by Catherine Porter. Durham, NC: Duke University Press, 2001.

Luhrmann, T. M. *Of Two Minds*. New York: Vintage, 2004.

Lukács, Georg. *The Historical Novel*. Translated by Hannah and Stanley Mitchell. Boston: Beacon, 1963.

Marcus, Sharon. *Between Women: Friendship, Desire, and Marriage in Victorian England*. Princeton, NJ: Princeton University Press, 2007.

Marder, Elissa. "Force and Translation or the Polymorphous Body of Language." *Philosophia* 3, no. 1 (winter 2013): 1–18.

Marx, Karl. *Capital*. Excerpted in *The Norton Anthology of Theory and Criticism*, edited by Vincent Leitch et al. New York: W. W. Norton, 2010.

———. *The Eighteenth Brumaire of Louis Napoleon*. New York: International, 1994.

———. "The German Ideology." In *The Marx-Engels Reader*, 2nd ed., edited by Robert C. Tucker. New York: W. W. Norton, 1978.

———. "Theses on Feuerbach." In *The Marx-Engels Reader*, 2nd ed., edited by Robert C. Tucker. New York: W. W. Norton, 1978.

Marx, Karl, and Friedrich Engels. "The Communist Manifesto." In *The Portable Karl Marx*, edited by Eugene Kamenka. New York: Penguin, 1983.

Massumi, Brian. *Parables for the Virtual*. Durham, NC: Duke University Press, 2002.

Mbembe, Achille. *On the Postcolony*. Berkeley: University of California Press, 2001.

McEleney, Corey. "Queer Theory and the Yale School: Barbara Johnson's Astonishment." GLQ 19, no. 2 (2013): 143–65.

McEwan, Ian. *Enduring Love*. New York: Anchor, 1998.

McFarland, Thomas. *Shapes of Culture*. Iowa City: University of Iowa Press, 1987.

McGurl, Mark. *The Program Era: Postwar Fiction and the Rise of Creative Writing*. Cambridge, MA: Harvard University Press, 2009.

McLuhan, Marshall. *From Cliché to Archetype*. New York: Viking, 1970.

Mellard, James M. "'No Ideas but in Things': Fiction, Criticism, and the New Darwinism." *Style* 41, no. 1 (spring 2007): 1–28.

Melzer, Arthur M. *Philosophy between the Lines: The Lost History of Esoteric Writing*. Chicago: University of Chicago Press, 2014.

Michael, John. *Anxious Intellects: Academic Professionals, Public Intellectuals, and Enlightenment Values*. Durham, NC: Duke University Press, 2000.

Miller, D. A. *Jane Austen, or The Secret of Style*. Princeton, NJ: Princeton University Press, 2003.

Miller, Laura. "Ian McEwan Fools British Shrinks." *Salon*, September 21, 1999.

Millett, Kate. *Sexual Politics*. Garden City, NY: Doubleday, 1970.

Mitchell, W. J. T. "The Commitment to Form; or, Still Crazy after All These Years." PMLA 118, no. 2 (2003): 321–25.

Moi, Toril. "The Adventure of Reading: Literature and Philosophy, Cavell and Beauvoir." *Literature and Theology* 25, no. 2 (June 2011): 125–40.

———. "Hedda's Silences: Beauty and Despair in *Hedda Gabler.*" *Modern Drama* 56, no. 4 (2013): 434–56.

Montag, Warren. *Althusser and His Contemporaries: Philosophy's Perpetual War.* Durham, NC: Duke University Press, 2013.

Moon, Michael. *Disseminating Whitman: Revision and Corporeality in Leaves of Grass.* Cambridge, MA: Harvard University Press, 1991.

Mumford, Lewis. *The Golden Day: A Study in American Literature and Culture.* Boston: Beacon Hill, 1955.

Muñoz, Jose Estaban. *Cruising Utopia: The Then and There of Queer Futurity.* New York: New York University Press, 2009.

Nancy, Jean-Luc. *The Inoperable Community.* Edited by Peter Connor, translated by Peter Connor, Lisa Garbus, Michael Holland, and Simona Sawhney. Minneapolis: University of Minnesota Press, 1991.

Ngai, Sianne. "Network Aesthetics." In *American Literature's Aesthetic Dimensions,* edited by Cindy Weinstein and Christopher Looby, 367–92. New York: Columbia University Press, 2012.

———. "Stuplimity: Shock and Boredom in Twentieth-Century Aesthetics." *Postmodern Culture* 10, no. 2 (2000). Accessed August 14, 2016. http://pmc.iath.virginia.edu /text-only/issue.100/10.2ngai.txt

———. *Ugly Feelings.* Cambridge, MA: Harvard University Press, 2007.

Nietzsche, Friedrich. *The Birth of Tragedy and Other Writings.* Translated by Ronald Speirs. Cambridge: Cambridge University Press, 1999.

Olsen, Niklas. *History in the Plural: An Introduction to the Work of Reinhart Koselleck.* New York: Berghahn, 2011.

Orwell, George. "Politics and the English Language." In *The Orwell Reader: Fiction, Essays, and Reportage by George Orwell.* New York: Harcourt Brace Jovanovich, 1984.

Osborn, Ian. *Tormenting Thoughts and Secret Rituals: The Hidden Epidemic of Obsessive-Compulsive Disorder.* New York: Pantheon, 1998.

Paine, Thomas. *Common Sense.* In *The Thomas Paine Reader,* edited by Michael Foot and Isaac Kramnick. New York: Penguin, 1987.

Papoulias, Constantia, and Felicity Callard. "Biology's Gift: Interrogating the Turn to Affect." *Body and Society* 16, no. 1 (March 2010): 29–56.

Patai, Daphne, and Will H. Corral. Introduction to *Theory's Empire: An Anthology of Dissent,* edited by Daphne Patai and Will H. Corral. New York: Columbia University Press, 2005.

Pease, Donald E. "Moby-Dick and the Cold War." In *The American Renaissance Reconsidered,* edited by Walter Benn Michaels and Donald E. Pease. Baltimore: Johns Hopkins University Press, 1985.

———. *The New American Exceptionalism.* Minneapolis: University of Minnesota Press, 2009.

Pinker, Stephen. *The Sense of Style.* New York: Viking, 2014.

Pippin, Robert. *Modernism as a Philosophical Problem.* London: Blackwell, 1989.

Pocock, J. G. A. *Barbarism and Religion*, vol. 1: *The Enlightenments of Edmund Gibbon, 1737–1764*. Cambridge: Cambridge University Press, 1999.

———. *The Machiavellian Moment, Florentine Political Thought and the Atlantic Republican Tradition*. Princeton, NJ: Princeton University Press, 1975.

Poirier, Richard. *A World Elsewhere: The Place of Style in American Literature*. New York: Oxford University Press, 1966.

Potts, Jason, ed. "Dossier: Surface Reading." Special issue, *Mediations* 28, no. 2 (2015).

Poulet, Georges. "Phenomenology of Reading." *New Literary History* 1, no. 1 (October 1969), 53–68.

Pratt, Lloyd. "Unfinished Business." Panel introduction, Modern Language Association Convention, January 8–11, 2015, Vancouver. Unpublished manuscript.

Rancière, Jacques. *Dissensus: On Politics and Aesthetics*. Translated by Steven Corcoran. New York: Continuum, 2010.

———. *The Emancipated Spectator*. London: Verso, 2009.

———. *The Politics of Aesthetics*. Translated by Gabriel Rockhill. London: Bloomsbury, 2013.

Redfield, Marc. *The Politics of Aesthetics*. Stanford, CA: Stanford University Press, 2003.

Ricks, Christopher. "Clichés." In *The State of the Language*, edited by Leonard Michaels. Berkeley: University of California Press, 1980.

Ricoeur, Paul. *Freud and Philosophy*. Translated by Denis Savage. New Haven, CT: Yale University Press, 1970.

Roberts, William. *A Dawn of Imaginative Feeling: The Contribution of John Brown (1715–66) to Eighteenth Century Thought and Literature*. Carlisle: Northern Academic Press, 1996.

Rooney, Ellen. "Better Read Than Dead: Althusser and the Fetish of Ideology." *Yale French Studies* 88 (1995): 183–200.

———. "Form and Contentment." In *Reading for Form*, edited by Susan J. Wolfson and Marshall Brown, 25–48. Seattle: University of Washington Press, 2006.

———. "Live Free or Describe: The Reading Effect and the Persistence of Form." *Differences* 21, no. 3 (2010): 112–39.

———, ed. "A *Novel* Forum: What Can Reading Do?" Special issue, *Novel* 45, no. 1 (2012): 1–29.

Rorty, Richard. *Philosophy and Social Hope*. New York: Penguin, 2000.

Rosenblatt, Louise. *The Reader, the Text, the Poem: The Transactional Theory of the Literary Work*. Carbondale: Southern Illinois University Press, 1992.

Roth, Marco. "The Rise of the Neuro-Novel." *n+1* (fall 2009). Accessed August 14, 2016. https://nplusonemag.com/issue-8/essays/the-rise-of-the-neuronovel/.

Roth, Michael. *Beyond the University: Why Liberal Education Matters*. New Haven, CT: Yale University Press, 2014.

Said, Edward. *Culture and Imperialism*. New York: Knopf, 1993.

———. *The World, the Text, and the Critic*. Cambridge, MA: Harvard University Press, 1983.

Saldívar, Ramón. "Historical Fantasy, Speculative Realism, and Postrace Aesthetics in Contemporary American Fiction." *American Literary History* 23, no. 3 (fall 2011): 574–99.

Sartre, Jean-Paul. "What Is Literature?" In *What Is Literature? and Other Essays*, edited by Steven Ungar. Cambridge, MA: Harvard University Press, 1988.

Scott, David. *Conscripts of Modernity: The Tragedy of Colonial Enlightenment.* Durham, NC: Duke University Press, 2004.

Scott, Jonathan. *Algernon Sidney and the English Republic, 1623–1677.* Cambridge: Cambridge University Press, 1988.

Sedgwick, Eve Kosofsky. "Paranoid Reading and Reparative Reading, or, You're So Paranoid, You Probably Think This Essay Is about You." In *Touching Feeling: Affect, Pedagogy, Performativity.* Durham, NC: Duke University Press, 2003.

Sheehan, Jonathan. *The Enlightenment Bible: Translation, Scholarship and Culture.* Princeton, NJ: Princeton University Press, 2005.

Shelley, Percy Bysshe. "A Defense of Poetry." In *Shelley's Poetry and Prose*, edited by Donald H. Reiman and Neil Fraistat. New York: W. W. Norton, 2002.

Shouse, Eric. "Feeling, Emotion, Affect." *M/C* 8, no. 6 (December 2005). http://journal.media-culture.org.au/0512/03-shouse.php.

Shulman, George. "Hope and American Politics." *Raritan* 21, no. 3 (2002): 1–19.

Slater, Avery. "American Afterlife: Benjaminian Messianism and Technological Redemption in Muriel Rukeyser's *The Book of the Dead.*" *American Literature* 86, no. 4 (December 2014): 767–97.

Sloterdijk, Peter. *Critique of Cynical Reason.* Translated by Andreas Huyssen. Minneapolis: University of Minnesota Press, 1988.

———. *Rage and Time: A Psychopolitical Investigation.* Translated by Mario Wenning. New York: Columbia University Press, 2010.

Smith, Dinitia. "A Stone's Throw Is a Freudian Slip." *New York Times*, March 10, 2001, http://www.nytimes.com/2001/03/10/arts/a-stone-s-throw-is-a-freudian-slip.html?scp=1&sq=%22edward+said%22&st=nyt.

Smith, Paul. *Primitive America: The Ideology of Capitalist Democracy.* Minneapolis: University of Minnesota Press, 2007.

Snediker, Michael D. *Queer Optimism: Lyric Personhood and Other Felicitous Persuasions.* Minneapolis: University of Minnesota Press, 2008.

Snow, C. P. *The Two Cultures.* Cambridge: Cambridge University Press, 1998.

Soler, Colette. "The Paradoxes of the Symptom in Psychoanalysis." In *The Cambridge Companion to Lacan*, edited by Jean-Michel Rabaté. Cambridge: Cambridge University Press, 2005.

Solnit, Rebecca. *Hope in the Dark: Untold Histories, Wild Possibilities.* New York: Nation Books, 2005.

Sommer, Doris. *The Work of Art in the World: Civic Agency and Public Humanities.* Durham, NC: Duke University Press, 2014.

Spinoza, Benedict. *Theological-Political Treatise.* Edited by Jonathan Israel. Cambridge: Cambridge University Press, 2007.

Spivak, Gayatri Chakravorty. *An Aesthetic Education in the Era of Globalization.* Cambridge, MA: Harvard University Press, 2012.

———. *A Critique of Postcolonial Reason: Toward a History of the Vanishing Present.* Cambridge, MA: Harvard University Press, 1999.

———. "Lie Down in the Karoo: An Antidote to the Anthropocene." *Public Books,* June 1, 2014.

———. "The Rest of the World: A Conversation with Gayatri Spivak." In *Hope: New Philosophies for Change,* edited by Mary Zournazi. New York: Routledge, 2003.

Sprinker, Michael. "Textual Politics: Foucault and Derrida." *boundary 2* 8, no. 3 (spring 1980): 75–98.

Stacey, Jackie. "Wishing Away Ambivalence." *Feminist Theory* 15, no. 1 (2014): 39–49.

Starr, G. Gabrielle. *Feeling Beauty: The Neuroscience of Aesthetic Experience.* Cambridge, MA: MIT Press, 2013.

Stengers, Isabelle. *Thinking with Whitehead: A Free and Wild Creation of Concepts.* Cambridge, MA: Harvard University Press, 2014.

Stoler, Ann Laura. *Along the Archival Grain: Epistemic Anxieties and Colonial Common Sense.* Princeton, NJ: Princeton University Press, 2010.

Swift, Jonathan. *The Prose Works of Jonathan Swift.* Vol. 3. Edited by Herbert Davis. Oxford: Basil Blackwell, 1940.

———. *A Tale of a Tub and Other Works.* Edited by Marcus Walsh. Cambridge: Cambridge University Press, 2010.

Taussig, Michael. "A Carnival of the Senses: A Conversation with Michael Taussig." In *Hope: New Philosophies for Change,* edited by Mary Zournazi. New York: Routledge, 2003.

Taylor, Charles. *A Secular Age.* Cambridge, MA: Harvard University Press, 2007.

Teskey, Gordon. *Allegory and Violence.* Ithaca, NY: Cornell University Press, 1996.

Thompson, Jim. *The Killer inside Me.* New York: Vintage, 1991.

Thrailkill, Jane. *Affecting Fictions: Mind, Body, and Emotion in American Literary Realism.* Cambridge, MA: Harvard University Press, 2007.

Todorov, Tzvetan. *Hope and Memory: Lessons from the Twentieth Century.* Princeton, NJ: Princeton University Press, 2003.

Turner, James. *Philology: The Forgotten Origins of the Modern Humanities.* Princeton, NJ: Princeton University Press, 2014.

Wallen, Jeffrey. *Closed Encounters: Literary Politics and Public Cultures.* Minneapolis: University of Minnesota Press, 1998.

Warburton, William. *Letters from a Late Eminent Prelate to One of His Friends.* Edited by Richard Hurd. London: T. Cadell and W. Davies, 1809.

Ware, Owen. "Dialectic of the Past/Disjuncture of the Future: Derrida and Benjamin on the Concept of Messianism." *Journal for Cultural and Religious Theory* 5, no. 2 (April 2004): 99–114.

Warner, Michael. "Uncritical Reading." In *Polemic: Critical or Uncritical,* edited by Jane Gallop, 13–38. New York: Routledge, 2004.

Watkins, Evan. "The Self-Evaluations of Critical Theory." *boundary 2*, nos. 12/13 (1984): 359–78.

Watts, Carol. *The Cultural Work of Empire: The Seven Years' War and the Imagining of the Shandean State*. Edinburgh: Edinburgh University Press, 2007.

Weber, Max. "Politics as Vocation." First published July 1919. Accessed November 21, 2014. http://anthropos-lab.net/wp/wp-content/uploads/2011/12/Weber-Politics-as -a-Vocation.pdf.

———. *The Protestant Ethic and the Spirit of Capitalism*. Translated by Talcott Parsons. London: Routledge, 1992.

———. "Science as a Vocation." In *From Max Weber: Essays in Sociology*, edited and translated by H. H. Gerth and C. Wright Mills. New York: Oxford University Press.

Weed, Elizabeth. "The Way We Read Now." *History of the Present* 2, no. 1 (2012): 95–106.

White, Hayden. *The Content of the Form: Narrative Discourse and Historical Representation*. Baltimore: Johns Hopkins University Press, 1987.

———. *Metahistory: The Historical Imagination in Nineteenth-Century Europe*. Baltimore: Johns Hopkins University Press, 1973.

Whitman, Walt. *Poetry and Prose*. Edited by Justin Kaplan. New York: Library of America, 1996.

Wiegman, Robyn. "The Ends of New Americanism." *New Literary History* 42, no. 3 (2011): 385–407.

———. "The Times We're In: Queer Feminist Criticism and the Reparative 'Turn.'" *Feminist Theory* 15, no. 1 (2014): 4–25.

Williams, Jeffrey J. "The New Modesty in Literary Criticism." *Chronicle Review*, January 5, 2015.

Wittgenstein, Ludwig. *Philosophical Investigations: The German Text, with an English Translation*. Rev. 4th ed. Translated by G. E. M. Anscombe, P. M. S. Hacker, and Joachim Schulte. Malden, MA: Wiley-Blackwell, 2009. First published 1953.

Wolfson, Susan J., and Marshall Brown, eds. *Reading for Form*. Seattle: University of Washington Press, 2006.

Wootton, David. *The Invention of Science: A New History of the Scientific Revolution*. New York: HarperCollins, 2015.

Yack, Bernard. *The Longing for Total Revolution: Philosophical Sources of Social Discontent from Rousseau to Marx and Hegel*. Berkeley: University of California Press, 1992.

Zakaria, Fareed. *In Defense of Liberal Education*. New York: Barnes and Noble, 2014.

Zalewski, Daniel. "The Background Hum." *New Yorker*, February 23, 2009.

Zijderveld, Anton. *On Clichés: The Supersedure of Meaning by Function in Modernity*. London: Routledge and Kegan Paul, 1979.

Žižek, Slavoj. *The Fragile Absolute*. New York: Verso, 2000.

Zournazi, Mary. *Hope: New Philosophies for Change*. New York: Routledge, 2003.

Zunshine, Lisa. *Why We Read Fiction*. Columbus: Ohio State University Press, 2006.

ABOUT THE CONTRIBUTORS

ELIZABETH S. ANKER is associate professor in the English Department at Cornell University and associate member of the faculty of Cornell Law School. Her first book is *Fictions of Dignity: Embodying Human Rights in World Literature* (2012). Her current work focuses on the status of paradox within theory and the common metaphors that lend political and legal authority to constitutionalism.

CHRISTOPHER CASTIGLIA is Liberal Arts Research Professor of English and Women's, Gender, and Sexuality Studies at the Pennsylvania State University. He is cofounder of C19: the Society of Nineteenth-Century Americanists and is coeditor of the society's journal, *J19*. He is the author of *Bound and Determined: Captivity, Culture-Crossing, and White Womanhood from Mary Rowlandson to Patty Hearst*; *Interior States: Interiority and Institutional Consciousness in the Antebellum United States*; *If Memory Serves: Gay Men, AIDS, and the Promise of the Queer Past*, coauthored with Christopher Reed; and *The Practices of Hope: Literary Criticism for a Disenchanted Age* (forthcoming).

RUSS CASTRONOVO is Tom Paine Professor of English and Dorothy Draheim Professor of American Studies at the University of Wisconsin–Madison. He is written or edited eight books, including, most recently, *Propaganda 1776: Secrets, Leaks, and Revolutionary Communications in Early America*. He is the winner of the 2016 Chancellor's Distinguished Teaching Award. His current research examines the intellectual and literary history of U.S. conservatism.

SIMON DURING is a research professor at the Institute for the Advanced Study of the Humanities at the University of Queensland. He is the author, most recently, of *Against Democracy: Literary Experience in the Era of Emancipations* (2013). He is currently working on the relation between religion and literature in Britain between about 1688 and 1945.

RITA FELSKI is William R. Kenan, Jr., Professor of English at the University of Virginia and the editor of *New Literary History*. She is the author of *Beyond Feminist Aesthetics*, *The Gender of Modernity*, *Doing Time: Feminist Theory and Postmodern Culture*, *Literature after Feminism*, and *Uses of Literature*, and the editor of *Rethinking Tragedy* and coeditor of *Comparison: Theories, Approaches, Uses*. She has received a William Riley Parker Prize for best essay in *PMLA* and a Guggenheim Fellowship, and her work has been translated into twelve languages. Her most recent book, *The Limits of Critique*, was published in 2015.

JENNIFER L. FLEISSNER is associate professor of English at Indiana University, Bloomington. She is the author of *Women, Compulsion, Modernity: The Moment of American Naturalism* (2004), along with numerous essays published in such journals as ELH, *Critical Inquiry, American Literary History, American Literature, Novel, J19, differences,* and *Studies in Romanticism,* as well as in such collections as *The Cambridge History of the American Novel.* She is presently working on a project titled *Maladies of the Will: The American Novel and the Symptomatology of Modernity.*

ERIC HAYOT is Distinguished Professor of Comparative Literature and Asian Studies at the Pennsylvania State University. He is the author of four books, including *On Literary Worlds* (2012) and *The Elements of Academic Style* (2014).

HEATHER LOVE is the R. Jean Brownlee Term Associate Professor at the University of Pennsylvania, where she teaches courses in gender and sexuality studies, twentieth-century literature and culture, affect studies, film and visual culture, and critical theory. She has also taught at Harvard University, New York University, and Princeton University. She is the author of *Feeling Backward: Loss and the Politics of Queer History* (2009) and the editor of a special issue of GLQ on Gayle Rubin ("Rethinking Sex"). She is currently completing a book project on practices of description in the humanities and social sciences.

JOHN MICHAEL is professor of English and of Visual and Cultural Studies at the University of Rochester. He has published many articles on American literature, contemporary cultural studies, and critical theory. He is the author of *Emerson and Skepticism: The Cipher of the World* (1988), *Anxious Intellectuals: Academic Professionals, Enlightenment Values, and Democratic Politics* (2000), and, most recently, *Identity and the Failure of America from Thomas Jefferson to the War on Terror* (2008). He is completing a book called *The Secular Lyric* and beginning one on the contemporary need for humanistic study.

TORIL MOI is James B. Duke Professor of Literature and Romance Studies and professor of English, philosophy, and theater studies at Duke University. Trained in comparative literature, she works on feminist theory and literary theory and in the field of literature and philosophy. Among her books are *Sexual/Textual Politics: Feminist Literary Theory* (1985), *Simone de Beauvoir: The Making of an Intellectual Woman* (1994), *What Is a Woman? and Other Essays* (1999), and *Henrik Ibsen and the Birth of Modernism: Art, Theater, Philosophy* (2006). She has just finished a book on ordinary language philosophy and literary theory, entitled *Language, Theory, Reading: Literary Studies after Wittgenstein, Austin, and Cavell.* Toril Moi also writes a monthly column for the Norwegian cultural weekly *Morgenbladet.*

ELLEN ROONEY is professor and chair of Modern Culture and Media and professor of English at Brown University. She is the author of *Seductive Reasoning: The Pluralist Problematic of Contemporary Literary Theory* and the editor of *The Cambridge Companion to Feminist Literary Theory.* She serves as coeditor of *differences: a journal of feminist cultural studies* and associate editor of *Novel: A Forum on Fiction.* Her essays on the topics of reading and form include "Live Free or Describe: The Reading Effect and the Persistence of Form" (2010) and "Form and Contentment" (2007), and her current project, *The Reading Effect and the Persistence of Form*, is addressed to contemporary efforts to rethink reading practices and their troubled relation to the category of form.

C. NAMWALI SERPELL is a writer and critic who is currently associate professor of English at the University of California, Berkeley. Her research in contemporary fiction and film concerns the relationship between aesthetics, affect, and ethics. Her first book of literary criticism is called *Seven Modes of Uncertainty* (2014). Other scholarly work has appeared in *The Comparatist, Critique, Narrative,* and a collection called *On the Turn: The Ethics of Fiction in Contemporary Narrative in English.* Her essays and reviews have been published in *Bidoun, The Believer, n+1, Public Books,* the *L.A. Review of Books,* the *San Francisco Chronicle, The Guardian,* and *Should I Go to Grad School?* (2014). You can find her fiction in *Callaloo, Tin House, n+1, McSweeney's, Triple Canopy, The Best American Short Stories, The Caine Prize Anthology,* the *Africa39* anthology, and the collection *Reader, I Married Him* (2016). She is working on a book of essays about faces and intention, *Face Books,* and on a novel, *The Old Drift* (forthcoming 2018).

INDEX

Abraham (biblical figure), 35, 45
absence, 100, 157–58, 175
absolutism, 76–77, 79, 80
actor-network theory, 17, 48n15, 56
Adams, Henry, 106, 119
Adorno, Theodor, 18, 80, 156–57, 231, 247, 256, 272, 278n43
Aesthetic Democracy (Docherty), 245, 251n51
aesthetics, 16–17, 71n19, 101, 116
affect, 2, 10–12, 70n7, 114–15, 121n11, 124n53, 133, 150n21, 151n39, 165, 272, 278n43
Agamben, Giorgio, 187
agglutination, 168–69
Ahmad, Aijaz, 192
Ahmed, Sara, 11, 12, 203, 226
allegory, 6–7, 24, 191–94, 199–203
alterity, 195, 198–99, 277nn35–37
Althusser, Louis: on cliché, 22, 159–60, 162; on a constitutive subject, 140; on guilty reading, 119, 129, 131; on ideology, 179n27; narrator as agent of repressive state apparatus, 171; on play on words, 129, 131, 135–38, 145–46, 148n9; on the problematic, 132–36, 149n18, 150n21; on the production of knowledge, 167; on reading and writing, 133–34, 140, 150n24; "reading" in works of, 131–33, 137, 138, 146, 149n18, 152n56; on surprise, 144; on the surveillance state, 283; on symptomatic reading, 33, 119, 130–31, 142, 158. *See also Capital* (Marx); *Reading*

Capital (Althusser and Baliban); symptomatic reading
The American (James), 113, 114, 116
American academia: author's experiences in, 281–84, 293; change in, 285–86; creative writing programs in, 190; moving beyond critique in, 288–93; neoliberalism, 18, 64–65, 70n11, 290–91, 295n8; political intervention in, 18, 230–31, 236, 241–42, 289–92; radicalism in, 14, 239–40; temporalities in, 285–86, 292; theory in, 280, 287
amorous language, 166–67, 168–69
Amossy, Ruth, 159, 170, 174, 175, 177n3
anagnorisis, 44
Anglicanism, 80–81, 85, 88–89, 91
antibiologism, 203
Appadurai, Arjun, 275n19
Apter, Emily, 142, 277n35
Arendt, Hannah, 156–57, 160, 173, 187
Armstrong, Paul B., 181n52
Arnold, Matthew: on criticism, 24, 128, 232, 237–38, 242, 248; "disinterestedness," 124n42; migration of ideas into secular world of action, 239; role of "Dover Beach" in McEwan's novel, 124n42; social effect of criticism, 236–37; in works of Edward Said, 235, 236
art, 16–20, 18, 247, 260–63, 265, 276n29
Arvin, Newton, 218, 219
Asad, Talal, 13
Attridge, Derek, 198

llave universal/llave maestra, 187, 188, 192, 200, 205; metaphor in, 186, 187, 188, 192, 200, 205; Novilla, 185, 187, 191, 199, 202; The Other in, 199; philosophical digressions in, 187; plot in, 186–87, 191; readings of, 186–87; Simón, 185, 186–87, 188, 191, 195, 199, 200; theory in, 187–88, 205–6; title of, 186. *See also* David (*The Childhood of Jesus* [Coetzee])

Christian, Barbara, 128

Christianity, 78, 80–81, 83, 85, 86, 88–89, 91

Citizen: An American Lyric (Rankine), 191

civil liberties, 232, 282–84

civil society, 77–78, 83–84, 90–92, 94n17

Clarissa (*Enduring Love* [McEwan]), 100, 107, 108, 109, 110–12, 114–15, 118, 123n37

Clark, Dorothy G., 182n62

Claudel, Paul, 32

cliché: critique, 159–60; experience of language, 22; hermeneutics of suspicion, 153, 157, 158, 161; hiddenness of, 159–60, 163–64; invisibility of, 159, 166–67; narrative speech patterns, 170–71; origins of, 154–55, 160–61, 179n33; phenomenology, 164, 165, 168–69; poetic language, 163–64; political uses of, 84, 156, 180n42; psychology of, 173–74; repetition, 22, 155, 156–57, 162, 169, 174–75; self-invention of, 156–57, 161; symptomatic readings of, 159–60, 163–64, 173–74; transparency of, 159–62, 163–64; as trash talk, 163–64; Zijderveld on, 161–63, 168, 173–74, 178n13, 179n33, 180n42, 180n48

close reading, 17, 64, 133, 137, 150n21, 252–53, 271

Coetzee, J. M.: allegory in works of, 24, 187, 191–94, 193, 200, 205; citations used by, 187; elusiveness of, 187–89, 191–92; emergence of alterity in works of, 195; ethical encounters in works of, 195; imaginative experiments of, 189; interpretations of, 188–89; philosophical complexity of, 187; theory in works of, 183–85, 187–90, 192, 202, 205–6, 257; thought experiments in works of, 192–93; title of *Childhood of Jesus*, 186

The Cognition of the Literary Work of Art (Ingarden), 164

Colbert, Stephen, 214

Cold War, 24, 215–19, 223–24, 240

Collins, Anthony, 83–84, 85

commerce, 91–92, 258–59, 275n19

communism, 216, 217

The Communist Manifesto (Marx), 258, 282

communities of belief: art, 261; in intellectual discourse, 259

The Conduct of the Allies (Swift), 84

conjectural knowledge, 44

conservatism/conservative movement, 218, 236–40, 239, 244, 291, 292, 295n8

consilience (Wilson), 109–10

Corral, Will, 241

coteries, 75, 81, 82, 88

crime fiction, 267–68

critique: absolutism, 76–77, 79, 80; crisis in, 104, 206, 283–85; critique of, 287, 295n5; deconstructive ethics, 24, 194–97, 199, 202–3; development of, 3–4, 20, 22, 32, 69n5, 74–75, 81, 93n1, 293; diagnosis, 4–6, 16, 19, 107, 128, 173, 185; fact/fiction distinctions, 101, 183, 290, 295n7; history of, 13–14, 20, 76–82, 85–88, 255–56, 283–85; and how we read, 129–30, 184–87, 189–91, 194–205; moving "beyond critique," 288–93; and politics, 230–31, 234–35, 240, 242–44, 245, 246–48; satire as, 22, 75, 79, 84–85, 88–92; in the

two-cultures split, 105–7, 109–10, 113, 118–19, 122n30

England: civil society and private judgment in, 77; commercial interests of, 91; constitution of, 77; religious tolerance in, 80–82; societal interests in, 91; state formation, 80–81, 94n17; war against France (1756), 90

English, James, 239–40

Erasure (Everett), 190–91

An Essay on Satire: Occasioned by the Death of Mr Pope (Brown), 22, 88–89

Essay upon Ancient and Modern Learning (Temple), 82–83

An Estimate of the Manners and Principles of the Times (Brown), 80, 90–91

ethics: deconstructive ethics, 24, 194–97, 195, 199, 202–3; limitations of democratic ethics, 267–68; literature, 194–95, 199, 265–66; Otherness, 143, 195–99, 201, 202, 266–67; political aspects of, 196; singularity of literature, 198; temporality of, 196–97; tragic knowledge, 259, 269–70; of translation, 264–65, 271, 277n35

Everett, Percival, 190–91

evidential paradigm, 44

fact/fiction distinction, 101, 183, 290, 295n7

family resemblances, theory of (Wittgenstein), 4

fantasy, 220–21, 228n26, 267–68

fascism, 15, 156

Fear and Trembling (Kierkegaard), 34, 44, 45

Felski, Rita, 181n53; on the concept of ideology, 157; on critique, 34, 139, 238–39; hermeneutics of suspicion, 31; *Limits of Critique* (Felski), 69n5; on the objects of knowledge, 270; phenomenology of reading, 165, 289; on poststructuralism's tendency to "stand back," 165–66

feminism, 8–9, 11, 35, 53, 58–61, 72n22, 291

fetishism, 134, 135

Fetterley, Judith, 6

fictional imagination, 199–201, 225

Fish, Stanley, 70n11

Flaubert, Gustave, 155–56, 157, 160, 166, 261

Fleissner, Jennifer L., 22

Fletcher, Angus, 6–7

"Force of Law" (Derrida), 197

forensic hermeneutics, 267–68

form (term), 22, 129

formalism, 130, 148n11

Foster, Hal, 18

Foucault, Michel, 5, 75, 108, 239, 283

Frank, Adam, 10–11, 14, 203

Frankfurt School, 13, 14, 104, 252, 271, 279

Freedgood, Elaine, 142

Freud, Sigmund: conjectural knowledge, 44; "Dream of Irma's injection" (Freud), 42–43; and the hermeneutics of suspicion, 42, 158, 201; on human behavior, 100, 124n29; interpretation of, 21; as the master hunter, 43; on modern rationalism, 104; symptom defined by, 100–101, 125n61

Friedman, Geraldine, 137

Gaddis, John Lewis, 215

Garner, Dwight, 123n37

Gates, Henry Louis, Jr., 281

Gay, John, 82

Geertz, Clifford, 59, 71n19

Geist (progress), 261

gender, 6, 16, 54–57, 58, 143, 253, 282, 295n8

Geulen, Eva, 276n29

Geuss, Raymond, 76

Ginzburg, Carlo, 43, 44, 46

glossary: in English translation of *Reading Capital*, 145–46, 147

Goffman, Erving, 221

Goodall, Jane, 62
Goodlad, Lauren M. E., 70n12
Gordimer, Nadine, 192, 197
Gourgouris, Stathis, 262
grammatical investigation, 38, 48n22
Gramsci, Antonio, 240, 294
Grossberg, Lawrence, 17
Grotius, Hugo, 77
Gubser, Michael, 11
guilty reading, 119, 129, 131
Gulliver's Travels (Swift), 84–85

Habermas, Jürgen, 76, 77, 80
habit, 169–70
Hadley, Elaine, 124n42
Haraway, Donna: car repair analogy of,
    59, 72n20; on construction v. decon-
    struction, 64; critique of knowledge
    production (the temptations), 58,
    60, 61, 62–63, 67; on epistemological
    disruption, 53; feminist objectivity,
    60–61, 72n22; knowledge production,
    53, 54–56, 58, 61–62, 68; on Latour,
    56–57; on objectivity, 59, 61, 66; on
    reality, 59–61; science in works of,
    53–55, 58–63, 67–68; on social trans-
    formation, 53; strong objectivity, 60,
    72n22; uses of realism, 58–59, 72n20
Harding, Sandra, 60
Hardouin, Jean, 78
Hardt, Michael, 13
Harley, Robert, 82
Harney, Stefano, 15
Hartley, Daniel, 154, 155
heap (use of term), 170, 175, 177, 182n59
Hedda Gabler, 38
Hegel, Georg Wilhelm Friedrich, 254,
    255, 260–61, 276n29
Heidegger, Martin, 104
Hemmings, Claire, 70n7
Hensley, Nathan K., 65
hermeneutics of suspicion. *See* suspi-
    cion, hermeneutics of

Hess, Moses, 79
Heywood, John, 161
hiddenness: of cliché, 158–60, 163–64;
    detective process, 41–42; Freudian
    psychoanalysis, 4, 158–59; Greek
    drama, 44–45; knowledge, 159–60;
    in language, 36; in literary criticism,
    35; repression, 4, 6, 10, 16, 33, 125n61,
    171, 189; revelation of/exposure of,
    159–60; Wittgenstein on, 39–40
historicism, 124n49, 134, 150n21
historicity, 292
history: art, 260; and a new theory
    of reading, 133–34; perceptions of,
    285–86; reading, 134; symptomatic
    reading, 142; temporalities of, 285–86,
    292; writing, 134
Hitchens, Christopher, 123n37
Hobbes, Thomas, 77, 78, 84, 85, 86, 88,
    94n17
Holliger, David, 257
holophrase, 168–69
hooks, bell, 11, 281
hopefulness: criticism, 212–13, 218–20,
    247–48; critique and, 24, 216–17,
    247–48; deconstructive ethics, 24,
    194–97, 202–3; imagination, 216–17,
    224–26, 228n34, 229n37; Sedgwick
    on, 116; social transformation, 222;
    strong hope (Scott), 272; susceptible
    reading, 133, 142, 150n21. *See also*
    messianism
Horkheimer, Max, 156, 256, 278n43
Howard, Richard, 168–69
Howells, William Dean, 105, 113
humanities: *Ceci n'est pas une pipe*
    (Magritte), 71n12, 99; crisis in, 64–65,
    127–28; critique in, 243–44; impor-
    tance of, 255–58; and the sciences, 22,
    103–7, 109–13, 118–19, 122n24, 122n30;
    two-cultures split, 22, 105–7, 109–13,
    118–19, 122n30
Hume, David, 88

Lear, Jonathan, 12
Leaves of Grass (Whitman), 263–64
Lesjak, Carolyn, 33, 64–65
De l'esprit des lois (Montesquieu), 91
Leviathan (Hobbes), 77, 85
Leviathan and the Air Pump (Shapin and Schaffer), 54, 55–56
Lewis, C. L. R., 219
Lewis, R. W. B., 226
Life and Times of Michael K (Coetzee), 195
Limits of Critique (Felski), 69n5
Locke, John, 77, 78, 83, 85, 86, 94n17
Love, Heather, 16, 21–22, 102
Lukács, Georg, 5, 104, 126n63
Luntz, Frank, 290

Mabillon, Jean, 78
Madame Bovary, 166
Magistrate (*Waiting for the Barbarians* [Coetzee]), 194, 198
Magritte, René, 71n12
Mahmood, Saba, 14
Mailer, Norman, 32
Marcus, Sharon: on contemporary ideological technique, 157–58; Fredric Jameson's application of Althusser's lens to literature, 158–59; Freudian psychoanalysis as hermeneutics of suspicion, 158; on reading, 16, 35, 69n5, 189; on surface reading, 32, 33, 52, 64, 69n5, 102, 115, 160, 181n58, 191, 219; symptomatic reading, 33, 111, 150n24, 158, 191, 211, 290; on work of demystification, 220
Marder, Elissa, 277n36
Marx, Karl: on Adam Smith, 158; on capitalist modernity, 104; *The Communist Manifesto*, 258, 282; on critique, 244; on Hegelian dialectic, 254; on interpretation, 201; optimism of, 255; play on words, 137, 139–40, 144; and the politics

of emancipation, 79; as reader, 23, 132, 133–34, 149nn16,17; on the social order, 258; surplus value, 91; symptomatic reading of, 158–59; *Wortspiel*, 137. See also *Capital*; Jameson, Fredric
masculinity, 54, 55, 108
Massumi, Brian, 182n65
materialism, 102–3, 121n16, 142, 267
materiality, 169–70, 175
mathematics, 104, 121n16
McCarthy, Tom, 190, 191
McEwan, Ian: on contemporary culture, 124n49; Darwinism, 108–9; influences on, 123n37; Latour compared with, 118; postcritique embraced by, 108–9; realism of, 112; on religion, 123n37; symptomatic reading of, 107–11, 118, 124n49; on the third culture, 109–10
McFarland, Thomas, 276n32
McGurl, Mark, 190
McLuhan, Marshall, 180n48
meaning, 111–12, 264, 267–68, 277n36
Merleau-Ponty, Maurice, 11
messianism: Benjamin on, 232, 246, 247, 248, 272; *The Childhood of Jesus*, 202, 203–4; critique and, 25, 246–48, 272; ethical encounter stimulated by, 198; and politics, 246–48; redemption, 289; weak messianism, 25, 196, 246, 247
metamateriality, 169–70
metaphor: allegory, 6, 192, 199–203; in *The Childhood of Jesus* (Coetzee), 187; inversion metaphor, 136; llave universal/llave maestra, 187, 188, 192, 200, 205; paraphrases as demanded by, 41; vision, 202–3
method, 2, 17, 34–35, 48n15, 54, 56
Miller, D. A., 141–42
Miller, Henry, 32
Millett, Kate, 32

Saldívar, Ramón, 228n34
Sand, George, 155
Sartori, Andrew, 70n12
Sartre, Jean-Paul, 47, 181n54
satire, 22, 75, 79, 85, 88–90, 92
Saturday (McEwan), 100, 112, 124n42
Saussure, Ferdinand de, 34
Scarry, Elaine, 64, 165
Schaffer, Simon, 54, 55–56
"the schizophrenic" (Zijderveld), 173–74
Schleiermacher, Friedrich, 277n35
Schmitt, Cannon, 69n5, 76, 83
Schopenhauer, Arthur, 73
science/science studies: fact/fiction distinctions, 101, 183, 290, 295n7; faux-scientific documents in *Enduring Love* (McEwan), 101, 107; in fiction, 107, 108, 111; gender, 54–57, 72n20; humanities and, 22, 109–13, 118–19, 122n24, 122n30; impact of politics on, 18, 236, 289, 290; martial rhetoric of, 54, 55, 56, 57–60, 64; the modest witness in, 54, 55; neuroscience, 100, 102, 103, 107, 121n11, 121n16, 123n37; objectivity, 62, 63–64; and obsessiveness, 114–15; Romanticism, 122n24; scientism v., 66–67, 101; the scientist as reader, 100; technoscience, 54, 55, 56, 57–60, 67, 72n20; two-cultures split, 22, 105–7, 109–12, 118–19, 122n30
Scott, David, 255–56, 258, 272
Scott-Heron, Gil, 232
Scriblerus Club, 82, 88
secularism, 25, 247; capitalism, 259; and the end of art, 260, 276n29; fundamentalisms, 254; modernity, 254, 261; progress, 261; reading *The Childhood of Jesus* (Coetzee), 186; secular criticism, 235–36, 245; translation, 262, 268
Sedgwick, Eve: antibiologism, 203; on a critical suspicion of pain, 278n43; on critique, 32, 51, 116–17; on dramas of exposure, 8, 196; ethical readings

as dramas of exposure, 196; hermeneutics of suspicion, 31, 32; Lesjak on, 65; on paranoia, 65–66, 117, 149n13; on paranoid reading, 11–12, 16, 116, 141–42, 211; plentitude, 16, 141, 151n39; on the reparative, 51, 67, 69n5, 116–17, 149n13
the self, 8–9, 100, 109, 194, 251n51, 264
semiotic analysis, 199–203
Seven Years' War, 90
sexual identity, 6, 16, 54–57, 58, 143–44, 282, 295n8
Shaftesbury, Anthony, 89
Shakespeare, William, 161, 179n33
Shapin, Steven, 54, 55–56
Shelly, Percy Bysshe, 260, 263
Sherlock Holmes, 21, 34, 41–42, 43, 44
Shrouse, Eric, 175, 182n65
signs, 199–200, 201–3, 271
silence, 38, 42
Simon, Richard, 78
"Situated Knowledges: The Science Question in Feminism and the Privilege of Partial Perspective" (Haraway), 58, 61
skepticism, 22, 32, 52, 53, 60, 101–2, 239, 274n14
Slingerland, Edward, 109
Sloterdijk, Peter, 14–15
Smith, Adam, 158
Smith, Zadie, 190
Snow, C. P., 101, 105, 108, 109, 124n52
Sobchack, Vivian, 11
Solnit, Rebecca, 211, 222
Sommer, Doris, 20
"Song of Myself" (Whitman), 267
Sontag, Susan, 16
Spinoza, Benedict, 78
Spivak, Gayatri Chakravorty, 68, 183–84, 194–95, 205, 222, 271
Stacey, Jackie, 70n7
Steele, Richard, 22
Stein, Gertrude, 164

stereotypes, 143–44, 155

Stewart, John, 149n18

stigma (Goffman), 221

St. John, Henry, 82

Stoler, Ann Laura, 16

strong objectivity (Harding), 72n21

Stuart, House of, 80–81

stuplime, 182n59

surface reading: and critique hermeneutics, 32, 52, 273n4, 290; depth reading, 16, 21, 33, 34, 35, 41; descriptions of texts in, 39; obsessions with innocence, 115; play on words, 136–37; political aspects of, 219–20; the problematic in, 133, 150n21; science, 100; and symptomatic reading, 16, 111

surplus value (Marx), 91

surprise, 23, 141–42, 144–45, 151n43

susceptible reading, 133, 142, 150n21

suspicion, hermeneutics of: allegory, 6–7, 24, 191–94, 199–203; art, 201, 261, 262; cliché, 153, 157, 158, 161; during Cold War, 215–16; critique, 31, 252–53, 262, 288–89; detection process, 21, 34, 41–42, 43, 44; Freud and, 42, 158, 201; New Criticism, 253; political uses of, 15, 32; reading practices, 16, 22, 34–36, 37, 40–41, 116, 133, 150n21. *See also* hiddenness; symptomatic reading

suspicious reading, 101, 183, 290, 295n7

Swift, Jonathan, 22, 80, 82, 84–88, 92, 155

symptomatic reading: alternatives to, 32, 219; changes in, 100–101, 140–41; cliché, 157, 159–60, 163–64, 173–74; depth analysis, 16, 35, 100, 252; *Enduring Love* (McEwan), 107–11, 118, 124n49; gaze in, 4, 5, 158; master codes in, 150n24; obsessions with innocence, 115; paranoid reading, 141–42; play on words in, 135, 139, 144–45; the problematic in, 129, 133, 135, 150n21; as provisional, 147; psychoanalysis in, 124n49, 173–74;

surprise in, 23, 144–45; "terrain" in, 131, 133, 139–40, 141, 143, 146, 150n21; and "What it is to read?," 136–37. *See also* hiddenness

A Tale of a Tub (Swift), 80, 84, 85–88

Tarde, Gabriel, 105, 119

Taussig, Michael, 221, 222

Taylor, Charles, 254, 255, 276n29

technoscience, 55–60, 67, 68, 102

Temple, William, 82–83

the temptations (Haraway), 58, 60, 61, 62–63, 67

terrain (Althusser), 131, 133, 139–40, 141, 143, 146, 150n21

theory: actor-network theory, 17, 48n15, 56; affect, 2, 10–12, 70n7, 114–15, 121n11, 124n53, 133, 150n21, 151n39, 165, 272, 278n43; in Coetzee's works, 183–85, 187–90, 192, 202, 205–6, 257; deconstructive ethics, 24, 194–95, 195–97, 196, 197, 199, 202–3; Eagleton's works in, 18, 184, 241–42, 281–82, 283–86; of the Frankfurt School, 13, 14, 104, 252, 271, 279; history of, 279–81, 283–84, 287–88; intellectual development in the theory era, 279–80, 287–88; method, 2, 17, 34–35, 48n15, 54, 56; militarization of, 50, 54, 242; psycho-biological development of members of, 292; of reading, 131–35, 138, 144, 146, 148n8, 150n24, 152n56; rhetoric of, 240–41, 250n34; of the "split sign," 36

Theory's Empire: An Anthology of Dissent, 240–41, 250n34

Thévanot, Laurent, 14

"Thing-in-itself" (Latour), 122n30

This Is Not a Pipe (Magritte), 70n12, 99

Thompson, Jim, 22, 154, 170–77, 182n62

Toland, John, 83

Tomkins, Silvan, 10, 11, 151n39

Tompkins, Jane, 11

torture, 194, 207n14

Tory party, 81–82, 84

tragedy, 259, 269–70, 271–72

translation: critique and, 271–73; ethics of, 264–65, 271, 277n35; of experience, 263–65, 277n36; meaning, 111–12, 264, 267–68, 277n36; reading, 145–46, 147; in the secular age, 268

transparency, 54, 135, 136, 161–62

trauma, 194, 207n14

Treaty of Utrecht, 84

triangulated narration, 170–71, 172

truth, 4, 52, 114, 271

truthiness (Colbert), 214–15

The Turn of the Screw (James), 115

two-cultures split, 22, 105–7, 109–13, 118–19, 122n30

two poles of interpretation (Ricouer), 201

Übersichtliche Darstellung (Wittgenstein), 39, 40

unconcealment, goal of, 195

violence, 194, 202–5

Voltaire, 79, 91

Waiting for the Barbarians (Coetzee), 194, 195

Warburtonian school (William Warburton), 88, 89, 90

Warner, Michael, 252

Watkins, Evan, 7

Weber, Max, 104, 106, 110, 118–19, 126n66, 231

We Have Never Been Modern (Latour), 100, 103–4, 115

What is it to read?, 132–33, 137, 149n18

Wheeler, Bonnie, 55

Whig party, 81–82, 84

Whitehead, Alfred North, 105, 119

Whitehead, Colson, 190, 191

Whitman, Walt, 25, 262–67

"Why Has Critique Run Out of Steam?" (Latour), 50–51, 56, 103, 289–90

"Why this?" question, 21, 36–38, 42, 43, 46

Wiegman, Robyn, 13, 70n7, 195–96, 243–44, 245

Williams, Raymond, 5

Wilson, E. O., 108, 109, 110

Wittgenstein, Ludwig, 4, 21, 33, 36, 37–41, 42, 48n22, 163

Wood, James, 190

"Work of Art in the Age of Mechanical Reproduction" (Benjamin), 260

The World, the Text, and the Critic (Said), 235

Wortspiel, 137

Wotton, William, 83

writing, 100–101, 120n9, 133–34, 138, 140, 150n24

Young, Iris, 11

Zijderveld, Anton, 161–62, 163, 168, 173–74, 178n13, 179n33, 180n42, 180n48

Žižek, Slavoj, 5, 7, 88

Zone One (Whitehead), 191